Signs and Voices

Signs and Voices:

DEAF CULTURE, IDENTITY, LANGUAGE, AND ARTS

Kristin A. Lindgren,
Doreen DeLuca,
and Donna Jo Napoli,
Editors

Gallaudet University Press
Washington, D.C.

Gallaudet University Press
Washington, DC 20002

http://gupress.gallaudet.edu

© 2008 by Gallaudet University

Published in 2008

Printed in the United States of America

Library of Congress Cataloging-in-Publication Data

Signs and voices : deaf culture, identity, language, and arts / Kristin A. Lindgren,
Doreen DeLuca, and Donna Jo Napoli, editors. — 1st ed.

   p. cm.

ISBN-13: 978-1-56368-363-3 (alk. paper)

  1. Deaf—United States—Social conditions. 2. Deaf—Means of communication—
United States. 3. American sign language. 4. Deaf—Psychology. 5. Identity
(Psychology) I. Lindgren, Kristin A. II. DeLuca, Doreen. III. Napoli, Donna Jo,
1948–

HV2545.S54 2008

305.9′0820973—dc22

2007050880

♾ The paper used in this publication meets the minimum requirements of American
National Standard for Information Sciences—Permanence of Paper for Printed Library
Materials, ANSI Z39.48-1984.

Contents

Contents of the DVD, by Chapter Number

To watch the DVD in its entirety, click on Play All on the DVD menu page. To watch individual clips in a particular chapter, click Contents on the menu page, then click on the specific chapter and clip.

Acknowledgments

This volume grew out of the Signs and Voices conference at Swarthmore, Haverford, and Bryn Mawr colleges in November 2004. The editors are grateful to the many individuals, departments, and offices at all three colleges that provided financial, logistical, and moral support. Without this support, neither the conference nor the book would have been possible. We owe a special thanks to the Linguistics Department at Swarthmore, which generously offered help at many stages of the production of this volume. We are grateful to the Andrew W. Mellon Foundation for supporting the Tri-College Forum that provided the seed money for the conference, and we thank the many organizations that provided additional support, including the Center for Peace and Global Citizenship at Haverford, the Center for Science in Society at Bryn Mawr, the John B. Hurford Humanities Center at Haverford College, the Lang Center for Social Responsibility at Swarthmore, the Office of Distinguished Visitors at Haverford, the Pennsylvania School for the Deaf, the Sager Foundation at Swarthmore, and the William J. Cooper Foundation at Swarthmore. For their enthusiasm and interest in this project, we thank our colleagues and students at all three colleges, particularly Joe Alberti and the students in Linguistics 62 at Swarthmore in fall 2004 and the students in Disability and Difference at Haverford in fall 2004. For helpful advice along the way, and for connecting us with others working on d/Deaf matters, we thank Dirksen Bauman, Brenda Jo Brueggemann, Michael Davidson, Sister Kathleen Schipani, Bob Shillings, Paul Sommers, and Rebecca Weinberger. For producing the DVD that accompanies this book, we thank Mark Mai and Robert Furrow. For skilled assistance with copyediting and formatting, we thank Bill Reynolds and especially Will Quale. Alex Pearson generously provided round-the-clock technical support. For expert guidance at every stage, we thank Ivey Wallace at Gallaudet University Press. And for keeping us smiling and allowing us the space and time to do this work, we thank our families: Alex, Anders, and Elias; Joe, Jadian, Brenna, and Kyle; and Barry, Robert, Eva, Nicholas, Michael, and Elena.

Introduction

In recent years, the rapid pace of cultural and technological change has necessitated a continual rethinking of what it means to be deaf, hard of hearing, or culturally Deaf.[1] A growing number of deaf children receive cochlear implants and are educated in mainstream settings, posing new challenges for defining both individual and collective identities. The development of genetic testing, gene manipulation, and other genomic technologies raises difficult questions for bioethicists, medical researchers and practitioners, and d/Deaf people. New research on sign languages, building on William Stokoe's groundbreaking research on American Sign Language (ASL) in the 1960s, has led to a greater understanding of and respect for the language, literature, and ways of life of signing Deaf people. At the same time, however, the widespread use of new communication technologies such as video relay services, text messaging, and electronic pagers has altered how people who are d/Deaf communicate with one another and with the hearing world. New video and digital technologies also play an increasingly important role in the creation and dissemination of ASL poetry and other forms of ASL literature. As these various technologies are reshaping d/Deaf identities and communities, hearing high school and college students are enrolling in ASL courses in record numbers. What does this mean for ASL, for d/Deaf people, and for Deaf culture? The chapters in *Signs and Voices: Deaf Culture, Identity, Language, and Arts* address these and other cultural issues that are changing the landscape of d/Deafness. The book is divided into three sections— Culture and Identity, Language and Literacy, and American Sign Language in the Arts—each of which focuses on a particular set of theoretical and practical concerns.

The editors of this volume first came together to organize the Signs and Voices conference, a four-day event in November 2004 that took place at Swarthmore, Haverford, and Bryn Mawr colleges. Many of the chapters in this volume grew out of work presented at that conference. The Signs and Voices

---

1. Following a convention first established by James Woodward, we use *deaf* to refer to individuals who are audiologically deaf and *Deaf* to refer to those who use sign as their primary language and identify with Deaf culture. Because these categories are overlapping and not always easy to tease apart, we also adopt the more recent practice of using *d/Deaf* to represent deaf, hard of hearing, and culturally Deaf people. See Brenda Jo Brueggemann's chapter in this volume for a discussion of the usage of *deaf*, *Deaf*, and *d/Deaf*.

conference was catholic, striving to be as inclusive as possible of different view-points, and eclectic, presenting research in many disciplines as well as visual, literary, and performance art and work related to assistive technologies and civil rights. We came away from the conference newly aware of important and exciting work in many fields of endeavor and committed to introducing our readers to some of that work. Other chapters included here were presented in an earlier form as part of the Presidential Forum on American Sign Language at the December 2004 Modern Language Association Convention in Philadelphia. Still others were solicited for this volume, and one, a study of the development of Nicaraguan Sign Language, originally appeared in *Science* and is reprinted here with our thanks. The book is accompanied by a DVD that includes clips of ASL and of ASL poetry and theater discussed by our contributors.

Taken together, these chapters point to new directions in a broad range of fields, including cognitive science, Deaf studies, disability studies, education, linguistics, literary criticism, philosophy, and psychology. Although no single volume can cover every discipline and every new angle of research, this collection aims to showcase some of the innovative and rigorous work being done across the disciplines. We hope that it will prove useful to scholars and teachers in a variety of fields, to their students, and to general readers, both d/Deaf and hearing, who are seeking information about d/Deaf matters.

CULTURE AND IDENTITY

The chapters in Part One explore what it means to be d/Deaf in the twenty-first century. Examining the past and envisioning the future, these chapters reflect on the complex individual and cultural processes through which d/Deaf identities and communities are constructed. They underscore the importance of understanding key moments in history as we move into a future of new choices and dilemmas for people who are deaf, hard of hearing, and culturally Deaf. Many factors, including the development of new technologies and changes in educational practices, mark the early twenty-first century as a moment of rapid cultural change and potentially of cultural crisis for d/Deaf people. These chapters testify to the ability of d/Deaf individuals and communities to adapt, to survive, and to thrive.

In the first chapter, "Scientific Explanation and Other Performance Acts in the Reorganization of DEAF," Tom Humphries traces the development of a new discourse of Deaf language and culture, a discourse that challenges earlier scientific explanations of deafness based on degree of hearing loss, functional ability, and social isolation in a hearing world. In the 1960s, William Stokoe's sign language dictionary, as well as work by many other linguists, sociologists, and psychologists, introduced the revolutionary ideas that ASL is a bona fide language and that people who use it as their primary language belong to a Deaf culture. Humphries emphasizes the crucial role played by cultural processes within the Deaf community in disseminating these ideas. When Deaf people entered into "talk" about their own language and culture, offering explanations to one another and to the hearing public via performance, the revolution had truly begun. In addition to "talking culture," Humphries argues, Deaf people made their culture visible by performing their language in public venues; by teaching one another, as well as hearing people, about ASL and Deaf culture; by collecting and displaying cultural artifacts; and by differentiating who and what is or isn't Deaf. Their new understanding that "everything DEAF had value" not only transformed perceptions of self and society but also effected long over-due changes in the sociopolitical and economic status of Deaf people.

In "Who Am I? Deaf Identity Issues," Irene W. Leigh asks, "What does it mean to say 'I am deaf'"? She reviews the literature on deaf identity develop-ment, exploring the definition of identity as both self-perception and social con-struct and considering the influence of language and communication, hearing ability, and family and social environment, including ethnic background. Leigh points out that for the 96 percent of deaf children born to hearing parents, a growing number of whom are receiving cochlear implants and being educated in mainstream settings, the paths toward deaf identity are not clear-cut. She re-views several theoretical models of deaf identity development and reports on a study by Deborah Maxwell McCaw showing that both deaf acculturation and biculturalism are associated with a healthy sense of well-being and that "being comfortable with one's deafness is as critical for psychological well-being as is the ability to switch comfortably between Deaf and hearing environments." Leigh concludes that deaf identity is mutable rather than fixed, that it is defined by both individual and cultural experiences, and that today's deaf identities will inevitably be reshaped by historical, cultural and technological forces.

Brenda Jo Brueggemann, in "Think-Between: A Deaf Studies Commonplace Book," introduces a theory of "betweenity" that challenges us to create new con-ceptual spaces between *deaf* and *Deaf, deafness* and *disability,* and other terms that attempt to name and differentiate deaf identities. She goes on to map several fruitful sites of inquiry for Deaf studies. These include the study of the "ever-shifting deaf cyborg" and the rhetorical relationship between technology and identity; the "euthanasia" of deaf people as part of the T-4 program in Nazi Germany in 1941–42; the evolution of new sign languages in developing coun-tries and places such as reunified Germany; the proliferation of ASL courses for hearing students in high school and college curricula; and the relationship be-tween writing and signing. While urging us to view the "identity kaleidoscope" from varied perspectives, Brueggemann makes clear that the shifting boundaries of Deaf-world do not entail the end of Deaf culture or of ASL but instead com-pel us to develop more capacious theories of self and community, theories that incorporate spaces of "betweenity."

Next, in her chapter " 'I Thought There Would Be More Helen Keller': *History through Deaf Eyes* and Narratives of Representation," Kristen Harmon describes the evolution of a proposed exhibit about Deaf culture, planned jointly by Gallaudet University and the Smithsonian Institution. This exhibit, later renamed "History through Deaf Eyes" and reframed as "a narrative that places culturally Deaf, hard of hearing, and deafened people within the context of American history," has been exhibited at several sites in the United States, including the Smithsonian's Arts and Industries Building in Washington, D.C. Drawing on the letters of protest and support generated by the exhibit proposal and also on the comments and drawings entered in visitors' logbooks at the Smithsonian posting, Harmon examines how the emotionally charged responses to the exhibit reveal competing discourses of deafness and Deaf culture in American life. The written responses to the exhibit—from parents of deaf children, audiologists and other medical professionals, and d/Deaf and hearing children and adults—stake out deeply felt positions about language choice, education, and technology. Harmon articulates the poignant question that the varied responses to the exhibit invoke: "Who owns the deaf child?"

In the final chapter in this section, "Bioethics and the Deaf Community," Teresa Blankmeyer Burke takes up this question as she surveys bioethical issues that affect d/Deaf individuals and communities and offers an analytical framework for examining these issues. Burke explores how Beauchamp and Childress's four ethical principles of autonomy, beneficence, nonmaleficence (the duty to do no harm), and justice raise bioethical issues for d/Deaf people. For example, she explains that interpretation of the dictum to do no harm depends on how an individual or community defines the concepts of health and harm, and she asks whether the principle of autonomy grants potential parents the freedom to use genetic technologies to select for genes associated with deafness as well as to screen out these genes. Burke argues for a nuanced, case-based bioethics and points out that most bioethics decisions are driven not by policy but by individuals making choices in specific contexts. "Granted," she writes, "this generates a messier picture of bioethics, but one that more accurately reflects the reality of bioethics in the greater deaf community." In closing, she emphasizes that emerging technologies make it critically important for members of this community—whether hard of hearing, deaf-blind, oral deaf, late-deafened, or culturally Deaf—to engage in dialogue with bioethicists and researchers.

LANGUAGE AND LITERACY

The chapters in Part Two highlight new research on sign languages and examine the implications of this research for educating deaf children. The first three chapters present evidence from linguistics and cognitive neuroscience research that enables us to better understand the similarities and differences between sign and speech, the relationship between linguistic and other types of cognitive processing, the development of new sign languages, and the semantic and syntactic behavior of specific signs. The remaining three chapters in this section draw on linguistic and pedagogical research to discuss the theory and practice of teaching deaf children, emphasizing a bilingual approach and the early use of sign language.

In "Cognitive and Neural Representations of Language: Insights from Sign Languages of the Deaf," Heather Knapp and David P. Corina offer an overview of the linguistic, psycholinguistic, and neurolinguistic properties of sign languages. They reaffirm that sign languages are natural languages, pointing out many structural similarities between sign and oral languages, but also noting the important difference that sublexical elements of sign occur simultaneously (both hands articulate as they move through space) without any problem of reception. Knapp and Corina note that psycholinguistic findings thus far have shown that sign languages and oral languages are accessed in the same way with regard to whether the signs/words are real or nonsense and with regard to whether the signs/words are frequent or rare. They argue for another similarity: Signs and words are stored and accessed along both structural and semantic dimensions.

And they note that evidence from research on aphasia, cortical stimulation mapping, and brain imaging shows that the same parts of the left hemisphere of the brain are responsible for linguistic structures in sign and oral languages. However, sign languages may also recruit parts of the right hemisphere, particularly when producing spatial information, such as that in classifier predicates and prepositions. Additionally, the production of ASL by signers who acquired sign during the critical period for language (whether they are hearing or not) involves the right hemisphere in a way that production of ASL by non-native signers does not.

In "Children Creating Core Properties of Language: Evidence from an Emerging Sign Language in Nicaragua," originally published in *Science*, Ann Senghas, Sotaro Kita, and Aslı Özyürek report on their study of children's sign in Nicaragua. In 1977, the first special education school opened in Managua, followed by a vocational school in 1981. The deaf children who attended these schools did not have a language in common prior to coming, instead having a variety of home sign systems. Once at school together, they began communicating with gestures, but soon this expanded to real sign. Preadolescent signers typically make changes in the grammar, teaching them to younger signers, but not to adults. Over the past twenty-five years, one cohort of children has taught the next cohort the sign language that was created at the school. In this study, Senghas, Kita, and Özyürek compare the signing fluency on complex motion events of deaf signers from three separate school cohorts (by the year they entered the school community) with the gestures used by hearing Nicaraguan Spanish speakers while speaking Spanish. They found that the younger the signing cohort, the less their signing is like gesture and the more fluent it is. In sum, the youngest signers are the most fluent, in contrast to most Deaf communities. Their findings give novel support to the claim that the language-learning mechanism in the brain is responsible for those attributes of language that are universal, and they contradict the claim that languages evolve solely through cultural transmission from generation to generation.

Carol Neidle and Robert G. Lee present us with another linguistic study in "WELL, 'WHAT' Is It? Discovery of a New Particle in ASL." They look at the frequently used sign often glossed as WHAT, articulated with a 5 handshape on (one or) both hands in neutral space with the palms upward and a single outward movement of the hand(s). This particle has received little attention in previous linguistic literature, being assumed to be either gestural (and not true sign) or an integral part of the other signs with which it occurs. They offer evidence that this particle is a bona fide sign, independent of other signs. It typically follows a semantically focused element and adds a sense of domain-widening or indeterminacy. That is, it serves to extend the set of referents under consideration to a larger group than one would normally expect. A somewhat comparable effect is found in English when we say "some boy or other" as compared with just "a boy." Neidle and Lee show that this particle is not to be identified as the wh-element WHAT because it behaves differently from WHAT syntactically (in terms of its distribution) and semantically; nor is it to be identified as an indefinite determiner, because it can co-occur with ordinary indefinite noun phrases. Indeed, this particle can also occur in sentence-final position, lending the same kind of expansive interpretation to the entire event of the sentence—giving a sense of "x or something like it happened."

The next three chapters examine the implications of research in linguistics for educating deaf children. In "Success with Deaf Children: How to Prevent Educational Failure," Ronnie Wilbur reviews research from linguistics and other fields that lends support to the use of natural sign languages in the early education of deaf children. She points out that success is multidimensional, involving doing grade-level work, feeling independent and happy, and choosing and working toward one's own career goals. Language is essential to any child's success, and this is true whether the language is a sign language or an oral language. She cites research showing that the use and mastery of sign language in the early years does not interfere with a deaf or hard of hearing child's development of speechreading and vocalization. Indeed, it is positively correlated with reading skills and general achievement. This should be no surprise: One must acquire language first in order to have the cognitive development that underlies successful skills in reading and writing. There is no substitute for the acquisition of a natural language. Signed Exact English (SEE), for example, cannot offer the cognitive benefits that ASL offers; because it is an artificial construct, it does not have those features common to all natural languages. Wilbur advocates the bilingual approach to deaf education, giving many arguments based on linguistic structures.

In "English and ASL: Classroom Activities to Shed Some Light on the Use of Two Languages," Shannon Allen, a teacher at the Pennsylvania School for the Deaf, describes her own practical methods for helping her deaf students express themselves in both ASL and English. She presents three activities that she has used in kindergarten and first grade classes, based on the work of others, but with her own spin. These activities explicitly address differences between the two languages with the goal of improving fluency in both. The first, Doing Words, involves daily one-on-one work with a student. The teacher begins by asking the student what word he'd like to focus on today. Then, together, they figure out what the child would like to say about that word and how to write the word or sentence that the child intends. The second, Morning Message, involves daily work with the whole class. The teacher writes the morning message—four simple lines in English—and the students greet each other and read the message, then sign it. They talk about differences between the way the English is written and the way the ASL is signed, such as the position of the verb. The third activity, ASL/English, is a group activity that calls for two teachers—the regular classroom teacher and a speech or ASL teacher. Each thirty-minute lesson focuses on a particular aspect of either English or ASL that the teachers want the children to master.

Doreen DeLuca and Donna Jo Napoli also apply linguistics to practical activities in educating children in "A Bilingual Approach to Reading." They explain why learning to read English for the child who is deaf or hard of hearing is similar to but even more difficult than learning to read Chinese characters for the child who is hearing and not a speaker of Chinese. English and ASL are quite different structurally. With respect to the lexicon, there are many mismatches. Some English words correspond to several different ASL signs, and some ASL signs correspond to several different English words. Also, the expression of predicates differs between the two: ASL uses classifiers in motion predicates while English does not. Syntax also presents many challenges to the new reader.

Word order alone is an issue, with the verb being medial in English but final in ASL. DeLuca and Napoli propose that initial reading materials for deaf and hard of hearing children offer stories told in one-word utterances, so that the child can focus on the concept of reading and on learning to recognize the individual words without having to face differences of linguistic structures between ASL and English at the outset. Later reading materials should revolve around particular differences between the two languages, explicitly confronting them. They present, as an example, their first story from *Handy Stories,* a reader with five stories in it, which will be published by Gallaudet University Press.

AMERICAN SIGN LANGUAGE IN THE ARTS

In recent years, ASL storytelling, poetry, and theater traditions have begun to receive the critical attention they have long deserved, and new artistic practices have developed and flourished. These emergent poetic and performative practices have been nourished by many factors, including research in linguistics (discussed in Part Two of this book), recognition among Deaf people that ASL is a rich natural language (discussed in Tom Humphries's chapter in this volume), the tremendous growth of ASL courses in colleges and universities, and new video and digital technologies used both to create and to preserve original ASL literature and translations. Presenting new work on the theory and practice of ASL poetry and the translation of Shakespeare into ASL, these chapters discuss the ways in which ASL draws on and reinterprets literary traditions in English and also how ASL expands these traditions, creating new possibilities for literature and performance. In particular, the visual and spatial dimensions of ASL provide unique poetic and dramatic resources, challenging us to rethink traditional notions of language, literature, and literary theory.[2]

In the opening chapter, "Body/Text: Sign Language Poetics and Spatial Form in Literature," H-Dirksen L. Bauman turns a Deaf eye toward literary theory and practice, revealing their phonocentric heritage and imagining a Deaf literary theory that would foreground the visual and spatial aspects of literature. Drawing on essays by G. E. Lessing, Joseph Frank, and W. J. T. Mitchell, he explores the relationship between the visual and literary arts and examines the notion of spatial form in literature. Bauman suggests that incorporating discussion of sign language and sign literature adds depth and perspective to theories of spatial form. He also shows that the embodiment of the text in a sign poem invites a phenomenological reading. The body performing a poem does not simply move through space, but collaborates with that space—in both oral poetry and sign poetry. But gesture and sign enable the mental grasping of space, which in turn carves out a place for the poem to occupy. A look at Clayton Valli's poem "Hands" offers a useful demonstration, as do examples from Ella Mae Lentz's, Debbie Rennie's, and Peter Cook's work. The Deaf poet's hand creates a form in space that allows the audience to see the poem, experience the image, and thus create with the poet the textual event. Bauman's analysis makes clear that

---

2. See *Signing the Body Poetic: Essays on American Sign Language Literature,* ed. H-Dirksen L. Bauman, Jennifer L. Nelson, and Heidi M. Rose, for an extended discussion of emerging traditions in ASL literature and critical analyses of this literature.

the growing recognition and appreciation of sign poetry expands our understanding of literary modalities and can lead to richer and more nuanced interpretations of poetry of all kinds.

Michael Davidson's "Tree Tangled in Tree: Re-siting Poetry through ASL,"
like Bauman's chapter, explores how sign poetry reshapes and expands our understanding of language and literature. After discussing the visual poetics of
modernist literature and the role of the optical in the Foucauldian notion of "bio-
power," he turns to a discussion of the literary strategies of three ASL poets.
First, he explains Ezra Pound's modernist experiments with poetic form, based
on Pound's reading of Ernst Fenollosa's theory of the Chinese character as a
method for poetry, and then he examines how the poet-pair The Flying Words
Project radically transforms two of Fenollosa's key examples: "Sun Tangled in
Branches of Tree" and "Man Sees Horse." Peter Cook, the Deaf poet of the pair,
combines the signs TREE and SUN, just as Chinese characters can be superimposed
to create new characters. And in translating into ASL the phrase "Man Sees
Horse," Cook wreaks havoc with the grammatical distinction between subject
and object. Davidson then turns to Clayton Valli's "Snowflake" and lays out how
Valli exploits ASL, SEE, fingerspelling, and nonsense signs to display a range
of levels of attempted communication between a deaf child and his hearing father. He examines a related theme in Patrick Graybill's "Paradox," in which the
poet explores generational and cultural tensions about language choice through
images of race and gender. In each of these poems, ASL poets reinterpret literary conventions through Deaf eyes, both building on the modernist project and
challenging us to rethink the metaphor of vision on which it is based.

In "*Nobilior est vulgaris*: Dante's Hypothesis and Sign Language Poetry,"
David M. Perlmutter traces the recent emergence of ASL poetry and argues that
two things set the stage for signers to produce original poetry in ASL. We needed
to realize both that ASL is a natural language and that natural languages offer
the noblest vehicles for poetry (an insight that the great medieval Italian poet
Dante offered when he chose to write his poems in the language of the people,
Italian, rather than in the literary language of scholarship at that time, Latin).
Perlmutter offers a detailed analysis of a single poem: Clayton Valli's "Deaf
World." He shows that three basic structural elements of oral poetry are found
in this sign poem: the stanza, the line, and the hemistich (half-line). Then he
delves into the relationship between the structure of the poem and its content.
He shows that the two stanzas of the poem have distinct syntactic structures and
distinct uses of handshapes, which correspond to the contrast Valli sets up between the descriptions of the hearing world in the first stanza and that of the
Deaf world in the second stanza. Having demonstrated that this sign poem uses
poetic devices found in oral poetry, Perlmutter goes on to show that sign poetry also uses resources not available to oral poetry. Through classifier predicates, body and face orientation, shifts in hand dominance, and eye gaze, the
poet is able to exploit linguistic patterns at multiple levels, underscoring Dante's
insight about why natural languages are the noblest vehicles for poetry.

Following these three tightly argued analyses of Deaf poetics and of a few
sign poems in particular, we turn to a discussion of creating ASL poems in "Flying Words: A Conversation between Peter Cook and Kenny Lerner." The editors
of this volume approached Cook, a Deaf poet, and his hearing collaborator,

Lerner, with a long list of questions about their work. They began responding to the first question—"Can you tell us a little about the way you two work?"—and turned it into an extended riff on their collaborative creative process. They never got to the other questions! The conversation flies back and forth between Cook and Lerner, giving the reader insight into the inventive and serendipitous nature of their work as they feel their way through creating a poem, sometimes across 500 miles, sometimes with one waking the other in the middle of the night, and often in a hotel room (as in the DVD clip that accompanies their chapter). What emerges is a sense of how a poem becomes full over time, often turning out very differently from the original conception. Cook and Lerner explain that their poems are always in process, even many years after they first created a poem or an image, and they discuss how video relay technology has given them a new way to create and rehearse poems. One of the striking features of this conversation is the way these poets play off one another's language and ideas; this aspect of their exchange may reveal as much about their creative process as their actual words. Their conversation shows how language games can produce serious contributions to art when those games are played by masters.

Next, in "Visual Shakespeare: *Twelfth Night* and the Value of ASL Translation," Peter Novak brings us to a discussion of theater. He describes the process of translating Shakespeare's *Twelfth Night* into ASL—a collaborative effort by two deaf translators, Adrian Blue and Robert De Mayo, and two hearing translators, Catherine Rush and Novak—and shows how the synergy of two languages and cultures creates a new, embodied text. Videotape proved to be a critical tool for establishing continuity in the team's work and for later analysis of the project. There are several film clips on the accompanying *Signs and Voices* DVD, some illustrating key moments in the translation process and others filmed during the play's production in Philadelphia. Novak explains how the ASL translation enhances the gestic element in Shakespeare's language; how it maps social notions of gender, class, and power onto the body; and how the performative nature of ASL enables visual augmentation of the text. He also describes the challenges of translating into ASL a play that opens and closes with music and details how the translators rendered rhymes, puns, double entendres, and other aspects of Shakespeare's text. Full of detailed examples from the original text and the translation, Novak's chapter provides a vivid demonstration of the literary and performative richness of ASL.

We end with "ASL in Performance: A Conversation with Adrian Blue," a companion piece to Novak's chapter. Blue is a director, storyteller, playwright, and actor who worked with Novak on the ASL translation of *Twelfth Night* and acted in the production. The editors' conversation with Blue touches on his childhood and schooling and traces the development of his career, from performing mime shows as a teenager to acting and directing with the National Theater of the Deaf, cowriting and producing the play *A Nice Place to Live* with Catherine Rush, and translating and performing Shakespeare's *Twelfth Night* and *Much Ado about Nothing*. Blue discusses how he approaches the use of both signs and voices onstage. He explains, for example, that when he writes a play with both Deaf and hearing characters, or when he directs a play featuring both Deaf and hearing actors, he finds ways of using voicing that enhance the dramatic structure of the play rather than simply making the play accessible to hearing audience members. In addition, he gives us further insight into the difficulties and pleasures of translating Shakespeare; focusing on specific scenes, he discusses the translation problems posed by these scenes and explains the translators' inventive solutions. The chapters in this final section underscore the vitality and creativity of Deaf culture as it faces both challenges and new possibilities in the twenty-first century.

Kristin A. Lindgren, Doreen DeLuca, and Donna Jo Napoli

REFERENCE

Bauman, H-Dirksen L., Jennifer L. Nelson, and Heidi M. Rose, eds. 2006. *Signing the body poetic: Essays on American Sign Language literature.* Berkeley: University of California Press.

Part One
Culture and Identity

1 Scientific Explanation and Other Performance Acts in the Reorganization of DEAF

TOM HUMPHRIES

If one was asked to explain who DEAF[1] people were in 1968, there were a few dominant choices. There was the "scientific" explanation that focused on the deafness or physical condition of the person. Usually this included a reference to the degree of hearing loss expressed in decibels (Davis and Silverman 1960) and categorized as mild, moderate, severe, or profound loss. Sometimes the explanation focused on the functional abilities of the deaf person: Could he/she hear and understand words without seeing the speaker's face and lips (Schein 1968)? Alternatively, the explanation was a social one with the condition of deafness as the defining factor: "And while his deafness has isolated the deaf person from the social groups of which he is overtly a member because of his residence and work, it has also been the main cause in the formation of social groupings of deaf persons" (Stokoe, Croneberg, and Casterline 1965, 300).

These ways of talking about DEAF were repeated in everyday talk and throughout the deafness literature almost by rote, with slight variations in form. The same phrases and words recurred in all of the narrative frames and units. They were a part of everyday discourse about deaf people. They evoked for the listener commonly prevailing images and ideas in 1960s society about people who don't hear. As ways of talking about deaf people, they were widely established in usage. To repeat one of these narratives required only that one be a part of the general discourse in public and scientific communities of this time. Deaf people themselves, as well as people who were not Deaf, engaged in this discourse. These types of narrative frames made up the sum of what we knew about DEAF. As explanations, they exactly represented what we, Deaf and hearing people alike, thought when we used the English word *deaf* and the American Sign Language (ASL) sign DEAF.

---

1. DEAF in small capital letters is used here to represent the sign in American Sign Language that Deaf people use for themselves. It is not the English word *deaf* and does not have the same definition.

However, they were mostly constructed and framed in English, and since this was the language of general society in the United States and the language of the scientific community, these English explanations dominated discourse about deaf people and migrated into ASL discourse.

There were alternative explanations that were not considered scientific. Historically, Deaf people talked of themselves in certain frames. They spoke of their sign language in terms of the ease with which they could communicate when using it and how it met their everyday needs for socializing (Krauel 1986). They spoke of it as having grace and beauty (Veditz 1913). They spoke of their social lives as a "Deaf world" in which Deaf people were very happy and content (Lane, Hoffmeister, and Bahan 1996).

When a group of people who live embedded within a much larger population of dominant others undergoes class change and a liberation movement, how can the resulting reorganization of the self be explained? How does the explanation of the self (and, therefore, the group) formulate and get circulated both within the group and in public space among others?

In the late 1960s and into the 1970s, a discourse of ASL and Deaf culture emerged with a narrative frame that rivaled and even contradicted traditional scientific explanations about DEAF (Baker and Battison 1980; Bellugi, Klima, and Siple 1975; Coye, Humphries, and Martin 1978; Lane 1976; Padden and Markowicz 1975; Siple 1978; Stokoe et al. 1965; Supalla and Newport 1978). These new narrative frames refer to scientific descriptions not only of a vibrant American Deaf culture but also of Deaf cultures within America and elsewhere around the world (Baker and Battison 1980; Bragg 2001; Hairston and Smith 1983; Lane 1984; McKee and Connew 2001; Padden and Humphries 1988, 2005). And even more interesting and detailed descriptions of the sign languages of these communities appeared (Armstrong, Karchmer, and Van Cleve 2002; Bragg 2001; Brentari 2001; Chamberlain, Morford, and Mayberry 2000; Padden 1988; Supalla and Newport 1978; Wilbur 1979).

As the newer discourse of culture emerged, older scientific explanations became problematic in several ways. The older way of talking about Deaf people was a preexisting code of English speakers (strongly influencing ASL users). Preexisting codes, or habits of talk, are, in a sense, narrative determinants. Acquiring a language involves much more than acquiring its internal structure; each language we learn carries intricate sets of meaning and images constructed by the people from whom the language comes (Kaplan 1994). Acquiring this code determines more than our ability to produce grammatical sentences; it determines what words and sentences mean and how we will use language in expressing intricate social discourses (Baker 1985; Basso 1979; Wertsch 1997). For Deaf people to imagine themselves differently than the way they were represented in the preexisting code of English speakers required that they break the hold that such narratives had on their own consciousness as well as defy public discourse dominated by English speakers.

What we have overlooked, perhaps, in our focus on the content of these new narratives of the "story" of DEAF is an understanding of how these explanations emerged in the first place. What did it mean for groups of people in 1965–1980 to construct new narratives that explained the language, the consciousness, and the very nature of DEAF, narratives that broke from previous explanations and became a widespread set of discourses about DEAF today? How did these everyday explanations, both scientific and ordinary, get constructed? What did they look like? Who formulated them? Some of these questions will be explored here, but a different set of questions are the actual focus of this chapter. How did these emergent narratives and frames take hold in scientific explanations? How did they travel through people and between people, using what mechanisms, to spread within the United States and throughout the world? And what role did the performing of these explanations play in the circulation of these new ways of talking?

A NARRATIVE SHIFT

Carol Padden and this author have written elsewhere about the significant class change that occurred after World War II and resulted in a larger Deaf middle class (Padden and Humphries 2005). One reason for this class change was the general improvement in economic conditions in the United States after World War II. Deaf people's access to better paying trades and professions fueled the growth of a Deaf middle class. Class change brought with it a desire for different images of the self that reflected a new class status. Desiring a different image of themselves, this Deaf middle class was open to change in the old language and discourse about them, which suddenly seemed to be inaccurate, inappropriate, and undignified. The older story of Deaf people that was characterized by descriptions of their hearing loss, ritualized statements of their inability to function in different ways, and social and educational underachievement no longer fit the image of themselves as people of middle-class affluence and position.

New scientific narratives were probably inevitable. A shift to a discourse of language and culture in talking about Deaf people and their lives, however, may not have been inevitable. Why did the new discourse take this particular form and not the forms of discourse taken by other people with disabilities? People who were seen to be in the same general human category with deaf people, such as people who use wheelchairs or people who are blind, were using a discourse of access and independent living in the 1960s and 1970s. Deaf people seemed not to embrace this discourse in the same way (Kailes and Weil 1985; Klienfield 1979; Owen 1987). In fact, they moved right past it and on to a discourse of language and culture.

Linguistic autonomy is one logical explanation for why Deaf people moved on to a discourse of language and culture in the 1960s. Having a language separate from English does set Deaf people apart from other people with disabilities. Their identities have always been wrapped up in their signed language, even as society failed to recognize it as language. We can speculate that it was inevitable (but, of course, we can't know it) that a newly affluent, middle class of Deaf people demanding a new image of themselves would want to feature their linguistic identity. We can also speculate that it was inevitable that the word *culture* would emerge as a group identifier. After all, American Deaf people, as a linguistic entity, have a long history going back several hundred years and have roots in Deaf societies in the old world. Was it only a matter of time until this people with a linguistic and social heritage would be considered a "cultural" group? Maybe, but it took work. Ironically, it took the work of cultural processes within the Deaf community to produce the discourse of "culture" that was, in turn, to produce a new scientific explanation of who Deaf people are.

CULTURAL PROCESSES AT WORK

William Stokoe's *Dictionary of American Sign Language* was a linguistic study of the parameters of signs (Stokoe et al. 1965). Stokoe painstakingly analyzed and cataloged hundreds of signs according to their articulatory or "phonological" structure. This was shocking to both Deaf and hearing people, not because signs were cataloged, but because Stokoe employed linguistic analysis and terminology to explain a finding—that sign language is indeed a language—which seemed to contradict all earlier scientific explanations (Eastman 1980).

What began then cannot be described too narrowly because, in fact, the processes that helped to formulate a new Deaf identity as a people of language and culture were myriad, complicated, and expansive. However, it is possible to attempt to identify some of the mechanisms and how they worked. The primary mechanism for the transformation that was to come was *talk,* or what I have referred to as "talking culture" (Clifford 1988; Humphries, 2008). As soon as there was a crack in the door—Stokoe's recognition that ASL was, indeed, a language—Deaf people began to talk about it, argue about it, and, interestingly, to do so in public. Prior to this time, Deaf people had never wanted, dared, or been able to talk about ASL as a language in public (Kannapell 1980). It could not have been done because the dominant scientific minds of hearing society had determined again and again in professional literature and in everyday English talk that ASL was not language (Fusfeld 1958; Myklebust 1960; Tervoort 1958).

Early talk about ASL was an invitation to an argument or at least a spirited discussion among Deaf people. Most Deaf people had to have it explained to them that Stokoe had shown that ASL has linguistic structure, just as spoken languages do. Many could not see how that could be true, as it had not been true for centuries. No one had ever let it be said that a sign language was really a language. One believed either that Stokoe's ideas were harebrained nonsense or that they were a brilliant admission that science had been completely wrong about signing behavior (Eastman 1980; Maher 1996). Many Deaf people, following the dominance of ideas of hearing people about them, were content to say that ASL was not a language. Some few were not, however. It's not that Deaf people had to be told that signs had parts. We can see in creative play with signs, which was a part of Deaf peoples' lives, that they knew what the parts were and how to manipulate them.

This knowledge is evident in such play as the traditional "ABC stories," which attempted to tell a story by linking the manual alphabet to handshapes that Stokoe was to identify as "cheremes" (the equivalent of phonemes; Stokoe et al. 1965). In short, in telling an ABC story, the signer starts with a sign containing a handshape that resembles the manual alphabet A and next uses a sign that resembles the manual alphabet B and so on to Z. The choice of signs with these manual alphabet-like handshapes had to form a coherent story. In other types of stories, the signer attempted to pick one handshape, for example, the handshape that corresponds with the number 1 on the finger (also identified by Stokoe as a chereme/phoneme). The signer proceeds to string together signs that contain this handshape to tell a story from beginning to end using just this handshape. There is other evidence that Deaf people knew how to disassemble their signs, but they could not talk about what they were doing in any language of science.

This brings us to a second mechanism, or cultural process, by which Deaf people transformed the narrative about themselves and their language: *performance*. *Performance* is used here in two ways: to refer to the performance of everyday life and also to refer to theatrical performance (Goffman 1959; Striff 2003). More than just talking about the language, Deaf people began to perform the language in public. And not just to perform it but also to foreground, highlight, and dissect it. The ABC stories, for example, were not inherently self-conscious, meaning they did not call attention to the parts of a language even though the production of them involved a lot of thought about the parts of signs. These ABC stories were rarely performed for anyone other than Deaf people, and they did not say, "Look at me, I am showing you my language" in the way that the National Theater of the Deaf's performance of some of the skits in *My Third Eye* in the early seventies did, for example (National Theatre of the Deaf 1973). In these performances, there was a joyful and deliberate effort by the actors to depict ASL as language on a very public national tour.

Performance was an important tool that Deaf people adopted in several ways. First, it was used to bring their language and culture into the public sphere. Second, performance had the power, through aesthetic and entertainment qualities, to compel an audience of both Deaf and hearing people to listen. It was not enough to just talk culture; Deaf people had to offer something that would compel attention. And third, performance was used to bridge the gap between folk explanation and scientific explanation. Emerging scientific explanations of ASL having linguistic features and processes were initially too foreign, too intellectual, and too abstract for consumption by most Deaf and hearing people. Performance allowed the introduction of the same ideas and the demonstration of the same processes without jargon and in traditions that people recognized or in forms that people were willing to attend.

A third mechanism in the creation of a new narrative of Deaf people and their language was explicit *instruction*. Adopting a stance of teaching others about themselves, particularly about that which had been private and previously thought of as unworthy of public instruction, was an important process. Instruction within one's own culture is often overlooked because one learns one's native language through a process of acquisition. As children, we acquire our language and our cultural identities and knowledge through a process of exposure and interaction with our families and communities. Some things, however, are learned through direct explanation, demonstration, and highlighting in conscious ways. We are taught, often explicitly in the form of classes, schools, colleges, and even workshops, certain ways of knowing and doing. Prior to the 1970s, Deaf people had nothing to teach hearing people. There were no classes in ASL because no one thought it was something to teach or worth teaching. There was no value attached to the mental or material artifacts of Deaf peoples' lives. Deaf people did not think hearing people were interested, and hearing people did not know there was something interesting to be learned from Deaf people.

But suddenly they did have something to teach. ASL and Deaf culture became commodities; they became content for public instruction (Welles 2004). Adopting the stance of having something to teach to hearing people was entirely new to

Deaf people. They had no experience with this process and had to create it as they went. Sometimes instruction was combined with performance to create interesting and attractive public displays of a new consciousness. This is discussed further on in this chapter.

A fourth process that Deaf people adopted in creating the new public story and image of themselves was *collecting* and *displaying* (Clifford 1988). To prove in a new public arena that they were a people of language and culture, Deaf people were compelled by forces outside the community to identify and display their cultural artifacts. Skeptics about a culture of Deaf people wanted to see evidence, wanted proof that a culture existed. In ASL they had visible and fascinating evidence of Deaf people's cultural lives. But the public demanded more and so Deaf people began to "collect themselves." In this process, Deaf people searched for and found other artifacts of Deaf culture. Their art, their literature, their jokes, and their technologies were some of the artifacts that they collected, displayed, and explained in an effort to show that they were a cultured people (Gannon 1981). Pressure from those outside the community to prove that, as a people, they had all the prerequisites of a cultural group became a catalyst for an urgent search for themselves.

And finally, a fifth process or mechanism worth mentioning here is the *differentiating* that Deaf people engaged in to create distance between themselves and others. This idea was explored in an earlier book (Humphries 1996) and will not be discussed in detail here, but this process involved at one level the differentiation of people (who is and who isn't Deaf), and at another level, it involved differentiation of artifacts (what is and what is not Deaf). Thus, defining who is deaf became a challenge among people within the community and among researchers seeking to draw a boundary around the Deaf culture (Markowicz and Woodward 1975; Padden and Markowicz 1976). The differentiation process proved crucial in propagating an understanding of the meaning of DEAF in the modern era, even as it led to bouts of identity politics in the Deaf community in the United States and other parts of the world. It extended beyond identities to behaviors and material artifacts. The cataloging of behaviors that were Deaf, or behaviors that differentiated them from hearing people, became a way to address the vacuum that was created by the introduction of the idea that cultures are different. If Deaf people have a culture of their own, we should be able to see the difference. Listing behaviors, such as Deaf people congregate in the kitchen at parties, Deaf people are blunt, and Deaf people have long and protracted leave-taking practices, were all early attempts, right or wrong, to differentiate Deaf people from hearing people (Holcomb 1977; Penilla and Taylor 2003).

These mechanisms and others like them, which make up the potential repertoire of cultural processes within a culture, did their work. Deaf people's folk knowledge of themselves, not previously explained in terms of ASL as a language and their "social group" as a cultural group, began to seep into scientific explanation. How did this happen? Some salient events best illustrate the convergence of the folk and the scientific.

PERFORMANCE AS SCIENTIFIC EXPLANATION— CHICAGO 1977 AND BOSTON 1980

By 1977, there had been almost a decade of rapidly accelerating linguistic research on ASL, a push to professionalize ASL teaching, and a new consciousness among

Deaf people of their cultural nature. However, all of these phenomena were just beginning, and the tone of discourse was tentative at best. Research laboratories had been established by hearing people in two key locations. At the Salk Institute in La Jolla, California, Ursula Bellugi had established a center that began intensive study of the structure and acquisition of ASL by Deaf children. At Gallaudet College (now Gallaudet University), William Stokoe had organized the Linguistics Research Lab (LRL) as a place to pursue linguistic studies of ASL. Other researchers at such places as the University of California at Berkeley and at San Diego as well as Northeastern University were growing interested in ASL as a potential vehicle for studying human languages and human development. But what was happening outside of these laboratories was equally fascinating. The Deaf community was experiencing an energetic and heated period of talking culture. During the early and mid-1970s, just a few years after the publication of Stokoe's dictionary, which shocked the sensibility of those who thought ASL was not a language, some "strange" talk begin to appear.

First, the words *Deaf* and *power* were juxtaposed to become a rallying cry for those who saw a political advantage in the newly emerging talk of Deaf culture. In fact, the words *Deaf* and *culture,* although commonly used together today, when combined to create the phrase "Deaf culture," had the power to cause consternation and debate within the Deaf community in 1975. There was even a short-lived struggle within the community to find a name for their language, which had been called "signing" or "the sign language" up to that point in time. Older generations of Deaf people were initially uncomfortable with labels for their signing behavior and resisted new names for it. After Stokoe referred to it as "the American Sign Language" (Stokoe et al. 1965), there was a brief flirtation with "Ameslan" (Fant 1972) and, finally, the community settled on "ASL." Other strange talk emerged. Audism came into being in 1975 (Humphries 1977; Wax and Danek 1982) but did not achieve widespread use until the '90s. *Deaf* and *pride* were juxtaposed and appeared in talk from time to time (Kannapell 1980).

Although the talk about ASL and Deaf culture was accelerating by 1977, it was by no means certain that the discourse of culture would last. Many Deaf people still had very little idea what it meant to think of themselves as a cultural group. The majority of society still had no understanding of signing behavior as possible language behavior. But there were organized efforts to recognize and facilitate understanding among both Deaf and hearing peoples. For example, the Communicative Skills Program of the National Association of the Deaf under Terence O'Rourke had started a move to professionalize the teaching of ASL by securing government grants to promote teacher training. Out of this effort, a plan grew for a National Symposium on Sign Language Research and Teaching in May 1977 in Chicago. The symposium was to bring together researchers and teachers and focus on the theme of research on ASL and the utilization of this research. This was probably the first time that linguists, psycholinguists, and sociolinguists had the opportunity to interact face to face with the early generation of ASL teachers and teacher trainers.

The symposium was more than an academic event. There was a level of emotion and excitement not usually present at such events. Deaf people at the conference were excited by research evidence establishing firmly that ASL was a language. ASL teachers were excited to learn new ways to analyze and explain the linguistic structure of ASL in their teaching. And researchers were excited about the potential for answering questions about the nature of language and the human capacity for language. All this excitement contributed to Deaf people's growing sense of affirmation and celebration of the emergence of their language into public view.

Researchers from the Salk Institute, from the LRL, and others, including a newly emerging cadre of graduate students doing work on ASL, found themselves in the presence of what can only be characterized as a groundswell of Deaf determination to place their language and culture at center stage in a very public way. ASL teachers and teacher trainers, for their part, found affirmation and validation at the symposium that would remain with them for years to come. Although the research presentations and the talks on teaching methods and practices were in themselves significant, there was another aspect of the symposium that is important to an analysis of how scientific and folk explanation converged at this crucial point in time.

When scholars began to look at ASL after Stokoe's critical introduction of the notion that there were patterns of internal structure, it is interesting that they were drawn to artistic expression and language play in ASL. In other words, they were fascinated by the performance of ASL. Edward Klima and Ursula Bellugi's book, *The Signs of Language*, published in 1979, contains two chapters on wit and humor, poetry, and "song" in sign.

> We have often been asked whether linguistic play—puns, plays on signs, linguistic wit—is natural or even possible in American Sign Language. Sometimes the question arises along with the much older question of whether or not the gesturing of the deaf does or does not constitute a language in the sense that English, say, is a language. Perhaps, or so this question sometimes implies, the existence or nonexistence of such plays on signs could give us clues to the status of ASL. Certainly the older literature on signs and signing contains much that would lead the uninitiated to question whether such possibilities exist. It has been suggested that the spontaneous use of signs in even an ironical or metaphorical way is virtually nonexistent. One might be led to suppose that creativity in the form of playful manipulation of linguistic units is also absent. (Klima and Bellugi 1979, 319)

The book goes on to show how ASL does, indeed, have spontaneous and metaphorical forms in expression. But in 1977, there was still much general skepticism of ASL's properties of language creativity. There was another even more insidious skepticism. Many felt that the language was limited to the everyday, the ordinary, and could not handle complex explanation, description, or instruction (Myklebust 1960). The old view of sign languages as rudimentary and unspecific systems with limited vocabulary choice was still very much present. People questioned whether ASL could be used to teach university subject matter or to explain how complex processes worked in everyday life. Initial impressions of ASL were that its vocabulary was too limited and its processes for expansion too primitive to incorporate modern knowledge.

Partly because of this misconception, Carlene Canady Pedersen and Carol Padden decided to perform explanations in ASL at a plenary session during the symposium. On stage and in front of an audience of hundreds, Pedersen explained in ASL how to change the oil in a car. Her detailed explanation was captivating for the simple reason that it was so elegantly clear and nuanced. The audience was fascinated by the generative nature of the language, how Pedersen displayed the stunning richness of the classifier system in ASL as she explained how to change the oil in a car. Because many in the audience were familiar with this procedure, they were able to match their knowledge to her explanation.

Then Carol Padden replaced Pedersen on stage and proceeded to give an explanation of how DNA is structured and works. Using the same language resources as Carlene Pedersen, Padden gave an equally detailed and visually striking depiction of Crick and Watson's double helix and how cells reproduce, down to the smallest detail of the matching of strands of matter. If the audience had been fascinated by the performance of changing the oil in ASL, they were amazed at the revelation that ASL could depict even the most abstract and modern of ideas; many confessed afterwards that they had not understood the concept of DNA before Padden's explanation. Unlike Pedersen's explanation of a process that they knew, Padden explained a process that was an abstraction.

As inspiration, these performances played an important role in this historical moment. These performances and many others like them across the country, performed by many other Deaf people, had the ability to do several things. They confirmed what Deaf people knew or wanted to believe about ASL. They convinced disbelievers that they had been wrong or at the very least that they should re-examine their beliefs. They took on legendary roles in the talk of ASL and Deaf culture. Padden's DNA explanation became the example of how ASL could do anything, including provide abstract academic explanation. And, probably most important of all, they bridged a gap between the work of research and the work of culture talking. As a process, performance served as both the substance of research examination and as the inspiration for Deaf people to continue to talk culture.

In 1980, when a third symposium was held in Boston, performance was again a part of it; however, now it was not so crucially involved with talking culture, but stood apart as "entertainment" rather than as a scientific demonstration. At this symposium, a featured event was an "Evening in ASL." It featured four Deaf performers, three well known and one newcomer. The three well-known performers were Dorothy Miles, Patrick Graybill, and Ella Mae Lentz. Miles was known for her work as an actress with the National Theater of the Deaf and as a poet. She had published English versions of her ASL poetry. Graybill was also known as an actor with the National Theater. Lentz was known as an ASL poet and as a trainer of ASL teachers. All three had been involved as research assistants or research subjects in the early linguistic studies of ASL. The newcomer was Clayton Valli, a young man just making his debut as an ASL poet. These four performers, one by one, performed both original and translated works in ASL to an appreciative audience who were entertained but not quite as amazed as they had been in 1977 to see Pedersen's and Padden's demonstrations of the extension of ASL. In the time between those 1977 performances and the 1980 performances, a subtle transformation had taken place. While in 1977 it was still necessary for Deaf people to perform the language in order to convince science that it existed in various forms and had the capacities that all language had, Deaf people by 1980 could perform in ASL merely to entertain. The folk science of Deaf people had converged with the science of others to create new ways of thinking and talking about ASL over the course of the 1970s.

SCIENTIFIC EXPLANATION AS PERFORMANCE

The convergence of Deaf people's "science" of themselves and the science of others (notably linguistics, sociolinguistics, and anthropology) was not only about hearing people accepting and adopting what Deaf people knew but was also about Deaf people accepting and learning to use the scientific explanations of others in describing their own language and culture. Talking culture started with the adoption of new terms like *ASL* and *Deaf culture,* but being able to explain these terms to each other was a much bigger task than just asking people to change their labels for things that already existed. Deaf people in the period from 1965 to 1980 were learning to accept that signing was language and that their way of being was culture (Padden and Humphries 1988). It was difficult for many Deaf people to overcome within themselves deeply held views of being languageless and cultureless.

> Here are some misconceptions about ASL widely held among the deaf population: "Poor English" (because it has no articles, no "to be" verbs, and no inflectional endings); "Shortcut English" (translating to ASL, you have to eliminate so much to have good ASL); "Simple language" (because for one 'big' English word you have to explain so much to get the same meaning, and it's easy to learn—just look at all those hearing people learning how to sign in such a short time); "deaf deaf language" (the language that uneducated deaf not having 'hearing' English use); "street language" (the kind of signing the deaf use 'on the street,' never in formal situations because it is limited and derogatory). (Lentz 1977, 239)

How did it happen that these views were changed? It is not possible to encompass all the things that transpired to bring about this rapid change in consciousness; but one aspect of it was that Deaf people instructed each other.

Many of the Deaf individuals involved in the early stages of ASL research made conscious decisions to change the ways that they talked about ASL and about their community. Some hearing people as well took it upon themselves to try to engage Deaf people in the new scientific way of talking about ASL. Sometimes Deaf and hearing people collaborated. When Deaf people (and hearing people as well) first began to explain ASL to themselves, there was no preexisting code for how to do so. No script or blueprint existed from which they could draw in explaining the most basic of concepts about ASL as a language. Terms we apply to ASL today without a second thought, such as *syntax, verb agreement,* and *inflection,* were alienated from sign language at that time. Does ASL have grammar? Does it have articles? Does it have prepositions? Although these questions seem preposterous on some level today, they were crucial questions then, and everything depended on how well they could be answered.

These attempts to instruct often took the form of workshops, courses, retreats, training sessions, and other organized instructional forms. Sometimes they were casual and part of everyday talk with other Deaf people individually or in small groups. Performance played a role in both types of instruction inasmuch as the instruction took on elements of rehearsed and ritualized explanations. As Deaf people began to develop effective ways to explain ASL to other Deaf people, they created among themselves certain means of explaining, certain language that they used, and ways of organizing information that became frozen in performance. Although they were instructing, they were also performing the instruction in very prescribed ways. Many who took up explaining or instructing their peers copied the performance of explanation about ASL used by those from whom they learned. The performances were sometimes rehearsed to the extent that they were practiced beforehand. And the performances were scripted to the extent that they relied on commonly used ways of explaining that were passed around and handed down. Instruction as performance became quite sophisticated and a sameness to the performances emerged.

For example, the performances often began with a discussion of myths about ASL. (These myths were incorporated into a booklet by Harry Markowicz and widely distributed [Markowicz 1977].) The following myths were most commonly addressed in these performances: Sign language is universal; sign language is transparent (iconic); ASL is not abstract (or is concrete); ASL has no grammar (or is ungrammatical); and ASL has a limited vocabulary. Whether in casual conversation (and this author both participated in and witnessed many such casual conversations) or during formal presentations, the explanations that addressed these myths invariably had the same form. For example, to counter the myth that ASL has no grammar, a French sentence would be glossed in English, producing an ungrammatical English sentence. Then the question would be asked: Does that mean French has no grammar?

Following the debunking of these myths, these performances commonly focused on phonology, showing that ASL signs have parts. Almost always, this was done by showing how ASL minimal pairs work and engaging the audience in discovering more minimal pairs. Many of these performances used exactly the same list of minimal pairs, which were explained in exactly the same way, as if scripted. The performances often went on to address grammatical processes in ASL, commonly focusing on directional verbs versus nondirectional verbs and pronominal incorporation, and they often ended with demonstrations of derivational processes in ASL, such as the derivation of nouns from verbs.

This instruction became more like performance because the people doing the explaining had just learned to think and talk about ASL in a new way and in a very short time span. Many Deaf people among those who originally performed these explanations were novices at doing it themselves. Many had little scientific training of their own; at best, they were paraprofessionals who were self-taught, learned by observation, had brief workshop-type training, learned from mentors, or had served as research or teaching assistants. Performing explanations that they had learned was a way to be sure that they had the information correct and was also a prescribed way to talk, which they felt had been effective in their own consciousness raising.

SHAPING SCIENTIFIC EXPLANATION

Because scientific explanation is, at bottom, explanation, it is fair to ask: Whose explanation? This is the scene in the late 1960s and early 1970s. William Stokoe has published his dictionary. It is not well received. Most people consider it misguided and idiosyncratic. There is no immediate move to change long-held beliefs about the nature of signing or claim that Deaf people, as a people of language, might be a people of culture. Reaction, what there is of it, is limited to a handful of hearing researchers and another handful of Deaf people who happen to interact with them. The scientific explanation of who Deaf people are and what their signing behavior constitutes is still unchanged, and although challenged, it is not likely to change soon. Unless Deaf people can find a way to accelerate alternative explanations, older scientific explanations seem likely to continue to dominate. Large-scale self-transformation of deaf individuals to new consciousness as *Deaf* individuals seems unlikely without an impetus. Despite the existence of a theoretical stance on sign language espoused by Stokoe and those who followed him "out there," it is mostly still only a theory.

Although it's not possible to pinpoint in this period of time when Deaf people started to talk culture and transform the dominant scientific explanation, it is possible to see the crucial elements of the transformation and to see what initial articulations of new explanations looked like.

One of the first articulations linked the new idea that ASL was a language to a larger idea that it was an artifact of a consciousness of a group of people. For example, Barbara Kannapell writes the following after a decade of personal self-examination and professional study of ASL and the Deaf community:

> So I know that a critical factor in understanding ASL is understanding that ASL is very much a part of a deaf person. If you want to change ASL, or take ASL away from the person, you are trying to take his or her identity away. I believe "my language is me." To reject a language is to reject the person herself or himself. Thus to reject ASL is to reject the deaf person. Remember ASL is a personal creation of deaf persons as a group. . . . Once I learned that ASL is my native language, I developed a strong sense of identity as a deaf person and a more positive self-image. (Kannapell 1980, 111–112)

She is echoing the general recognition within the community that, although it is exciting and important to hearing scientists that they have a new language to study that promises to yield interesting new approaches to questions of language and human development, it is much more than that for Deaf people. ASL springs from the consciousness of Deaf people; it is their creation and at the same time inseparable from their very identity. At the second National Symposium on Sign Language Research and Teaching, convened in San Diego in October 1978, Harlan Lane and Gilbert Eastman gave a performance which is notable in itself for the way it created a space in the midst of all of the talk about ASL research and teaching for the audience to consider Deaf people and their internal lives. Called "My Name Is Laurent Clerc," this performance by Lane, a hearing professor of psychology at Northeastern University, and Eastman, a deaf actor and teacher of drama at Gallaudet College, departed from the usual process of interpretation between ASL and English. In the usual process, a hearing person speaks the presentation and another hearing person interprets it in sign. Or, a Deaf person signs the presentation and a hearing person interprets it in voice. In this performance, they synchronized their presentations side by side. Eastman may have memorized his performance, and they may have worked out cues for each other to stay in synchronization. Lane spoke in character as Laurent Clerc, and Eastman signed in character as Laurent Clerc. Clerc, as is well known, was a Deaf French school teacher who migrated to the United States in 1816 and subsequently helped to found the first schools for the deaf in this country. He is a folk hero to many American Deaf people. With Lane speaking and Eastman signing, they simultaneously, as Clerc, told the story of his upbringing, his education, and the important people in his life (Sicard and Massieu to name two).

This performance captured the imagination of the audience for several reasons. The novelty of using the two voices of Clerc, one in English and one in ASL, was striking. But equally striking was the fact that this performance offered a previously unknown level of detail and suggested the emotional and mental life of a Deaf folk hero. The audience was stunned by the newness of the information about a historical figure and the suggestion of how he felt and thought. It is what is suggested by this collaboration of Lane and Eastman, whether intentional or not, that compelled attention. Near the end of this long performance, the character Clerc, as performed by Eastman and Lane, has been transported to San Diego in 1978 and says:

> In some ways, things have changed quite a lot over the century since then. Sign language has really evolved, hasn't it? I confess I don't understand very well many of the conversations I've looked in on here. I myself have always signed in the order of the words. That's the way I'm speaking to you now; I hope you don't mind. That's the way I learned it from the Abbé Sicard and that's the way I taught it to Gallaudet. I dare say your method's better. Real communication. "Language in another mode," they call it out here. Oh, yes, I've been looking in from time to time on what they do out here and on the East Coast, and, of course, in Washington and lots of other places and I've tried to keep up. I have a fair background in linguistics, the Abbe Sicard was very particular about that, and I even know some psychology, though they called it mental medicine when I went to school. I don't pretend to follow all the technical arguments that show that sign language has its own vocabulary, and its own ways of modifying that vocabulary to convey parts of speech, and its own syntax, and all that. The way I look at it is this, what is a language for? Why to love your parents, worship your God, raise your children, buy your food, keep your home, receive your friends, and share your joys—in a word, you need a language for living. And since sign language meets the needs of living, loving people, it surely is a language. (Eastman and Lane 1978, 333–334)

New scientific explanations of ASL, begun by hearing researchers in the 1960s and developed more fully as time went on, initially contained little reference to or interest in Deaf people themselves or a possible "culture" of Deaf people. Most interest was like Stokoe's; his 1965 *Dictionary of American Sign Language* finally talks about Deaf people in Appendix C:

> The deaf man is not essentially different any more than a Jew or Negro
> or Roman Catholic is essentially different from other segments of the
> American population. Like these, he is first and foremost an American in
> national and regional belonging, in education, in his way of earning a liv-
> ing, in his outlook on life, in his family and marriage patterns, in his rec-
> reational interest, in his successes and failures. (Stokoe et al. 1965, 301)

Although Klima and Bellugi's 1980 book, *The Signs of Language*, explains in great
detail their research on ASL during the 1960s and 1970s, it contains no reference
to Deaf people except to briefly comment on the native language status of the ASL
signers in their studies.

Contrary to a general assumption that it was the research on ASL that alerted
the world to Deaf people and their culture, it was actually cultural processes
within the Deaf community that brought into public view the people behind the
language. Situating ASL firmly within the consciousness of Deaf people, instead
of "out there" as a disconnected subject of research, these cultural processes
made an important contribution to a new scientific explanation of Deaf people.
Hearing people's science was interested in ASL for a different reason. Deaf
people quickly recognized that ASL and the performance of ASL (with the access to their interior lives that such performances gave to hearing people) were
a form of capital.

Performing deaf

Scientists studying ASL were, at first, only interested in seeing Deaf people sign
so as to see samples of the language in use. Poetry, stories, jokes, sign play, and
so on were all ways to tease out the internal and deep structure of the language.
But for Deaf people, realization grew that if there was interest among researchers
in seeing ASL and knowing ASL, there might also be interest among the general
public. A strong indicator of this was the experience of the National Theater of
the Deaf in attracting national interest in ASL theater during the 1960s (Padden
and Humphries 2005). This was a significant realization because Deaf people had
never felt that hearing people were remotely interested in their signing behavior.
Hearing people had always explained signing as un-language-like, primitive, and
lacking.

To suddenly notice that there might be a possible value attached to signing,
that there was a certain capital vested not just in ASL but also in the performance
of ASL, was a turning point for Deaf people in the 1960s. That it coincided with
researchers' interest in ASL as an object of study may or may not have been accidental, but the processes described earlier in this chapter took over within the
Deaf community. As talking, performing, instructing, collecting, and differentiating accelerated within the community, it became clear that there was a new
marketplace, a public space, where everything DEAF had value. Deaf identity
became coveted to the point that it was sometimes even contested by Deaf
people themselves. It was contested as if there was a limited supply of it, and
cheap claims of being DEAF were not to be allowed. How Deaf did you have to
be to be DEAF? This was an important question and one that still lingers. Being
DEAF became a desired state with tremendous status and economic advantage.

The state of DEAF-ness itself became valuable; job announcements began to seek "experience with Deaf culture."

Fluent ability in signing ASL became quite valuable in both Deaf and hearing people in such professions as teaching and interpreting—so valuable, in fact, that an industry of teaching ASL emerged, one that provided thousands of jobs to Deaf people (Freedman 2002). And the new scientific explanation of Deaf people took the form of "culture," a term in anthropology that had not been applied to Deaf people before. Performing in everyday talk, expressing themselves in public forums such as print and television, and instructing both Deaf and hearing people in thousands of classes across the country, Deaf people reveled in this new commodity.

In turn, this new value placed on Deaf people and their culture accelerated changes to the ways that science accounted for Deaf people. Scientific explanations in education, for example, which once described Deaf people as deficient and ASL as useless in pedagogy, acknowledged a culture of Deaf people and a possible advantage to bilingual, ASL-English, pedagogy. New bodies of scientific literature, often written by Deaf people themselves, emerged in literature, anthropology, and sociology. A field of Deaf studies emerged. In a very short time, a span of 10 to 15 years, Deaf people projected their language and the substance of their lives into public space in ways that produced new sociopolitical status and enormous economic gain.

NOVEL PRODUCTIONS

ASL and Deaf culture are new representations of DEAF and, as such, are novel productions. They are manifested in performance acts by Deaf people in private space and in public space. They are novel productions of a different consciousness but are also crucially involved in the formation of this new consciousness. DEAF has come to mean something different than it did in the first half of the twentieth century. But what it means to be DEAF has also changed. Some have theorized that the social movements of the 1950s and 1960s, the civil rights movement and the feminist movement to name two, made it more possible for a "DEAF movement" to occur (Jankowski 1997). Although it may be plausible that such movements, and the environment that existed in the United States as a result of them, set the stage for what occurred with Deaf people, it may be more realistic and more accurate to say that internal and accelerative processes within Deaf people's culture drove the formation of a new consciousness and novel external productions. It seems unlikely that, left to themselves, hearing researchers could have produced consciousness change for Deaf people. It was left to Deaf people, through their own means, to do that.

The performative acts described in this chapter can be seen as accelerative acts in producing new forms, explanations, representations, and identities. Metaculture, or culture about culture, as Urban and Lee call it, is its own accelerative force.

> The force behind such accelerative culture is the interest it generates, which stems in part from its novelty. It moves because it generates interest, catches the attention. How it accomplishes this task is what we . . . must investigate. (Urban and Lee 2001, 16)

With the accelerative power of their own internal processes, as well as the ability and resources to compel interest, Deaf people were able to create space for change. Realizing that the hearing people's science found their signing behavior interesting, Deaf people found ways to make their traditions new beyond the scientific laboratory and in public space. And they found that performing, or displaying, their talents and strangeness combined to compete better in public space for attention/thought than straightforward arguments that were likely to be rejected or seen as emotive or subjective. They made use of the public fascination with the aesthetics and exoticness of their language, their poetry, and the very idea of a human culture of deaf people. In doing so, they have been able to shape scientific explanation about themselves in specific ways.

Ultimately, what has emerged is a new voice of Deaf people, one that is an expression of the new science of themselves that is more aligned with the science of others. In earlier times, when the science of others convincingly portrayed Deaf people as a class of people without a language or culture of their own, Deaf people's notions of themselves survived only in nonscientific explanations. When an opportunity arose in the science of others for a possible alternative explanation, Deaf people embraced it and generated a new scientific explanation of their own that more closely paralleled that of others. It is not sufficient to say that the science of others recognized the existence of ASL and Deaf culture. For ASL to become a language and for a Deaf culture to emerge, it took the work of culture: Deaf people's culture.

REFERENCES

Armstrong, David F., Michael A. Karchmer, and John Vickrey Van Cleve. 2002. *The study of signed languages: Essays in honor of William C. Stokoe.* Washington, D.C.: Gallaudet University Press.

Associated Press. 2002. Enrollment in sign language classes swells. May 13.

Baker, Charlotte, and Robbin Battison, eds. 1980. *Sign language and the Deaf community: Essays in honor of William C. Stokoe.* Silver Spring, Md.: National Association of the Deaf.

Baker, Houston A., Jr. 1985. Autobiographical acts and the voice of the southern slave. In *The slave's narrative,* ed. Charles T. Davis and Henry L. Gates, 242–61. New York: Oxford University Press.

Basso, Keith H. 1979. *Portraits of "The Whiteman": Linguistic play and cultural symbols among the western Apache.* New York: Cambridge University Press.

Bellugi, Ursula, Edward S. Klima, and Patricia Siple. 1975. Remembering in signs. *Cognition* 3:93–125.

Bragg, Lois, ed. 2001. *Deaf world: A historical reader and primary sourcebook.* New York: New York University Press.

Brentari, Diane, ed. 2001. *Foreign vocabulary in sign languages: A cross-linguistic investigation of word formation.* Mahwah, N.J.: Lawrence Erlbaum Associates.

Chamberlain, Charlene, Jill P. Morford, and Rachel I. Mayberry. 2000. *Language acquisition by eye.* Mahwah, N.J.: Lawrence Erlbaum Associates.

Clifford, James. 1988. *The predicament of culture: Twentieth-century ethnography, literature, and art.* Cambridge, Mass.: Harvard University Press.

Coye, Terry, Tom Humphries, and Bette Martin. 1978. A bilingual, bicultural approach to teaching English. Paper presented at the Proceedings of the Second National Symposium on Sign Language Research and Teaching, Silver Spring, Md.

Davis, Hallowell, and S. Richard Silverman. 1960. *Hearing and deafness.* New York: Holt, Rinehart and Winston.

Eastman, Gil. 1980. From student to professional: A personal chronicle of sign language. In *Sign language and the Deaf community,* ed. Charlotte Baker and Robbin Battison, 9–32. Silver Spring, Md.: National Association of the Deaf.

Eastman, Gil, and Harlan Lane. 1978. My name is Laurent Clerc. Paper presented at the National Symposium on Sign Language Research and Teaching, San Diego.

Fant, Louie. 1972. *Ameslan: An introduction to American Sign Language.* Northridge, Calif.: Joyce Motion Picture Co.

Fusfeld, Irving S. 1958. How the deaf communicate—Manual language. *American Annals of the Deaf* 103:264–82.

Gannon, Jack R. 1981. *Deaf heritage: A narrative history of Deaf America.* Silver Spring, Md.: National Association of the Deaf.

Goffman, Erving. 1959. *The presentation of self in everyday life.* Garden City, N.Y.: Doubleday.

Hairston, Ernest, and Linwood Smith. 1983. *Black and Deaf in America: Are we that different?* Silver Spring, Md.: T.J. Publishers.

Holcomb, Roy K. 1977. *Hazards of Deafness.* Northridge, Calif.: Joyce Media.

Humphries, Tom. 1977. *Communicating across cultures (deaf-hearing and language learning).* PhD diss., Union Institute.

———. 1996. Of deaf-mutes, the strange, and the modern deaf self. In *Culturally affirmative psychotherapy with deaf persons,* ed. Neil S. Glickman and Michael A. Harvey, 99–114. Mahwah, N.J.: Lawrence Erlbaum Associates.

———. 2008. Talking culture and culture talking. In *Open your eyes: Deaf studies talking,* ed. H-Dirksen L. Bauman. Minneapolis: University of Minnesota Press.

Jankowski, Katherine. 1997. *Deaf empowerment: Emergence, struggle, and rhetoric.* Washington, D.C.: Gallaudet University Press.

Kailes, June I., and Marie Weil. 1985. People with physical disabilities and the independent living model. In *Case management in human service practice,* ed. Marie Weil and James M. Karls. San Francisco: Jossey-Bass.

Kannapell, Barbara. 1980. Personal awareness and advocacy in the deaf community. In *Sign language and the Deaf community: Essays in honor of William C. Stokoe,* ed. Charlotte Baker and Robbin Battison, 105–16. Silver Spring, Md.: National Association of the Deaf.

Kaplan, Alice Y. 1994. On language memoir. In *Displacements: Cultural identities in question,* ed. Angelika Bammer, 59–69. Bloomington: Indiana University Press.

Klienfield, Sonny. 1979. *The hidden minority.* New York: Atlantic-Little, Brown.

Klima, Edward S., and Ursula Bellugi. 1979. *The signs of language.* Cambridge, Mass.: Harvard University Press.

Krauel, Charles. 1986. *Charles Krauel: Profile of a deaf filmmaker.* Produced by Ted Supalla. San Diego: DawnSign Press.

Lane, Harlan. 1976. *The wild boy of Aveyron.* Cambridge, Mass.: Harvard University Press.

———. 1984. *When the mind hears: A history of the Deaf.* New York: Random House.

Lane, Harlan, Robert Hoffmeister, and Benjamin Bahan. 1996. *A journey into the DEAF-WORLD.* San Diego: DawnSign Press.

Lentz, Ella Mae. 1977. Informing the deaf about the structure of ASL. Paper presented at the National Symposium on Sign Language Research and Teaching, Chicago.

Maher, Jane. 1996. *Seeing language in sign: The work of William C. Stokoe.* Washington, D.C.: Gallaudet University Press.

Markowicz, Harry. 1977. *American Sign Language: Fact and fancy.* Washington, D.C.: Gallaudet College.

Markowicz, Harry, and James Woodward. 1975. Language and the maintenance of ethnic boundaries in the deaf community. Paper presented at the Conference on Culture and Communication, Philadelphia.

McKee, Rachel L., and Bruce Connew. 2001. *People of the eye: Stories from the Deaf world*. Wellington, New Zealand: Bridget Williams Books.

Myklebust, Helmer R. 1960. *Psychology of deafness*. New York: Grune and Stratton.

National Theatre of the Deaf. 1973. *My third eye*. West Hartford, Conn.: Author.

Owen, Mary Jane. 1987. The 504 demonstrations of 1977. *Rehabilitation Gazette*, 231.

Padden, Carol. 1988. *Interaction of morphology and syntax in American Sign Language*. New York: Garland Press.

Padden, Carol, and Harry Markowicz. 1975. Crossing cultural boundaries into the Deaf community. Unpublished manuscript.

———. 1976. Cultural conflicts between hearing and deaf communities. Paper presented at the Proceedings of the VII World Congress of the World Federation of the Deaf, Washington, D.C.

Padden, Carol, and Tom Humphries. 1988. *Deaf in America: Voices from a culture*. Cambridge, Mass.: Harvard University Press.

———. 2005. *Inside Deaf culture*. Cambridge, Mass.: Harvard University Press.

Penilla, Adan, and Angela Lee Taylor. 2003. *Signing for dummies*. New York: Wiley Publishing, Inc.

Schein, Jerome D. 1968. *The Deaf community: Studies in the social psychology of deafness*. Washington, D.C.: Gallaudet College Press.

Siple, Patricia, ed. 1978. *Understanding language through sign language research*. New York: Academic Press.

Stokoe, William C., Carl Croneberg, and Dorothy Casterline. 1965. *A dictionary of American Sign Language on linguistic principles*. Washington, D.C.: Gallaudet College Press.

Striff, Erin. 2003. Introduction: Locating performance studies. In *Performance studies*, ed. Erin Striff. New York: Palgrave Macmillan.

Supalla, Ted, and Ellisa L. Newport. 1978. How many seats in a chair? The derivation of nouns and verbs in American Sign Language. In *Understanding language through sign language research*, ed. Patricia Siple, 91–132. New York: Academic Press.

Tervoort, Bernard T. 1958. Acoustic and visual language communicating systems. *Volta Review* 60: 374–80.

Urban, Greg, and Benjamin Lee. 2001. *Metaculture: How culture moves through the world*. Minneapolis: University of Minnesota Press.

Veditz, George W. 1913. *The preservation of the sign language* [film]. Silver Spring, Md.: National Association of the Deaf.

Wax, Teena, and Marita M. Danek. 1982. Deaf women and double jeopardy: Challenge for research and practice. Paper presented at the Sociology of Deafness, Washington, D.C., 178–96.

Welles, Elizabeth B. 2004. Foreign language enrollments in United States Institutes of Higher Education. *ADFL Bulletin*, Winter.

Wertsch, James. 1997. Collective memory: Issues from a sociohistorical perspective. In *Mind, culture, and activity: Seminal papers from the laboratory of comparative human cognition*, ed. Michael Cole, Yrjo Engestrom, and Olga Vásquez, 226–32. New York: Cambridge University Press.

Wilbur, Ronnie. B. 1979. *American sign languages and sign systems*. Baltimore: University Park Press.

2 | Who Am I?
    | Deaf Identity Issues

Irene W. Leigh

"I am deaf." What a seemingly simple phrase! But in actuality, "I am deaf" is a complex phrase, with various meanings depending on the background and experience of the individual making that statement. The person diagnosed as audiologically deaf from birth, the person who navigates a progressive or late-life hearing loss, and the deaf person growing up in a culturally Deaf family: Each one has a different self-perception of *deaf*. Whatever *deaf* means to each deaf individual has great salience for that person's identity evolution.

While the concept of identity has long been explored in the psychology, sociology, and anthropology literature, its relevance has exploded in recent decades, as evidenced by increased publications on the topic. This explosion has been fueled by the increase in cultural diversity and subsequent interest in cultural or ethnic group membership and social identity within the United States and other countries (Sue and Sue 2003). Because of the present acknowledgment of a long-existing Deaf culture (Padden and Humphries 2005), researchers interested in the implications of diversity and deaf people have begun to move from the traditional focus on self-concept and self-esteem toward developing studies that explore deaf identity, how it evolves in deaf individuals, and its role in the psychological health of deaf individuals. The role of group perspectives in the reinforcement of deaf identity evolution is also of interest to researchers.

As we know, people have multiple identities, depending on their environment and what is most salient at any given point in time. These identities, which help individuals define and understand themselves as well as align with social groups, tend to be forged through perceptions of differences and classifications, including

This chapter is based on material that originally appeared in the following two chapters: I. W. Leigh, Being a Deaf adult: Viewpoints from psychology. In *Deaf people: Evolving perspectives from psychology, education, and sociology,* ed. J. F. Andrews, I. W. Leigh, and T. Weiner. Boston: Allyn & Bacon, 2004; I. W. Leigh, Deaf: Moving from hearing loss to diversity. In *Culturally diverse mental health: The challenges of research and resistance,* ed. J. Mio and G. Iwamasa, 323–39. New York: Brunner-Routledge, 2003.

gender, ethnicity, educational levels, career categories, sexual orientation, hearing status, and so on (Corker 1996; Waterman 1992; Woodward 1997). Healthy identity development is a critical component of positive psychological adjustment (Erikson 1980).

Exactly what is identity? Identity consists of self-perceptions that evolve out of social constructions (Baumeister 1997; Holland, Lachicotte, Skinner, and Cain 1998). These social constructions are based on interactions with others in multiple ongoing social contexts (Baumeister 1997; Grotevant 1992; Harter 1997; Kroger 1996). As new information about oneself emerges, mostly through lifelong, ongoing experiences and the responses of others toward the self, there is often a process of identity restructuring (Grotevant 1992). In turn, as Woodward (1997) indicates, identities influence how people select their self-representations and behaviors, depending on social context.

SOCIALIZATION INFLUENCES

The interface of language, communication, and hearing ability, in tandem with social environments, has a powerful impact on how deaf individuals conceptualize their deaf-related identity. It is a well-known axiom that ease in communication and socializing leads to enhanced social competence (e.g., Andrews, Leigh, and Weiner 2004; Antia and Kreimeyer 2003; Calderon and Greenberg 2003; Marschark, Lang, and Albertini 2002). The degree of social ease, however, is based on the reference group (hearing, deaf, or culturally Deaf groups), the specific language/communication being used within each group setting, and the naturalness of this communication. For example, a deaf person with well-developed spoken language capability and minimal American Sign Language (ASL) skills will typically not find it easy to feel a strong sense of social competence in gatherings attended by culturally Deaf individuals and will develop a culturally Deaf identity only after having increased positive contact with these individuals and improving his or her facility in the use of ASL. In turn, culturally Deaf individuals may rely on paper and pencil, pagers, or speech to communicate with spoken language users. In such situations, the degree of felt social competence may vary according to the level of comfort with written and/or spoken language use. These social experiences and feelings of social competency will significantly impact the process of internalizing deaf identities.

When a deaf child grows up in a family in which both parents are culturally Deaf, *Deaf* means using ASL, developing Deaf ways of being and communicating, and going to events frequented by Deaf people. "Deaf" becomes the normal center of being. Being able to hear with the assistance of auditory devices is seen as ancillary rather than paramount. The social environment of Deaf culture and the trend toward sending these children to educational settings where ASL is used (Mitchell and Karchmer 2005) reinforces the development of a culturally Deaf identity.

Estimates are that approximately 4 percent of the children born to deaf parents are deaf (Moores 2001, 24). It is often assumed that all of these children will be assimilated into Deaf culture, but there are exceptions, such as when the deaf parents use only spoken language. For these deaf children, deaf identity will emerge in somewhat different frames, possibly modeled after their deaf parents and incorporating the nature of their own varied experiences, including social experiences with hearing, deaf, or both hearing and deaf peers in school and outside school.

For the remaining 96 percent born to hearing parents, the paths toward affirming some kind of deaf identity are less clear-cut. More of those hearing parents will focus on communicating with their children using spoken language rather than sign language, which requires a commitment to learning a new language. Greater numbers of this population are receiving their education in mainstream settings (Karchmer and Mitchell 2003). Ever-increasing percentages of this group are being fitted with cochlear implants, rather than hearing aids, at a young age (Christiansen and Leigh 2005).

Overall, hearing parents typically view being deaf through the lens of audiology, hearing loss, and difference, and not as a cultural phenomenon. Based on a Gallaudet Research Institute survey and participation in interviews about their experiences, the majority of parents of children with cochlear implants report not meeting deaf adults, whether oral or signing, at the time of diagnosis of deafness or when deciding on cochlear implantation for their deaf children (Christiansen and Leigh 2005). For deaf children of hearing parents, exposure to deaf peers or to Deaf culture comes, if at all, when the children get older and are provided with opportunities for interacting either in educational programs that include deaf children or during social functions that involve large groups of deaf people (Andrews, Leigh, and Weiner 2004). Very often, this exposure hinges on the advice, guidance, and information provided by professionals specializing in working with deaf and hard of hearing individuals, typically within early intervention, audiology, or educational settings. These professionals can significantly influence the perceptions about deafness of the parents they work with and in turn influence their children's self-perceptions. However, professionals have their own biases (Mertens, Sass-Lehrer, and Scott-Olson 2000). How these professionals convey implicit messages about successfully integrating into hearing worlds or interacting with other deaf peers can play a significant role in framing the meaning of deaf identity, whether as a minuscule difference (not hearing), a stigmatized concept to be minimized, or as a significant core identity.

Corker (1996) addresses the question of whether deaf identity can be considered a "core identity," particularly for those deaf children and youths who do not grow up within deaf families. She claims that incorporating deaf identity becomes an additional developmental task, dependent in large part on the nature of the deaf child's environment, including family and school situations. The presence of stigma or feelings of difference when in the presence of hearing persons can heighten the salience of a deaf identity. In contrast, when these feelings are minimal or absent, the desire to focus on deafness as an integral part of one's identity may be lessened.

DEAF IDENTITY AND MULTICULTURALISM

According to Corker (1996), in families consisting of hearing parents, ethnic or racial identity related to the culture of the family is a more critical determinant than deaf identity during the early years of core identity construction. Ethnic diversity is increasingly present in the population of deaf people. The Gallaudet

Research Institute's (2002) demographic information, collected from schools and programs enrolling deaf and hard of hearing children between 1974 and 2001 (representing approximately 65 percent of this specialized population), reveals a 22 percent drop in the number of White students together with a 14.8 percent increase in Hispanic students and a 3.2 percent increase in Asian-Pacific Islander students, while the percentage of African American students has remained relatively consistent at 16 percent. The Native American and multiethnic categories show modest increases (0.4 percent and 1.3 percent, respectively). It is important to note that ethnic demographic patterns for deaf children in school programs as indicated here (Gallaudet Research Institute 2002) are very similar to the projections made by the U.S. Bureau of the Census (1996, as cited in Delgado 2000).

Consequently, the ethnic backgrounds of deaf persons will influence the salience of deaf identities, depending on which "community" the deaf person is in. In general, deaf individuals are likely to be involved with up to four communities: the majority hearing community, the larger deaf community, their ethnic hearing community, and their ethnic deaf community (Corbett 1999; Leigh, Corbett, Gutman, and Morere 1996; Wu and Grant 1999). Specifically, they may adapt their method of communication and behavior appropriately to suit the specific community in which they find themselves and switch as they move from one community to another. Depending on the situation, for example, they may identify themselves as deaf and Latino in their ethnic community, and as Latino and Deaf in the Deaf community. This fits the alternation model of LaFromboise, Coleman, and Gerton (1993), which essentially encapsulates the ability of individuals to alter their behavior to fit the social context while still being true to their inner sense of self. In this way, neither deaf identity or ethnic identity is denied.

THEORETICAL FOUNDATIONS

What are the classifications that constitute deaf identity? How do deaf identities develop? Researchers have worked to develop categories based on theoretical frames of reference in order to answer these questions.

The medical model reflects a conventional perception of what it means to be deaf (Gonsoulin 2001). Specifically, the focus is on hearing loss per se, with the basic approach being that of detection, cure, or rehabilitation. This model is often applicable to those who identify themselves as audiologically deaf, hearing impaired, hard of hearing, or some other similar term (Leigh 1999). Weinberg and Sterritt (1986) used this disability (meaning deficit)-based framework to create the following categories: hearing identity meaning able-bodied or, in other words, when the deaf person psychologically identifies as a hearing person and endeavors to hide the deafness; deaf identity conceptualized as disability related; and dual identity reflecting identification with both deaf and hearing peers. In exploring the relationship between identity categories and adjustment using a brief questionnaire, they found that dual identity was associated with more positive adjustment outcomes.

Stinson and Kluwin (1996) relied on a conceptual model of social orientation to categorize identities as deaf oriented, hearing oriented, or oriented to both groups. Specifically, identity categories were determined primarily on the basis of whether social peers were deaf, hearing, or both. Differences in identity choices were predicated on the perceived quality of social experiences, which is related to comfort in communicating and socializing with specific peer groups (Leigh 1999; Stinson, Chase, and Kluwin 1990).

Using cluster analysis, Bat-Chava (2000) derived three identity categories: culturally hearing, culturally Deaf, and bicultural, using four criterion variables related to communication and socialization: importance of signing, importance of speech, group identity, and attitudes toward deaf people. These criterion variables highlight the importance of language and communication, socialization, and societal perceptions in forging deaf or hearing-related identities. This represents an attempt to move away from the medical model of disability and capture the sociolinguistic aspect of deafness, which incorporates shared perspectives about a Deaf way of life, with a common language, common attitudes, social obligations to each other, and a unique quality of life.

An in-depth examination of theoretical conceptualizations of deaf identities was undertaken by Neil Glickman (1996). His theoretical model is based on a compendium of cultural and racial identity development models. Paralleling these models, he lists four different stages of deaf identity, which he originally viewed to be developmental. The first stage is defined as the culturally hearing stage. In this stage, deafness is perceived as based on the medical model, as described earlier. To achieve parity with hearing peers, the deaf person needs to emulate hearing ways of speaking, understanding, and behaving. Taking advantage of auditory rehabilitation techniques and ameliorating the need for support services are seen as avenues for integrating into hearing society. Glickman views this stage as most relevant to individuals who lose their hearing in adulthood, but also applicable to deaf users of spoken English who interact primarily with hearing peers, and who may belong to organizations advocating the teaching of spoken language to deaf children. His basic assumption is that this stage tends not to be a healthy one emotionally for those growing up deaf, since they are essentially denying their deafness.

The next stage is that of cultural marginality for deaf persons who do not fully identify with either Deaf or hearing culture. They find themselves on the fringe of both cultures and experience difficulties interacting within deaf or hearing groups. Glickman theorizes that this category is applicable to deaf children born into hearing families who initially are naïve to deafness. These children start off with little to no exposure to deaf groups and are not fully part of the hearing environment because of limited access to sound and spoken language.

Deaf individuals in the third stage move toward immersing themselves in the "Deaf-World" (Lane, Hoffmeister, and Bahan 1996). They embrace a positive, uncritical, and idealized identification with the Deaf-World and act the way they believe authentic "Deaf" people are supposed to. Hearing values, including speech, are denigrated. Hearing people are perceived through a negative lens, as are deaf people with "hearing minds" who speak English. Persons who are culturally Deaf can do no wrong.

The fourth stage is reflective of Deaf people who have recognized the strengths and weaknesses of both culturally Deaf and hearing people. They are now more capable of integrating the values of both hearing and Deaf cultures and participate in each environment. ASL and English are respected. For this reason, the fourth stage is labeled the bicultural stage. This is a stance increasingly adopted by individuals identifying with Deaf culture because current technology (e.g., e-mail, text messaging, the Internet, and video relay services) and work settings offer more opportunities for interaction with hearing peers (Padden 1996), albeit not without some dissonance (see below).

Careful scrutiny of Glickman's (1996) theory demonstrates that the development of deaf identities does not occur in a linear fashion. Not every deaf person starts at the first stage. For example, deaf children of culturally Deaf parents tend to start off identifying as culturally Deaf and eventually may perceive themselves as bicultural, depending on life experiences. Those who are culturally marginal may remain stuck in that stage, or move toward hearing, culturally Deaf, or bicultural stances.

Glickman (1996) constructed the Deaf Identity Development Scale (DIDS) to assign the four identity categories listed above. The psychometric properties appear sound with the possible exception of the bicultural scale, which may have been impacted by social desirability factors (seeing oneself as bicultural is perceived as a positive attribute by most people filling out this scale) (Leigh, Marcus, Dobosh, and Allen 1998). Fischer and McWhirter (2001) revised the DIDS. While improved reliability for the bicultural scale was demonstrated, this reliability was lower compared to the other scales.

Deborah Maxwell-McCaw (2001) has adapted acculturation models that explain how immigrants adjust to life in the United States to account for how people gravitate toward identity categories. These models incorporate acculturation patterns, which may vary in terms of the level of psychological (or internalized) identification with each culture (the culture of origin and the new host culture), the degree of behavioral involvement in the two cultures, and the level of cultural competence in these cultures. In applying these to deaf individuals, she retains Glickman's (1996) four identity categories, which she conceptualizes as varying in terms of the level of psychological identification with Deaf and hearing cultures, the degree of behavioral involvement in both cultures, and the level of cultural competence in each culture.

To test this idea, Maxwell-McCaw (2001) developed the Deaf Acculturation Scale (DAS), which consists of two scales: a Deaf Acculturation Scale and a Hearing Acculturation Scale. Based on a median split of the Hearing and Deaf Acculturation scales, the overall scale will produce four kinds of acculturation in Deaf people: hearing acculturated (high scores in hearing acculturation and low scores in deaf acculturation), marginal (low scores in both hearing and deaf acculturation), deaf acculturated (high scores in deaf acculturation and low scores in hearing acculturation), and bicultural (high scores in both deaf and hearing acculturation). Reliability and validity were demonstrated to be in the acceptable range.

Maxwell-McCaw (2001) also explored the relationship between psychological well-being and DAS acculturation styles. Her results indicated that for deaf and hard of hearing subjects, deaf acculturation and biculturalism were equally associated with a healthy sense of well-being, more so than for those who were hearing acculturated. Marginalism was found to be the least adaptive of the four acculturation styles. In essence, being comfortable as a Deaf person is as critical for psychological well-being as is the ability to switch comfortably between Deaf and hearing environments. This finding has also been substantiated in other studies (Bat-Chava 2000; Jambor and Elliott 2005).

While assuming that a bicultural identity facilitates psychological well-being, this identification basically incorporates self-perceptions of the ability to move between Deaf and hearing cultures. How it may actually play out in practice depends greatly on whether the bicultural person is seen as "true" to Deaf culture. Deaf and hard of hearing individuals who are comfortable with spoken English have expressed feelings of being torn between Deaf and hearing circles and being doubted or not accepted by culturally Deaf persons (Leigh 1999). Framing a deaf person as having a "hearing mind" rather than as capable of respecting both cultures carries with it the possibility of placing the deaf person in a position of uncomfortable marginality with respect to Deaf culture. In turn, if there is difficulty in fully integrating into hearing environments, the sense of marginality or of being rooted within Deaf culture will prevail over the capability of being bicultural.

In this chapter, we have included hard of hearing in addition to deaf persons throughout the discussion of deaf identities. However, the literature has begun to entertain the notion of a hard of hearing identity. Hard of hearing adults do struggle with issues of marginalization and identification, whether with hearing or deaf communities (Leigh et al. 1998). Interestingly, current research suggests that those hard of hearing youth placed in special education programs gravitate more readily to a hard of hearing identity (Israelite, Ower, and Goldstein 2002) in contrast to those who are in the mainstream and dealing with negative perceptions of being "different" (Kent 2003). Now that there is renewed interest in studying the hard of hearing population, we can anticipate more studies of hard of hearing identity issues.

CONCLUSION

Based on McAdams's (1997, 5) perspective, "identity is a life story." In this vein, deaf identity, whatever its manifestation, evolves throughout life as a deaf person experiences specific family, school, and outside environments and develops specific linguistic and communication capabilities in responding to these environments. These individualized experiences and capabilities work in tandem to create one's self-perception of deaf identity. Thanks to the nature of human variation, deaf identity is not a fixed construct, but one that is defined by individual experiences and cultural exposure. As we move further into the twenty-first century, we will see how historical, cultural, and technological forces reshape today's deaf identities.

REFERENCES

Andrews, J., I. W. Leigh, and M. Weiner. 2004. *Deaf people: Evolving perspectives from psychology, education, and sociology.* Boston: Allyn & Bacon.

Antia, S., and K. Kreimeyer. 2003. Peer interaction of deaf and hard-of-hearing children. In *Oxford handbook of Deaf studies, language, and education,* ed. M. Marschark and P. Spencer, 164–76. New York: Oxford University Press.

Bat-Chava, Y. 2000. Diversity of deaf identities. *American Annals of the Deaf* 145 (5):420–28.

Baumeister, R. 1997. The self and society: Changes, problems, and opportunities. In *Self and identity,* ed. R. D. Ashmore and L. Jussim, 191–217. New York: Oxford University Press.

Calderon, R., and M. Greenberg. 2003. Social and emotional development of deaf chil-
    dren. In *Oxford handbook of Deaf studies, language, and education*, ed. M. Marschark
    and P. Spencer, 177–89. New York: Oxford University Press.
Christiansen, J. B., and I. W. Leigh. 2005. *Children with cochlear implants: Ethics and choices.*
    Washington, D.C.: Gallaudet University Press.
Corbett, C. 1999. Mental health issues for African American deaf people. In *Psychotherapy
    with deaf clients from diverse groups*, ed. I. W. Leigh, 151–76. Washington, D.C.: Gallaudet
    University Press.
Corker, M. 1996. *Deaf transitions.* London: Jessica Kingsley.
Delgado, G. 2000. How are we doing? In *Deaf plus: A multicultural perspective*, ed. K.
    Christensen. San Diego: DawnSign Press.
Erikson, E. 1980. *Identity and the life cycle.* New York: W. W. Norton.
Fischer, L. C., and J. McWhirter. 2001. The Deaf Identity Development Scale: A revision
    and validation. *Journal of Counseling Psychology* 48 (3):355–58.
Gallaudet Research Institute. 2002. Race/ethnic background of deaf children in U.S. re-
    gional and national summary report of data from 1973 to 2001. *Annual surveys of deaf
    and hard of hearing children and youth.* Washington, D.C.: GRI, Gallaudet University.
Glickman, N. 1996. The development of culturally deaf identities. In *Culturally affirmative
    psychotherapy with Deaf persons*, ed. N. Glickman and M. Harvey, 115–53. Mahwah, N.J.:
    Lawrence Erlbaum Associates.
Gonsoulin, T. 2001. Cochlear implant/Deaf world dispute: Different bottom elephants.
    Otolaryngology—Head and Neck Surgery 125 (5):552–56.
Grotevant, H. D. 1992. Assigned and chosen identity components: A process perspective
    on their integration. In *Adolescent identity formation*, ed. G. R. Adams, T. P. Gullota, and
    R. Montemayor, 73–90. Newbury Park, Calif.: Sage.
Harter, S. 1997. The personal self in social context. In *Self and identity*, ed. R. D. Ashmore
    and L. Jussim, 81–105. New York: Oxford University Press.
Holland, D., W. Lachicotte, D. Skinner, and C. Cain. 1998. *Identity and agency in cultural
    worlds.* Cambridge, Mass.: Harvard University Press.
Israelite, N., J. Ower, and G. Goldstein. 2002: Hard-of-hearing adolescents and identity
    construction. *Journal of Deaf Studies and Deaf Education* 7 (2):134–48.
Jambor, E., and M. Elliott. 2005. Self-esteem and coping strategies among deaf students.
    Journal of Deaf Studies and Deaf Education 10 (4):63–81.
Karchmer, M. and R. Mitchell. 2003. Demographic and achievement characteristics of deaf
    and hard-of-hearing students. In *Oxford handbook of Deaf studies, language, and educa-
    tion*, ed. M. Marschark and P. Spencer, 21–37. New York: Oxford University Press.
Kent, B. 2003. Identity issues for hard-of-hearing adolescents aged 11, 13, and 15 in main-
    stream settings. *Journal of Deaf Studies and Deaf Education* 8 (3):315–24.
Kroger, J. 1996. *Identity in adolescence.* New York: Routledge.
LaFromboise, T., H. Coleman, and J. Gerton. 1993. Psychological impact of biculturalism:
    Evidence and theory. *Psychological Bulletin* 114 (3):395–412.
Lane, H., R. Hoffmeister, and B. Bahan. 1996. *A journey into the Deaf-World.* San Diego:
    DawnSign Press.
Leigh, I. W. 1999. Inclusive education and personal development. *Journal of Deaf Studies
    and Deaf Education* 4 (3):236–45.
Leigh, I. W., C. Corbett, V. Gutman, and D. Morere. 1996. Providing psychological services
    to deaf individuals: A response to new perceptions of diversity. *Professional Psychol-
    ogy: Research and Practice* 27 (4):364–71.
Leigh, I. W., A. Marcus, P. Dobosh, and T. Allen. 1998. Deaf/hearing identity paradigms:
    Modification of the Deaf Identity Development Scale. *Journal of Deaf Studies and Deaf
    Education* 3 (4):329–38.
Marschark, M., H. Lang, and J. Albertini. 2002. *Educating deaf students: From research to prac-
    tice.* New York: Oxford University Press.

Maxwell-McCaw, D. L. 2001. Acculturation and psychological well-being in deaf and hard-of-hearing people. Ph.D. diss., George Washington University. Abstract in *Dissertation Abstracts International* 61 (11-B): 6141.

McAdams, D. 1997. *The stories we live by.* New York: Guilford.

Mertens, D., M. Sass-Lehrer, and K. Scott-Olson. 2000. Sensitivity in the family-professional relationship: Parental experiences in families with young deaf and hard of hearing children. In *The deaf child in the family and at school,* ed. P. Spencer, C. Erting, and M. Marschark, 133–50. Mahwah, N.J.: Lawrence Erlbaum Associates.

Mitchell, R., and M. Karchmer. 2005. Parental hearing status and signing among deaf and hard of hearing students. *Sign Language Studies* 5 (2):231–44.

Moores, D. 2001. *Educating the deaf: Psychology, principles, and practices.* Boston: Houghton Mifflin.

Padden, C. 1996. From the cultural to the bicultural: The modern deaf community. In *Cultural and language diversity and the deaf experience,* ed. I. Parasnis, 79–98. New York: Cambridge University Press.

Padden, C., and T. Humphries. 2005. *Inside Deaf culture.* Cambridge, Mass.: Harvard University Press.

Stinson, M., K. Chase, and T. Kluwin. April 1990. Self-perceptions of social relationships in hearing impaired adolescents. Paper presented at the American Educational Research Association Convention, Boston, April 16–20.

Stinson, M., and T. Kluwin. 1996. Social orientations toward deaf and hearing peers among deaf adolescents in local public high schools. In *Understanding deafness socially: Continuities in research and theory,* 2nd ed., ed. P. C. Higgins and J. E. Nash, 113–34. Springfield, Ill.: Charles C. Thomas.

Sue, D. W., and D. Sue. 2003. *Counseling the culturally diverse: Theory and practice.* New York: John Wiley and Sons.

Waterman, A. S. 1992. Identity as an aspect of optimal psychological functioning. In *Adolescent identity formation,* ed. G. R. Adams, T. P. Gullotta, and R. Montemayor, 50–72. Newbury Park, Calif.: Sage.

Weinberg, N., and M. Sterritt. 1986. Disability and identity: A study of identity patterns in adolescents with hearing impairments. *Rehabilitation Psychology* 31 (2):95–102.

Woodward, K. 1997. Concepts of identity and difference. In *Identity and difference,* ed. K. Woodward, 7–50. Thousand Oaks, Calif.: Sage.

Wu, C., and N. Grant. 1999. Asian American and Deaf. In *Psychotherapy with deaf clients from diverse groups,* ed. I. W. Leigh, 203–26. Washington, D.C.: Gallaudet University Press.

3 | Think–Between:
A Deaf Studies
Commonplace Book

Brenda Jo Brueggemann

For some time now, I have been imagining a theory of "betweenity," especially as it exists in Deaf culture, identity, and language. And because I teach a great deal in the larger umbrella of disability studies these days, I've also been thinking about the expansion of that deaf-betweenity to disability more largely. (Of course, I've also then been thinking about the way that deafness itself occupies an interesting "betweenity" in relationship to disability identity.) In any case—whether deaf, disabled, or between—I'm finding that I'm generally more interested in the hot dog rather than the bun, the cream filling in the Oreo (which, if you've noticed, has been changing a lot lately) rather than just the twinned chocolate sandwich cookies on the outside. Give me a hyphen any day. To be sure, the words on either side of the hyphen are interesting too; but it is what's happening in that hyphen—the moment of magic artistry there in that half-dash—that really catches my eye.

I owe a great debt to several colleagues for their roles in making this chapter happen. First, and most significantly, there is Dirksen Bauman, who helped instigate—and inspire—the ideas here when he invited me to be a part of the summer 2002 "Deaf Studies Think Tank." He encouraged me to write an introductory personal statement for the think tank that became, in essence, the genesis of this chapter's content. Later, as we continued to hold vibrant electronic and face-to-face conversations about my ideas and examples under development, he further influenced not only the content but also the very form of this chapter. In a sense, I think of this piece as a collaboration with Dirksen. Colleagues Cathy Kudlick (University of California–Davis) and Jim Ferris (University of Wisconsin) also came to play a part in the production of this piece as the three of us shared a kind of "trialogue" performance in a session, called simply "Between," at the 2004 Society for Disability Studies meeting in St. Louis. When they helped me further expand the signing and body space to create a six-armed insect, I knew then that after nearly two years of tinkering with this chapter, I had finally reached the (between) place where I not only felt comfortable—but now actually wanted—to put the ideas in print. This essay is adapted from my chapter in *Open Your Eyes: Deaf Studies Talking* published by University of Minnesota Press and used here by permission.

Between "Deaf" and "deaf" (or, the Names We Call Ourselves)

In disability culture and studies, as well as in Deaf culture and studies, we often get back to—or maybe, yes, we also get forward to—discussions about what we do and don't want to be called. Deaf culture, in particular, has been around the block with this discussion for a long, long time. I offer three exhibits (call them angles) for consideration:

Exhibit A
(from the University of Brighton, U.K. http://staffcentral.brighton.ac.uk/ clt/disability/Deaf.html)

Note on terminology:
The term "Deaf" (with a capital D) is the preferred usage of some people who are either born profoundly deaf or who become deaf at a very early age and who regard themselves as belonging to the Deaf community. Like people in many communities, those within the Deaf community are bound together by a feeling of identifying with other Deaf people. People in the Deaf community share, amongst other things, a sense of Deaf pride, traditions, values, lifestyles, humor, folklore, art, theatre, as well as a rich common language . . .

Exhibit B
(From a copyedited essay on interpreters that I received from university press editors):

I do not understand the distinctions between use of upper- and lowercase D for deafness? Please clarify for my own knowledge and for the general scope of this book.

Exhibit C
(From Gina Oliva, author of *Alone in the Mainstream: A Deaf Woman Remembers Public Schools,* the first book in the new "Deaf Lives" series of auto-biography, biography, and documentary from Gallaudet University Press that I edit. This is a memo Gina sent to me after the copyeditors asked her to double-check and "clarify" her use of Deaf/deaf in the manuscript):

Subject: deaf vs. Deaf

To: brueggemann.1@osu.edu

Hi Brenda. . . . I took a look at Padden and Humphries and decided it made sense to use Deaf when referring to adults in the Deaf community. If they are oral deaf, I will call them deaf. As for children, I would stick with deaf and hard of hearing children (lower case). This means that the "big D" will appear much in my book, as I say "Deaf adults this" and "Deaf adults that" a lot. I also say "deaf and hard of hearing children" a lot.

Then I looked at *Journey into the Deaf-World* (Lane, Hoffmeister, Bahan) and see that they advocate using Deaf for any child who is deaf and couldn't access info without assistance.

Hmmmmm. . . . Do you have any opinion about this???? I checked some other books. . . . Wrigley uses Deaf predominantly. Preston does not. I have others I can check . . . but my guess is there is little consensus about this.

Whether we capitalize or do not capitalize *deaf* is a common issue. In Deaf studies, we can explore, and perhaps even expand upon, the definitions of the terms of d/Deaf operations—subtracting, adding, dividing, and multiplying the possibilities—for the key naming terms like *deaf, Deaf, hard of hearing, late deafened, hearing-impaired, has hearing loss, think-hearing,* and my mother's personal favorite for me, *selective hearing.* But we can also move further out in the concentric circles by studying, for example, the mapping and meaning of many medical conditions and mental proficiency labels, alongside audiometric ones, noting their in-common categorizations—"moderate," "severe," "profound." Medicine commonly uses those labels when designating degrees of pathological conditions; deafness then becomes pathology. Additionally and interestingly enough, these labels also parallel those assigned to IQ, and both sets of terms (audiological and IQ) came on the diagnostic screen in our culture at about the same time. What's more, if you simply rotate the axes of the two bell curves created by either the IQ or audiometric charts as they plot out "normal," "moderate," "severe," and "profound," you would find them folding neatly right on top of each other. Is this parallel only circumstance, or do the angles make more meaning in their overlay and intersections?

For one way to further explore this curious commonplace, we might consider that in 1940s Germany under the Nazis, people with disabilities in psychiatric institutions throughout the Reich became subject to "euthanasia" at the hands of their own doctors and nurses. In what became known as the T-4 program during 1941–42, at least 70,273 patients from these institutions were transported to seven designated killing centers and were murdered in gas chambers that became the experimental locations of the Final Solution targeted at Jewish people a few years later. Before the T-4 program, in the 1930s, many of these patients/people were also sterilized. What is more, after the T-4 program officially ended in 1942—because of considerable alarm and pressure from churches and from German citizens, as well as Hitler's fear that the United States would find out about the program and enter the war over it—an estimated additional 100,000 people in these institutions may have died as victims of what is now called the "wild euthanasia" period, when they were administered drug overdoses or starved to death unofficially. My point in telling these troubling facts is that at this time—as well as other times both past and present—people who were deaf in Germany (*taubstumme*—deaf and dumb) were often as not collapsed in diagnoses of other mental disabilities as well. I have looked at remaining records from one of these killing centers (which is still, eerily enough, a fully functioning psychiatric institution even today) as well as some records from the T-4 program housed in the German federal archives (*Bundesarchiv*) and I have, for myself, seen this conflation written on the records of several patients.

My point is that in the commonplace book of "deafness," things are not always clearly or singularly defined, designated, or determined as "just," or "pure," or "only" deafness. And however much some deaf people may want to resist being labeled as "disabled," the fact remains that they are often labeled as such and that these labels—in all cases—are not always accurate but may have consequences. Certainly deaf people should want to resist the easy conflation of their "condition" with others that coexist in degrees of "moderate," "severe," and "profound"—realizing the violence that can be done (and has been done) by such an overlay. Yet also, just as certainly, I would suggest that to resist and distance one's self-identity and group identity from those whose condition has been deemed (for better or worse, for right or wrong) affiliated with hearing loss, would also be, in essence, to do further violence to those others that "authorities" have placed us (deaf people) in categorical similarity with. Who—or what—are deaf people so afraid of when they resist placement in the commonplace of "disability"?

This unnamed fear also has us (and them) working (hard, very hard) to contrast *deaf* and *Deaf*. The source of the Deaf/deaf divide dates to around 1972, purportedly from coined usage in a seminal Deaf studies essay by James Woodward, *How You Gonna Get to Heaven if You Can't Talk to Jesus? On Depathologizing Deafness.* Thus, the definitional divide has been around for more than 30 years. Yet aside from its usage in presses and publications long familiar with the commonplaces of "deafness," it must commonly still be footnoted in an academic text in order to explain, once again, what the distinctions between Big D "Deafness" and little d "deafness" are. Even when the distinctions are used, they are most often used, interestingly enough, in direct relation to each other; one is just as likely to see "d/Deaf" or "D/deaf" written as one is to see just "Deaf" or even "deaf" in a text that has set up this distinction. Thus, the divisional/definitional terms *Deaf* and (or versus) *deaf* more often than not come in tandem as *d/Deaf.* As such, they are twinned—doppelgangers. "Mirror mirror on the wall," they whisper and sign back and forth to each other.

The twinning of d/Deaf is perhaps safer that way since often, when pressed, it will be hard to determine at any one moment in a text whether the Big D cultural/linguistic arena is where we are or if we are just in the small d audiological/medical space. And what if we are both places at the same time? The long-standing and footnoting practice of establishing some kind of border patrol between these terms tries to define and differentiate—apples here, oranges there—but more often than not the aliens still wind up looking very much like the natives. And perhaps it is really an avocado that is wanted, anyway? In most cases, for example, deaf students can't enroll in a state residential institution—long deemed the center of American Deaf culture and the sanctuary for American Sign Language (ASL; and thus, a commonplace for Big D cultural/linguistic Deafness)—without offering an audiogram and first being able to claim their little d deafness. Until 2002, when Gallaudet University's new HUGS (Hearing Undergraduates) program was established, you could not get to the world's only liberal arts college for deaf and hard of hearing students without proof of (flawed) audiogram: You had to be (little d) deaf in order to go there and engage in the particular Gallaudet cultural practices that might also then mark you as (big D) Deaf (see http://admissions.gallaudet.edu/admprocedures/HUG.htm).

Yet when the question is posed about the differences between *deaf* and *Deaf*—as it was by a recent editor I worked with (see Exhibit B above) and really by almost every editor I've ever had in twenty years of writing about, in, from, around deafness[1]—most often the answer given is either "language—the use of ASL" or even more simple (yet complex) "attitude." And suddenly, there you are again, in another dark and thick forest without a working compass: "What kind of *attitude?*" you have to wonder. And what *levels* and *types* and *uses* of signed communication?

And what does it mean, anyway, to locate the choice position within the capital D? Is this not also an assault and an oppression—a dominance of one way of thinking (epistemology) and being (ontology) over another? This think-between space between deaf and Deaf is a rock and a hard place for Deaf studies. I wonder what happens if we squeeze (more) in there? What if we don't draw the line on, around, through, or under where someone is (and isn't) culturally Deaf or not? What if we stop footnoting and explaining (and educating them again and again and again, as we have for almost thirty years now) what we've learned to chant from almost rote memorization when we endeavor, once again, to explain the difference between little d and big D deafness? But hearing people never seem to hear a word of any of this, and so we go on footnoting and explaining and educating about the distinctions between Deaf and deaf. If a (deaf) tree falls in the (hearing) forest, does anyone really hear it?

Can we create a new geometry, a new space for deaf (and thus Deaf as well) to be in and for those trees to fall in? To answer such questions might be to enter into questions of perspective. How, for example, might we follow both the dynamic and static flow of terms like *deaf,* while along the way working also to understand our culture's long-standing cure-based obsessions with definitive causes and effects where deafness matters? What were—and are—the circumstances that create *deaf* or *Deaf* to begin with (and in continuance)? Whose testimony counts—and when and where and why and how—when it comes to authorizing d/Deaf identity or the condition of deafness? What I am suggesting is that we might begin in Deaf studies to push beyond the mere recitation of the d/Deaf pledge in our footnotes and to explore instead all the rhetorical situations that arise from the d/D distinctions, that bring the distinctions to bear, and that, most importantly, keep shifting them like an identity kaleidoscope in our own hands.

The (Deaf) Cyborg Space

> *A cyborg is a cybernetic organism, a hybrid of machine and organism, a creature of social reality as well as a creature of fiction.*
>
> —Donna Haraway, "A Cyborg Manifesto"

Within the deaf kaleidoscope is the fragmented but also contained—and beautiful—image of the ever-shifting deaf cyborg. The seamed and seeming boundaries between cure and control in constructing the deaf cyborg body is a potent

---

1. Here you can now imagine a Big D if you want; but for now, I'm going to just let one term stand and use *deaf* or *deafness* (little d) to represent both the deaf and Deaf positions since, as I have been arguing, no one really seems to completely understand the differences and distinctions between the two terms to begin with.

commonplace, especially for late twentieth- and early twenty-first-century Deaf studies. Obviously, this seamed space might be illustrated in the controversy over cochlear implants and the deaf cyborg who, borrowing cultural critic Donna Haraway's terms, becomes the "hybrid of machine and organism," the creation of "a creature of social reality as well as a creature of fiction" that has already "change[d] what counts as [deaf people's] experience in the late twentieth century" (Haraway 1991, 149).

What Haraway's cyborg myth foretells is that deaf people and the Deaf world won't likely disappear, implanted as alien others. This is instead likely to be a tale of "transgressed boundaries, potent fusions," as Haraway's cyborg myth suggests: The boundaries might change, but the fusion will likely remain potent. At Gallaudet University, for example, they have been counting the numbers of their students who arrive with cochlear implants, and since 2000, the number has virtually doubled itself each year. In effect, the cochlear implant seems to be squaring itself as the technology advances and the next generation of young deaf and hard of hearing people come of counting age. At the Kendall School, the demonstration elementary school on the Gallaudet campus, education about the implant (for those who have them as well as for those who don't) takes the form of several children's books and a Barbie-like doll, "C. I. Joe" (who also happens to be African American). Even at hearing-dominated state universities like my own (Ohio State University), the cochlear implant makes headlines as one of the major Friday feature stories in the campus newspaper—and this at a university that records only two students with cochlear implants (among the 54,000 enrolled here).

In Deaf studies, we might begin to rethink the potent fusions in the boundaries created by cochlear implants—between then (the past) and now (the present), as well as between now (the present) and then (the future). Tough, opportunistic, interesting, and sometimes even beautiful things grow in the cracks of structures seemingly well established and impenetrable; the cochlear implant cyborg might just be such a crack dweller. It will take far more than an implant to make deaf identity (whatever it might be) go away. Like dandelions on the hearing lawn, deaf people greet the cultivated green with sunny color and tenacious bearing season after season, generation upon generation. Hearing aids have never pulled the rug entirely out from under deafness; eugenicists couldn't either (although they are tugging very hard again), and oral-focused educators mostly just continue to sweep things under the rug so the house looks pretty on the surface.

This is not to suggest that we should not worry. We should. We need only glance over our shoulders at the specter of those doctors during the Nazi era who had themselves (and important others) convinced that life with a disability was a life simply not worth living. Under such a conviction, these doctors killed more than 270,000 of those lives deemed unworthy in gas chambers (as well as through nurse-administered drug overdoses or even through starvation) in a program they termed "euthanasia." Deaf people were one of the eight categories of people targeted for these "mercy deaths" in the T-4 program of 1941–1942, as well as being common victims of the sterilizations that occurred for a decade before the T-4 euthanasia program. Those Nazi doctors also thought they were improving the lives of their patients, and they developed chilling technologies (the gas chambers) to efficiently carry out those "improvements." The smoke rising in thick acrimonious billows day and night from the psychiatric institute set up on the hill over the sleepy little village of Hadamar, Germany, during 1941–1942 (as but one example, captured with disturbing clarity in several photos of the time) makes at least one thing very clear: Where there is smoke, there is fire.

Still: While we look for the fire, we should also be critically careful not to let cochlear implants create a smoke screen that hides other strong magic at work. Even the technology in hearing aids, FM systems, real-time captioning, video conferencing, instant messaging, the Internet, and e-mail matters in the cyborg mix here. If you have been to Gallaudet University lately, you would have surely noticed how electronic pagers (instant e-mail) have radically changed "the Deaf gaze." These days, when you walk across Gallaudet's campus, you are just as likely—perhaps even more likely—to see an individual deaf student with head bent and thumbs flying at her pager as she walks from place to place as you are to see the older scene of two students signing with hands high above their head, "shouting" at each other from across Kendall Green, the oval grassy area at the center of Gallaudet's campus.

Do these pagers and other devices of instant communication really connect—or disconnect—deaf people? What distortions and/or enhancements are aided by the electronic eye extension of the Deaf gaze in these instances? What might be the form of the [SEE] sign for extended pager gazing? And why are such devices, when used to aid the deafened ear, commonly referred to as "assistive" or "adaptive" technologies, when technologies are, by definition, assistive and adaptive to begin with? Why is it, for example, that a Blackberry in the hands of a hearing person suddenly sheds its adaptive or assistive skin and becomes instead just another device to fill up one's airport or driving time or to conduct one's business incessantly?

With questions like these—as well as attempts at critical discussions about them—Deaf studies would be attending to the rhetorical relationships between our technologies and our identity. In essence, we would be investigating the shape and substance of purpose, intention, motivation, and communication (rhetoric, in sum) that such small but strong technology has in refiguring the Deaf gaze, in changing deaf people's status as "people of the eye." We would be considering the dynamic or static perspectives that these technologies—as adaptive or assistive technologies—play not just in our (deaf) lives but also in hearing lives, as well as in the relationships and lives between those spaces. Deaf studies would do well to gaze here.

Lingering in the (Un)Common Space of Language

> "No man fully capable of his own language ever masters another."
>
> —George Bernard Shaw,
> "Maxims for Revolutionists," 1903

Deaf people and their uses of sign (or even/additionally/predominately oral) languages offer a rich commonplace site for the study of how language inherently oppresses, standardizes, and yet also resists—all at the same time—whatever it comes into contact with and even whatever it makes for and of itself. Language duplicates, replicates, and reinforces itself (so that "no man fully capable of his own language ever masters another") while it also resists its own pure replication and dominance. This is not to signify that deaf people have no respect for their sign language (or their multiple other forms of language), but only to suggest that language is always refiguring its own space just as it makes that space operate much like a kaleidoscope—where elements and perspectives may shift but the whole and its contents remain the same. Thus, to aim for some sort of standardization of (a/the) language is only, in effect, to assure that it is awfully (and awesomely) darn slippery to begin with; sooner or later, something or someone comes along and bumps the kaleidoscope—a little or a lot—and a new image (still with the same basic contents) appears. Perspectives shift.

Such shifting also happens to represent the slippery business of rhetoric in which the communication triangle and its emphasized angles are always in changing relationships to each other. Aristotle's entire second book of the *Rhetoric* emphasizes this contextually dependent shifting as he attempts to categorize and consider all the kinds of audiences a rhetor might be dealing with and how those audiences might react to given kinds of subjects presented in certain kinds of ways. "Discovering all the available means of persuasion," which was how Aristotle defined the art of rhetoric, becomes much like the number of patterns one can view in a kaleidoscope.

In this space of ever-unfolding possibilities, Deaf studies (which is, often as not, associated with the study and teaching of sign languages) could consider the way that sign languages are themselves reaching for, lurching toward, grasping at, and pushing against standardization. And this is not uncommon. Language is only a tool—and an often inadequate one—for trying to get at or toward or even around the truth.

Dictionaries and attempts to capture or standardize any language also operate under such perspective-oriented prevailing paradigms. Yet dictionaries are definitely needed—if for no other reason than to record the revolutionary and rhetorical shifts that language can make. "Hold still, we're going to do your portrait," writes French feminist theorist Hélène Cixous (1990, 1244) about the rhetorical act of representation, "so that you can begin looking like it right away." In Deaf studies, we should be focusing on the portrait-making involved in developing and publishing any kind of sign language. No scholar has yet, for example, to undertake a serious study of even the earliest representations of hand alphabets or published sign systems (by Pierre Desloges and others). To be sure, these early printed representations can often be found in histories written about deaf people and their use of sign languages. But they are more often than not simply gestured toward and not ever (yet) analyzed in terms of what their shifting representations might mean and say for language systems in general or even in comparison with each other as commonplace sign systems.

We might also then look backward (yet still forward) to the commonplaces of a sign language's (near) disappearance or considerable reconfiguration. For an example of its reconfiguration, there are sites such as seventeenth-century English educator and rhetorician John Bulwer's (1975, 1652) adaptation of signs, gestures, body configurations, and facial expressions in his classical and seminal rhetorical-elocutionary treatises, *Chirologia* and *Chironomia*. Bulwer is credited for founding the "elocutionary movement" in the history of rhetoric with his elaborately detailed descriptions (and prescriptions) of what the hands, body, and face could do in the act and art of persuasion in his two treatises on "the art of the hand." We now also know that he was one of the earliest English deaf educators and what is more, we now know that he had a deaf daughter whose name happened to be *Chirolea*. Yet Bulwer himself never credits any "language of gestures" he might have acquired from these two deaf sites in his life that would, most likely, have had a significant influence on his ability to create these two rhetorical treatises to begin with.

We could also contemplate, for example, the changing shape of sign language in places like rural Nebraska, now that the state residential institution for deaf students has been closed. How does the lack of such an important site for developing and sharing language among deaf and hard of hearing children who are more often than not isolated and singular in their deafness change the face of ASL overall? Or too, we might explore more about how deaf people negotiated sign language in Germany during the Nazi regime when they were not only the targets of forced sterilization but also the potential victims of the T-4 euthanasia program of 1941–1942. How did deaf people sign when their lives likely depended on not marking themselves as deaf in any way? And after World War II, what happened to deaf ways—their schools, clubs, workplaces, and shared language—between East and West Germany? Further, how have (or haven't) German signs "reunified" since the Berlin Wall fell in 1989? We would also want to look forward—to the development of new sign languages in developing, or third-world, countries, or in places like reunified Germany, or even say, across the city of Berlin where not so long ago, four nations occupied the city limits. What can we learn about standardization and the values of language—any language—from these developments?

And finally, we would also do well to look across the plains of the present, to squint our eyes in the startling sunlight of ASL's immense popularity on high school and college campuses where it is now taught (usually as a foreign language requirement). While the Deaf world frets over the loss of Deaf culture and identity at the hands of geneticists, cochlear implant surgeons, and hearing parents (to name but a few of the largest threats), the truth of another matter is that on campuses where it is offered, no language except Spanish enrolls better than ASL right now. In summer 2003, the Modern Language Association's new report on college foreign language offerings marked ASL courses in higher education as up a remarkable 432 percent in the past five years (Welles 2004). (The next closest increased figure was Arabic at 94 percent.) This put ASL officially in the fifth-place seat for "most commonly taught language in college." Yet, if we were also to factor in that the four languages ahead of ASL in this survey are likely taught at each and every college where foreign language is offered—and that ASL is still very much a lesser-taught language that is, in fact, still rarely taught at most colleges—the popularity of ASL probably outstrips the four languages that place ahead of it. In fact, demand almost never matches supply in the case of ASL instruction since qualified ASL instructors at the high school and university certification level are as rare, say, as ocean front property in Kansas.

How is this massively popular instruction changing the face—and shape—of ASL? (These issues over ASL and its place in the academy and its relationship to "foreign language" instruction were the subject of a three-session "Presidential

Forum" at the 2004 Modern Language Association Annual Convention in Philadelphia.) And what should be the "perspective" of Deaf studies on these issues
when, ironically, more and more deaf and hard of hearing children are mainstreamed and implanted and often kept *away* from sign language while their hearing peers flock to ASL classes? What interesting rhetoric is at work on the two
sides of this single language-learning coin? Who profits from such a great increase
in ASL instruction? The wise owl of Deaf studies should be forming this "who?"
on its own lips and hands.

Writing (and) Deafness

> *To say that writing extends the field and the powers of
> locutory or gestural communication presupposes, does it
> not, a sort of homogeneous space of communication? Of
> course the compass of voice or of gesture would encounter
> therein a factual limit, an empirical boundary of space and
> of time; while writing, in the same time and in the same
> space, would be capable of relaxing those limits and of
> opening the same field to a very much larger scope.*

—Jacques Derrida, "Signature Event Context"

The wise owl should also ponder writing. As a form of expression typically (and
too often) considered oppositional for modern deaf people, what in fact might
writing have in common with signing? How might writing extend signing—and
signing, too, extend writing? Derrida, of course, raises this question at hand, and
some of my colleagues in Deaf studies—Lennard Davis most notably—keep it
raised (1995). In Deaf studies, I think we have some remarkable and rich work
still left to do, philosophically and practically, in the space between writing and
signing. Not only can we perhaps de-Derrida Derrida himself in expanding the
philosophical space between writing and signing, but we can, just as importantly,
work to find better ways to translate and transliterate what happens in the space
between English and ASL. This perspectival orientation would be especially important for both deaf and hearing students who are struggling to enter that between space.

It will be most fruitful to do this practical and philosophical perspectival
work, not from the center of English studies (where it has already been tried and
yet never true), but rather from the center (and margins) of Deaf studies. When
Deaf studies starts thinking about how to translate, transliterate, and teach in the
space between English and ASL, for example, we are likely to become all the more
"capable of relaxing those limits and of opening the same field to a very much
larger scope." Why leave it up to English departments and deaf education and
sociolinguistics? These three sites, in particular, have long skewed the center and
arranged themselves as the triangle of matters associated with "deaf language and
literacy instruction."[2] Why keep the location of locution always already there?
Certainly, English studies and deaf education and scientific linguistic study have
things to offer the study of sign languages—and they should continue to do so.

But how much longer must we continue to look for the keys to the uses and power of sign languages for deaf people under the brighter lamps of these more dominant (and better funded) areas of the academy just because the light is there when, in fact, we know the keys are in a less well-lighted place a few steps back or around the next corner?

Let Deaf studies take up the questions often left to the long legacy of Western philosophy—from Plato to Derrida and back again: What difference does writing make? Do feminist theories about writing the body (see Cixous 1990) apply to and invigorate, or further erase, deaf people and their way of performing literacy? If writing is a performance (as the latest theoretical rage proclaims)—and sign language is also performative—do these two have even more in common than we have yet begun to explore? Is deafness the hiccup—the errant locution in the location—of the all-too-standardized connections between reading and writing that are chanted in our educational history? Deaf studies might attend to asking and exploring a question that one professor of philosophy at my own university recently used to title his own campus lecture with (even though he did not have sign languages in mind)—"how can language change your hearing?"

Let us begin, now more than ever, to answer that question from within Deaf studies. Not only should we begin, for example, to critically engage the construction of "deaf lives" from these other fields, but we should also (and this is very important) be encouraging the creation, production, and reception of deaf lives through such channels as biography, autobiography, and documentary. As I revised an earlier version of this chapter from a café in Berlin, Germany, I was reminded, you see, that I am deaf in any and all languages and cultures; the German language does not, in essence, seem to change my hearing.

"How can language change your hearing?" Indeed, that is no small question. It is also not an unfamiliar question since deaf education has been around the block with it at least several times over. What if we also began to ask instead how it is that deaf ways can actually be used as a method and means of changing even dominant Western classroom and pedagogical practices? And what if we just stopped rehearsing the already well-articulated history of deaf education in the United States? What if instead we asked, for example, "What does this history (of deaf education) show us about all of Western education?" As Margret Winzer (1993) has challenged us in her excellent history of special education, we might think more of how deaf education ripples in the larger pond:

> The way that children are trained and schooled is a crucial demonstra-
> tion of the way that they are perceived and treated in a given society . . . .
> Discovering who was taught, and when and how, is related far more to
> the social, political, legislative, economic, and religious forces at work in
> a society than it is to the unique social and educational needs of disabled
> persons. At the same time, this history mirrors our progress toward ap-
> preciating the basic humanity of all people. (Winzer 1993, xi)

---

2. For more discussion on the consequences of the lack of contextually and cultur-ally based approaches to scholarship in "deaf language and literacy," see the introduction to *Literacy and Deaf People: Cultural and Contextual Approaches,* Brenda Jo Brueggemann, ed., Gallaudet University Press, 2004.

Deaf education did not—and does not—occur in a socioeconomic-historical vacuum. We can get so hung up on A. G. Bell and his legacy, for example, that we forget to answer the other incoming calls about the interplay of speech, education, and "normalcy" as this tangled braid brought us into the twentieth century.

THINK-EYE

> *"Perspective, as its inventor remarked, is a beautiful thing."*
>
> —GEORGE ELIOT [MARY ANN EVANS],
> *DANIEL DERONDA*, 1876

Some days I am so energized by all the possibilities of Deaf studies that I am exploding. Other days, I am so daunted by all the possibilities that I am imploding. I come to Deaf studies as a hard of hearing (the only term my family could use) girl from the extremely rural region of western Kansas; there are still less than twenty-five people per square mile in Greeley County, Kansas. I come as someone who didn't even know that sign language or, say, Gallaudet University existed (let alone a single sign or the idea of deaf education) until the age of 29. I come as the granddaughter of a deaf woman (although she was called hard of hearing too) and the inheritor and carrier and engenderer of a complicated string of hearing loss and kidney abnormalities in my family. I come with two children (one has the kidney abnormalities) who perhaps understand my "deafness" in ways that my own parents didn't and in ways, too, that I myself still don't. (They are perhaps more "deaf" than me, I've written elsewhere [Brueggemann 1999].)

I come always wanting to fit in. Yet I also come always wanting to ask questions and *not* fit in. I arrive doubly hyphenated (hard-of-hearing)—with a lot going on in those multiple hyphenated between spaces. I come, I suppose, thinking between—thinking in another kind of between space, between think-deaf and think-hearing: [THINK-EYE]. For the deaf space is a visual space—an eye space—and also too, an I-space. We still have a lot to learn from each "I" and from each "eye." Perspective (the eye) really matters; the personal (the I) experience really matters as well. This little between space can be, in fact, rather expansive. It is a space of potent possibilities, contained and yet kaleidoscopic in its perspectives. As the late nineteenth-century English novelist George Eliot (Mary Ann Evans) knew, since she was writing a novel named for a male protagonist and using a male pseudonym herself, perspective really matters.

There are so many ways to bump and see the same pieces again, but now all arranged differently. In keeping our eyes out for deaf commonplaces while also admiring the ever-shifting capabilities of perspective (in both our "eyes" and our "I's") and attending to the value of being between worlds, words, languages, and cultures—even as we can be contained in either one—the sites and sights of Deaf studies promise us ever-enchanted explorations.

REFERENCES

Aristotle. 1991. *On rhetoric: A theory of civic discourse,* trans. George A. Kennedy. New York: Oxford University Press.

Bulwer, John. 1975. *Chirologia; or, the natural language of the hand.* New York: AMS Press.

Brueggemann, Brenda. 1999. Are you deaf or hearing? In *Lend me your ear: Rhetorical constructions of deafness.* Washington, D.C.: Gallaudet University Press.

———, ed. 2004. *Literacy and Deaf people: Cultural and contextual approaches.* Washington, D.C.: Gallaudet University Press.

———. 2008. Think-between: A Deaf studies commonplace book. In *Open your eyes: Deaf studies talking*, ed. H-Dirksen Bauman. Minneapolis: University of Minnesota Press

Cixous, Hélène. 1990. From the laugh of the Medusa. In *The rhetorical tradition: Readings from classical times to the present*, ed. Patricia Bizzell and Bruce Herzberg. Boston: Bedford.

Davis, Lennard. 1995. Deafness as insight: The deafened moment as critical modality. *College English* 57 (8): 881.

Derrida, Jacques. 1982. Signature, event, context. In *Margins of philosophy*, trans. Alan Bass, 307–30. Chicago: University of Chicago Press.

Eliot, George. 1984. *Daniel Deronda*, ed. Graham Handley. New York: Oxford University Press.

Gallaudet University Admissions. Hearing undergraduate student. http://admissions .gallaudet.edu/admprocedures/HUG.htm (accessed April 15, 2006).

Haraway, Donna. 1991. A cyborg manifesto: Science, technology, and socialist-feminism in the late twentieth century. In *Simians, cyborgs and women: The reinvention of nature.* New York: Routledge.

Shaw, George Bernard. 2000. Maxims for revolutionists. In *Man and superman: A comedy and philosophy*, 251–63. New York: Penguin.

Welles, Elizabeth B. 2004. Foreign language enrollments in United States institutions of higher education, fall 2002. *ADFL Bulletin* 35 (2–3): 7–26. http://www.adfl.org/ resources/enrollments.pdf (accessed October 1, 2007).

Winzer, Margret. 1993. *The history of special education: From isolation to integration.* Washington, D.C.: Gallaudet University Press.

Woodward, James. 1982. *How you gonna get to heaven if you can't talk with Jesus: On depathologizing deafness.* Silver Spring, Md.: T.J. Publishers.

4 | "I Thought There Would Be More Helen Keller": *History through Deaf Eyes* and Narratives of Representation

Kristen Harmon

The purpose of this letter is to express extreme opposition to the proposed Smithsonian Institution/Gallaudet University exhibit titled "DEAF: A Community of Signers."

—An audiologist[1]

This exhibit must be cautious in presenting any viewpoint which would encourage withdrawal into a small, confined, and poorly informed cultural entity.

—A medical professional[2]

Please—the Deaf community has a rich culture with intense bonds. I ask you to let the world experience, as only the Smithsonian Institute can do, a glimpse into this unique, beautiful, and fascinating cultural group.

—A hearing ASL student[3]

---

1. Letter to the Smithsonian, November 27, 1995. Gallaudet University Archives. Due to restrictions placed upon the research-related use of this archival material, the letter writers to the Smithsonian in this exhibition-related collection are cited as anonymous. For the same reason, logbook entries are also cited as anonymous.

2. Letter to the Smithsonian, November 27, 1995. Gallaudet University Archives.

3. Letter to the Smithsonian, June 19, 1996. Gallaudet University Archives.

I do not care what the "deaf culture" do with their lives. If they want to go off into a ghetto, that's fine with me. Just don't try to drag me, and others like me, along with you.

—A LETTER TO SILENT NEWS,
a DEAF COMMUNITY PUBLICATION[4]

Thanks to Deaf culture, I have thrived as a Deaf person. . . . Deaf culture is real and is a part of American history.
—A DEAF ADULT WHO USED PURE ORALISM IN HIS EARLY YEARS[5]

YOUR PROPOSED EXHIBIT OF DEAF AMERICANS EXCLUDES ME!! [Followed by a picture of a child.] PLEASE REMEMBER THOSE OF US WHO HAVE CHOSEN TO BE AURAL AND ORAL—WE ARE PART OF THE HISTORY AND THE FUTURE

—A PARENT[6]

The Smithsonian . . . is in a unique position. You have the opportunity to strike down barriers and open up doors. . . . For those who are not familiar with deaf culture and the deaf community, you have the rare opportunity to open their world. To paraphrase Jesse Jackson, the problem is not that the deaf can't hear, it's that the hearing world doesn't listen.

—A HEARING VISITOR TO THE SMITHSONIAN[7]

In the early 1990s, Gallaudet University and the National Museum of American History, part of the Smithsonian Institution in Washington, D.C., planned a joint production, a permanent exhibition called "DEAF: A Community of Signers." However, as a result of a series of conflicts over the original conception, the focus changed, and the exhibition became a traveling installation called "History through Deaf Eyes." A committee based at Gallaudet University handled the design and fundraising, and the Smithsonian's Arts and Industries Building eventually became the host site for one of the exhibition's early postings. In moving from "DEAF" to "Deaf Eyes," this particular exhibition sheds light on American d/Deaf identities and the conflicted nature of representation. It also shows how hearing, deaf, and culturally Deaf people define and describe themselves

---

4. Wells 1994.

5. Letter to the Smithsonian, April 22, 1996. Gallaudet University Archives.

6. Letter to the Smithsonian, February 16, 1996. Gallaudet University Archives.

7. Letter to the Smithsonian, May 27, 1996. Gallaudet University Archives.

and others in relation to the concept of a subjectivity that sees through "Deaf eyes."

In its original conception as "DEAF: A Community of Signers," the exhibition set out to provide a series of short narratives that would inform and educate a hearing audience. As such, it was intended to focus upon signing Deaf people as members of a unique sociolinguistic community. In the early stages, the planning committee deliberated on what one idea, one concept, they wanted visitors to understand. That one idea was to show the audience an *alternative* narrative concerning Deaf people, a group that many hearing visitors would know simply as a subsection of the disabled population. Hearing people with no knowledge of the Deaf community or of Deaf history were the intended audience of the original exhibition. According to exhibition director Jean L. Bergey, viewers would feel as though they had "met" a Deaf person.[8]

As we shall see, the ensuing controversy arose by asking a simple question: What sort of Deaf person is the visitor meeting?

Please stop the myth that the deaf are mute and dependent on Deaf culture to thrive.[9]

I urge you to make sure the exhibit, funded by public monies, tells the complete history of deaf people in America in a fair and objective way.[10]

I understand that the present focus of the exhibit is . . . [that] deafness is a culture and not a disability. . . . There are other views held by many people that deafness is a disability that may be immensely minimized by Auditory-Verbal/Oral approaches.[11]

The deaf or hearing impaired who have learned to use what hearing they have proficiently, and are able to speak intelligibly, are far better able to cope with life than the cloistered community of those who must rely entirely on sign language because they have rejected oralism for whatever reason, be it the lack of opportunity, misinformation, or insufficient intestinal fortitude to stay the course.[12]

It seems to be a "Generation Thing" to think of deafness as "living in a silent world." Most of our friends . . . accept + expect our adopted son will be oral while our own loving parents sometimes, inadvertently, just can't believe that he's not going to be using sign language. Like I said—I believe these ideas of only signing to communicate were of that generation. Please don't pass this misguided view on to our children.[13]

8. Jean Bergey, personal communication with author, June 25, 2004.

9. Letter to the Smithsonian, n.d., Gallaudet University Archives.

10. Letter to the Smithsonian, n.d., Gallaudet University Archives.

11. Letter to the Smithsonian, n.d., Gallaudet University Archives.

12. Letter to the Smithsonian, November 16, 1995. Gallaudet University Archives.

13. Letter to the Smithsonian, n.d., Gallaudet University Archives.

It is improper for the Smithsonian to display a political view regarding oralism vs. manualism. If the exhibit were to remain the way it is, the Smithsonian would in fact be supporting one approach over another, and therefore be telling parents of deaf children what choices to make for their children. I am certain that the Smithsonian is not in the business of telling people how to raise their children.[14]

In 1995 and 1996 hundreds of letters were written to the Smithsonian in order to protest the exhibition's initial focus upon the signing Deaf community. The protest letters, several of which are excerpted above, initiated a dialogue within the planning committee that eventually reshaped the content of the exhibition in order to "present the deaf population in a context to which many people can relate, aligning deaf experiences with U.S. history."[15] Now known as "History through Deaf Eyes," a narrative of deaf people within the context of American history, the exhibition opened in 2002 and has since been posted in numerous U.S. cities.

In changing the focus, the exhibition shifted paradigms of knowledge; instead of looking through a sociological lens and using sociolinguistic and anthropological terms of description, the exhibition reinserted the story of deaf people within American history. Instead of focusing upon community-based verbal arts genres of American Sign Language (ASL), a section of the exhibition focused on the conflicted educational history of deaf people in America. Another section focused upon deaf people in the war industry during World War II. Yet another focused upon the great strides made in civil rights recognition. The director, Jean L. Bergey, noted that "[c]onceptual alignment with American social and political movements opens visitors' eyes to parallels in minority/majority experiences."[16] This shift in paradigm became an act of recovery because, as a minority culture and as users of a minority language, hard of hearing, deaf, and Deaf people have largely been erased from the narratives that constitute the American public's understanding of history. As a result of this focus on common experiences—regardless of cultural affiliation—the exhibition intentionally did not include an explicit message or definition of what is or is not Deaf identity and what is or is not the American Deaf community.

Understandably, many in the Deaf community saw this shift in focus from "DEAF: A Community of Signers" to "History through Deaf Eyes" as a lost opportunity to explain Deaf culture and community to an international audience. However, by responding to contested notions of d/Deaf identity, this exhibition ended up elucidating competing narratives of representation, and as such, the texts generated by the making of this exhibit—that is, the letters of protest and support and the entries in the visitors' logbooks posted at each site—are enormously revealing of discourses describing and defining Deaf culture and deafness in American social life. It is within these texts that we see the juxtaposition of imposed, adopted, and organic social theories of deafness and Deaf lives and bodies. In addition to the letters reiterating the idea of deafness as absence and the perceived need for inclusion of deaf people within the national "hearing" body, there are also letters

14. Letter to the Smithsonian, January 25, 1996. Gallaudet University Archives.

15. Bergey 2004, 45.

16. Bergey 1998, 83.

and logbook entries that show an emerging sensibility arising from Deaf and deaf viewers, theorizing the representation of their lives and experiences in ways that both overlap with and depart from politicized social discourses. As such, these texts provide a map of the discursive conflicts in representation.

Because of the increasing numbers of cochlear-implanted and mainstreamed deaf children, as well as the development of genetic screening and related technologies, this is a historically important moment for examining what is at stake when we talk about representing Deaf, deaf, and hard of hearing people.

Questions raised, but not necessarily answered, by the exhibition include:

- Are d/Deaf, hard of hearing, cochlear-implanted, and late-deafened people all members of a larger disability community in which the only commonality is deafness, and what purposes does such a pulling together serve?

- Is there such a thing as a shared experience that can be said to be common to all deaf and hard of hearing people, and if so, is that shared experience a matter of living through a shared historical moment?

- In the struggle to become visible and politically viable, which grouping, which narrative, which frame, is the most compelling and productive?

- Which narrative trope is most empowering for Deaf people and yet still accessible to a larger American public, particularly when stigma, misunderstanding, and pathologizing discourses are omnipresent in regards to deafness?

- Interestingly enough, for an exhibition focused upon history, the most emotionally weighted questions have to do with children: Where does the deaf child fit into all of this? Who "owns" the deaf child?

These and other questions informed the exhibition's evolution. In 1995, after the National Museum of American History (part of the Smithsonian Institution) had approved the original proposal for "DEAF: A Community of Signers," an audiologically diverse national review group was put together to generate feedback. Members of this review committee included several representatives from the Deaf academic community as well as from the oralist deaf community. As Bergey recounts,

> [T]here was vigorous discussion about the exhibition, even shouting, in both voice and sign. . . . Soon a campaign to shift the project focus became evident. Oral schools and associations wrote to the Smithsonian, urging . . . [the Institution] to alter the exhibition. Of the more than 300 letters [written between October 1995 and December 1996], most came from oral school administrators, parents and grandparents of deaf children, primarily hearing people.[17]

What the original planners, in all their initial excitement, didn't realize is that some reviewers of this original plan would feel as though the exhibit meant to reject hearing people, and by extension, oral deaf individuals.

---

17. Bergey 1998, 82.

Parents of deaf children felt that because their children did not sign, they—and their hearing families—were erased from this public discourse on deafness. One such letter included a picture of a deaf child, with an emphatic caption that read, "I AM DEAF—BUT I LISTEN AND SPEAK. I DON'T USE SIGN. CHANGE YOUR EXHIBIT TO INCLUDE ME."[18] The concept of "inclusion" popped up again and again in the letters, a truncation of a hugely conflicted history of deaf education in the United States. This was often accompanied by an implied argument that "exclusion" is a form of treason. A large part of the emotional outcry had to do with the sense that a parent's own deaf child (or oneself, in the case of a deaf adult) would be "left out" or excluded . . . a sort of nationwide shunning. The parent works so hard, these letters suggest, to "include" the deaf child in every way, and yet this child is left out of a national exhibition that is "funded by public monies." This perceived oversight felt very personal to many letter writers. "[W]e have a fourteen year old son," wrote one mother, "who was born with a profound loss and has been educated all his life with hearing kids. He has worked very very hard to accomplish this."[19]

Many of the letters, especially those from parents and oral school administrators, also stressed "choice." One deaf adult wrote, "I am proud that my parents have chosen the oral communication mode for my upbringing."[20] This excerpt calls up a particular and persistent discourse, or narrative, about a "hearing impaired" child's choices, ostensibly to live as either a member of the hearing world or of the Deaf world. An audiologist wrote in with thoughts on the matter: "Although ASL is one option for people who are deaf, there are other options in which children who are deaf learn to listen, talk, and communicate in the hearing world. . . . More than anything, it is critical to present the OPTIONS of deafness and the OPTIONS of the use of technology to provide hearing to deaf people" (emphasis in original).[21] Again and again in the letters of protest, words like these were highlighted, underlined, or capitalized. This suggests not only extreme opposition but also extreme emotion, with a resulting and reiterated emphasis upon inclusion accompanied by the hope that inclusion will blend the deaf child into "mainstream" American life. "This is what makes our country so great," one parent of a ten-year-old deaf son wrote, "that is, having choices!"[22] What is left out of this love letter to the melting pot is that the deaf child rarely chooses.

What is also clear in these protest letters is that, due to stigmatizing social discourses about deafness, the use of ASL, a visual language, is rarely presented as a valid "option." One parent of a profoundly deaf child wrote that "[a]fter . . . studying the manual method of helping [our daughter] with her deafness, it became obvious to me that there must be something better, something modern and more scientific. . . . The manual method . . . seemed primitive. It was born in the 18th century. It compared to my patients wearing wooden dentures."[23] Similarly, other

18. Letter to the Smithsonian, March 1996. Gallaudet University Archives.
19. Letter to the Smithsonian, n.d., Gallaudet University Archives.
20. Letter to the Smithsonian, December 1, 1995. Gallaudet University Archives.
21. Letter to the Smithsonian, November 27, 1995. Gallaudet University Archives.
22. Letter to the Smithsonian, November 6, 1995. Gallaudet University Archives.
23. Letter to the Smithsonian, n.d., Gallaudet University Archives.

writers also referenced notions of modernity and of technological progress in their case against "manualism." To wit: "The Smithsonian was supposed to be up-to-date and modern. Hopefully, ["DEAF: A Community of Signers"] was simply a mistake, a case of being uninformed or misinformed."[24] By suggesting that sign language was a tool that people used until better technology came along, the letter writers portrayed the Deaf community as a retrogressive throwback that was out of synch with the modern era, and they maintained a postwar sensibility toward science and medicine. A particularly 1950s' understanding of culture as a set of tangible and visible features was also pervasive in these letters. "Frankly, I am tired of the so-called 'deaf culture' tearing parents of hearing-impaired and the hearing-impaired down for making it easier for their children to hear," wrote one mother of a profoundly deaf son. "Show me their anthropological roots, relics . . . to prove that they have a 'culture.' How can the Smithsonian Institution recognize only one side of such a rapidly changing technological field with something so outdated?"[25] Notions of the Progressive Era and of deafness (in the manner of common perceptions of Helen Keller) surfaced with surprising consistency.

A parent of a cochlear-implanted deaf child wrote, "Parents need to be given accurate information on all the available options and then be free to make their own decisions. . . . Technology is a miracle and a gift. . . . However, this is a two-sided issue that has created factions as divided and as militant as those in the abortion issue."[26] The analogy made between the exhibition and the abortion debate suggests that what is at stake is a potentially aborted child, so to speak, an undeveloped child that the hearing parents try their best to bring to term, with the attendant implications that in doing so, the child will become "born again" into normalcy, into the narratives of completion and bodily integrity. This parent also references the ownership issue when she says that parents should be "free" to make their own decisions, as if the Deaf community were waiting to snatch her deaf child. This unstated concern about "ownership" appeared in letter after letter, suggesting both great concern and anxiety about the ways in which family and marital bonds are highlighted in the presence of a child who forces the family to consider what integration and belonging mean when there is love but perhaps little meaningful, easy, or consistent communication.

Many of these letters present short "protonarratives" that the letter writers felt compelled to offer as a kind of anecdotal evidence in the case against "exclusion." These were not fully developed narratives or personal stories; instead these proto-narratives were short kernels of often agonized, sometimes angry, narratives that focused primarily on the struggle with choices and emphasized the perceived threat to the integrity of the family. "This was all new to my wife and myself," wrote the father of a profoundly deaf daughter. "We knew no one deaf."[27] And similarly, "As a working mother, my time is of utmost importance to me. However, I feel the need to send this letter to you," wrote the mother of a seven-year-old "oral deaf" son. "I am not opposed to signing, and I hope my son will

---

24. Letter to the Smithsonian, n.d., Gallaudet University Archives.

25. Letter to the Smithsonian, November 24, 1995. Gallaudet University Archives.

26. Letter to the Smithsonian, November 15, 1995. Gallaudet University Archives.

27. Letter to the Smithsonian, n.d., Gallaudet University Archives.

eventually learn this beautiful language, however, now we are communicating orally and are having much success at it."[28]

These letters insist over and over again: "We are doing just fine, thank you very much!" "Through the use of powerful hearing aids," our deaf child succeeds, they reiterate. "By using her remaining hearing effectively," my deaf child has learned "to listen and to speak." Again and again, parents list sports activities, dean's lists, and various academic achievements: "My son is a recent graduate of [a prestigious college in the Northeast] and communicates by speech, but he is just as much a part of the story as a recent graduate of Gallaudet who signs!"[29]

I have yet to read one letter that tells the story of the other deaf children in the mainstream, the children who are deemed "oral failures" or who struggle with low self-esteem, social isolation, academic failure, and frustration with incomplete communication. Instead, these letters are reiterations of ability vis-à-vis the American Dream: "It was a joy raising [our daughter]. I guess we can be compared to parents centuries ago who refused to accept their child's blindness and used the early eyeglasses. That is the way scientific breakthroughs happen."[30]

The most agonized letters came not only from parents but also from oral deaf adults themselves. Because what is at stake is essentially the self, or rather, the validity of a self-concept centered around not-hearing-but-hearing, self-representation takes on an urgent, and at times fierce, tone, as can be seen in protonarratives written by deaf adults: "I am profoundly deaf and oral. . . . I feel that it is significantly important for the public to see the 'big picture' of the deaf population, not just one half."[31] This writer also described how frustrated she felt when people, upon finding out that she is deaf, assumed that she also knew signs. She seems personally assailed by this assumption, as if it were an accusation of some kind of failure on her part to be hearing (enough).

Most dismaying were the letters that contain echoes of ethnocentrism. As a center with services for deaf children noted: "Our approach is TOTALLY auditory. . . . Infants are fitted as early as possible even at 21 days old . . . WE DO NOT DO SIGNING . . . They can communicate with anyone, not just those who use the local 'dialect' of the manual language" (emphasis in original).[32] There is a sense of logic being constructed here; the "local dialect" is seen as inferior rather than as a culturally valid form of communication for that group. The suggestion is also that the local dialect will limit the signer, with no recognition of the fact that oral languages also have local dialects, yet we don't try to stop hearing people from using their local language. The writer also seems to think that by "doing" signing, one espouses a particular worldview that she finds repugnant.

In a similar vein, a parent of a cochlear-implanted child expressed her frustration: "Many strangers ask about the equipment [my daughter] wears behind her ear (she wears a CI) and upon learning she is deaf, EVERY SINGLE PERSON has asked, Does she know sign language yet? She does not. She speaks English"

28. Letter to the Smithsonian, November 14, 1995. Gallaudet University Archives.
29. Letter to the Smithsonian, January 17, 1996. Gallaudet University Archives.
30. Letter to the Smithsonian, n.d. Gallaudet University Archives.
31. Letter to the Smithsonian, February 21, 1996. Gallaudet University Archives.
32. Letter to the Smithsonian, July 2, 1996. Gallaudet University Archives.

(emphasis in original).[33] Again, the sense of xenophobic logic: the mother insists that her daughter "speaks" English, which she then argues will ensure her child's membership in a monolingual society. Taken far enough, this kind of statement smacks of historically similar statements made about immigrants to America.

Those in the medical sciences also bolstered xenophobic logic and amplified it by focusing upon the colonialist corollary, the desire to segment the other's (the deaf person's) body by focusing solely upon one fetishized body part: the ear. The deaf person is reduced to a broken-down ear, an absence that must then be medicalized and theorized. An audiologist wrote, "Such an exhibition runs contrary to the Smithsonian's purpose of advancing and disseminating knowledge."[34] This writer also noted, "The agenda of the planned exhibition is clearly political in nature; it is not founded on verifiable, incontrovertible facts which lead to a better understanding of the subject."[35] The writer uses the trope of science; the exhibition is meant to coolly and methodically sort through and display decontextualized bits of information for pseudo-medical decisions about the deaf child.

In these letters, there's not only the sense of the exhibition content being put under a microscope and analyzed accordingly but there's also a sense that the proposed and future exhibition viewer is being constructed as a detective, in search of facts that lead to a better understanding of what exactly happened. Thus the deaf child becomes both the site of a murder of normalcy and a medical aberration that needs to be fixed.

The letters raise their voices, even howl, in upper case, at the proposed indignity of the exhibition "DEAF: A Community of Signers." Perhaps the shrill or sentimental or agonized tone of many of the letters arises from the sense of an undefined and persistent threat to deaf children, grandchildren, deaf students, and clients: the threat of invisibility and exclusion, of being disabled, disconnected. Certainly, there are "successful"—whatever that really means—oral deaf adults, who also pay a social and personal price for such success. However, what is not mentioned in the letters is that the child is still deaf, no matter the superhuman efforts put into including, offering options, choices, technology, exhibitions, and so forth. A deaf child will not grow up to be hearing.

In contrast to these letters, the exhibition visitors' logbooks represent more varied responses, more possible ways to represent others and one's own self and community. Visitors began viewing the exhibit in 2002, and at each posting, a logbook was left for visitors to sign. Many viewers took the opportunity to write their thoughts, and one of the significant differences between the letters and logbooks is that the logbooks contain fewer anguished protonarratives and many more comments explicitly addressing the perceived conflicts in self- and other-representation. Perhaps this shift is due to the nature of writing one's individual responses to a visual and textual experience, as opposed to making a defensive and polemical point, but it could also be that the shift is due to a different demographic attending the exhibition. It may well be that the people who protested,

33. Letter to the Smithsonian, September 10, 1996. Gallaudet University Archives.
34. Letter to the Smithsonian, March 12, 1996. Gallaudet University Archives.
35. Letter to the Smithsonian, March 12, 1996. Gallaudet University Archives.

and eventually influenced, the exhibition were not the same people who viewed the exhibition. The majority of exhibition postings were held at deaf schools around the nation or in cities with a large culturally Deaf population. However, in this chapter, to keep some level of consistency between the inclusion of excerpts from far-flung letter writers and then far-flung visitors, I focused mainly on the logbooks from the Smithsonian posting.

In addition to registering one's presence and intimacy with the exhibition's subject matter, the short texts in the logbooks evince protonarratives that position the visitor within yet another set of perceived discursive conflicts regarding deafness, Deaf identity, Deaf history, familial and community connections, "hearing," and minority identity. Although anxious or defensive protonarratives similar to those in the protest letters also are present, in some ways, the logbooks represent those "voices" that are not present consistently in the body of protest letters.

With these responses and protonarratives, provocative and revealing intersections emerge between discursive terms used to represent or describe d/Deaf people and deafness and the ways in which hearing and d/Deaf people described their individual experiences with the exhibition. Excerpts from the "outsider's" perspective on the exhibition show some of the misconceptions and stereotypes that the exhibition had always hoped to correct. A few hearing visitors counted their blessings that they were not deaf. However, most had the good sense to attempt to step out of their "audiocentric" worldview: "This exhibit was amazing! It showed how smart 'dumb' people are. I know ASL myself, but I am not deaf."[36] With this visitor, the exhibition was clearly successful with its act of recovery and reinscription of deaf people within the context of American history; it was able to normalize and reincorporate deaf citizens for visitors who might otherwise stigmatize the subject of the exhibition.

Some hearing visitors chose to respond by focusing upon deaf people as individuals rather than as a group; but once again, the impulse was to reinscribe deaf people into a normalized category of sensory experience. One visitor wrote, "Does anyone read this? . . . What would be a good addition is a room set up where there were (movies of) people talking that you couldn't hear and other things that showed what it is like to be deaf."[37] This visitor imagines that by simulating lack of hearing she might become better able to understand the experience of deaf people. Until that happens, she can only imagine, in a very limited way, what Deaf people experience in a deafened body. This lack of something essential in her understanding does not quite square with what she describes as an otherwise "excellent and extremely informative" exhibit. Perhaps that sense of disjunction between what is already described and normalized and then an intriguing encounter with someone who doesn't easily fit those categories is the reason that quite a few felt compelled to describe encounters with deaf people:

> I was a kindergarten teacher . . . at [a school] in Washington, D.C. One of my students . . . was a hearing child of a deaf parent. She provided me with my first experience outside my family with a hearing impaired per-

---

36. Excerpt, Smithsonian Logbook. 2002. Gallaudet University Archives.

37. Excerpt, Smithsonian Logbook. 2002. Gallaudet University Archives.

son. Our "Teacher's Conference" was a wonderful experience. She and I "talked" about her charming son's progress. . . . I pray all has gone well for this lovely family.[38]

Praise the Lord! . . . The Lord guided me to this exhibit. We have a "Silent Music Ministry Choir" at our church. . . . [T]he Silent Mission Choir signs sign so beautifully. It's as if their fingers are literally speaking.[39]

Attention Musicians: Perhaps the most rewarding gig you can play is for an audience who cannot hear you perform. Turn up the Bass and keep a smile on your face. The vibration (and good vibes) will keep your gracious Audience Dancin' All Night![40]

In most cases, with these kinds of responses, the encounter with a deaf person "enriches" or enhances the hearing person's understanding of commonplace sensory experiences. In that respect, deaf people serve as arbiters of a sensory and sensual liaison that nonetheless is still framed within the context of "hearing": "talking," "hands literally speaking," "vibration (and good vibes)" set to the tones of loud bass music.

In a similar vein, still others used common tropes of diversity to describe what they saw and how they perceived the exhibition: "Exhibits like this help little by little to dispell [sic] the ignorance of Americans about people. . . . We are a diverse people."[41] The very frame of the exhibition encourages this kind of reinsertion of deaf people into what has largely been an "able-bodied" narrative, that of American history—hence the overlay of distinctly hearing terms of description onto d/Deaf experiences, d/Deaf bodies.

Other hearing visitors chose to connect to the exhibition by writing proto-narratives that, unlike those described earlier, shifted the focus away from the writer and instead signaled intimacy with the Deaf community through the naming of deaf family members:

The exhibit is wonderful! I have a deaf bro and it meant a lot to see such a tribute.[42]

My deaf daughter now 33 went through the entire revolution depicted in this remarkable and bright (?) [sic] exhibit. Thank you indeed.[43]

After 41 years of married life to my deaf wife, I, a hearing person, have not fully mastered sign language.[44]

---

38. Excerpt, Smithsonian Logbook. 2002. Gallaudet University Archives.

39. Excerpt, Smithsonian Logbook. 2002. Gallaudet University Archives.

40. Excerpt, Smithsonian Logbook. 2002. Gallaudet University Archives.

41. Excerpt, Smithsonian Logbook. 2002. Gallaudet University Archives.

42. Excerpt, Smithsonian Logbook. 2002. Gallaudet University Archives.

43. Excerpt, Smithsonian Logbook. 2002. Gallaudet University Archives.

44. Excerpt, Smithsonian Logbook. 2002. Gallaudet University Archives.

Those who named a relationship with a culturally Deaf person were enacting the same kind of inter- and intracommunity networking that one does with another Deaf person; by doing so, one establishes a relation to the community as a member, as an ally, or as a participant on the fringes. This sort of relational matrix is common for the culturally Deaf community. In contrast to the letters, these protonarratives do not describe an immediate threat to a family "body" or to the national body. They expand on the representation of Deaf and deaf people through the addition of more bodies and more narratives allied to those on display rather than asserting the deaf child's inclusion within an already homogenized U.S. history.

On the other hand, some visitors, like the man married to a deaf woman for forty-one years, seem to register in their responses a question mark, a blank that continued in their consciousness even after seeing the exhibition. It is as if this man had hoped for some clarity, some insight, into what it means to be deaf. Many, many visitors registered the same response, the same kind of continuing question mark about what it means to inhabit a perceived absence: "How does it feel to be deaf?"[45]

Others tried to position themselves as gatekeepers at the gate of inclusion: "As an employer of the deaf, I believe it is important to educate the public that the hearing impaired are normal people not freaks to be pointed at. Keep up the good work."[46] Teachers, principals, speech therapists, and other education-related professionals wrote similar notes.

However, throughout, there are oblique mentions of freakishness, of unease with a "disabled," not-hearing body, and these sensations were often distanced from the viewer by being recorded in the form of jokes and observations:

Nothing on Helen Keller? How come?[47]

Q: Why was Helen Keller's socks yellow?
A: Her dog was blind too.
Q: Why did Helen Keller's dog jump off a cliff?
A: You would too if your name was arrrrgggh.[48]

Interesting and admiring to see how hearing impaired have developed new ways to live life.[49]

I thought there would be more Helen Keller.[50]

Such an insistence upon Helen Keller's presence as the cultural icon of embodied deafness points to a desire to see disabled bodies on display, to view the spectacle of seemingly incomprehensible physical difference.

---

45. Excerpt, Smithsonian Logbook. 2002. Gallaudet University Archives.
46. Excerpt, Smithsonian Logbook. 2002. Gallaudet University Archives.
47. Excerpt, Smithsonian Logbook. 2002. Gallaudet University Archives.
48. Excerpt, Smithsonian Logbook. 2002. Gallaudet University Archives.
49. Excerpt, Smithsonian Logbook. 2002. Gallaudet University Archives.
50. Excerpt, Smithsonian Logbook. 2002. Gallaudet University Archives.

Similarly, non sequiturs mark an unease and apparent need to register one's presence or reaction:

I am sexy and hot ☺.[51]

Not so cool. Not cool at all.[52]

It could be that the writers felt discomfort or disconnection with the display and chose instead to simply register their presence, their physicality and able-bodiedness.

In contrast, others deliberately wrote their bodies directly into the text on display by reading their own embedded history into the culturally Deaf content:

Thanks for an excellent overview of the good old days and the latest developments. It was highly nostalgic to both of us (in 60's) who experienced many of the events.[53]

It brought back memories of our Deaf school![54]

My Grandpa + Grandma are deaf. This place makes me think of them. . . . Me and my twin are deaf and we are proud.[55]

These writers focus on their own relationship to the events depicted, and by doing so, recover the individual stories that comprise some of the history on display.

The textual inscriptions of dialogue between one writer and another are very revealing, particularly when what is at stake is representation of Deaf people as opposed to pathological representations of deafness. One visitor suggested incorporating information on cochlear implants because that "would help people with normal hearing to understand the implant is not a 'cure.' " Another visitor circled the word *normal* and wrote in the margins, "ouch!"[56] (See figure 1.)

Another visitor responded using the phrase "hearing impaired," and a separate visitor wrote, again in the margins, "many deaf people prefer the word DEAF, not hearing impaired!"[57] (See figure 2.)

In figure 3, someone drew a human figure with the caption "Deaf people Rule!" On the other side of the page, another person, probably a younger child than the one who drew the first figure, wrote "I wish we knew a way to help deaf people." That same person had drawn a human figure holding up a hand to his ear, with a word balloon asking, "What did you say!"[58] Clearly, what is being

51. Excerpt, Smithsonian Logbook. 2002. Gallaudet University Archives.
52. Excerpt, Smithsonian Logbook. 2002. Gallaudet University Archives.
53. Excerpt, Smithsonian Logbook. 2002. Gallaudet University Archives.
54. Excerpt, Smithsonian Logbook. 2002. Gallaudet University Archives.
55. Excerpt, Smithsonian Logbook. 2002. Gallaudet University Archives.
56. Excerpt, Smithsonian Logbook. 2002. Gallaudet University Archives.
57. Excerpt, Smithsonian Logbook. 2002. Gallaudet University Archives.
58. Excerpt, Smithsonian Logbook. 2002. Gallaudet University Archives.

FIGURE 1.

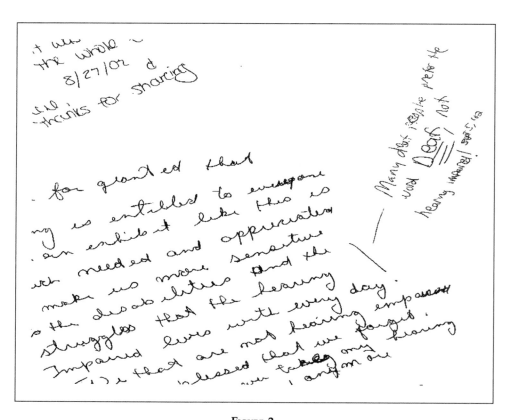

FIGURE 2.

Figure 3. Contrasting views of deafness in exhibition feedback.

contested here are very different ways of conceptualizing and embodying deafness and Deaf lives.

Many comments by Deaf people about the Deaf subjectivities on view echo current narratives of and about Deaf identity and history, particularly through references to Deaf President Now (DPN)—a protest by Gallaudet students, alumni, and their allies in 1988 that resulted in the appointment of the first Deaf president of Gallaudet University—and through the use of common discursive elements for describing Deaf identity through the sociolinguistic and sociological/anthropological model:

> What a great start! . . . Its [*sic*] in a good location for "deaf-impaired" (hearing) people to see and start to understand and accept that deaf people can do anything, but hear![59]

> Deaf Can!![60]

> Great exhibit, but perhaps some info about how deaf people do not consider themselves disabled, but rather a "language minority."[61]

> Great exhibit but only scratches the surface of Deaf history, deaf issues, and deaf culture. Remember: hearing people *must* learn to perceive deaf people in a humanistic light instead of a scientific one.

---

58. Excerpt, Smithsonian Logbook. 2002. Gallaudet University Archives.

59. Excerpt, Smithsonian Logbook. 2002. Gallaudet University Archives.

60. Excerpt, Smithsonian Logbook. 2002. Gallaudet University Archives.

61. Excerpt, Smithsonian Logbook. 2002. Gallaudet University Archives.

P.S. Cochlear implants are not the cure. It's just a way for doctors and un-
aware parents to "try" to assimilate those deaf children into the hearing
world. There's nothing wrong w/ being deaf. Believe it.[62]

By and large, these responses tended to be from professionals in the Deaf community who are largely college-educated and well versed in academic discourse
about Deaf people. As such, these writers consciously and directly positioned
themselves in contrast to the pathological and medical discourses on deafness.

Points of critique reveal cultural values and an awareness of gaps in social
representation, particularly in regards to real deaf people, not just the faces on the
storyboards:

Very informative and non-confrontational in portrayal of deafness and deaf
culture. I would like to have seen more of the uniqueness of deaf gatherings as an emotional event. The finding of sameness in being deaf always
seems to bring an emotional relief when shared with other deaf people.
Perhaps this relief shows itself in emotions similar to love but whatever it
is it brings us together with such a bond: I wish that bond had been more
described.[63]

People said Deaf are dumb or mute? But . . . mute means cannot talk. Hearing people cannot talk through sign languages so they are mute too? I don't
think so. . . . Nobody are dumb or mute. Deaf people could do anything like
hearing people. [Handwriting reveals a young teen wrote this.][64]

Interesting exhibit, but when a deaf person comes in, shouldn't the men
checking bags be able to sign?[65]

In the logbooks from the Smithsonian posting, there is relatively little mention of the controversial issues facing the community, such as cochlear implants,
but there is some discussion of culture and cochlear implants in the logbooks from
a posting at a nearby residential school: "It was wonderful. But I don't like cochlear implants because it is not part of deaf. Deaf Power!"[66] Similar comments
throughout this logbook from Hartford, Connecticut, the site of the American
School for the Deaf, echoed the same sentiment. However, there was one writer
who noted, "Cochlear implant is a good technology! It is better than hearing aid!
I'm getting C.I. in TWO WEEKS!!"[67] Interestingly enough, in contrast with the
debate and dialogue in the Smithsonian logbooks on deaf education and "options"
or "choices," especially in regard to technology, there was no extended or nuanced
discussion of cochlear implants other than comments that they are "good" or
"bad" and that they do not fit with the current model of Deaf sociolinguistic iden-

---

62. Excerpt, Smithsonian Logbook. 2002. Gallaudet University Archives.

63. Excerpt, Smithsonian Logbook. 2002. Gallaudet University Archives.

64. Excerpt, Smithsonian Logbook. 2002. Gallaudet University Archives.

65. Excerpt, Smithsonian Logbook. 2002. Gallaudet University Archives.

66. Excerpt, Hartford, Conn., Logbook. 2001. Gallaudet University Archives.

67. Excerpt, Hartford, Conn., Logbook. 2001. Gallaudet University Archives.

tity. Only time will tell whether these cochlear-implanted children will grow up to learn ASL and to integrate a Deaf, hearing, or bicultural identity; this may explain the lack of extended discussion. Generally speaking, however, those deaf or hard of hearing people who saw themselves as somehow marginalized through oral education, cochlear implantation, or lack of fluency in sign language tended to write themselves into the exhibit with long, autobiographical narratives, none of which are published here because they are not easily quoted in short excerpts.

What's striking about these logbook entries by Deaf visitors, in contrast to the letters to the Smithsonian, is the relative lack of protonarratives; many did not seem to feel a compelling need to narrate themselves as individuals within the larger context of competing discourses. Instead, these visitors often position themselves solidly within a Deaf cultural community identity. Perhaps this shift away from the particulars of an individual autobiography outwards to a kind of dialogue has to do with the perceived audience, someone, anyone, who would be reading in English. As one young writer from a deaf school wrote, "Hello anyone. . . . It is cool. I'm deaf. . . . Thank you."[68]

By addressing a generalized, presumably not Deaf, but allied, reader, many visitors register the desire to record what they found most touching: their own presence within history, on storyboards, within a public building, and in printed English ("Wow, because I am Deaf person, too!" [This] "make me feel like good because I'm Deaf," and "I think it's interesting because we're learning all their things about yourselves that you didn't know").[69] Registering one's presence within a heretofore opaque discourse, that of American (hearing) history, was the subtext of many comments.

Some writers, particularly children, young teens, and young adults, chose to use pictograms or drawings to inscribe ASL sign glosses or to convey a sense of what a Deaf life, as lived, could look like, and how it could be represented on the page, on the storyboards, as living the life of "the people of the eye." In figures 4, 5, and 6, people chose to draw "ILU" hands, or hands waving in the sign for applause, or as in the last example, pictograms: a heart shape with the word *fun* enclosed, and then an eye. [70, 71, 72]

However, the competing narratives of self and community, one within a sociological community that insists upon a visual subjectivity and the other within a pathologizing discourse that denies agency and subjectivity, are everywhere present. Juxtaposed below (see figures 7 and 8) are, first, a beautiful line drawing of an eye, with the word, *thanks*,[73] and second, a line drawing of a girl with her hands behind her back (her hands cannot be seen) and her face scrawled over. Above this figure is the word *grazie!*, Italian for "thanks," in the same ink used to draw the faceless, armless figure.[74]

---

68. Excerpt, Smithsonian Logbook. 2002. Gallaudet University Archives.

69. Excerpt, Smithsonian Logbook. 2002. Gallaudet University Archives.

70. Excerpt, Smithsonian Logbook. 2002. Gallaudet University Archives.

71. Excerpt, Smithsonian Logbook. 2002. Gallaudet University Archives.

72. Excerpt, Smithsonian Logbook. 2002. Gallaudet University Archives.

73. Excerpt, Smithsonian Logbook. 2002. Gallaudet University Archives.

74. Excerpt, Smithsonian Logbook. 2002. Gallaudet University Archives.

FIGURE 4.

FIGURE 5.

Hello This is   I
enjoy The Deaf eyes.
I am Deaf and my family
is Deaf Too! (fun)

Figure 6.

Figure 7.

Although the exhibition intended to place Deaf and deafened people within the context of American history, the challenge remained: how to take the deaf person out of a debilitating and pathologizing social discourse and to place that body within another one that is still largely invisible for hearing visitors. For members of the culturally Deaf community, there was a clearly delineated personal and academic set of narratives of representation, as seen in the references to a common narrative of empowerment and sociolinguistic community.

FIGURE 8.

With these texts—the letters and the logbooks—provocative and revealing interstices emerge between discursive terms used to represent d/Deaf people and deafness and those that hearing and d/Deaf people use to describe their experiences. These texts shed light on the conflicted nature of representation and particularly on how hearing, deaf, and culturally Deaf people define and describe themselves and others in relation to the concept of a subjectivity that sees through "Deaf eyes."

REFERENCES

Bergey, Jean L. 1998. Creating a national exhibition on Deaf life. *Curator* 4 (2):81–89.
———. 2004. "History through Deaf Eyes." Presentation at the University of Virginia, November 11, Charlottesville, Va.
Letters, "History through Deaf Eyes." 1995–1996. Gallaudet University Archives, Washington, D.C.
Visitors' Logbooks, "History through Deaf Eyes." Installation at Hartford, Conn., March 5–April 14, 2001. Gallaudet University Archives, Washington, D.C.
Visitors' Logbooks, "History through Deaf Eyes." Installation at the Arts and Industries Building, Smithsonian Institution, Washington, D.C., May 9–September 22, 2002, Gallaudet University Archives, Washington, D.C.
Wells, Tommie G. 1994. Don't drag me into ghetto. *Silent News* 26 (4) (April).

5 | Bioethics and the
Deaf Community

Teresa Blankmeyer Burke

When the editors of this volume asked me to submit a chapter explaining the importance of bioethics to the deaf community, my first inclination was to refuse this daunting task.[1] Bioethics is a discipline with amorphous boundaries; defining the deaf community is similarly challenging. Given the difficulty of carving out a niche in which to situate my discussion, how could I possibly bring together these two disparate fields of bioethics and Deaf studies and, at the same time, offer a substantive discussion of the issues in just a few pages? After some reflection, I decided that this task was insurmountable—defining bioethics and the deaf community would take more ink than I was willing to spill, and there would be no space left to discuss the intersection of these two disciplines. The best that I could possibly do would be to designate working definitions, survey some important bioethical issues that affect the deaf community, and highlight some of the key concepts and arguments that accompany these issues. By reframing this chapter as an initial exploration into the questions of bioethics that might be raised by those working in Deaf studies scholarship, I hope to create a roadmap locating issues important to both of these domains and to suggest some starting points for cross-disciplinary discussion in Deaf studies and bioethics.

Defining Terms

For the purposes of this chapter, I've designated bioethics as the discipline where ethical questions related to biological sciences emerge. The range of these questions affecting deaf and hard of hearing people is extensive—from concerns about the environmental impact of the manufacturing and disposal of technological

---

1. I have designated the lowercase version of *deaf* when it precedes *community* as an inclusive term that represents the variety of people with hearing variation (e.g., hard of hearing, oral deaf, late deafened, deaf-blind, cochlear implant users, and culturally Deaf). I maintain the standard practice of using uppercase *Deaf* to indicate those with a linguistic and cultural orientation.

devices used by deaf and hard of hearing people to questions about biomedical issues, such as the moral implications of genetic screening for deafness. Establishing a working definition for the larger deaf community is complicated; the history of bioethics has impacted this community in discrete and different ways. Sometimes the issues affect a specific group within the group, such as members of the signing deaf community, the hard of hearing population, or people with cochlear implants. In other instances, a bioethics issue may affect the entire population, from the signing Deaf to those who consider themselves persons with hearing loss. Rather than establish one comprehensive definition, I will identify particular groups with each example I consider. In this way, I hope to avoid the pitfall of wrongly generalizing the population commonly referred to as "the deaf community." Having said this, I want to emphasize that the categories Deaf, oral deaf, hard of hearing, and so forth are fluid and not easily defined. By classifying issues as affecting certain groups, I merely intend to indicate a primary orientation from which to analyze an issue and not to exclude or dismiss other perspectives from within these groups.

In spring of 2006 I taught a course called Bioethics and Deafness at Gallaudet University. Although this was not the first course on bioethics offered at Gallaudet University, it was the first bioethics course specifically focused on ethical issues related to the signing Deaf community. These issues include the eugenics movement that began in the late nineteenth century and continued well into the twentieth century, the debate about the appropriateness of cochlear implant surgery for prelingually deaf children, genetic screening for hearing variation, and genetic selection. In addition to these issues, we also discussed the potential impact of future technology on the community, including nanotechnology, developments in cognitive and information science, and designer babies. Focused discussion on the ethical implications of emerging technologies has not been part of the everyday discourse at Gallaudet or in the greater signing Deaf community, but this is rapidly changing. One indication of increased interest in bioethics and biotechnology is the recently formed World Federation of the Deaf's ad hoc Task Force on Bioethics. Additionally, discussions about bioethics and biotechnology were featured for the first time at the 2007 Congress of the World Federation for the Deaf in Madrid.

As a philosopher and bioethicist, I chose to emphasize an Anglo-American philosophical approach to bioethics by using the method of argument analysis. Argument analysis is fairly straightforward: It involves identifying arguments, schematizing the premises and conclusion, assessing the truth of the premises, evaluating the strength of the link between the argument's premises and conclusion, and ultimately, deriving the argument's overall cogency. This approach comprises the core of analytic philosophy; the majority of American bioethicists trained as philosophers come from this background. This is the primary lens through which we evaluated bioethics in the Gallaudet course, although it was not the only one.

Determining the scope of bioethics for this course was much more difficult than determining the method of analysis. Typically, bioethics discussions related to specific communities within the broader population fall into two categories: (1) ethical issues that impact the specific community as a whole and (2) ethical issues that impact individual members of the community in particular ways. For example, the biomedical research agenda to eradicate deafness has the potential to affect the existence of the signing Deaf community as a whole, given the social construction of that community. The issue of whether to give a particular child a cochlear implant is an issue that impacts that particular child and her family. Of course, these two categories are not mutually exclusive. The decision of the parents to provide their child with a cochlear implant may result in the removal of that particular child from the signing Deaf community, but it is not necessarily the case that this will be the result.

Another way of looking at this is to consider bioethics from the macro-level of generally accepted institutional assumptions, values, and practices as well as to consider bioethics on a micro-level, where individual assumptions, values, and practices intersect. The fields of Deaf studies and bioethics typically posit two macro-level orientations at odds with each other; this is most commonly framed as the signing Deaf community that views itself as a cultural community versus the pathological definition of *deafness* espoused by the biomedical community. I believe that this framework omits an important consideration: Most, if not all, bioethics decisions are made at the level of the individuals directly involved and are not simply policy-driven. In order to consider bioethics as it plays out on the ground, we must pay just as much attention to the unique factors that influence each individual as we do to the viewpoints prescribed by the key institutions. Granted, this generates a messier picture of bioethics, but one that more accurately reflects the reality of bioethics in the greater deaf community.

A TRUNCATED HISTORY OF BIOETHICS: DEAF CONNECTIONS?

Before delving into the current relationship of bioethics to the Deaf community, a thumbnail sketch of the history of contemporary bioethics is in order. Some date the birth of present-day bioethics from the Nuremberg Doctors Trial, in which sixteen of the twenty-three German physicians tried were found guilty of euthanizing people and/or conducting human subject research without consent. The war crimes tribunal at Nuremberg is also notable for setting down a judgment of ten standards for morally permissible medical experiments, otherwise known as the Nuremberg Code, which established international conventions for the practice of medicine and protection of human subjects. Others date the beginning of bioethics from an American intellectual movement that began in the early 1960s with the advent of the so-called "God Squads," gatekeeper committees of community representatives who regulated access to kidney dialysis machines based on judgments of both the medical and moral worthiness of the candidates for dialysis. Still others consider that the discipline of bioethics coalesced when a series of egregious human subject experiments became public. This includes the infamous U.S. Public Health Services (USPHS) syphilis study at Tuskegee designed to track the natural outcomes of untreated syphilis in African American men. That study did not follow standard informed consent procedures established by the Nuremberg Code and did not provide information about standard anti-syphilitic treatment available to them, such as penicillin, once it became available.

Another government-approved experiment revealed to the public around the same time was the Willowbrook study on hepatitis, where children with mental retardation were injected with infected serum to induce hepatitis at the

Willowbrook State Hospital in Staten Island, New York. Conditions at Willowbrook were such that all the children were expected to contract hepatitis as well as other infectious diseases at some point; part of the rationale behind the study was that children who were deliberately exposed to hepatitis would benefit by being carefully monitored in a special unit, where exposure to other infectious diseases would be less likely.[2] Although this study purported to hold to a higher ethical standard than that of the USPHS syphilis study protocols in Tuskegee—because informed consent from the children's parents was obtained—several other ethical issues surfaced, including questions about the nature of informed consent when real or practical alternatives are beyond reach for the consenting parties.

What is striking about these noteworthy incidents in the history of bioethics is the documented and unexplored connections to deaf and hard of hearing people. While the Nazi euthanasia and human experimentation programs have been widely documented as affecting Deaf people, particularly the T-4 euthanasia program and the sterilization projects documented by Horst Biesold,[3] scholars have overlooked the potential connections of these other incidents to the Deaf community. In the case of Willowbrook State Hospital, there are at least two widely publicized instances of deaf adults mistakenly diagnosed with mental retardation who resided in Willowbrook during the time the hepatitis studies were conducted; it is not known if these people or other deaf people were participants in these studies. As for the Tuskegee syphilis experiment, one of the symptoms of advanced-stage syphilis is deafness; it would be worth investigating to determine whether any of the participants in this study were deaf or became deaf as a result of participation in this project. The suggested connection of the Tuskegee syphilis experiments to the deaf community may seem peripheral, given the standard summation of this case in which most emphasis is placed on how race and class issues played out to permit the continuation of the study long after it should have been discontinued. However, raising questions about participants' side effects, including deafness, offers the possibility of a new lens through which to analyze these cases. It goes without saying that the unethical practices that precipitated the development of contemporary bioethics are horrific on any reading—regardless of the presence or absence of deaf people. My point is that the hidden narrative of deaf and hard of hearing people as part of the history of bioethics is yet to be explored on many fronts. Stories of signing deaf people take center stage when people think of bioethics and deafness, but the stories about oral deaf and hard of hearing people are also part of this narrative and must be unearthed as well.

Although there is some debate over which events precipitated the birth of bioethics, by the 1970s, the National Commission for the Protection of Human Subjects of Biomedical and Behavioral Research was established to identify the guiding principles for ethically justifiable research on human subjects in the United States. The commission consisted of philosophers, theologians, community advocates, lawyers, researchers, and medical professionals. This commission authored the *Belmont Report*, one of the seminal documents of the American bio-

---

2. Veatch (1997, 275).

3. Biesold 1999.

ethics movement. The *Belmont Report* identified three ethical principles for evaluating human subject research: beneficence (do no harm), justice, and respect for persons. Shortly after this, philosopher Tom Beauchamp and religious studies scholar James Childress codified this approach into a school of thought now known as principlism, an amplification and explanation of the original principles identified in the *Belmont Report*.[4] Beauchamp and Childress (2001) argue that all ethical issues in biomedicine can be addressed by consideration of the following four principles: autonomy, or respect for persons; beneficence, the duty to do good; justice, as in fair treatment; and nonmaleficence, the duty to do no harm. Of course, individual cases will differ. Some cases may appeal to one or two principles, whereas others may merit consideration of all four principles.

Principlism held sway over bioethics as the dominant approach for a couple of decades. In the 1990s, it was challenged on several fronts; most notable of the criticisms was that this mid-level approach did not have sufficient theoretical grounding. Philosophers argued that principlism, by listing several principles without providing a coherent and consistent framework that justifies each principle, was inconsistent and insufficiently rigorous. Principlism could not be justified from a single theory of morality, such as (to use a few historical examples) John Stuart Mill's utilitarianism or Immanuel Kant's deontological theory, where one foundational concept grounds everything. The attacks on principlism mirrored other substantive challenges playing out on the battlefield of twentieth-century philosophy and applied ethics, including questions about the nature and justification of knowledge. The elegance of the top-down moral theories developed in the eighteenth and nineteenth centuries does not match up well to the real world of bioethics, where results tend to be messy and incomplete. Rather than using the top-down model where one foundational theory provides the supporting structure, Beauchamp and Childress's (2001) principlism bears more similarities to epistemic coherentism, where key mid-level concepts fit together supported in a web of beliefs. By weighing and balancing principles in the context of a particular case, principlism acknowledges the need for an approach that incorporates flexibility with some core concepts. Due to the difficulties of establishing theoretical grounding and consistency for principlism, this approach fell out of favor with many philosophers and bioethicists, who offered a variety of other approaches to bioethics. Another criticism levied at principlism was the tendency for health care professionals to use it as a checklist; by working through the list of principles, ethics committees developed a false sense of security that all important moral issues had been covered. In worst case scenarios, this meant that robust discussion of complex moral dilemmas was sacrificed for brief conversations regarding each principle, sacrificing the nuances and particularities of the case at hand.

Although I am in agreement that there are deep concerns about principlism as a theoretical approach, the four principles offered by Beauchamp and Childress (2001) are useful for the layperson in that they offer a succinct summary of several major traditions in Western philosophy. The principles of nonmaleficence and beneficence, with their moral imperative to "do no harm" and to "do good" bring consequentialist or utilitarian theories to mind. Here, actions are determined

---

4. Beauchamp and Childress (2001).

ethical or unethical according to the net benefit or harm resulting from the action. The principle of autonomy, or respect for persons, comes straight out of the deontological tradition in moral philosophy associated with Immanuel Kant. This family of ethical theories places the highest emphasis on making decisions that honor the intrinsic worth of the person and do not treat the person as a means to an end. Contemporary ethical theory bears part of the responsibility for the concept of justice; the release of the *Belmont Report* coincided with John Rawls's groundbreaking work in political philosophy, which stressed the importance of justice as a fundamental principle for creating a society fair to all, an important consideration for ethical decision making.

In some ways, the question of whether principlism can be justified as a robust theory is beside the point and best left to moral philosophers who care about such arcane matters. Those who wish to think critically about bioethics and the deaf community would be well served to ask how these principles might help to clarify the relationship of bioethics to the deaf community. One approach is to think about the kinds of issues that arise under each principle, setting up a rough classification scheme. In the following sections, I attempt to do just this by identifying how a given principle raises different questions and issues for bioethics within the greater deaf community. Although this list is by no means exhaustive, it is my hope that it will form a skeleton on which to build further discussion of bioethical issues affecting members of the deaf community.

First, Do No Harm

Primum non nocere, the command to do no harm, is one of the oldest in health care ethics. Yet what does harm mean in this context? Usually it is taken to mean that physicians and other health care providers have a duty not to worsen a person's state of health through their actions. A clear example of this would be performing a painful treatment that will worsen the patient's physical health. The harm in the paradigm case is twofold—the patient's health status is further compromised and the patient experiences pain and suffering. Health care providers have a duty not to increase a person's suffering when there is no benefit attached to the suffering, in contrast to short-term suffering in exchange for long-term health. Why should this be a pivotal issue for members of the signing Deaf community? This turns on how this community defines such concepts as health and harm; these are distinctly different than the definitions used by the dominant mainstream culture. The imperative of nonmaleficence occurs at the level of moral agents making decisions that affect individuals; the health care provider is charged with the responsibility of not harming her patients. At the most general level, nonmaleficence means avoiding actions that will likely bring about bad consequences overall. This differs from those actions involving pain or suffering that are expected to bring about a good result overall. For example, the child receiving a rubella vaccine briefly feels physical pain upon the act of immunization, but the morality of this action is generally not interpreted as harmful by mainstream culture—even if mild side effects occur or, more rarely, serious side effects occur.

When the focus shifts from the micro-level of particular individuals to the macro-level of a given population, the concept of harm takes on a different meaning. Asking a meta-level question related to harm raises the issue as to whether certain practices, such as the practice of medicine itself and the values subsumed under it, might be harmful to some and beneficial to others. Now, a connection to the signing Deaf community emerges. The medical approach that defines auditory status through the pathology of hearing loss brings with it a set of values that views individuals primarily through the lens of their disability; that is, people are seen as a broken set of ears in need of a fix. Defining a missing sense as harm drives all other determinations about harm and benefit related to hearing loss. According to this biomedical agenda, avoiding harm reduces to avoiding hearing loss. (This differs from taking actions to restore hearing, which would fall under the principle of beneficence for most health care workers.)

In general, health care providers subscribing to the definition of *hearing loss* as harm think of abiding by the principle of nonmaleficence for deaf people in a few ways, most notably through avoiding hearing loss. For example, this could be achieved by prescribing medications that do not have ototoxic side effects or by opting to prescribe ototoxic medications only when the risk of hearing loss is the lesser of two evils. Note that this position is not necessarily incompatible with a position of supporting a cultural conception of the signing Deaf community. One could simultaneously support the right of the signing Deaf community to continue to flourish and exist along with the right of hearing people to maintain their identity as "people of the ear." Also note that the issue of whether or not to prescribe ototoxic drugs to people who are already audiologically deaf is a different sort of issue than it is for hearing people. Additionally, the consequences of ototoxicity have different meanings for these communities and individuals residing within these communities. Hearing people, including most members of the medical community, equate the loss of a sense with being harmed; members of the signing Deaf community likely have a different orientation, especially if their experience of being in the world has never included auditory sensation.

Now, perhaps this is a bit too reductionistic. I'm not claiming that all medical professionals view members of the signing Deaf community as people whose ears must be fixed—certainly there are those who recognize that there is another aspect to this community. One important task is locating the putative harm. Hearing people would claim that the hearing loss itself is the harm; this however, is a privation, not a deprivation, to paraphrase Descartes. It is rare that one grieves for something that one has not lost. Consider gender as an analogy. A woman might wonder what it would be like to be a man, or vice versa; yet, this curiosity is not likely to be expressed in terms of loss. Granted, this is not a perfect analogy, since the range of hearing variation tends to be expressed as hearing or deaf (not hearing) by the dominant culture as a strictly audiological evaluation. In the case of the signing Deaf community, the range of hearing variation features, instead, cultural identification from Deaf to hearing-minded—a range that lessens the importance of audiological status. Many Deaf people would stake out a different claim about harm, arguing that the harms visited upon deaf people by the medical establishment are harms of bodily integrity—akin to those claimed by intersex people who are surgically forced into a particular social norm before they are old enough to decide for themselves. Another analogy would be the harm that is visited on the male infant who is circumcised—although medical reasons are offered for this procedure, it is also a procedure that has strong social (and sometimes religious or cultural membership) considerations.

At this point, I do not want to make the claim that a community is harmed. I think this is a difficult claim to establish philosophically, and I'll reserve this discussion for another essay. I do think it is clear that individuals within a community can be harmed; this issue must be considered in the context of how *hearing loss* or *being Deaf* is defined by professionals working in bioethics. Harms of bodily integrity are only part of this picture. Another issue important for bioethicists and health care professionals to consider when making decisions that affect people who are deaf or hard of hearing is the importance of broadening the definition of *harm* to include not just physical or bodily harm, but psychological harm. For example, is an individual harmed when he or she is not able to have full access to communication? Are decisions about treatment for hearing loss fully informed if this issue is not on the table? These questions are worthy of vigorous discussion and should be part of the informed consent process.

Beneficence

As any good utilitarian will tell you, sometimes a bit of harm is necessary to achieve the greater good. Health care providers do not set out to harm individuals with hearing loss, but rather to help them by doing good. Granted, some health care providers and scientists pursue their work from a paternalistic standpoint, but many others go into medicine because of a desire to ease suffering. The inability to hear is translated into potential suffering by most health care providers, who accordingly see their actions aimed at increasing hearing status as doing good.

Just as the notion of harm varies depending on who is defining the term, the notion of beneficence is also relative. A broad utilitarian definition of *doing good* rests on the concept of creating more benefit than harm. If we consider the dominant cultural view that the capacity to hear is a good, then it follows that the pursuit of actions toward this goal is beneficent. If we turn to the view that cultural Deafness is simply a human variation, a different kind of argument ensues. In biological terms, diversity is thought to be a good. The benefits of diversity are justified through both instrumental and intrinsic reasons. For example, environmentalists might offer both intrinsic and instrumental reasons for saving the Brazilian rain forests. An intrinsic reason would appeal to the value of the rain forest in itself. Here, an appeal is made by considering the nature and intrinsic worth of the rain forest as an object that deserves moral consideration. However, intrinsic arguments may not convince everyone. Sometimes instrumental arguments are also necessary for persuasion. In the case of preserving the rain forests, an instrumental reason commonly offered is the claim that plant species in danger of extinction might have the potential to cure disease; another instrumental reason relates to the importance of maintaining vast amounts of vegetation on the planet to counter the effects of greenhouse gases on global warming. Roughly stated, instrumental arguments can be persuasive to those who think in utilitarian terms; intrinsic arguments are more likely to convince those with a deontological bent.

The analogy of diversity can be extended to cultural diversity. For the person who accepts the idea that all cultural communities have intrinsic value, beneficent actions would include any actions that preserve a cultural good. For the signing Deaf community, this would include actions taken to preserve various aspects of the Deaf community, including its language and practices that encourage and maintain sufficient numbers of signing Deaf community members, thus benefiting individual members within that community. An instrumental argument supporting practices that encourage the flourishing of the signing Deaf community is to point to linguistic research on sign languages and the promise that sign languages offer the promise of gaining different kinds of knowledge about the development and structure of human language and cognition.

So far, I have posited a fairly strict duality between signing Deaf community members and the dominant mainstream culture, suggesting that research aimed at eradicating deafness is typically seen as a good by members of the dominant culture and that this same research agenda is seen as harmful by members of the signing Deaf community. In reality, it is not quite so simple. Those who occupy liminal space, such as hard of hearing people who sign, or culturally Deaf people who wear cochlear implants or hearing aids, must also be attended to. These people may find themselves in the position of supporting a research agenda aimed at improving technology that increases listening comprehension, but disavowing practices that threaten the existence of the signing Deaf community, such as genetic screening and selection. This position is not necessarily a contradiction, although it initially may appear to be so. Discussion of such complex positions is merited and likely to become more important as the numbers of signing Deaf adults with cochlear implants increase.

JUSTICE

Just as nonmaleficence and beneficence are opposite sides of the same coin, so do justice and autonomy fit together. The principle of justice refers to the treatment and constraints imposed on an individual from outside. The sordid history of eugenic practices under Nazi Germany is a classic example of injustice perpetuated against deaf people, among others. Much of the discussion in bioethics related to justice deals with unfair treatment regarding vulnerable populations; most commonly these are separated into the categories of children, prisoners, and people with cognitive disabilities. Although it is of course true that there are deaf people who fit into each of these categories, in the bioethics literature, little attention has been paid to the unique nature of hearing loss (I use this term to illustrate the dominant viewpoint) and the consequences of communication breakdown for people with decisional capacity. In this context, decisional capacity refers to one's ability to make health care decisions. As such, it requires the ability to comprehend the information provided and to appreciate this information in the context of the situation at hand. Ideally, when a person uses a language other than the dominant language of that medical institution, an interpreter will provide a translation to the person with decisional capacity so that the person can make an informed decision. In the case of a person with a hearing loss, the issue is not always one of providing language translation, but of providing communication access so that an informed decision can be reached.

This issue breaks down further. If we consider Deaf people who sign, one approach to making sure that justice is served is to provide equal treatment by ensuring equal access to communication through the use of sign language interpreters. If a patient or research subject is hard of hearing, amplified communication and the use of assistive listening devices allow that person to be treated on an equal footing with hearing people. The ideal of providing services to secure the basic conditions for just treatment depends on a number of factors, ranging from the awareness of the health care providers, researchers, and institutions of various laws governing access to communication, to the practical matter of availability of resources, both economic resources and scarcity or abundance of service providers and equipment. It is rare that the reality matches this ideal.

The population of late-deafened individuals, particularly elderly individuals, may be most at risk of injustice in medical and research settings. This is not to say that institutions deliberately set out to discriminate against such people. Rather, it is a statement about how existing stereotypes about elderly people and deaf people combine in a way that supports paternalistic social attitudes towards this population. Consider the process of informed consent, in which a person is given appropriate and relevant information about medical treatment options. If communication with a late-deafened individual is difficult due to a lack of residual hearing, a health care worker with time pressures may be more likely to presume choices or hurry through the process rather than take the time to ensure that effective communication has occurred. Unfair treatment has occurred through denying the late-deafened person the option of making his own choices. Typically, this occurs because the task of communicating with a late-deafened person is made more difficult; it can also occur because the late-deafened person has developed the habit of "bluffing" in an attempt to hide the extent of her hearing loss. Informed consent is a two-part process that requires both the act of notifying the patient about her treatment options and checking to be sure that the patient has understood this information. The process of checking for understanding with elderly late-deafened patients takes more time; this, coupled with the practice of bluffing, can lead to patient's granting consent without fully understanding or even misunderstanding what they have consented to.

Autonomy

The principle of autonomy, or respect for persons, goes hand in hand with justice. The central issue here is that one should have the freedom to make decisions about one's body and health. Unlike justice, the constraints here focus on the individual's right to make choices, even choices that may be out of step with mainstream medicine. A prototypical case is hearing parents faced with making a decision about providing their deaf child with a cochlear implant. In most cases, parents are presumed to be the best surrogate decision makers for their child because they have the child's best interests at heart. (An exception to this is surrogate decision making by parents who deny life-saving medical treatment to their child for religious reasons; typically, government intervention occurs in these cases because the state's interest in the child's right to continued existence supersedes the parent's right to religious freedom.) Cochlear implant surgery is not a life or death matter—to the best of my knowledge, the state has not mandated medical intervention in these cases, but has left these matters to the parents. Yet, the parents are making a decision about their child's body that will have enormous consequences on that child's quality of life.

A more complex version of this problem exists with genetic screening and genetic selection against deafness. Now that it is possible to identify genes that have been associated with hearing variation, potential parents with a family history of deafness have the option to screen embryos for this genetic trait. Some Deaf people may want to have a Deaf child and will want to use the technology to increase their odds of having such a child; others will use the technology to screen out deafness. Imagine two sets of potential parents who have undergone in vitro fertilization and have learned that some of their fertilized eggs about to be implanted code for deafness, and some of them do not. Do these sets of potential parents have equal freedom of choice regarding which fertilized eggs can be implanted? It is clearly the case that the potential parents who wish to screen out embryos carrying genes associated with deafness will be supported by the mainstream agenda of science and medicine. It is not so clear that this freedom to choose holds for Deaf parents who wish to have a Deaf child that will become a full-fledged member of their community. Yet, if we are to promote the principle of autonomy, with parents having the right to make decisions about the future of their offspring, it seems that both options must be permitted. This is without considering the question of autonomy for the potential person, which adds more complexity to this matter.

There are several other issues related to the principle of autonomy, or respect for persons. The twin issues of privacy and confidentiality take a new twist when a language is more public by its very nature, such as sign language in the case of culturally Deaf people. Privacy considerations are also an issue for late-deafened or hard of hearing people who may not realize that their health care provider is speaking loudly enough to be overheard or that they are projecting their own voice loudly in a very quiet environment. Confidentiality, or the duty to keep private information private, becomes more of a concern when other individuals are brought in to facilitate the communication process. Although most sign language interpreters are keenly aware of the ethical obligation of their profession to maintain confidentiality, there are differences in how this duty is perceived and practiced. Additionally, uniform standards of confidentiality for real-time captioning providers are unclear; some of these providers who defer to the standards of the court reporting profession may not realize how small the Deaf community is and may inadvertently breach confidentiality with the disclosure of one or two identifying characteristics. A right to autonomy includes the right to keep one's private information private; yet this may not always be the case.

CONCLUSION

In many ways, the history of bioethics parallels the recent history of the deaf community. Although the previous pages do not come close to providing a comprehensive list of the ethical concerns and issues related to bioethics and the deaf community, I hope that they will provide food for thought and a starting point for further discussion. The convergence of emerging technologies has put us at a crossroads; the future of the deaf community is in the hands of today's medical and scientific researchers. Positing the signing Deaf community as a cultural community that has resisted the biomedical establishment's attempts to eradicate it has opened people's eyes to a different viewpoint on hearing variation. The need for deaf people to engage in more discussion about bioethics with bioethicists and researchers is more critical today than ever. From the eugenics movement of the late nineteenth century to the current dialogue about the use of genetic technology in the deaf community, questions about the morality of curing, abating, or preventing hearing loss abound. Opening up dialogue between researchers and different members of the deaf community, whether hard of hearing, deaf-blind, oral deaf, late-deafened, or culturally Deaf, is imperative. Although these discussions may prove to be difficult and painful and may not result in universal agreement regarding a "deaf bioethic," encouraging this discussion to unfold in the realm of academic bioethics as well as Deaf studies scholarship offers the potential of better understanding, and one hopes, more thoughtful and ethical practices.

REFERENCES

Beauchamp, Tom L., and James F. Childress. 2001. *Principles of biomedical ethics,* 5th ed. New York: Oxford University Press.

Biesold, Horst. 1999. *Crying hands: Eugenics and Deaf people in Nazi Germany.* Washington, D.C.: Gallaudet University Press.

Veatch, Robert M. 1997. *Case studies in medical ethics.* Cambridge, Mass: Harvard University Press.

Part Two
Language and Literacy

6 | Cognitive and Neural Representations of Language: Insights from Sign Languages of the Deaf

HEATHER P. KNAPP AND DAVID P. CORINA

The past forty years have witnessed remarkable developments in our understanding of the languages used in Deaf communities around the world. Sign languages are complex and naturally emerging communicative systems that display all of the linguistic, cognitive, and biological hallmarks of human spoken language. Their mere existence provides important insights into the remarkable diversity of human language, and their linguistic structure yields invaluable clues as to the flexibility of the cognitive and neurological systems that support their use. In this chapter, we highlight several important findings that have emerged from these fascinating studies.

LINGUISTIC STATUS OF SIGN LANGUAGES

Two of the most important (but often misunderstood) facts about the sign languages of Deaf people are that there are many different sign languages and that these communication systems are real, natural languages. Sign language is not universal. Just as there are a multitude of spoken language communities around the world (e.g., speakers of Quechua, Farsi, Portuguese, and English) there are many different sign language communities (e.g., signers of Langue des signes québécoise [LSQ], Deutsche Gebärdensprache [DGS], Taiwan Ziran Shouyu [TZS], and British Sign Language [BSL], to name but a few). Although the histories and geographical ranges of sign languages have been less documented than those of spoken languages, it is known that sign languages arise spontaneously, over several generations, from isolated communities that have a preponderance of deaf

This work was supported by predoctoral National Research Service Award 5F31DC006796-02 to Heather Knapp and by NIH-NIDCD grant R01DC003099-06 to David P. Corina.

individuals. As community members migrate, their linguistic influences travel with them. Thus, just as spoken languages have formal similarities due to historical connections (for example, Dutch, German, and English are all Germanic languages), so do sign languages (e.g., American Sign Language [ASL], Langue des signes québécoise [LSQ], and Lenguaje de signos mexicano [LSM] all have origins in Old French Sign Language).

Second, sign languages themselves are not collections of invented hand symbols that simply represent the words of a spoken language, nor are they elaborate and codified systems of pantomime. They are complete, natural languages in their own right, with forms and grammatical rules that are abstract, linguistically complex, and largely independent of their surrounding spoken language communities. Although individual sign languages often correspond to the same geographical and political regions that separate users of spoken languages (e.g., both German spoken language and DGS are found in Germany, while English and BSL are found in England), sign languages are independent of the spoken languages used within these regions (e.g., ASL is also used in Nigeria [Kiyaga and Moores 2003] and in the Philippines, and ASL is no more dependent on English than BLS is). This common confusion stems in part from the fact that many sign languages do have auxiliary systems for borrowing elements of spoken languages into a manual form (i.e., fingerspelling systems, initialized signs). However, these subsystems are not considered to be native, core components of Deaf sign languages.

Units of Language Perception and Production

Languages are systems in which a small number of distinct and contrastive units (e.g., sounds) are combined in a finite number of ways to produce an infinite number of words. This process is recursive: Each distinct sound in a spoken language, for example, can be described uniquely by a complex of distinct features, which itself results from a unique combination of articulatory features that vary along such parameters as the horizontal and vertical position of the tongue in the mouth and the modulation of airflow from the lungs through the vocal tract (e.g., Ladefoged 1993).

Not until William Stokoe's pioneering work on sign language structure (Stokoe 2005; Stokoe, Casterline, and Croneberg 1965) did linguists and psychologists understand that sign languages are composed of abstract representational units comparable to those in speech. When Stokoe described the principal physical components of ASL signs—the hand configurations, path movements, and spatial positions (locations) that form the closed set of combinatorial units used during sign formation—he, in essence, instigated a minor revolution in the way linguists and psychologists conceptualize the human capacity for language.

While listening to their own language, speakers are able to effortlessly segment a continuous stream of sound into a comprehendible sequence of individual words (Miller 1990). As hearing people know from listening to spoken foreign languages, words are not separated by temporal pauses as they are (spatially) in text. In order to parse speech signals into separate words, speakers likely refer to their own memories of words and to their respective composite sounds.

Thus, the physical problem of speech recognition involves (1) the online segmentation of utterances into discrete and well-known linguistic units (i.e., breaking the word *kitten* into syllables and individual speech sounds) and (2) the mapping of those sounds onto memory representations of speech sounds. In the same way, the efficient perception of a sign language requires a parsing of a continuous visual sign signal into separate signs and their constituents (i.e., handshapes, movements, places of articulation, and hand orientation [a parameter proposed by Battison in 1978] stored in an abstract form in memory).

Modality and Sign Language Form

Sign language structure can be described in terms of the symbolic linguistic units used to describe speech (e.g., syllables, segments, consonants, vowels, and distinctive features), although there are continuing theoretical debates concerning the homologies of these units across modalities. These units are particularly fascinating to study in the context of sign because their physical expression varies radically from that of speech. Signs are articulated with the arms and hands (and modulations of facial features) and perceived with the eyes, whereas spoken words are articulated with the vocal tract (e.g., larynx, pharynx, parts of the oral and nasal cavities) and perceived with the ears. A central issue in the research of sign languages has been the extent to which the form or modality of expression of sign and speech influences the cognitive and neurological processes involved in perceiving and producing them.

One of the biggest differences between sign and speech is the degree to which the sublexical elements of signs occur simultaneously during sign production. For example, for any given sign to be recognized (e.g., DADDY), the handshape (5), location (forehead), and movement type (to-and-fro) expressed in the service of that sign must appear at the same time or very close together during a short time window. This is in contrast to speech, wherein the sounds that make up a word (e.g., *daddy*) unfold more gradually over time (/dædi/). This modification of the expression of sign language no doubt reflects the greater flexibility afforded by the visual system's encoding of physical space. The visual system is capable of perceiving multiple objects and movements simultaneously, whereas a comparable multiplicity of cues delivered to the auditory system would be jumbled beyond recognition. In spite of this important modality difference, to date, there have been many more studies stressing the structural commonalities between sign and speech than there have been papers emphasizing their differences (see Meier, Cormier, and Quinto-Pozos 2002 for a collection of papers devoted to this latter issue).

PSYCHOLINGUISTICS OF SIGN LANGUAGES

The broad goal of psycholinguistic research is to discover the relationship between linguistic and cognitive processing. Much work in this field has concentrated on understanding the organizational system used to store and access words from the mental dictionary, or lexicon. Although sign language psycholinguistics is a new field in which much important work remains to be done, preliminary evidence indicates that many psycholinguistic processes appear to be similar across sign and speech. A variety of well-documented psycholinguistic effects, such as the *lexicality effect*, the *word frequency effect*, and semantic and phonological *priming*, have enabled researchers to make some general claims about the nature of the lexicon.

For example, it is known from speech research that real (lexical) words are recognized faster than phonetically possible nonsense (made-up) words. This has been termed a *lexicality effect*. Lexicality effects have been found both in ASL (Corina and Emmorey 1993; Emmorey 1991; Emmorey 1995) and BSL (Dye and Shih 2006). The greater time taken to identify a possible non-word (relative to a lexical item) is thought to be due to its absence in the lexicon: Although a mental search for a real word will eventually end in success, a search for a phonetically possible nonsense word will continue until the entire lexicon has been searched, then eventually fail.

Another common speech psycholinguistics finding is the *word frequency effect* (Savin 1963). Words that are heard and spoken very often can be identified or recognized much faster than rare words. This is thought by many to be due to differences in the level of cognitive activation required for common and rare words to reach awareness. Very common words are thought to have low thresholds for activation, whereas rare words are thought to have higher thresholds, relative to resting levels (e.g., Luce, Pisoni, and Goldinger 1990; Morton 1969).

Although published sign frequency counts are currently unavailable for most sign languages, the word frequency effect has been demonstrated for sign lexical access. For example, ASL signs rated as common on a scale from 1 to 10 (e.g., FIND) have been found to be recognized, on average, 120 ms faster than signs rated as rare on the same scale (e.g., DRAPES; Emmorey 2002).

The Sign Lexicon

Although the evidence above suggests that signs are accessed in the lexicon more quickly if they are real and if they occur frequently in the language, questions remain regarding how individual signs are stored in the lexicon and what cues people use to access them. One question is whether signs are stored according to their structural properties—their handshape, location, or movement values— much the way spoken words are purported to be stored by sounds. If so, does the nearly simultaneous appearance of these components affect how signs are retrieved over time? This appears to be the case. Signs can be identified within the first 240 ms (35 percent) of their total 686-ms average length, which is quite fast compared to spoken words, which require the presentation of 83 percent of their total length (330 ms of 398 ms, on average) before reliable recognition can be achieved (Grosjean 1980). This difference between the amount of time it takes to identify a word and sign is probably due to the near-simultaneous presentation of phonological information in signs. In other words, if the handshape, movement, and location values of a sign occur very close together in time, the sign will be recognized quickly—as soon as all three values appear.

However, recognition isn't perfectly simultaneous. The parameter values that the signer produces first are, in fact, recognized first by the person watching the sign. For example, when signers were shown 33-ms videotaped clips of ASL signs (presented cumulatively) and asked to guess what ASL sign they were watching

(Emmorey and Corina 1990), they first suggested signs that shared the location and handshape with the signs being viewed, but that differed in the movement of the actual sign. Only when the final movement information was available did complete recognition occur. Thus, it is possible that signs in the mental lexicon are stored according to their sublexical structure, and more particularly, in a fashion that corresponds to the parameters that appear over time during sign production. One possible working hypothesis is therefore that incoming signs are first "looked up" in the lexicon by their place of articulation and/or handshape values, and that the final match is made from a subset of only the signs that share these values with the input. This is consistent with the general idea of a model of speech lexical access in which the sounds at the beginning of the word iteratively constrain the set of target words.

Another question is whether signs are stored according to their meanings, with signs with similar meanings being stored in closer mental "proximity" than unrelated signs. Despite the physical differences between the two language modalities, early evidence suggests that signs are stored and accessed along both structural and semantic dimensions, similar to spoken words. We know, for example, that signs and words are stored and retrieved from the lexicon similarly because both signs and spoken words can be primed by semantically and phonologically related lexical items. *Priming* occurs when the recognition of a word is faster or more accurate because it (or a close relative) has recently been seen. For example, recognition of the word *dog* (the target) will be faster if it is preceded by the semantically related word *cat* (a prime that shares the category "animal" with the target) than if it is preceded by the unrelated word *cup* (a prime that shares no obvious relationship with the target). This is an example of *semantic priming*, a phenomenon that is well attested in sign. For example, the ASL sign HOT strongly primes its semantic associate COLD (Corina and Emmorey 1993).

Similarly, *phonological priming* occurs when the recognition of a word changes because it has been preceded by a word that shares a sound, or a group of sounds, with the target. In sign, the analog is priming by a sign that shares a handshape, a location, or a movement with the target sign. Sometimes a shared structural relationship between prime and target may interfere with recognition, rather than facilitate it. This is true for both speech and sign. In sign, it is additionally an open question as to which of the three parameters has the strongest effect on recognition. In general, it appears that signs that share both a location and movement with a target will have the strongest effect on recognition speed (Corina and Hildebrandt 2002; Dye and Shih in press). Handshape especially seems to exert little influence in this realm.

Semantic and phonological properties of signs also exert different degrees of influence during sign language production. For example, in a recent sign production study, signers were asked to rapidly name common, everyday objects shown to them in colored photographs (Corina and Knapp 2006). They had to do so while ignoring a superimposed video image of a person signing the name of a different object. This interference naturally caused the process of retrieving an object's name from memory to be more challenging. Interestingly, when the ASL sign for the pictured object (the target) and the ASL sign produced by the signer (the interfering sign) shared a semantic relationship, signers were slower to name the pictured object than when the object and sign shared no values in common. But when the target and interfering sign shared both movement and location values, picture naming was faster! Effects of other phonological parameters on picture naming were much smaller and more variable.

Taken together, these findings suggest that, like spoken words, lexical entries of a sign language are stored within a searchable mental lexicon from which common signs can be more readily retrieved than rare words. These signs are likely organized and accessed according to both their semantic and phonological properties, although the precise relationship between a sign's semantic and phonological "entries" is not yet well understood. Moreover, the phonological parameters of handshape, location, and movement themselves do not exert equal influence on the retrieval of signs during language perception or production.

NEUROLINGUISTICS OF SIGN LANGUAGES

Linguistic and psycholinguistic research have provided corroborative evidence that sign languages are legitimate human languages that call upon many of the same cognitive processes as spoken languages during perception and production. Similarly, recent work has begun to lay bare the neurological correlates of sign languages—including the identification of particular regions of the brain that are specialized for linguistic activity. In large part, the findings from aphasiology, cortical stimulation mapping (CSM), and brain imaging studies converge to suggest that sign language localization and processing overlap extensively with those in speech.

Aphasia

The easiest access to the study of the biology of language has historically been through accidents of nature—unfortunate cases of stroke or brain injury that result in aphasia, a loss of a person's ability to speak and/or understand language. Aphasias do not affect a person's ability to see, hear, or understand nonlinguistic information. Importantly, they also do not affect a person's ability to gesture: It is not uncommon for aphasic patients to use gestures in an attempt to communicate. It is therefore an interesting question as to whether Deaf signers who experience comparably located strokes or other brain injuries will lose the ability to use manual sign language while retaining the ability to gesture. Additionally, it is critical to understand whether the specific locations of brain injuries result in similar kinds of language disturbances across sign and speech.

Since the 1860s, it has been known that speech aphasias occur when left hemisphere brain structures are damaged. Several reports have now documented cases in which, following damage to the left hemisphere, a Deaf signer completely or partially lost the ability to use sign language but retained an ability to use pantomime and nonlinguistic gesture (e.g., Corina 1998; Corina et al. 1992; Hickok, Love-Geffen, and Klima 2002; Poizner, Klima, and Bellugi 1987). For example, an interesting case study describing a Deaf user of BSL who suffered a left hemisphere stroke makes clear that sign and gesture production in BSL can be highly dissociated, even when the signs and gestures in question are physically quite similar (Marshall et al. 2004). This patient, Charles, was frequently unable to remember BSL signs for common objects, instead substituting gestures or related signs. For example, when asked to produce the BSL sign for BICYCLE, he panto-mimed a bicycling motion. When attempting to sign TUNNEL, he produced the se-mantically related signs TRAIN and BRIDGE.

Cases of sign aphasias such as these are highly comparable to the difficulties experienced by hearing persons with aphasias. They suggest that like speech use, sign language use is reliant upon an intact left hemisphere, and, moreover, is dissociable from visual perception and from the comprehension and production of nonlinguistic gestures of the arms and hands. This type of dissociation makes it clear that the left hemisphere is crucial in the mediation of complex language systems, whether spoken or sign, and provides additional evidence that sign lan-guages are formal language systems that are different from more general non-linguistic gestural abilities.

More specific commonalities between the breakdown of spoken and sign lan-guages have also been identified. Lesions that are localized to anterior or poste-rior left hemisphere regions can result in specific types of aphasia, such as Broca's aphasia and Wernicke's aphasia, respectively (for more information, see Blumstein 1973; Goodglass 1993). Broca's aphasia is associated with damage to a relatively small anterior area of the cortex. Hearing patients with Broca's aphasia can typi-cally understand language, but struggle to produce speech sounds. It is thought that they have an inability to access the articulatory motor programs associated with the sublexical units of speech. Wernicke's aphasia is associated with lesions to more central and posterior left hemisphere areas. These patients struggle to comprehend language, and although their language production is fast and smooth, it often contains many errors and may not fully make sense. The language problems seen in patients with Wernicke's aphasia are thought to reflect a distur-bance in the ability to associate sound sequences with meaning representations.

When signers experience neurological damage to anterior and posterior re-gions of their left hemispheres, these familiar language function dissociations occur. One classic example is patient G. D. (Poizner et al. 1987), who had a stroke that damaged anterior sections of his left hemisphere. G. D. was able to under-stand ASL, but his own signing was effortful and dysfluent. This is highly con-sistent with the standard description of Broca's aphasia. Another example is patient W. L. (reported in Corina et al. 1992), who had a stroke that damaged pos-terior parts of the left hemisphere. This patient had difficulties understanding sign language and also produced many signs that were phonologically and semanti-cally incorrect, as is typical of Wernicke's aphasia. Critically, both of these patients exhibited relatively normal gesture comprehension and production.

Cognitive Neuroscience Methodologies

Often the lesions of aphasic patients are quite large and nonspecific, encompass-ing portions of both frontal and parietal cortex. These injuries do not allow for conclusions to be drawn about which regions of the left hemisphere are engaged during specific aspects of language use. It is situations such as these when cogni-tive neuroscience techniques are particularly valuable. CSM, positron emission tomography (PET), and functional magnetic resonance imaging (fMRI) have be-gun to be useful tools, answering more specific questions about particular rela-tionships between language structure and function.

Cortical Stimulation Mapping

CSM, for example, is commonly employed as part of a very important preliminary assessment of brain functioning in epileptic patients. Because patients with severe epilepsy must have brain surgery to reduce the severity of their seizures, it is vital to learn which areas of their brain are required for language functioning so that these can be left undisturbed during surgery. The most precise way of learning which brain regions are critical for language is to apply very small electrical currents to selective parts of the brain while the epileptic patient uses language (e.g., reading or naming objects viewed on a video screen). This electrical activity will temporarily interrupt behaviors controlled by these brain regions. In rare cases in which these epileptic patients are Deaf signers, these same CSM procedures can be used to ensure that regions vital to sign language production and perception are not damaged during epilepsy surgery. This testing has the added benefit of informing researchers about which brain regions support select aspects of sign language use.

As with aphasia, clear dissociations emerge between the types of errors that result from stimulation to anterior and posterior brain regions in Deaf epileptic patients. A prominent example is that of patient S. T., a right-handed Deaf signer (reported in Corina et al. 1999). When S. T. was asked to sign the ASL names of line-drawn pictures with his left hand while twenty-three potential language sites were tested, two sites were consistently associated with sign naming problems.

The first, an anterior site corresponding to Broca's area, resulted in S. T. producing signs with reduced, unspecified handshapes and movements. These handshapes were not real, allowable ASL hand configurations, but they were lax, closed-fist hand forms that he produced for nearly every sign, regardless of his goal. Similarly, the movements S. T. made were general, unspecified rubbing motions that were not real ASL movements. These findings again emphasize that Broca's area does not only mediate the link between speech sounds and their corresponding motor plans, but rather serves to link linguistic and motor representations in both spoken and sign modalities.

Errors made by S. T. when posterior brain regions were stimulated were quite different from those made during anterior stimulation. In the case of posterior disruption, he produced both formational and semantic errors. His formational errors were characterized by the selection and production of real but inaccurate ASL handshapes and/or movements, followed by successive attempts to produce the sign correctly. Interestingly, all of the semantic errors also involved the selection of signs that were themselves formationally related to the target sign. For example, when S. T. was shown a picture of a pig, he produced the sign FARM, which is related to PIG both by semantic association and by similar place of articulation and hand configuration. Taken together, these data suggest that in S. T., posterior brain regions were normally involved both in the selection of appropriate phonological specification of signs and with mapping between semantic and phonological forms.

Neuroimaging

Neuroimaging techniques like PET and fMRI also provide unique contributions to our current understanding of the neurological processing of signs. In particular, these studies reaffirm the importance of left hemisphere anterior and posterior brain regions for sign language use and emphasize that some neural areas appear to participate in language perception and production regardless of the modality of the language.

Sign language tasks that are especially likely to recruit the left hemisphere involve the production of signs. For example, when signers name objects (Emmorey et al. 2003), generate verbs to go with nouns (e.g., CHAIR → SIT) (McGuire et al. 1997; Petitto et al. 2000; Corina et al. 2003), or sign whole sentences (Braun et al. 2001), their left hemispheres show significant increases in blood flow, relative to control tasks. It has been suggested that this heightened blood flow reflects, in part, the activation of motor systems needed for the production of complex linguistic actions.

Sign language comprehension also recruits the left hemisphere in some studies, for both word-level and sentence-level tasks. For example, classic Broca's area has been found to be involved in sign comprehension when subjects observe single signs (Levanen et al. 2001; Petitto et al. 2000) and sentences (Neville et al. 1998; MacSweeney et al. 2002). This activation is not limited to anterior regions: When signers of BSL view their language, posterior left hemisphere regions are activated, including the posterior superior temporal gyrus and sulcus (*gyri* and *sulci* being anatomical terms for the elevated folds and intervening narrow fissures, respectively, on the surface of the brain) as well as the supramarginal gyrus (MacSweeney et al. 2004). This heightened activation is relative to complex nonlinguistic gestures and does not occur for nonsigners.

Interestingly, there is growing evidence that right hemisphere regions may also be recruited for aspects of sign language processing in ways that are not required in the processing of spoken languages. At least one sign language production task is known to recruit right hemisphere brain regions: When Deaf signers were asked to use classifier constructions to describe the relative positions of two objects depicted in a line drawing, both left and right hemisphere regions were found to be active (Emmorey et al. 2002). When ASL prepositions were used instead of classifiers, only the right hemisphere was recruited.

Other evidence suggests that right hemisphere posterior parietal regions may contribute to the processing of some aspects of sign comprehension (Bavelier et al. 1998; Capek et al. 2004; Corina 1998; Newman et al. 2002). For instance, both left and right hemisphere cortical regions were recruited when hearing native signers of ASL passively watched ASL sentences (Newman et al. 2002) but not when they viewed English consonant strings or sentences. The basis of right hemisphere involvement during sign comprehension may be the involvement of spatial processing: Comprehension of BSL signed sentences depicting a reversible spatial relationship between two lexical items (i.e., a pen is on a book vs. under a book) was found to be impaired in right hemisphere–damaged signers (Atkinson et al. 2005). The comprehension of spatial relationships was the only difficulty these signers exhibited.

Moreover, right hemisphere involvement may be related to the age at which the signer first acquired a sign language: In the Newman study (2002) one particular structure, the right angular gyrus, was found to be active for hearing participants only when they were native users of ASL. When hearing signers who learned to sign after puberty performed the same task, the right angular gyrus failed to be recruited. Thus, the activation of this neural structure during sign language perception may be a neural "signature" of sign being acquired during the critical period for language (ibid.). There is ample evidence that Deaf children acquiring sign master the linguistic depiction of spatial relationships (i.e., *you/me* pronoun reversals and classifier constructions) much later than the nonlinguistic concepts these forms are predicated on (Emmorey 2002). This may reflect a critical stage of conceptual and linguistic "linking" of spatial relationships in the right hemisphere.

In sum, while left hemisphere regions are indisputably recruited in a similar fashion for both sign and speech, it has been argued that the right hemisphere activation seen during sign language comprehension is more robust than that observed in studies of spoken language processing and may be particularly relevant to spatial processing. Continued research using cognitive neuroscience tools such as PET and fMRI will provide more opportunities to investigate these exciting findings.

CONCLUSION

In this chapter we have provided a broad overview of linguistic, psycholinguistic, and neurolinguistic properties of sign languages of Deaf people. Both speech and sign can be described in terms of well-known symbolic linguistic units, such as syllables and segments. The physical form of these units is quite different between the two modalities, with sign language being articulated by the hands and arms and perceived via the visual system, and speech being articulated by parts of the speech tract and perceived through auditory channels. Surprisingly, in spite of this difference, both sign and speech have been found to be organized and processed by similar cognitive conventions and neurological structures.

Psycholinguistic evidence of these commonalities is found in the fact that information about the identity of signs and spoken words is accrued gradually, as information is made available (by the signer or speaker) over time. Matching or retrieving signs from memory (from the mental lexicon) can be speeded or disrupted by the presence of related semantic or phonological (handshape, movement, location) information in ways that are only now becoming understood.

Neurological commonalities between sign and speech come from three independent literatures: aphasia, cortical stimulation, and neuroimaging. Evidence from these fields converges on the view that left hemisphere anterior and posterior brain regions are recruited for both speech and sign language processing. Sign language production, in particular, is reliant upon left hemisphere structures. Additionally there is preliminary evidence that aspects of sign language use involving visual-spatial encoding may recruit right hemisphere regions to a greater extent than is seen for speech and that this may depend on the age at which a sign language is acquired.

Ideally, linguistic, cognitive, and neurological experiments will be conducted with an eye toward constructing neurocognitive models of both speech and sign language perception and production, in order to tell a coherent and encompassing story of language processing. These models of language should be flexible enough to incorporate new psycholinguistic and cognitive neuroscience data, but conservative enough to provide explanatory value for both naturalistic and experimental linguistic observations. It is thus vital that the body of information from sign language linguistics, psycholinguistics, and neurolinguistics be available for incorporation into the larger body of spoken language data and that the commonalities and differences between sign and speech be reflected in such models.

REFERENCES

Atkinson, J., J. Marshall, B. Woll, and A. Thacker. 2005. Testing comprehension abilities in users of British Sign Language following CVA. *Brain and Language* 94 (2):233–48.

Battison, R. 1978. *Lexical borrowing in American Sign Language*. Silver Spring, Md.: Linstok Press.

Bavelier, D., D. P. Corina, P. Jezzard, V. Clark, A. Karni, A. Lalwani, J. P. Rauschecker, A. Braun, R. Turner, and H. J. Neville. 1998. Hemispheric specialization for English and ASL: Left invariance–right variability. *Neuroreport* 9 (7):1537–42.

Blumstein, S. E. 1973. *A phonological investigation of aphasic speech*. The Hague: Mouton.

Braun, A. R., A. Guillemin, L. Hosey, and M. Varga. 2001. The neural organization of discourse: An H2O-PET study of narrative production in English and American Sign Language. *Brain* 124 (10):2028.

Capek, C. M., D. Bavelier, D. P. Corina, A. J. Newman, P. Jezzard, and H. J. Neville. 2004. The cortical organization of audio-visual sentence comprehension: An fMRI study at 4 Tesla. *Brain Research: Cognitive Brain Research* 20 (2): 111–19.

Corina, D. P. 1998. Studies of neural processing in Deaf signers: Toward a neurocognitive model of language processing in the Deaf. *Journal of Deaf Studies and Deaf Education* 3(1):35–48.

Corina, D. P., and K. Emmorey. 1993. Lexical priming in American Sign Language. Presented at the 34th Annual Meeting of the Psychonomics Society, Washington, D.C., November 1993.

Corina, D. P., and U. C. Hildebrandt. 2002. Psycholinguistic investigations of phonological structure in ASL. In *Modality and structure in sign and spoken languages*, ed. R. P. Meier, K. Cormier, and D. Quinto-Pozos, 88–111. New York: Cambridge University Press.

Corina, D. P., and H. P. Knapp. 2006. Lexical retrieval in American Sign Language production. In *Laboratory phonology 8: Varieties of phonological competence*, ed. L. M. Goldstein, D. H. Whalen, and C. T. Best, 213–39. Berlin: Mouton de Gruyter.

Corina, D. P., S. L. McBurney, C. Dodrill, K. Hinshaw, J. Brinkley, and G. Ojemann. 1999. Functional roles of Broca's area and SMG: Evidence from cortical stimulation mapping in a Deaf signer. *Neuroimage* 10(5):570–81.

Corina, D. P., H. Poizner, U. Bellugi, T. Feinberg, D. Dowd, and L. O'Grady-Batch. 1992. Dissociation between linguistic and nonlinguistic gestural systems: A case for compositionality. *Brain and Language* 43(3):414–47.

Corina, D. P., L. San Jose-Robertson, A. Guillemin, J. Hugh, and A. R. Braun. 2003. Language lateralization in a bimanual language. *Journal of Cognitive Neuroscience* 15(5):718–30.

Dye, M. W. G., and S. Shih. 2006. Phonological priming in British Sign Language. In *Laboratory phonology 8,* ed. L. M. Goldstein, D. H. Whalen, and C. T. Best, 241–63. Berlin: Mouton de Gruyter.

Emmorey, K. 1991. Repetition priming with aspect and agreement morphology in American Sign Language. *Journal of Psycholinguistic Research* 20(5):365–88.

———. 1995. Processing the dynamic visual-spatial morphology of sign languages. In *Morphological aspects of language processing*, ed. L. B. Feldman, 29–54. Hillsdale, N.J.: Lawrence Erlbaum Associates.

———. 2002. *Language, cognition, and the brain: Insights from sign language research*. Mahwah, N.J.: Lawrence Erlbaum Associates.

Emmorey, K., and D. P. Corina. 1990. Lexical recognition in sign language: Effects of phonetic structure and morphology. *Perceptual and Motor Skills* 71(3):1227–52.

Emmorey, K., H. Damasio, S. McCullough, T. Grabowski, L. L. Ponto, R. D. Hichwa, and U. Bellugi. 2002. Neural systems underlying spatial language in American Sign Language. *Neuroimage* 17(2):812–24.

Emmorey, K., T. Grabowski, S. McCollough, H. Damasio, L. L. Ponto, R. D. Hichwa, and U. Bellugi. 2003. Neural systems underlying lexical retrieval for sign language. *Neuropsychologia* 41(1):85–95.

Goodglass, H. 1993. *Understanding aphasia.* San Diego: Academic Press.

Grosjean, F. 1980. Spoken word recognition processes and the gating paradigm. *Perception and Psychophysics* 28(4):267–83.

Hickok, G., T. Love-Geffen, and E. S. Klima. 2002. Role of the left hemisphere in sign language comprehension. *Brain and Language* 82(2):167–78.

Kiyaga, N. B., and D. F. Moores. 2003. Deafness in sub-Saharan Africa. *American Annals of the Deaf* 148(1):18–24.

Ladefoged, P. 1993. *A course in phonetics,* 3d ed. Orlando: Harcourt Brace Jovanovich.

Levanen, S., K. Uutela, S. Salenius, and R. Hari. 2001. Cortical representation of sign language: Comparison of Deaf signers and hearing non-signers. *Cerebral Cortex* 11(6):506–12.

Luce, P. A., D. B. Pisoni, and S. D. Goldinger. 1990. Similarity neighborhoods of spoken words. In *Cognitive models of speech processing: Psycholinguistic and computational perspectives,* ed. Gerry T. M. Altmann, 122–47. Cambridge, Mass.: MIT Press.

Marshall, J., J. Atkinson, E. Smulovitch, A. Thacker, and B. Woll. 2004. Aphasia in a user of British Sign Language: Dissociation between sign and gesture. *Cognitive Neuropsychology* 21(5):537–54.

MacSweeney, M., R. Campbell, B. Woll, V. Giampietro, A. S. David, P. K. McGuire, G. Calvert, and M. J. Brammer. 2004. Dissociating linguistic and nonlinguistic gestural communication in the brain. *Neuroimage* 22(4):1605–18.

MacSweeney, M., B. Woll, R. Campbell, G. A. Calvert, P. K. McGuire, A. S. David, A. Simmons, and M. J. Brammer. 2002. Neural correlates of British Sign Language comprehension: Spatial processing demands of topographic language. *Journal of Cognitive Neuroscience* 14(7):1064–75.

McGuire, P. K., D. Robertson, A. Thacker, A. S. David, N. Kitson, R. S. J. Frackowiak, and C. D. Frith. 1997. Neural correlates of thinking in sign language. *NeuroReport* 8(3):695.

Meier, R. P., K. Cormier, and D. Quinto-Pozos, eds. 2002. *Modality and structure in sign and spoken languages.* New York: Cambridge University Press.

Miller, J. 1990. Speech perception. In *An introduction to cognitive science,* vol. 1: *Language,* ed. D. N. Osherson and H. Lasnik, 69–94. Cambridge, Mass.: MIT Press.

Morton, J. 1969. Interaction of information in word recognition. *Psychological Review* 76(2):165–78.

Newman, A. J., D. Bavelier, D. P. Corina, P. Jezzard, and H. J. Neville. 2002. A critical period for right hemisphere recruitment in American Sign Language processing. *Nature Neuroscience* 5(1):76–80.

Neville H. J., D. Bavelier, D. P. Corina, J. Rauschecker, A. Karni, A. Lalwani, A. Braun, V. Clark, P. Jezzard, and R. Turner. 1998. Cerebral organization for language in Deaf and hearing subjects: Biological constraints and effects of experience. *Proceedings of the National Academy of Sciences* 95(3):922–29.

Petitto, L. A., R. J. Zatorre, K. Gauna, E. J. Nikelski, D. Dostie, and A. C. Evans. 2000. Speech-like cerebral activity in profoundly deaf people processing sign languages: Implications for the neural basis of human language. *Proceedings of the National Academy of Sciences* 97(25):13961–66.

Poizner, H., E. S. Klima, and U. Bellugi. 1987. *What the hands reveal about the brain: MIT Press series on issues in the biology of language and cognition.* Cambridge, Mass.: MIT Press.

Savin, H. B. 1963. Word frequency effects and errors in the perception of speech. *Journal of the Acoustical Society of America* 35(2):200–6.

Stokoe, W. 2005. Sign language structure: An outline of the communication systems of the American Deaf. *Journal of Deaf Studies and Deaf Education* 10(1).

Stokoe, W., D. C. Casterline, and C. G. Croneberg. 1965. *A dictionary of American Sign Language on linguistic principles.* Washington, D.C.: Gallaudet University Press.

7 | Children Creating Core Properties of Language: Evidence from an Emerging Sign Language in Nicaragua

Ann Senghas, Sotaro Kita, and Asli Özyürek

A new sign language has been created by deaf Nicaraguans over the past twenty-five years, providing an opportunity to observe the inception of universal hallmarks of language. We found that in their initial creation of the language, children analyzed complex events into basic elements and sequenced these elements into hierarchically structured expressions according to principles not observed in gestures accompanying speech in the surrounding language. Successive cohorts of learners extended this procedure, transforming Nicaraguan signing from its early gestural form into a linguistic system. We propose that this early segmentation and recombination reflect mechanisms with which children learn, and thereby perpetuate, language. Thus, children naturally possess learning abilities capable of giving language its fundamental structure.

We thank the Nicaraguan participants for their enthusiastic participation; the Melania Morales Center for Special Education, the National Nicaraguan Association of the Deaf (ANSNIC), and the Nicaraguan Ministry of Education, Culture, and Sports for their assistance and cooperation; Quaker House, Managua, for providing testing facilities; A. Engelman, M. Flaherty, E. Housman, S. Katseff, S. Littman, J. Pyers, M. Santos, and P. Shima for assistance with data collection and analysis; and S. Bogoch, P. Hagoort, S. Pinker, and R. Short for comments on earlier versions of the manuscript. We were supported by the Language and Cognition Group at the Max Planck Institute for Psycholinguistics, the Netherlands Organization for Scientific Research (NWO) project 051.02.040 (A.Ö.), National Institutes of Health (NIH) National Institute on Deafness and Other Communication Disorders (NIDCD) grant R01 DC00491 (S. Goldin-Meadow and A. Ö.), Turkish Academy of Sciences grant HAO/TUBA-GEBIP/2001-2-16 (A. Ö.), a visiting faculty position in psychology at Harvard University (A. S.), and NIH NIDCD grant R01 DC05407 (A. S.).

Certain properties of language are so central to the way languages operate, and so widely observed, that Hockett (1987) termed them "design features" of language. This study asks whether these properties can arise naturally as a product of language-learning mechanisms, even when they are not available in the surrounding language environment. We focus here on two particular properties of language: discreteness and combinatorial patterning. Every language consists of a finite set of recombinable parts. These basic elements are perceived categorically, not continuously, and are organized in a principled, hierarchical fashion. For example, we have discrete sounds that are combined to form words, which are combined to form phrases, and then sentences, and so on. Even those aspects of the world that are experienced as continuous and holistic are represented with language that is discrete and combinatorial. Together, these properties make it possible to generate an infinite number of expressions with a finite system. It is generally agreed that they are universal hallmarks of language, although their origin is the subject of continued controversy (Christiansen and Kirby 2003; Hauser, Chomsky, and Fitch 2002; Jackendoff 2002; Kirby 1999; Pinker and Bloom 1990; Tomasello 2003).

Humans are capable of representations that lack these properties. For example, nonlinguistic representations such as maps and paintings derive their structure iconically, from their referent. That is, patterns in the representation correspond, part for part, to patterns in the thing represented. In this way, half a city map represents half a city. Unlike language, such nonlinguistic representations are typically analog and holistic.

The present study documents the emergence of discreteness and combinatorial patterning in a new language. Over the past twenty-five years, a sign language has arisen within a community of deaf Nicaraguans who lacked exposure to a developed language. This situation enables us to discover how fundamental language properties emerge as the nonlinguistic becomes linguistic.

Before the 1970s, deaf Nicaraguan children and adults had little contact with each other. Societal attitudes kept most deaf individuals at home, and the few schools and clinics available served small numbers of children. Interviews with former students reveal little evidence of contact with classmates outside school or after graduation (Polich 2005; Senghas 1997). In this context, no sign language emerged, as evidenced by the lack of language in today's adults older than the age of forty-five.

In such situations, deaf people will often develop "home signs": communication systems built up out of common gestures used with family members. Although not full languages, home signs exhibit some of the rudiments of language (Goldin-Meadow 1982; Morford 1996). The home sign systems developed by Nicaraguans appear to have varied widely from one deaf person to another in form and complexity (Coppola 2002).

This situation changed abruptly with the opening of an expanded elementary school for special education in 1977, followed by a vocational school in 1981, both in Managua. Deaf enrollment in the programs initially comprised about 50 students, growing to more than 200 by 1981, and increasing gradually throughout the 1980s. For the first time, students continued their contact outside school hours, and by the mid-1980s deaf adolescents were meeting regularly on the weekends (Polich 2005). Although instruction in school was conducted in Spanish (with minimal success), these first children began to develop a new, gestural system for communicating with each other. The gestures soon expanded to form an early sign language (Kegl, Senghas, and Coppola 1999; Senghas 1995). Through continued use, both in and out of school, the growing language has been passed down and relearned naturally every year since, as each new wave of children entered the community (Senghas and Coppola 2001).

Today there are about 800 deaf signers of Nicaraguan Sign Language (NSL), ranging from four to forty-five years of age. Previous research on NSL has found that changes in its grammar first appear among preadolescent signers and soon spread to subsequent, younger learners, but not to adults (Senghas 2003). This pattern of transmission, when combined with the rapid and recent expansion of NSL, has created an unusual language community in which the most fluent signers are the youngest, most recent learners. Consequently, much of the history of the language can be surveyed by performing a series of observations, progressing from the older signers, who retain much of NSL's early nature, to younger, more recent learners, who produce the language in its expanded, most developed form.

Following this logic, the present study compares the signed expressions of thirty deaf Nicaraguans, grouped into cohorts according to the year that they were first exposed to NSL: ten from a first cohort (before 1984), ten from a second cohort (1984–1993), and ten from a third cohort (after 1993). All of the deaf participants have been signing NSL since the age of six or younger. Their signed expressions are compared with the gestures produced by ten hearing Nicaraguan Spanish-speakers while speaking Spanish.

In particular, we examined the gestures and signs in expressions that describe complex motion events, such as rolling down a hill or climbing up a wall. We chose descriptions of motion for two reasons. First, previous research has found that when speakers describe motion events, they often produce co-speech gestures that iconically represent the movement (Kita and Özyürek 2003; McNeill 1992). Such gestures (unlike speech) are fully available to deaf observers, likely providing raw materials to shape into a sign language. Second, the description of motion offers a promising domain for detecting the introduction of segmented, linear, and hierarchical organization of information into a communication system. Motion events include a manner of movement (such as rolling) and a path of movement (such as descending). These characteristics of motion are simultaneous aspects of a single event and are experienced holistically. The most direct way to iconically represent such an event would be to represent manner and path simultaneously. Languages, in contrast, typically encode manner and path in separate elements, combined according to the rules of the particular language (Talmy 1985). For example, English produces one word to express manner (rolling) and another to express path (down), and assembles them into the sequence "rolling down." Signing that dissects motion events into separate manner and path elements, and assembles them into a sequence, would exhibit the segmentation and linearization typical of developed languages, and unlike the experience of motion itself.

To collect samples of signing and gesturing that describe motion events, we presented participants with an animated cartoon and videotaped them telling its story to a peer. Deaf subjects signed their narratives. Hearing subjects spoke Spanish, and only their co-speech gestures were analyzed. Those expressions that included both manner and path information were coded with respect to how the information was integrated: (a) simultaneously, as a single hand movement, and/or (b) sequentially, articulated separately in a string of simple manner-only and path-only elements (figure 1 and **clips 7.1 and 7.2**). Note that a single multigesture expression can include both means of integration.

Two analyses compared, across groups, the use of each method of integration. Figure 2A shows the proportion of the expressions produced by each participant that include manner and path simultaneously. All of the Spanish speakers' gestures (100 percent) and most of the first-cohort signers' expressions (73 percent) use this approach. Second- and third-cohort signers produce relatively fewer expressions of this type (32 percent and 38 percent). Figure 2B shows the proportion of expressions produced by each participant that articulate manner and path sequentially. Such sequences are never observed in the Spanish speakers' gestures (0 percent). First-cohort signers sometimes include such sequences (27 percent); second- and third-cohort signers include such sequences in most of their expressions (78 percent and 73 percent).

In appearance, the signs very much resembled the gestures that accompany speech. The movements of the hands and body in the sign language are clearly derived from a gestural source. Nonetheless, the analyses reveal a qualitative difference between gesturing and signing. In gesture, manner and path were integrated by expressing them simultaneously and holistically, the way they occur in the motion itself. Despite this analog, holistic nature of the gesturing that surrounded them, the first cohort of children, who started building NSL in the late 1970s, evidently introduced the possibility of dissecting out manner and path and assembling them into a sequence of elemental units. As the second and third cohorts learned the language in the mid-1980s and 1990s, they rapidly made this segmented, sequenced construction the preferred means of expressing motion events. NSL thus quickly acquired the discrete, combinatorial nature that is a hallmark of language.

Note that this change to the language, in the short term, entails a loss of information. When representations express manner and path separately, it is no longer iconically clear that the two aspects of movement occurred simultaneously within a single event. For example, ROLL followed by DOWNWARD might have instead referred to two separate events, meaning "rolling, then descending."

However, the communicative power gained by combining elements more than offsets this potential for ambiguity. Elements and sequencing provide the building blocks for linguistic constructions (such as phrases and sentences) whose structure assigns meaning beyond the simple sum of the individual words. We observed one such structured sequence pattern that has emerged specifically for expressing simultaneity. A sign can be produced before and after another sign or phrase in an A-B-A construction, essentially embedding the second element within the first, yielding expressions such as ROLL DESCEND ROLL. This string can serve as a structural unit within a larger expression like CAT [ROLL DESCEND ROLL], or can even be embedded within another sign, as in WADDLE [ROLL DESCEND ROLL] WADDLE, and so on. These A-B-A constructions appeared in about a third of the coded expressions (37 percent) by participants from all three cohorts: four first-cohort signers, seven second-cohort signers, and six third-cohort signers. They were used to link various simultaneous aspects of events, including agent and action (CAT CLIMB CAT),

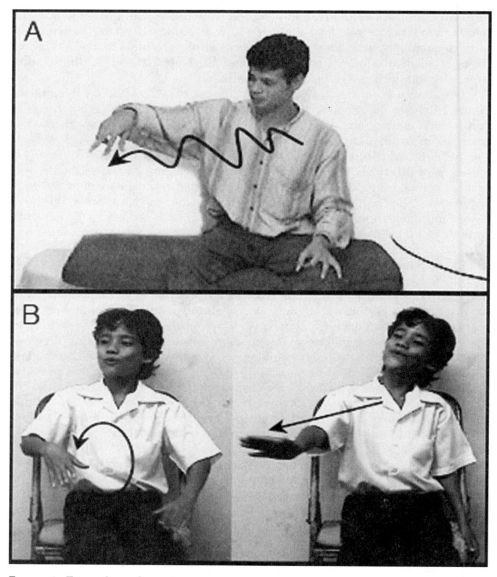

FIGURE 1. Examples of motion event expressions from participants' narratives. (A) Manner and path expressed simultaneously. This example shows a Spanish speaker describing an event in which a cat, having swallowed a bowling ball, proceeds rapidly down a steep street in a wobbling, rolling manner. The gesture shown here naturally accompanies his speech. Here manner (wiggling) and path (trajectory to the speaker's right) are expressed together in a single holistic movement. (B) Manner and path expressed sequentially. This example shows a third-cohort signer describing the same rolling event in Nicaraguan Sign Language. Here manner (circling) and path (trajectory to signer's right) are expressed in two separate signs, assembled into a sequence. The video clips from which the frames were drawn can be viewed on the DVD accompanying this book (clips 7. 1 and 7.2).

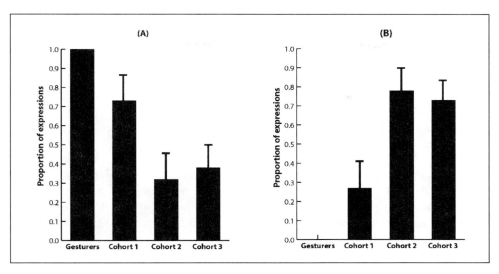

FIGURE 2. (A) The proportion of expressions that include manner and path that articulate them simultaneously within a single gesture or sign. Proportions were computed for each participant. Bars indicate mean proportions for each of the four groups; error bars indicate standard error. All of the co-speech gestures and most of the first-cohort signers' expressions articulate manner and path simultaneously. Second- and third-cohort signers produce relatively fewer expressions of this type. Proportions differ significantly across the four groups (Kruskal-Wallis, $p < .02$, $df = 3$, $\chi^2 = 10.8$). Post-hoc analyses with Bonferroni adjustment indicate that the Spanish speakers differ significantly from second-cohort signers (Mann-Whitney, $p < .04$) and marginally from third-cohort signers (Mann-Whitney, $p < .06$). (B) The proportion of expressions that include manner and path that articulate them sequentially in a string of manner-only and path-only elements. Proportions were computed for each participant. Bars indicate mean proportions for each of the four groups; error bars indicate standard error. These sequential expressions are never observed in the co-speech gestures. First-cohort signers sometimes produce such sequences; second- and third-cohort signers include them in most of their expressions. Proportions differ significantly across the four groups (Kruskal-Wallis, $p < .01$, $df = 3$, $\chi^2 = 14.7$). Post-hoc analyses with Bonferroni adjustment indicate that the Spanish speakers differ significantly from both second-cohort signers (Mann-Whitney, $p < .02$) and third-cohort signers (Mann-Whitney, $p < .03$).

ground and action (CLIMB PIPE CLIMB), and manner and path (ROLL DESCEND ROLL). We observed fifteen examples of these constructions applied specifically for combining manner and path information, again by signers of all three cohorts: two first-cohort signers, four second-cohort signers, and four third-cohort signers. They never appeared in the gestures of the Spanish speakers, and they represent a temporal hierarchy not found in motion events themselves.

Such hierarchical combinations are central to the language engine, enabling the production of an infinite set of utterances with a finite set of elements. Thus, the emergence of this construction in NSL represents a shift from gesture-like to language-like expression.

It is informative that the first-cohort signers, who originated the language when they were children in the late 1970s, continue to produce it today in a form closer to its gestural model. We take this as an indication of the extent of their impact on NSL before the mid-1980s, when they reached adolescence. The children who were arriving in the mid-1980s then became NSL's second wave of creative learners, picking up where the first cohort left off and making changes that were never fully acquired by now-adolescent first-cohort signers (Senghas 2003; Senghas and Coppola 2001). The difference today between first- and second-cohort signers therefore indicates what children could do that adolescents and adults could not. It appears that the processes of dissection, reanalysis, and recombination are among those that become less available beyond adolescence. Such an age effect is consistent with, and would partially explain, the preadolescent sensitive period for language acquisition discussed in other work (Lenneberg 1967; Newport 1990). Using their early learning skills, those who were still children in the mid-1980s developed NSL into the more discrete and combinatorial system that they, and the children who followed in the 1990s, still exhibit today.

Because NSL is such a young language, recently created by children, its changes reveal learning mechanisms available during childhood. Our observations highlight two of these mechanisms. The first is a dissecting, segmental approach to bundles of information; this analytical approach appears to override other patterns of organization in the input, to the point of breaking apart previously unanalyzed wholes. The second is a predisposition for linear sequencing; sequential combinations appear even when it is physically possible to combine elements simultaneously, and despite the availability of a simultaneous model. We propose that such learning processes leave an imprint on languages—observable in mature languages in their core, universal properties—including discrete elements (such as words and morphemes), combined into hierarchically organized constructions (such as phrases and sentences).

Accordingly, these learning mechanisms should influence language emergence and change as long as there are children available to take up a language. Consistent with this account, linear sequencing of elements (even when representing simultaneous aspects of an event) appears to be an initially favored device in language emergence (Newport 1981). For example, strong word order regularities are well documented in creoles, young languages that arise out of particular social situations of language contact (Anderson 1983; DeGraff 1999; Holm 1988). Some theories of creolization hold that child learners drive this process (Bickerton 1984; Sankoff and Laberge 1973). Our findings, in line with these approaches, favor a degree of child influence in identifying and sequencing elements.[1]

However, these learning predispositions will not fully determine a language's eventual structure. For example, many sign languages use simultaneous combinations in addition to sequential ones. Nonetheless, even in cases where adults use simultaneous constructions, the pattern of children's acquisition points to a

---

1. Unlike NSL, creoles draw much of their vocabulary and possibly some grammatical structure from the languages in contact where they arise; much debate surrounds the question of the nature and degree of this influence.

preference for linear sequencing (Newport 1981). For example, research on the acquisition of American Sign Language (ASL) (Meier 1987; Newport 1981) has shown that children initially break complex verb expressions down into sequential morphemes, rather than produce multiple verb elements together in the single, simultaneous movement found in adult models. In ASL, over-segmentation during acquisition was observed across a number of element types, including the agent and patient of a transitive event, and, as in NSL, the manner and path of a motion event. These elements correspond to semantic units that are relevant to lexicalization patterns in many (possibly all) languages (Talmy 1985). Thus, the elements chosen for segmentation may reveal the very primitives that children are predisposed to seek out as basic, grammatical units.

Such primitives, and the processes that isolate and recombine them, are central to children's language-learning machinery today. Whether these drove the formation of the very first human languages depends on whether languages shaped learning abilities, or vice versa. We speculate that a combination of the two was the case. Once language developed a discrete and hierarchical nature, children who tended toward analytical and combinatorial learning would have an advantage acquiring it (Jackendoff 2002). In this way, evolutionary pressures would shape children's language-learning (and now, language-building) mechanisms to be analytical and combinatorial. On the other hand, once humans were equipped with analytical, combinatorial learning mechanisms, any subsequently learned languages would be shaped into discrete and hierarchically organized systems (Hauser et al. 2002; Pinker and Bloom 1990).

Although our findings are consistent with both directions of effect in the evolution of learners and languages, they are at odds with accounts in which such attributes evolved externally, were passed from generation to generation solely through cultural transmission, and were never reflected in the nature of the learning mechanism (Tomasello 2003). In studies of mature languages, the potential imprint of the learning mechanism is redundant with, and hence experimentally obscured by, preexisting language structure. But the rapid restructuring of Nicaraguan Sign Language as it is passed down through successive cohorts of learners shows that even where discreteness and hierarchical combination are absent from the language environment, human learning abilities are capable of creating them anew.

REFERENCES

Anderson, Roger W. 1983. A language acquisition interpretation of pidginization and creolization. In *Pidginization and creolization as language acquisition*, ed. Roger W. Anderson. Rowley, Mass.: Newbury House.

Bickerton, Derek. 1984. The language bioprogram hypothesis. *Behavioral and Brain Sciences* 7(2):173–221.

Christiansen, Morten H., and Simon Kirby. 2003. Language evolution: Consensus and controversies. *Trends in Cognitive Sciences* 7(7):300–7.

Coppola, Marie. 2002. The emergence of grammatical categories in homesign: Evidence from family-based gesture systems in Nicaragua. Ph.D. diss., University of Rochester, Rochester, N.Y.

DeGraff, Michel, ed. 1999. *Language creation and language change: Creolization, diachrony, and development*. Cambridge, Mass.: MIT Press.

Goldin-Meadow, Susan. 1982. The resilience of recursion: A study of a communication system developed without a conventional language model. In *Language acquisition: The state of the art,* ed. Eric Wanner and Lila R. Gleitman. New York: Cambridge University Press.

Hauser, Marc D., Noam Chomsky, and W. Tecumseh Fitch. 2002. The faculty of language: What is it, who has it and how did it evolve? *Science* 298(5598):1569–79.

Hockett, Charles Francis. 1987. *Refurbishing our foundations: Elementary linguistics from an advanced point of view.* Philadelphia: J. Benjamins.

Holm, John. 1988. *Pidgins and creoles.* Vol. 1 of *Theory and structure.* New York: Cambridge University Press.

Jackendoff, Ray. 2002. *Foundations of language: Brain, meaning, grammar, evolution.* New York: Oxford University Press.

Kegl, Judy, Ann Senghas, and Marie Coppola. 1999. Creation through contact: Sign language emergence and sign language change in Nicaragua. In *Language creation and language change: Creolization, diachrony, and development,* ed. Michel DeGraff. Cambridge, Mass.: MIT Press.

Kirby, Simon. 1999. *Function, selection, and innateness: The emergence of language universals.* New York: Oxford University Press.

Kita, Sotaro, and Aslı Özyürek. 2003. What does cross-linguistic variation in semantic coordination of speech and gesture reveal? Evidence for an interface representation of spatial thinking and speaking. *Journal of Memory and Language* 48 (1): 16–32.

Lenneberg, Eric H. 1967. *Biological foundations of language.* New York: Wiley.

McNeill, David. 1992. *Hand and mind: What gestures reveal about thought.* Chicago: University of Chicago Press.

Meier, Richard P. 1987. Elicited imitation of verb agreement in American Sign Language: Iconically or morphologically determined. *Journal of Memory and Language* 6(3):362–76.

Morford, Jill P. 1996. Insights to language from the study of gesture: A review of research on the gestural communication of non-signing deaf people. *Language and Communication* 16(2):165–78.

Newport, Elissa L. 1981. Constraints on structure: Evidence from American Sign Language and language learning. In *Aspects of the development of competence: Minnesota Symposia on Child Psychology,* ed. by W. Andrew Collins. Hillsdale, N.J.: Lawrence Erlbaum Associates.

———. 1990. Maturational constraints on language learning. *Cognitive Science* 14(1):11–28.

Pinker, Steven, and Paul Bloom. 1990. Natural language and natural selection. *Behavioral and Brain Sciences* 13(4):707–84.

Polich, Laura. 2005. *The emergence of the Deaf community in Nicaragua.* Washington, D.C.: Gallaudet University Press.

Sankoff, Gillian, and Suzanne Laberge. 1973. On the acquisition of native speakers by a language. *Kivung* 6:32–47.

Senghas, Ann. 1995. Children's contribution to the birth of Nicaraguan Sign Language. Ph.D. diss., Massachusetts Institute of Technology, Cambridge, Mass.

———. 2003. Intergenerational influence and ontogenetic development in the emergence of spatial grammar in Nicaraguan Sign Language. *Cognitive Development* 18(4):511–31.

Senghas, Ann, and Marie Coppola. 2001. Children creating language: How Nicaraguan Sign Language acquired a spatial grammar. *Psychological Science* 12(4):323–28.

Senghas, Richard J. 1997. An "unspeakable, unwriteable" language: Deaf identity, language, and personhood among the first cohorts of Nicaraguan signers. Ph.D. diss., University of Rochester, Rochester, N.Y.

Talmy, Leonard. 1985. Lexicalization patterns: Semantic structure in lexical forms. In *Grammatical categories and the lexicon*, vol. 3, ed. Timothy Shopen. Cambridge: Cambridge University Press.

Tomasello, Michael. 2003. On the different origins of symbols and grammar. In *Language evolution*, ed. Morton H. Christiansen and Simon Kirby. New York: Oxford University Press.

8 | Well, "What" Is It? Discovery of a New Particle in ASL

Carol Neidle and Robert G. Lee

Here we describe a specific sign—which occurs with great frequency in American Sign Language (ASL)—in terms of its articulation, distribution, and meaning. In several articles about ASL, this sign had been noted and variously glossed as WELL or "WHAT" or WELL-WHAT.[1] However, the systematicity of its usage across a range of constructions had not been documented prior to Conlin, Hagstrom, and Neidle (2003). The first section, "The Indefinite Particle: Distribution," identifies the sign under consideration here and discusses the type of construction in which it occurs. The second section, "Background Information on ASL Constructions," provides some background information enabling us to formulate a linguistic generalization about its distribution. In the third section, "Distribution and Meaning of the Indefinite Particle," we consider the contexts in which this particle occurs and the meaning that is associated with this particle across the range of its uses.

This article presents an overview of facts originally presented in Conlin et al. (2003). We would like to thank the following people for their contributions: Lana Cook, Norma Bowers Tourangeau, Michael Schlang, Paul Hagstrom, Fran Conlin, Carla DaSilva, and Sarah Fish, as well as Stan Sclaroff, Vassilis Athitsos, Murat Erdem, and Sarah Fish for assistance in production of the video files illustrating the example sentences (which are copyrighted by the National Center for Sign Language and Gesture Resources at Boston University). The research discussed here was supported in part by grants to Boston University from the National Science Foundation (#EIA-9809340, #IIS-0329009, #CNS-04279883). For further information about the research conducted as part of the Boston University American Sign Language Linguistic Research Project (ASLLRP), please see http://www.bu.edu/asllrp/.

1. The use of quotation marks around the sign WHAT is conventional, to distinguish this sign from a different (less frequently used) sign glossed as WHAT. WHAT is articulated with a 5 handshape, palms facing upward and moving side to side, whereas WHAT is articulated with the index finger of the dominant hand brushing downward across the open palm of the nondominant hand. These signs differ significantly in their usage.

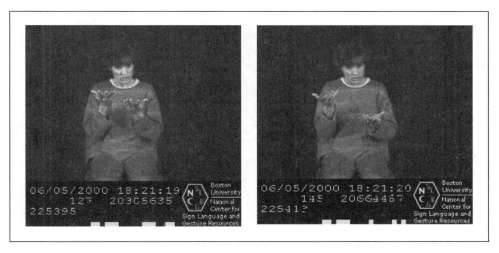

FIGURE 1. The beginning and end articulation of *part:indef.*

Finally, the fourth section, "Articulatory Variations," describes the possibilities for articulation of this focus particle on the dominant and/or nondominant hands.

THE INDEFINITE PARTICLE: DISTRIBUTION

This section describes the specific characteristics of the sign we will gloss as *part:indef* (for *part*icle of *indef*initeness, for reasons that will be explained later). The sign is articulated with a 5 handshape on both hands,[2] in neutral space with palms facing up (see figure 1); there is a single outward movement of the hands.

Previously, this sign has been described in a number of different ways in the literature. In some cases (e.g., Baker and Cokely 1980, 126), it has been called a discourse marker and glossed as WELL. In Emmorey (1999), this is considered to be a gesture (rather than a linguistic sign) and is glossed as '/well-what/.' Although there are gestures produced with somewhat similar articulation, here we focus on a specific usage that is distinguished by its articulation, syntactic distribution, and meaning.

In the transcription of our own data, we initially glossed the occurrences of this sign as "WHAT". It should be noted that the interrogative sign "WHAT", although having the same handshape, location, and palm orientation, differs from the *part:indef* in movement. The articulation of "WHAT" involves a repeated side-to-side movement, while the *part:indef* is signed with a single outward movement.[3] Another reason it has been easy to confuse this particle with "WHAT" is the fact that

---

2. The sign can also be articulated with one hand. Differences in articulation are discussed in the "Articulatory Variations" section.

3. In addition, "WHAT" is articulated with the nonmanual marking associated with wh-questions as described in section "Wh-Questions." As noted, the *part:indef* can occur in a variety of constructions (e.g., yes-no questions, declaratives) and thus appears with the nonmanual marking associated with the particular construction in which it is found.

the particle frequently occurs with wh-questions. However, this sign can also occur in a wide range of other constructions, including declaratives, negative sentences, and yes/no questions. Later we discuss the meaning that *part:indef* contributes to a sentence, but let us look first at examples in which this sign can occur:[4]

Declarative:

1. SOMETHING/ONE **part:indef** BOAT SINK CAPE COD IX
    "Some (kind of) boat sank (off) Cape Cod (over there)."

Negative:

$$\overline{\hspace{7cm}}^{\text{neg}}$$

2. MOTHER SHOULD NOT BUY CAR **part:indef**
    "Mother should not buy a car."

Wh-question:

$$\overline{\hspace{7cm}}^{\text{whq}}$$

3. JOHN SEE WHO YESTERDAY **part:indef**
    "Who did John see yesterday?"

Yes-no question

$$\overline{\hspace{7cm}}^{\text{y/n}}$$

4. IX-2p SEE SOMETHING/ONE **part:indef**
    "Did you see something (or someone)?"

Note that in the above examples, the rough English translation does not always reflect the meaning of the ASL sentence with the indefinite particle. That is because, in many cases, there is no direct equivalent in English to reflect the additional meaning contributed by the *part:indef*. We return to the meaning of the particle in the "Distribution and Meaning of the Indefinite Particle" section.

BACKGROUND INFORMATION ON ASL CONSTRUCTIONS

This section provides background information on some of the constructions in which the *part:indef* appears. In the "Wh-Questions" and "Determiners" sections, we briefly look at the structure of wh-questions and the presence of determiners in ASL.

---

4. ASL sentences are represented here using conventional gloss notation (i.e., signs are in capital letters representing the closest English approximation, and nonmanual markings are shown as labeled lines over the glosses with which they co-occur). For ease of exposition and reading, only relevant nonmanual markings are shown for any given sentence.

Wh-Questions

The structure of wh-questions in ASL is quite complex, and there have been various claims in the literature about the range of wh-question constructions that occur. Here we consider some basic facts about simple wh-questions (containing a single question word). Additional information can be found in Neidle, Kegl, Bahan, Aarons, and MacLaughlin (1997); Neidle, MacLaughlin, Lee, Bahan, and Kegl (1998a, 1998b); Neidle, Kegl, MacLaughlin, Bahan, and Lee (2000); and references contained therein.

Generally speaking, languages differ in how they construct wh-questions. In some languages, including English, a wh-phrase must appear in a specific position, regardless of whether the subject or object is being questioned. Consider the English sentences in examples 7 and 8 below. Note that even when questioning the object of the sentence (such as "house" in example 7), the wh-word normally appears at the beginning of the sentence in English.[5]

Wh-phrase moved (to left edge)—English

5. John bought a *house.*　　7. *What* did John buy?

6. *John* bought a house.　　8. *Who* bought a house?

Other languages, including Chinese, do not move the wh-phrase at all, as seen in example 9. In these cases, the wh-phrase is said to occur in situ. Still other languages allow for the wh-phrase either to remain in situ or to undergo wh-movement. French is a language of this kind, with examples of the two strategies shown in examples 10 and 11.[6]

Wh-phrase in situ—*Chinese*[7]

9. ni kanjian-le *shei?*
    you see-ASP who

"Who did you see?"

---

5. This is true for information-seeking questions. In the case of so-called echo-questions (where a listener does not hear—or is surprised by—a part of the sentence), the wh-phrase can occur in the position of the questioned argument. Consider a case where a speaker trails off and the listener does not hear the end of the sentence:

Speaker A: John bought a (*mumbles*).

Speaker B: John bought a *what*?

Speaker A: A house.

6. There has been much discussion (and disagreement) in the literature about the differences in usage of these constructions (e.g., Adli 2006; Boškovic 1998; Cheng and Rooryck 2000; Mathieu 1999).

7. This example is from Huang (1982, 253).

Wh-phrase in situ—French   *Wh-phrase moved (to left edge)—French*

10. Tu fais *quoi* maintenant?   11. *Que* fais-tu   maintenant?
     you do   what   now   what do you   now

"What are you doing now?"   "What are you doing now?"

ASL also happens to make use of both strategies. There are cases where the wh-phrase occurs in situ and other cases in which it moves. However, in ASL, the wh-phrase moves to the *right* edge of the sentence when it moves, rather than to the *left* (as in French and English). There is a meaning difference between an ASL question with a moved versus in situ wh-phrase, and there are also different possibilities for the spread of the nonmanual marking associated with wh-questions in the two cases.

First consider a simple declarative sentence, as shown in example 12.

12. JOHN ARRIVE

     "John arrived."

To question the subject, there are two possible positions for the wh-phrase, as illustrated in examples 13, 15, and 16. Note that the nonmanual wh-marking, consisting most notably of lowered brows and squinted eyes (Baker and Padden 1978; Baker and Cokely 1980; Baker-Shenk 1983, 1985) extends over the entire question in example 13, which contains an in situ wh-phrase. It cannot occur only over the wh-phrase, as shown by the ungrammaticality of example 14.[8] Examples 15 and 16 illustrate the fact that when the wh-phrase has moved to the right edge of the clause, it is possible for the nonmanual wh-marking to occur solely over the moved wh-phrase or over the entire wh-question.

Wh-phrase in situ—ASL   *Wh-phrase moved (to right edge)—ASL*

          _____ wh   _____ wh
13. WHO ARRIVE   15. ARRIVE WHO

     ___ wh   ___ wh
14. * WHO ARRIVE   16. ARRIVE WHO

     "Who arrived?"   "*Who* arrived?"

While sentences 13, 15, and 16 are grammatical, there are different contexts in which a sentence with a moved, as opposed to an in situ, wh-phrase would be used. The key difference is that sentences 15–16, with a wh-phrase at the right periphery, would be used in the context where it is known that someone had

---

8. We have argued elsewhere (e.g., Neidle et al. 2000; Neidle and MacLaughlin 2002) that certain nonmanual markings provide information about syntactic structure (e.g., those marking negative sentences and questions). These expressions are governed by principles that determine over which parts of a sentence a nonmanual syntactic marking may occur.

arrived, to ask who it was, whereas sentence 13 is a more neutral question. In sentence 13, there is no presupposition that someone did, in fact, arrive, so one possible felicitous answer is "Nobody."[9]

This same distinction occurs in English (Hajicová 1983); however, it is indicated by intonation. A sentence with this kind of presupposition, such as 18, exhibits a focal stress on the wh-word and a characteristic intonational contour that differs from that of the neutral question in sentence 17.

Wh-phrase without focal stress—English	*Wh-phrase with focal stress—English*
17. Who arrived?	18. *Who* arrived?
(neutral intonation: "Nobody" is a possible answer.)	(focal stress on *Who:* "Nobody" would be an infelicitous answer.)

This is similar to the distinction that is found in English affirmative sentences with and without focal stress on a noun phrase, as in the following examples:

NP without focal stress—English	*NP with focal stress—English*
19. John arrived.	20. *John* arrived.
(neutral intonation)	(focal stress on *John,* meaning "It is *John* who arrived.")
	21. John *arrived.*
	(focal stress on *arrived*)

In answer to a question like 17 or 18, 20—but not 21—would be a felicitous response.

The issue of focus in relation to wh-questions is complex.[10] For purposes of the present discussion, we will assume that the distinction between English questions like 17 and 18 is essentially the same as the distinction between ASL wh-constructions with moved versus in situ wh-phrases: The focus on the wh-phrase correlates with a particular intonational contour in English and with rightward wh-movement in ASL. We will return to this distinction in the readings of the ASL wh-questions in the "Particle Restricted to Focused Constituents" section. As we will see, the difference between wh-questions with moved and in situ wh-phrases with respect to focus has consequences for the allowable usage of this particle, as the particle is restricted to occurring with focused constituents.

---

9. An utterance is "felicitous" if it satisfies the conditions appropriate for the context in which it is uttered. For example, questions have certain sets of answers which would be felicitous; WHO questions would be felicitously answered by a name, WHERE questions by a location. It would be infelicitous to answer a question like "Who won the race?" with an answer like "blue" or "two o'clock." Note that an utterance can be grammatically well formed but still be infelicitous if it is not appropriate for the context in which it occurs.

10. For further discussion, see Neidle 2003; Neidle and Lee 2005, 2006.

Determiners

There have been disagreements in the literature about whether ASL has determiners.[11] There have been claims, on the one hand, that ASL completely lacks determiners (De Vriendt and Rasquinet 1990), and on the other, that index signs
occurring before and/or after nouns function as determiners (e.g., Hoffmeister
1977, 1978; Wilbur 1979; Zimmer and Patschke 1990). Part of the confusion may
stem from the fact that determiners in ASL are not obligatory; that is, there are
cases when a referent is semantically definite (in that it refers to an entity that has
already been introduced into the discourse), but no definite determiner is present.
In addition, the form used to realize the determiner (a pointing index finger) occurs productively in ASL for a variety of purposes (e.g., for expressing pronominal reference, shown in example 23 below, as well as location information, as in
examples 22 and 24b).[12]

22.   JOHN ARRIVE IX_{adv}
      "John arrived there."

23. IX_{pro} ARRIVE
      "He arrived."

Bahan, Kegl, MacLaughlin, and Neidle (1995) made a case for the existence
of determiners in ASL, and MacLaughlin (1997) argued convincingly that ASL
does indeed have both a definite and an indefinite determiner sign. The definite determiner is realized by an index sign that precedes the articulation of the
noun and that points to the location in space associated with the noun, as in
example 24.

24a. IX_{det} MAN ARRIVE
      "The man arrived."

24b. IX_{det} MAN IX_{adv} ARRIVE
      "The man over there arrived."

Furthermore, this definite determiner can appear without a following noun,
in which case it has a pronominal function, as was just seen in example 23. Thus,
as in many other languages (e.g., French—examples 25–26), the forms for the
definite determiner and the pronoun are the same in ASL.

---

    11. Determiners are words that precede a noun in an English noun phrase and mark,
for example, whether the noun is definite (as in English, "*The* boy walked home") or indefinite (as in "*A* boy walked home").

    12. The subscript on the gloss of the index shows the function of the sign: "adv" for
locative adverbial, "det" for determiner, "pro" for pronoun.

Definite determiner—French   *Pronoun—French*

25. *Le* garçon arrive.   26. Marie *le* voit.
     "The boy is arriving."   "Marie sees him."

MacLaughlin (1997) showed that ASL also has an indefinite determiner. The articulation of this sign involves the index finger, pointing upward, with the palm facing the back of the signer; there is a slight circling of the hand. Whereas the definite determiner is associated with a point in space, the indefinite determiner is associated with a region in space. Interestingly, the larger the region of articulation, the larger the uncertainty about the identity of the referent.

Like the definite determiner, the indefinite determiner can also be used pronominally, without a following noun. In such cases, the best English translation would normally be "something" or "someone" (as the ASL sign does not make an animacy distinction). Therefore, we have consistently glossed this sign as SOMETHING/ONE in both its determiner and pronominal uses, as illustrated in examples 27–28 and 29–30, respectively.

Indefinite determiner—ASL   *Indefinite pronoun—ASL*

27. SOMETHING/ONE$_{det}$ STUDENT HAVE VIDEOTAPE   29. SOMETHING/ONE$_{pro}$ HAVE VIDEOTAPE
     "Some/a student has (the) videotape."   "Someone has (the) videotape."

28. IX-1p FIND SOMETHING/ONE$_{det}$ BOOK   30. IX-1p FIND SOMETHING/ONE$_{pro}$
     "I found a/some book."   "I found something (or someone)."

In addition to the manual articulation of SOMETHING/ONE, there is an associated nonmanual marking consisting of slightly raised shoulders, tensed nose, squinted eyes, and a slight rapid headshake. MacLaughlin (1997) noted that many signs that express uncertainty are accompanied by this particular expression.[13] We will see in the "Nonmanual Correlates" section that a similar marking is found with the indefinite particle as well.

DISTRIBUTION AND MEANING OF THE INDEFINITE PARTICLE

This section describes the meaning contributed by the particle and the positions in the sentence where it can occur. Specifically, we show that the *part:indef* occurs only with focused elements and suggest that it has a "domain-widening" effect, serving to extend the set of referents under consideration beyond what would

---

13. MacLaughlin (1997) cites Petronio (1993), who claims there is a specific nonmanual expression associated with verbs involving mental pondering (e.g. MULL-OVER, WONDER, SUSPECT).

usually be expected. The *part:indef* can occur in a variety of places in a sentence. Consider the following examples:

31. [[[<u>SOMETHING/ONE</u>] part:indef] STRANGE] ARRIVE
     "Something (or other) strange arrived."

32. [[<u>SOMETHING/ONE STRANGE</u>] part:indef] ARRIVE HERE
     "Something strange (of some sort) arrived here."

In examples 31 and 32, the particle modifies the meaning of the phrase (highlighted by an underline) that it follows, as suggested by the translations provided.

The *part:indef* can also follow an ordinary indefinite noun phrase, as in example 34.

33. [SOMETHING/ONE BOAT] SINK CAPE COD
     "A boat sank (off) Cape Cod."

34. [[<u>SOMETHING/ONE BOAT</u>] part:indef]   SINK CAPE COD
     "A boat (or something like a boat) sank (off) Cape Cod."

Note that in example 33, the object being referred to is necessarily a boat of some type. In contrast, the addition of the *part:indef*, as in example 34, extends the domain of objects that can be referred to (to possibly some vaguely boat-like object). This function is similar to the English use of "any" as described by Kadmon and Landman (1993). Consider the difference in meaning of the following two English sentences:

35. John didn't see a boat.

36. John didn't see any boat.

In principle, these two sentences are true in the same set of circumstances. If he didn't see a boat, then he didn't see any boat. So, what meaning is "any" contributing? Kadmon and Landman (1993) suggested that it functions to extend the set of entities under consideration beyond the typical, in this case perhaps to a wider set of things than just typical boats. This could be used to indicate that he didn't see anything like a boat. We suggest that this is precisely the same type of expanded meaning that the ASL focus particle contributes in sentences like 31, 32, and 34, where the set of referents that would normally be associated with the underlined phrase is expanded in some way beyond the typical by the use of the particle.

In addition to its use with individual constituents, the *part:indef* can occur at the end of the sentence, modifying the meaning of the proposition as a whole, to extend it beyond what it would typically be expected to cover. Consider the following sentences:

37.   [<u>SOMETHING/ONE STRANGE ARRIVE</u>] part:indef

"Something strange arrived (or something *like that* happened)."

38.   [<u>SOMETHING/ONE BOAT SINK CAPE COD</u>] part:indef

"A boat sank off Cape Cod (or something *like that* happened)."

The indefinite particle can also occur twice within a sentence, for example with a noun phrase (or pronoun) and at the end of the sentence, as shown below. In these cases, the two occurrences of the particles are associated with the meanings just described.

39.   [<u>SOMETHING/ONE</u> part:indef <u>STRANGE ARRIVE</u>] part:indef

"Something (or other) strange arrived
(or something *like that* happened)."

40.   [<u>SOMETHING/ONE</u> part:indef <u>BOAT SINK NEAR CAPE COD</u>] part:indef

"Some boat or other sank near Cape Cod
(or something *like that* happened)."

Particle Restricted to Focused Constituents

It is interesting to note that this particle co-occurs only with the focused constituent in the sentence. Consider the contrast between the following discourse contexts.

41a.   Everyone in the group has been located, but one person appears to be missing, and we are concerned about that person. I ask:

"Has anyone seen *Joan?*"

41b.   We continue to search for Joan. I've asked many people in the group, and so far, nobody has reported having seen her. I wonder whether *anyone at all* has seen her, and I ask:

"Has *anyone (at all)* seen Joan?"

Note that the following sentence, although perfectly grammatical in ASL, would only be appropriate in a context like example 41b. It would not be an appropriate utterance in the context described by example 41a.

		y/n	
42. dominant:	[<u>SOMETHING/ONE</u>]		SEE JOAN
nondominant:	part:indef		

"Did *anyone (at all)* see Joan?"

Occurrence with Wh-Questions

As stated before, the *part:indef* has, in the past, been conflated (by some research-ers, including ourselves) with the wh-word "WHAT" with which it shares hand-shape, palm orientation, and location (although, as noted, the movements of the two signs are different). Part of the reason for this is that wh-constructions are a prime environment for its occurrence, as they frequently involve focused constitu-ents whose referents are unknown, and the questioner may often wish to probe beyond the expected set of possible responses. Nonetheless, as examples in pre-vious sections have demonstrated, this particle is definitely not restricted to en-vironments involving wh-questions.

Moreover, in wh-questions, there are also restrictions on the acceptability of the particle in particular types of constructions. As noted in the "Wh-Questions" section, rightward moved wh-phrases are necessarily in focus. If we return to the type of distinctions in discourse contexts discussed in the "Particle Restricted to Focused Constituents" section, we again find a contrast in the acceptability of the usage of the particle. It occurs felicitously with a constituent that is in focus, but not with one that lacks such focus.

> 43a. Everyone in the group has been located, but one person appears to be missing, and we are concerned about that person. I ask:
>
> "Who has seen *Joan?*"

> 43b. We continue to search for Joan. Bill says that she was spotted, but I want to confirm this. So, I ask Bill:
>
> "*Who* saw Joan?"

In the context described in example 43a, the appropriate ASL question would be the sentence in example 44. Note that in this case, the wh-phrase does not occur at the end of the sentence (for the reasons discussed in the "Wh-Questions" section) and the particle would not be felicitous following WHO, as shown in example 45.[14]

<pre>
                         wh
44.   WHO SEE   !JOAN!
      "Who saw Joan?"
</pre>

<pre>
                              wh
45.   ?* WHO^part:indef SEE !JOAN!
</pre>

However, in the context set up in example 43b, where the wh-phrase is in focus, the wh-phrase normally occurs at the right edge of the sentence and is per-fectly compatible with the presence of the focus particle, as shown in example 46.

---

14. The exclamation points in the gloss notation indicate a stressed articulation of the sign (JOAN in example 44). Contraction, discussed in the next section, is indicated in the glosses by the symbol "^," as in examples 45 and 46.

$$\overline{}^{\text{wh}}$$

46. SEE JOAN WHO^part:indef

"*Who* saw Joan?"

In summary, the claim that this particle co-occurs solely with focused constituents correctly predicts that it cannot co-occur with a nonfocused wh-phrase, as in example 45. In Neidle and Lee (2005), we also demonstrate that this makes correct predictions for constructions in which focus is marked by nonmanual expressions of syntactic agreement: specifically, that nonfocused constituents do not co-occur with this particle.

ARTICULATORY VARIATIONS

We conclude with a brief discussion of the variety of possible phonological expressions of this particle.

Manual Expressions

There is generally a phonological fusion (or contraction) of the particle with the sign that it follows. This occurs very frequently with signs such as WHO, WHY, and HOW, for example. For WHO and WHY, this occurs on the dominant hand, as these are one-handed signs; for HOW, a two-handed sign, it occurs on both hands simultaneously: There is a smooth transition from the wh-sign to the outward movement of the particle, as shown in figure 2. In fact, despite its frequency in colloquial signing, ASL signers have also generally not recognized this particle as

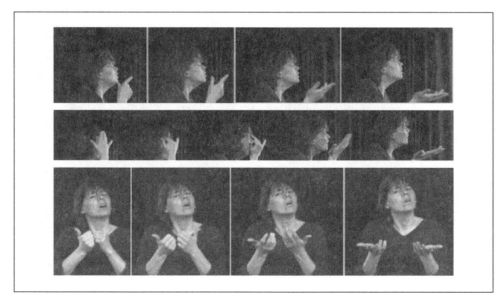

FIGURE 2. WHO^part (top), WHY^part (middle), and HOW^part (bottom).

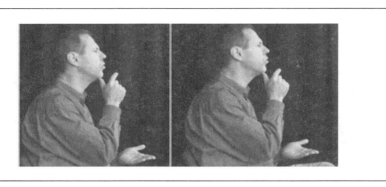

FIGURE 3. WHO **signed by the dominant hand, in parallel with particle on non-dominant hand.**

an independent sign, in many cases believing that the signs incorporating this particle (e.g., WHO^part:indef) represent articulatory variants of the canonical signs without the particle (e.g., WHO).

With one-handed signs, there are further variations in the expression of the particle that are possible:

i. What happens sometimes is that the dominant hand expresses the one-handed sign while the particle is expressed, in parallel, solely by the nondominant hand (which is cotemporal with the sign it modifies). This is the case in a sentence like 47, as illustrated in figure 3.

47. dominant: ARRIVE <u>W H O</u>
    non-dominant: <u>part:indef</u>

(with "wh" line above W H O)

  "*Who* arrived?"

ii. Frequently, however, the particle is expressed by the nondominant hand (throughout the entire duration of the sign produced by the dominant hand) as well as by a contracted form of the particle at the end of the sign articulated by the dominant hand, as in example 48, illustrated by figure 4. Thus, the two hands finish together in a joint articulation of the particle.

FIGURE 4. WHO^**part signed on the dominant hand co-occurring with particle on the non-dominant hand.**

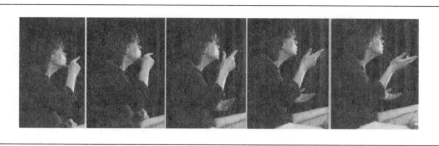

FIGURE 5. WHO **on the dominant hand followed by 2-handed articulation of the particle.**

$$\overline{\hspace{5cm}}^{\text{wh}}$$

48. dominant: FIND BOOK   WHO^part:indef
     non-dominant: part:indef

     "Who found the book?"

iii. And finally, the particle may be signed (by both hands) following the articulation of the (one-handed or two-handed) sign, as in example 49, as seen in figure 5.

$$\overline{\hspace{7cm}}^{\text{wh}}$$

49. dominant: JOHN SEE YESTERDAY   WHO^part:indef
     non-dominant: part:indef

     "Who did John see yesterday?"

Given that the particle in this sentence-final position may be associated solely with the right-peripheral wh-phrase, or it may modify the entire proposition, as discussed earlier, it is likely (although this remains to be confirmed in future research) that these differences in the timing of the articulation of the particle may correlate to some degree with differences in syntactic structure, and therefore in the semantic interpretation of the particle.[15]

Nonmanual Correlates

There are several nonmanual expressions that tend to co-occur with this particle. As mentioned in the "Determiners" section, the same types of facial expressions that typically occur with indefinite noun phrases, conveying some degree of uncertainty, also commonly occur with this particle. Notice that the type of extension of the set of referents that results from the use of the particle is compatible

---

15. It is also possible, of course, to have the particle articulated solely by the dominant hand, as in example 46.

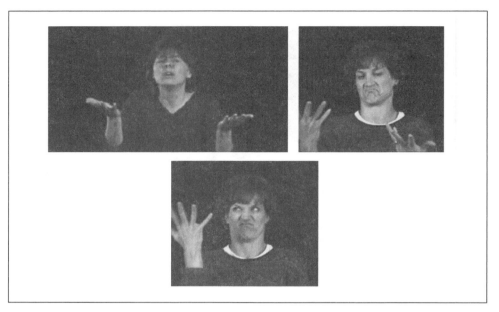

FIGURE 6. Facial expressions associated with the focus particle, which sometimes
includes an eye gaze to the extreme right or left (as shown on the bottom).

only with indefinite interpretations, often involving some degree of uncertainty.
Thus, it is perhaps unsurprising that the facial expression accompanying the particle frequently includes tensed nose, lowered brows, and sometimes also the raising of the shoulders. Examples are shown in figure 6.

In addition, there is sometimes a sudden shift in eye gaze to the left or right.
It is unclear whether this is strictly linguistic or whether it reflects the type of cognitive processing that may be associated with evocation of such uncertainty.

CONCLUSION

In summary, we have described here a particle that, despite its frequency in colloquial ASL, had escaped notice until recently, having been assumed either to be
gestural or to be a wh-sign, or else having been interpreted as an integral part of
other signs rather than a sign with its own identity and properties. We have argued that this particle co-occurs with focused constituents (or with entire propositions), serving the function of extending the set of referents (or propositions)
under consideration. This account makes correct predictions for the syntactic distribution of the particle in wh-constructions, where distinctions in the position of
the wh-phrase are analyzed as reflecting differing semantic interpretations.

REFERENCES

Adli, Aria. 2006. French wh-in-situ questions and syntactic optionality: Evidence from
three data types. *Zeitschrift für Sprachwissenschaft* 25(11):163–203.

Bahan, Benjamin, Judy Kegl, Dawn MacLaughlin, and Carol Neidle. 1995. Convergent evidence for the structure of determiner phrases in American Sign Language. In *FLSM VI: Proceedings of the Sixth Annual Meeting of the Formal Linguistics Society of Mid-America*, ed. Leslie Gabriele, Debra Hardison, and Robert Westmoreland, 1–12. Bloomington: Indiana University Linguistics Club.

Baker, Charlotte, and Carol A. Padden. 1978. Focusing on the nonmanual components of American Sign Language. In *Understanding language through sign language research*, ed. Patricia Siple, 27–57. New York: Academic Press.

Baker, Charlotte, and Dennis Cokely. 1980. *American Sign Language: A teacher's resource text on grammar and culture*. Silver Spring, Md.: T.J. Publishers.

Baker-Shenk, Charlotte. 1983. A micro-analysis of the nonmanual components of questions in American Sign Language. Ph.D. diss., University of California, Berkeley.

———. 1985. The facial behavior of Deaf signers: Evidence of a complex language. *American Annals of the Deaf* 130(4):297–304.

Boškovic, Zeljko. 1998. LF movement and the minimalist program. In *Proceedings of the Northeast Linguistic Society* 28, ed. Pius N. Tamanji and Kiyomi Kusumoto, 43–57. Amherst: University of Massachusetts, Graduate Linguistics Student Association.

Cheng, Lisa Lai-Shen, and Johan Rooryck. 2000. Licensing wh-in-situ. *Syntax* 3(1):1–19.

Conlin, Frances, Paul Hagstrom, and Carol Neidle. 2003. A particle of indefiniteness in American Sign Language. *Linguistic Discovery* 2; http://journals.dartmouth.edu/cgi-bin/WebObjects/Journals.woa/2/xmlpage/1/article/142.

De Vriendt, Sera, and Max Rasquinet. 1990. The expression of genericity in sign language. In *International Studies on Sign Language and Communication of the Deaf*, vol. 9, ed. Sigmund Prillwitz and Tomás Vollhaber, 249–55. Hamburg: Signum.

Emmorey, Karen. 1999. Do signers gesture? In *Gesture, speech, and sign*, ed. Lynn Messing and Ruth Campbell, 133–59. New York: Oxford University Press.

Hajicová, Eva. 1983. On some aspects of presuppositions of questions. In *Questions and answers*, ed. Ferenc Kiefer, 85–96. Dordrecht, Germany: Reidel.

Hoffmeister, Robert J. 1977. The influential point. In *Proceedings of the National Symposium on Sign Language Research and Teaching*, ed. William Stokoe, 177–91. Silver Spring, Md.: National Association of the Deaf.

Hoffmeister, Robert J. 1978. The development of demonstrative pronouns, locatives, and personal pronouns in the acquisition of ASL by deaf children of deaf parents. Ph.D. diss., University of Minnesota.

Huang, C.-T. James. 1982. Logical relations in Chinese and the theory of grammar. Ph.D. diss., MIT.

Kadmon, Nirit, and Fred Landman. 1993. Any. *Linguistics and Philosophy* 16(4):353–422.

MacLaughlin, Dawn. 1997. The structure of determiner phrases: Evidence from American Sign Language. Ph.D. diss., Boston University.

Mathieu, Eric. 1999. Wh in situ and the intervention effect. In *UCL Working Papers in Linguistics* 11, ed. Corinne Iten and Ad Neeleman, 441–72; http://www.phon.ucl.ac.uk/home/PUB/WPL/uclwpl11.html.

Neidle, Carol. 2003. Language across modalities: ASL focus and question constructions. *Linguistic Variation Yearbook* 2:71–93.

Neidle, Carol, Judy Kegl, Benjamin Bahan, Debra Aarons, and Dawn MacLaughlin. 1997. Rightward wh-movement in American Sign Language. In *Rightward movement*, ed. Dorothee Beerman, David LeBlanc, and Henk Van Riemsdijk, 247–78. Philadelphia: John Benjamins.

Neidle, Carol, Judy Kegl, Dawn MacLaughlin, Benjamin Bahan, and Robert G. Lee. 2000. *The syntax of American Sign Language: Functional categories and hierarchical structure*. Cambridge, Mass.: MIT Press.

Neidle, Carol, and Robert G. Lee. 2005. The syntactic organization of American Sign Language: A synopsis. *American Sign Language Linguistic Research Project no. 12*, Boston University.

———. 2006. Syntactic agreement across language modalities. In *Studies on agreement*, ed. João Costa and Maria Cristina Figueiredo Silva. Amsterdam: John Benjamins.

Neidle, Carol, and Dawn MacLaughlin. 2002. The distribution of functional projections in ASL: Evidence from overt expressions of syntactic features. In *Functional structure in DP and IP: The cartography of syntactic structures*, ed. Guglielmo Cinque, 195–224. New York: Oxford University Press.

Neidle, Carol, Dawn MacLaughlin, Robert G. Lee, Benjamin Bahan, and Judy Kegl. 1998a. The rightward analysis of wh-movement in ASL: A reply to Petronio and Lillo-Martin 1997. *Language* 74(4):819–31.

———. 1998b. Wh-questions in ASL: A case for rightward movement. *American Sign Language Linguistic Research Project no. 6*, Boston University; www.bu.edu/asllrp/publications.html.

Petronio, Karen. 1993. Clause structure in American Sign Language. Ph.D. diss., University of Washington, Seattle.

Wilbur, Ronnie B. 1979. *American Sign Language and sign systems: Research and application.* Baltimore: University Park Press.

Zimmer, June, and Cynthia Patschke. 1990. A class of determiners in ASL. In *Sign language research: Theoretical issues*, ed. Ceil Lucas, 201–10. Washington, D.C.: Gallaudet University Press.

9 | SUCCESS WITH DEAF CHILDREN: HOW TO PREVENT EDUCATIONAL FAILURE

RONNIE B. WILBUR

The objective of this chapter is to provide research support for the use of natural sign languages in the early education of deaf children, especially when the aim is to develop sophisticated language, literacy, academic, and social skills. To achieve this objective, the reader needs to understand several conceptual and terminological distinctions. The remainder of the chapter addresses the benefits to all deaf children of early sign language acquisition. The literature indicates that early learning of sign language benefits cognitive and memory development, overall socioeducational performance, and reading and writing ability by providing a complete language base. Also, it does not interfere with learning English or limit speech potential. A longstanding research conclusion is that knowledge of American Sign Language (ASL) is invaluable in the education of deaf children (Johnson, Liddell, and Erting 1989; Charrow and Wilbur 1975).

TERMINOLOGY

What We Mean by *Success*

Typically, the degree to which deaf children are considered successful is measured by speech production and perception, speechreading, and the ability to manage in mainstreamed (hearing) classrooms (Karchmer and Mitchell 2003). But several criteria carry much greater import in our definition of *successful*.

1. The student has access to grade-level material (Johnson, Liddell, and Erting 1989).
2. The adult is autonomous, confident, educated, and happy.

Special thanks to Evguenia Malaia for assistance with manuscript preparation. This research was funded, in part, by NIH DC005241 and NSF HRD-0622900.

3. In the United States, we also expect individuals to make choices about their career goals and to work toward them. Parents and schools do not decide a deaf person's future.

This last criterion is often overlooked, but the problem continues. I know a 2005 Deaf school graduate who wanted to be an economist but was trained in auto mechanics.

What We Mean by *Bilingual*

The goal of bilingual development is to maximize fluency in two natural languages. For deaf children, we mean one "oral" language (spoken, written) and one natural sign language. We do not include artificial signing systems, such as signed English (SE), which are designed to follow spoken language morphology and syntax. We also do not include speaking and signing at the same time (simultaneous communication).

What We Mean by *Normal Development*

Children who do not meet certain milestones at age-appropriate times are routinely referred for intervention and therapy. Critically, brain and cognitive development and memory organization go hand in hand with language development (Rönnberg 2003). Children must be able to communicate at expected levels for their age.

In order for children to develop age-appropriate communication, the language environment must be child-oriented: It must provide what the child needs, not what is convenient for parents and teachers. To provide for the child's psychosocial development, there must be effective communication. It must also be remembered that parents are not full-time teachers and must be able to interact with their children on levels other than teacher-student. Early bilingual communication makes this possible.

The Difference between Language and Speech

The term *language* is not synonymous with the word *speech*. Speech is one way of transmitting language between users. This distinction is demonstrated by talking parrots, which can "speak" (produce speech-like sounds) but do not "know a language." Other language transmission means (coding) include different styles of print and script as well as encoded alphabets such as Braille and fingerspelling. Language transmission does not have to be by alphabetical methods at all, as Chinese characters demonstrate. Furthermore, many languages do not have an associated written system other than what was invented by outsiders, such as missionaries (in order to translate the Bible), linguists (to be able to investigate the language), and others (conquerors solidifying dominance over the conquered). To distinguish between spoken and signed languages, linguists refer to the *modality of perception and production*; cross-modal investigations consider similarities and differences between spoken or signed languages.

This distinction between language and speech is critical to understanding why deaf education has been slow to fulfill deaf children's potential. Simply put, educational professionals have been able to dominate the field by focusing almost exclusively on speech. Let me illustrate several ways in which this happens.

Scenario 1: The professional says to parents: "Your child has to be able to get along in a hearing world." This is a nondebatable issue. They continue: "Hearing people speak; therefore your child must be able to speak; therefore we will concentrate on teaching your child to speak." Yes, your child should learn to speak. But when they say, "We will concentrate on teaching your child to speak," they mean "and that is our primary goal." Other needs may be overlooked.

This offer accomplishes several things simultaneously. Parents are reassured that their child will someday be perceived as "normal," that is, "able to speak like hearing people." Parents do not have to do anything special except continue to speak with their child, being careful to have eye contact and not talk too fast. The child's progress will be evaluated on the basis of speech production and perception and speechreading. Children who appear to meet certain criteria for success in speech will be placed in mainstream classrooms with other hearing/speaking children.

Scenario 2: "With a cochlear implant, your child will be able to hear." Of course, if your child can hear, she should be able to learn how to speak "normally." Return to scenario 1.

But, in fact, "being able to hear" and "being able to hear and understand speech" are also two different things. Your child may be able to hear environmental sounds (car horns, sirens, etc.) but not be able to distinguish words (pill, bill, mill) for many years. To understand connected speech, one must also know the language.

Scenario 3: "Don't you want your child to speak?" This question carries with it negative implications. If parents consider signing, the child will be in danger of not learning to speak, and the child's failure will be the parents' fault. Underlying is the assumption that signing interferes with the development of speech.

Yet researchers have known for more than forty years that there is no evidence to support the belief that early use of sign language interferes with the development of speech abilities. A study of children using Swedish Sign Language (Ahlström 1972) reported that "speech was not adversely affected by knowledge of signs" (Power 1974). A study comparing non-ASL users with early intensive oral training (deaf children with hearing parents) to ASL users with no intensive speech training (deaf children with deaf parents) showed no differences in oral skills, but the ASL users were superior in reading and general achievement (Vernon and Koh 1970). Moores (1971) summarized several studies that directly compared early oral preschool children with children who had no preschool. None of the studies reported any differences in oral skills (speech and speechreading) between the two groups. What is striking about these studies is the lack of any direct evidence that the use of signing is detrimental to the development of speech skills.

Other studies comparing deaf ASL users to deaf non-ASL users showed the ASL users to be superior on some or all of the English skills and measures of general ability. Three of these studies (Meadow 1966; Quigley and Frisina 1961; Stevenson 1964) reported no difference between the two groups on measures of speech production, but a fourth (Stuckless and Birch 1966) reported that the deaf children of hearing parents (the non-ASL users) were better at it. When these two groups are compared on measures of speechreading ability, the same three studies reported no differences between the two groups, and a fourth (Stuckless and Birch 1966) reports that the ASL users are better (For a description of these four studies, see Bonvillian, Charrow, and Nelson 1973; Moores 1971, 1974.)

Despite an impressive body of research more than thirty years old, current reaction tends to be that "those are old studies." But there is no research that *refutes* those general findings, and more recent research no longer focuses on the question of whether signing interferes with speech development, but rather on how early signing *contributes* to success in academic areas, including speech.

Another factor contributing to the research findings being overlooked is the general public's failure to separate language from speech. That this attitude has had practical implications for deaf education is undisputed. McDonnell and Saunders (1993, 257–58) discuss their oral education in Dublin, Ireland.

> Pupils who were caught signing were punished in a variety of ways; they were slapped, deprived of meals or privileges or humiliated in some way . . .
>
> Our teachers told us that if we signed, our speech would deteriorate and we would never learn anything. We believed them when they said that signing was bad and that it was stupid. . .
>
> In the classroom there was conflict between the learning needs of the pupils and the oral policy of the school.
>
> Understanding did not come first. No teacher used signs. Lip reading was very tiring. I tried to understand the words that were said but in the end I had no story. I could not understand long sentences.
>
> Oral schooling meant that the form of communication was more important than the content. It emphasized *how* the pupils communicated and not *what* they communicated.

The challenge facing deaf children is not really the acquisition of fluent speech skills, although those can be extremely useful in interactions with the hearing world, but rather the acquisition of the language skills that underlie successful use of speech, signing, reading, and writing. That is, it is critical to develop the underlying concepts (knowledge) and the linguistic mechanisms necessary to map those concepts onto meaningful forms of expression, regardless of the form that the output will take (spoken, written, signed, fingerspelled).

There is very strong evidence that deaf children can be taught to articulate speech at a decent level of intelligibility and can be taught to make perceptual distinctions in speech sounds, especially when properly aided. These skills, however, are not central cognitive and linguistic skills. Thus, it is possible to learn to produce speech without understanding what one is saying. Parrots do it. A linguist trained in phonetic transcription can read aloud any spoken language written in it and have no idea what the passage means. To be fully understood, the input (sound, print, sign) must be received by the brain centers that are involved in cognitive and linguistic skills, where the processing that is required to parse syntax, identify lexical items, and construct an understanding of the message takes place. Speech reception and production at the level of a parrot are not sufficient for a lifetime of human cognitive and linguistic potential.

The Difference between Naturally Evolved Languages and Artificially Created Systems

Another distinction that needs to be made is that between natural languages and artificially created systems. Natural languages are acquired by babies from birth without formal intervention (teaching and consistent correction). Two examples of natural languages are English (hearing babies with hearing parents) and ASL (deaf babies with deaf parents). In contrast, artificially created systems require formal procedures, such as training adult users to provide specific input in a specific way, and, as such, are not learned by babies in the home environment without intervention. An example of an artificially created system is SE, of which there are many variations, as different educators choose different pedagogical principles to follow (cf. Signing Exact English, Seeing Essential English; Wilbur 1987, 2000a).

The Distinctions *Bilingual*, *Bimodal*, and *Typical Bilingual Situation*

Here, the term *bilingual* is used to refer to naturally evolved languages, both spoken and signed. Much of the available research concentrates on ASL and English; hence they will be used in this discussion as examples representing the larger set of natural languages. It is important to note that artificial signing systems such as SE do not qualify as natural languages and hence cannot be included under the rubric *typical bilingual situation*. Critically, speaking and signing at the same time, as one can do with SE, is not bilingual but *bimodal*, that is, using two modes—speaking and signing—to convey a single message.

The global benefit of learning a natural sign language as a first language (L1) is that it creates a typical bilingual situation. This term refers first to situations in which young children (zero to five years of age) are exposed to, and interact with, at least one language in the course of daily home and family conversations. It also requires that there be no language disorders or other anomalies that prevent the children from acquiring at least one language fluently and fully (e.g., no specific language impairment [SLI]). In typical bilingual situations, the second language (L2) may come from a variety of sources, including family, community, school, and so on. Because at least one language is being acquired naturally, teachers and learners can take advantage of the L1 to assist children in learning the second language and in the transfer of general knowledge. Thus, the term *bilingual* does not require that the child develop competence in two languages at the same time, but rather that the second language is learned either simultaneously with, or sequentially dependent on, knowledge of the L1. This wording reflects the fact that balance and dominance between the two languages in these early stages is not important to the outcome. Instead, at least one language must be acquired naturally and the acquisition of the other, whether natural or taught or both, must utilize architecture established during the acquisition of the L1. Relevant to the present discussion, the L1 can be either (spoken) English for hearing children or ASL for deaf children, but not SE (because it is not a natural language). Another language can then be built on top of, or co-extensive with, the L1.

These definitions clarify the problem with early learning of SE as opposed to ASL. SE is not a natural language and its structure does not include many of the universal characteristics of natural languages, such as modality-appropriate intonation patterns (Wilbur and Petersen 1998). Thus it does not provide the necessary initial language learning experience or the basis for the acquisition of a second language, even if that language is English (see further discussion of this issue in Schick 2003).

These observations and conclusions are further confirmed by a recent study comparing the outcomes of two groups of Dutch deaf children with hearing parents. Hoiting and Slobin (2002) analyzed data from deaf children aged one year three months to three years collected over a twelve-year period, during which time the educational policy at the Guyot Institute was changed from Sign Supported Dutch (SSD, parallel to SE) to Sign Language of the Netherlands (NGT: Nederlandse Gebarentaal, a sign language parallel to, but unrelated to, ASL). The Guyot Institute abandoned SSD in 1995 because it was not succeeding as a primary language for parent-child communication beyond a basic level: It was difficult for teachers and service personnel to use, and Deaf staff workers found it unmanageable for advanced communication.

Hoiting and Slobin (2002) reported significant advantages to the children who received the NGT input compared to the SSD input, such as parental use of more varied structures, wider choice of lexical items, and more modeling of appropriate uses of language (requests, demands, plans). As for the children's output, those children receiving NGT input produced longer and more complex output than did the SSD children. Based on a sample of five SSD and five NGT children, two to three years old, they found that the NGT children produced 67 percent of the multiple-sign utterances in the sample, produced twice as many three-sign utterances as SSD children, produced four times as many four-sign utterances, and produced almost seven times as many more-than-four-sign utterances. Looking at the development of morphological complexity, they found that all five NGT children used complex verbs, whereas only two SSD children used complex verbs. Furthermore, looking at all complex verbs produced, 90 percent were produced by NGT children. Thus, signing while speaking does not provide the linguistic requirements for true bilingual development. All the developmental advantages are with the natural sign languages (Wilbur 2003). Now the policy of the Guyot Institute is that all parents should use NGT with their children, regardless of their hope for eventual success with cochlear implantation.

Because nearly all deaf children are born to hearing parents, the issue arises of how the parents and children are able to learn sign language and to what extent they develop fluency. With respect to the parents, there are various possible outcomes, all dependent on resources available and decisions made. In many countries and in many U.S. schools for deaf people, parents are encouraged to learn to sign as much as possible, and they are provided with opportunities to be in contact with fluent signing adults who can serve as teachers, tutors, motivators, and models. These same signing individuals can also sign with the hearing parents' deaf child, providing critical input during the critical period. Parental signing achievement levels can range from conversationally fluent to barely able to manage at their young child's level.

What of the deaf child? Fortunately for such deaf children, their acquisition of signing fluency is not critically dependent on their parents' achievement level—rather it is more dependent on the other people with whom they communicate, such as children their own age, teachers, and other members of the Deaf community. A parallel example is the acquisition of English by children of immigrant parents who may not be able to manage in English at all. Such children acquire English just like other children, and they may also be bilingual to varying degrees. This means that, provided with adequate input and interaction with fluent signing individuals, deaf children will acquire fluent signing, and, in most cases, will surpass the signing achievement level of their own parents. What I have observed is this: Fluent signers simplify their signing style for their own parents just the way they do for other nonnative, nonfluent (hearing) signers.

Given these outcomes, what the Guyot Institute and similar organizations in other countries are saying to hearing parents is this: Try to learn the natural sign language rather than trying to speak and sign at the same time. Let others who are fluent in the sign language help you and your children to communicate using sign language. The results in terms of your child's academic and linguistic achievement will be greatly improved.

WHAT IS THE PROBLEM THAT DEAF CHILDREN HAVE LEARNING ENGLISH AND WHAT CAUSES IT?

The overall difficulty that deaf children have learning English has been very well documented (Quigley and Kretschmer 1982; Quigley and Paul 1984; Wilbur 1979, 1987). As a general observation, by age eighteen, deaf students do not have the linguistic competence of ten-year-old hearing children in many syntactic structures of English, and studies report that less than 12 percent of deaf students at age sixteen can read at a fourth-grade reading level or higher, as measured on the Metropolitan Reading Achievement Test (see Wilbur 2000a for a detailed overview and Karchmer and Mitchell 2003 for recent statistics). These classic papers demonstrate clearly that whether or not deaf children are able to speak, there is still a larger overriding problem of language that renders the children unable to understand what they read (or speak, when reading out loud).

In contrast, by the time hearing children begin to learn to read, they have already developed conversational fluency in their native language, including sophisticated linguistic skills, and can transfer this knowledge to reading and to the learning of other languages. Deaf children who have lost their hearing at an early age do not have this knowledge; thus, they do not come to the task with the same skills as hearing children in sentence formation, vocabulary, and world knowledge.

The powerful role that early learning of sign language plays in linguistic and educational achievement is reflected by the fact that deaf children whose deaf parents use sign language at home with them are exceptional in their accomplishments (Karchmer and Mitchell 2003; Mayer and Akamatsu 2003). This success is a result of the fact that they have a fully established language base prior to learning to read. These children are more similar to hearing children who must learn to read and write in a second language (typical bilingual). For this group, early ASL use provides a significant advantage, not interference.

Early studies overwhelmingly reported better overall achievement for ASL users, although there are differences on some measures, and, in some cases, no differences at all (Moores 1974). More recent studies (Strong and Prinz 1997; Prinz 2002; Hoffmeister 2000; Padden and Ramsey 2000; Singleton, Supalla, Litchfield, and Schley 1998) have confirmed many of these findings. Significantly, there is, as indicated by the older research, a strong correlation between ASL fluency and English literacy. Furthermore, there is an improvement in English literacy as ASL skills improve, indicating that the early benefit of having deaf parents fades as children acquire ASL while in contact with other fluent users. This finding is significant because some have tried to suggest that the educational advantage shown by deaf children of deaf parents was not due to knowledge of sign language but rather to social development issues such as greater parental acceptance of a deaf child by deaf parents than by hearing parents, who might be distressed at the presence of a deaf child in their family. We now know that it is the ASL skills that are important, and that as deaf children, even those with hearing parents, become more fluent in ASL, they become better readers of English. Additional support for this finding comes from James and MacSweeney (2005) who conclude on the basis of their research on British Sign Language (BSL) and literacy development that "overall, BSL proficiency was the most powerful predictor of reading accuracy and reading comprehension."

How Can a Bilingual Situation Help with Respect to Language and Literacy Development?

Similarities of ASL Bilinguals and Hearing Children

Consider the benefits that all deaf children would receive from early exposure to ASL. One would be the fully developed language base that deaf children of deaf parents are already getting. A fully developed language base provides normal cognitive, perceptual, and memory development within the critical language acquisition period (Newport and Meier 1985; Petitto 1993; Lillo-Martin 1994). Like normally developing hearing children, early ASL bilinguals go through the language acquisition process more or less naturally, whereas later acquisition requires more conscious learning. With early ASL bilingualism, teacher-child and parent-child communication is vastly improved and there is no longer a limited input problem. Instead, ASL-signing deaf children become another bilingual minority learning English (Charrow and Wilbur 1975).

It is already known that deaf children learn English as though it were a foreign language. Charrow and Fletcher (1974) gave the Test of English as a Foreign Language (TOEFL) to deaf high school students of college-entrance age. Although the deaf subjects did not perform as well as foreign college entrants, in general, their results more closely resembled that of foreign students than that of native speakers of English. From the perspective of treating deaf children like other second language learners, one should expect on-grade-level performance, not the delays in educational development still seen today. Some of that performance may be demonstrated in the first, rather than the second, language. Hakuta (1986) has shown that there is no problem with the transfer of curricular material learned in one language to eventual use in the other language; thus this is not a concern. In short, with early ASL bilingualism, there is nothing to lose and everything to gain.

Advantages of Having a Fully Developed First Language

The research reviewed above indicates that early ASL bilinguals (deaf children of deaf parents) had overwhelmingly better overall achievement in 90 percent of the comparisons that were made with nonsigning deaf children (deaf children of hearing parents). They also noted that the deaf children of deaf parents had higher self-image and academic achievement (arithmetic, reading, and overall). Meadow (1966) also reported higher teachers' ratings for the deaf children of deaf parents on maturity, responsibility, independence, sociability, appropriate sex role, popularity, appropriate responses to situations, fingerspelling ability, written language, signing ability, absence of communicative frustration, and willingness to communicate with strangers.

How does sign language fluency contribute to this greater overall performance? One benefit of early sign language fluency is that it increases the quantity and quality of concepts and linguistic devices that the children know, which then serve as a base for learning written English vocabulary and syntax (Schick 2003; Paul 2003; Mayer and Akamatsu 2003). A high level of sign language ability also results in increased comprehension of classroom instructional materials.

From a linguistic perspective, knowledge of ASL as an L1 is beneficial because it taps normal capacities at the appropriate stage of development (Schick 2003). As Lillo-Martin (1993, 1994) discusses, when children have an L1 (ASL or other language), their linguistic competence is constrained by universal grammar; that is, the normal language acquisition process takes place within the confines of what all natural languages have in common (see also Petitto 1993; Newport and Meier 1985; Pinker 1993). Given knowledge of an L1, learners of a second language have some idea of what to expect, making the acquisition of the second language simpler.

Van Patten (1995, 1996) has argued that for successful language acquisition or learning, individuals need access to input which is communicatively and/or meaningfully oriented and comprehensible in nature. He notes that there are three corollaries to this observation: (a) The individual must interact with the input to maximize language acquisition or learning; (b) the input must not only be comprehensible, it must be comprehended with ease; and (c) the degree and quality of language competence is partially determined by degree and quality of input received. Deaf children of deaf parents are clearly provided with quality input that is easily understood, and they are able to interact with their parents and other signers. Thus, they have the basis for successful learning of English, and this is reflected in their academic and professional accomplishments.

Contributions of ASL to Improved Literacy in English

Learning to read requires an already developed language base (Padden and Ramsey 2000; Paul 2003). Deaf children are traditionally asked to learn English language structure, speech, and reading at the same time. The problem with this is that students cannot understand what they are being told until they have mastered English well enough to understand the teacher's instructions. This vicious cycle is broken when the children come to school with a fully established ASL language base—then a normal situation is encountered for teaching English as a second language (ESL). Properly trained teachers of deaf people should have substantial expertise in ESL methods, and speech-language pathologists and audiologists working to develop speech and listening skills should have conversational fluency in ASL in order to be able to work with the children.

Consider reading readiness, that is, what children are expected to be able to do with language before learning to read. They should have a well-developed vocabulary, otherwise they will not recognize a written word even if they sound it out. They should be able to handle sentences of some complexity. Finally, they should be able to draw on their conversational skills and their knowledge of story structure to draw inferences and conclusions so that they can "read between the lines." Deaf children with competency in a natural sign language should be expected to meet reading readiness milestones as well. Even though they might not be able to recognize words that they sound out, they should be able to do the equivalent with fingerspelling (Padden and Hanson 2000). Certainly, they should be able to understand those concepts when signed, and this is precisely where knowledge of ASL makes a difference. Deaf parents show their young deaf children the fingerspelling of common English words with the signs before children have any idea about spelling. As the children develop, they learn the fingerspelled letters in the words gradually and already know their meaning from the associated sign. Padden and Hanson (2000) argue that this forms the bridge to successful bilingual development and literacy.

Twenty-five years ago, Stuckless (1981) noted that whereas deaf children exposed only to a graphic form of English are working with a clear and complete code (written English), they still need to have an established language base in order to derive meaning from it. Similarly, Hirsh-Pasek and Treiman (1982) noted that deaf children rarely possess a strong language base that is compatible with the alphabetic writing system and that sounding out or spelling aloud in the absence of extensive articulatory or fingerspelled vocabularies is unprofitable. They suggested that teachers can increase signing deaf children's fingerspelled lexicons, but that explicit instruction in using fingerspelling as a coding strategy related to print may be necessary because children may not discover it without assistance. More recently, Padden and Hanson (2000, 442) argue that fingerspelling is a "mediating tool that provides a platform for the development of rudimentary phonological coding," such as an awareness of segments as units of fingerspelling, print, speechreading, mouthing, and sound. Thus, the process of learning to deal with printed material is separate from the task of learning a language in the first place (for both speakers and signers). As long as the two goals continue to be confused, progress toward both will continue to be hindered.

One of the most significant advantages of working with deaf children who already have a well-developed L1 base is that many opportunities for learning can be found outside of the traditional classroom situation. For example, a trip to the zoo becomes more than just an opportunity to learn the names of animals; with extensive communication provided through the sign language, teacher and students can have a discussion about which animals are more interesting to write stories about and why. Children can make up short stories and tell them in ASL, enjoying the experience without the frustration of English structure, spelling, and writing. When the children do finally write stories, the task is different, but typical for bilingual children: translating into another language. For children who do not know ASL, writing the story is not just a translation task, and it requires attention to factors other than just the structure of English (e.g., the notion of a story form has to be developed, whereas children who can use ASL will have already learned many things about normal story structure, such as creating the setting, introducing participants, etc.).

UNDERSTANDING ASL AS A NATURAL LANGUAGE

ASL is a naturally evolved complex language that varies significantly from English. Like many other languages (e.g., Russian, Spanish), it has a flexible word order, preferring that sentence elements reflect the discourse roles (topic, focus) rather than the grammatical relations (subject, object) that English prefers (Wilbur 1997). Another difference between ASL and English is that ASL has what is called fixed phrasal stress, that is, it does not allow stress to shift to different words in a sentence in order to focus on different items (Wilbur 1997). Instead, ASL takes advantage of its more flexible word order to ensure that the desired focus will receive stress only in sentence-final position.

An illustration of the differences between the two types may be helpful here. English allows the following sentences, each one with a different stressed item (in *italics*) but with the same word order:

1a. Virginia saw Elizabeth put the book on the *TABLE*.   (not the SHELF)

1b. Virginia saw Elizabeth put the *BOOK* on the table.   (not the MANUSCRIPT)

1c. Virginia saw *ELIZABETH* put the book on the table.   (not Alonzo)

1d. *VIRGINIA* saw Elizabeth put the book on the table.   (not Marina)

Stress movement cannot be done in languages with fixed phrasal stress. Instead, in ASL, the word order must be changed so that the item to be stressed is put in the reserved place for focused items; in ASL and many other languages, this position is at the end of a sentence (Wilbur 1994b, 1995b, 1996). ASL has a very common structure that translates into English in two ways, either as in examples

1a–d or as the wh-cleft, as in example 2; signs are glossed in small capitals, the extent of required brow raise (br) is marked with a line:

                                br
2a.   VIRGINIA SEE ELIZABETH PUT BOOK WHERE, TABLE

"The place where Virginia saw Elizabeth put the book was the table."

                                 br
2b.   VIRGINIA SEE ELIZABETH PUT-ON-TABLE WHAT, BOOK

"What Virginia saw Elizabeth put on the table was the book."

                               br
2c.   VIRGINIA SEE BOOK PUT-ON-TABLE WHO, ELIZABETH

"The person who Virginia saw put the book on the table was Elizabeth."

                              br
2d.   SEE ELIZABETH BOOK PUT-ON-TABLE WHO, VIRGINIA

"It was Virginia who saw Elizabeth put the book on the table."

This ASL structure can be expanded to create further structures that are considered exceptionally complex in English:

                      br
2e.   VIRGINIA SEE ELIZABETH DO++, BOOK PUT-ON-TABLE

"What Virginia saw Elizabeth do was put the book on the table."

            br
2f.   VIRGINIA DO++, SEE ELIZABETH BOOK PUT-ON-TABLE

"What Virginia did was see Elizabeth put the book on the table."

                            br
2g.   VIRGINIA SEE ELIZABETH DO++ WITH BOOK, PUT-ON-TABLE

"What Virginia saw Elizabeth do with the book was put it on the table."

The basic form of this construction in ASL is "old information + wh-word, new information," with the old information clause marked by a brow raise (Wilbur 1996). Brow raises and other nonmanual markers are integral components of the ASL grammatical system (Baker and Padden 1978; Battison 1974; Frishberg 1978; Siple 1978; Wilbur 1991, 1994b, 1995a, 1999b; Wilbur and Patschke 1999). These differences in prosodic structure are primary contributors to significant differences in syntactic structure between ASL and English (Wilbur 1999a, 1999c). The prosodic, intonational, and syntactic structures evolved together to provide natural language capability in the signed modality (Allen, Wilbur, and Schick 1991; Wilbur and Allen 1991; Wilbur 1997, 2000b).

The nonmanual markers comprise a number of independent channels: head; body position; eyebrow and forehead; eye blink and eye gaze; nose; and mouth, tongue, and cheek (Wilbur 1994a). Nonmanual cues provide morphemic information on lexical items, or they indicate the ends of phrases (boundary markers) or their extent (domain markers, such as the brow raise in the examples above). The nonmanual signals made on the face can be roughly divided into two groups: lower and upper. The lower portion of the face is used to provide adverbial and adjectival information. The mouth, tongue, and cheeks provide meaningful markers that associate with specific lexical items or phrases (Liddell 1978, 1980; Wilbur 2000b), and the nose can be used for discourse marking purposes (Wood 1996).

The nonmanuals supplied by the upper part of the face and the head (eyebrows, head nods, tilts, and shakes, eye gaze; Wilbur 2000b) occur with higher syntactic constituents (clauses, sentences), even if such constituents contain only a single sign (e.g., a topicalized noun). Liddell (1978, 1980) noted the larger scope of upper face/head nonmanuals when he discussed the nonmanual marking "q" (lean forward, head forward, brows raised) for yes/no questions, as in example 3:

$$\overline{\hspace{4cm}}^{\text{q}}$$
$$\overline{\hspace{3cm}}_{\text{mm}}$$

3. MAN FISH[I:continuous]

"Is the man fishing with relaxation and enjoyment?"

This single example illustrates inflectional modification on the predicate sign itself (continuous); lower mouth adverbial modification of the predicate (mouth position "mm"; meaning with enjoyment), and upper face, head, and body marking for the entire question, all on only two sequential lexical items. Information corresponding to English intonation is provided throughout the ASL clause from beginning to end by the upper face and head, and it differs in production from what hearing people might also do with their face and head (Veinberg and Wilbur 1990).

Similarly, spatial arrangement in ASL can convey syntactic, semantic, and morphological information. If a verb is inflected for its arguments by showing starting and ending locations, then the nouns or pronouns do not need to be separately signed. Aspectual information carried in English by adverbial and prepositional phrases can be conveyed in ASL by modifying the verb's temporal and rhythmic characteristics. Information is layered, and thus ASL does not need separate signs for many of the concepts that English has separate words for. In this respect, the fact that ASL is a naturally evolved language in the visual/manual modality can be fully appreciated—more information is conveyed simultaneously than in comparable English renditions.

Why Signing the Spoken Language, for Example, Signed English, Does Not Provide the Same Benefits

Two criterial features for defining a natural language are that (a) it has a community of users and (b) it can be learned by babies from birth. There must be a perfect fit between the perception and production characteristics of the human user, and over time, natural languages evolve to fit the modality in which they are produced and perceived. Obviously, spoken languages are designed to allow communication with ease by people who speak and hear. Similarly, signed languages have evolved to provide communication with ease by people who sign and see. It is only when spoken languages and signed languages are compared for what they have in common, despite their modality differences, that these linguistic design features become obvious.

What signing the spoken language lacks is adaptation to the signing modality, which would allow it to take advantage of simultaneity rather than sequentiality. For example, SE has not developed an intonational and rhythmic system that is designed to be seen by the eyes and produced by the hands and face. This evolution has not taken place because the goal of its usage is to mimic the lexicon, morphology, and syntax of English. Thus, when SE is learned by deaf children, it is learned with the overriding constraint that it must follow English word order. This means that the syntactic structure of SE cannot adapt over time in the ways that would be suitable for the manual modality. In particular, flexible word order cannot develop.

A perhaps bigger problem is that SE is supposed to follow English morphology, which cannot be modified to suit the manual modality. There is substantial overlap between the lexical vocabulary of ASL and SE (Wilbur 1987). But these signs do not provide an exact match with English because certain information in ASL is not carried by separate signs, but rather by morphological modifications in the form of spatial or temporal adjustments to the sign movement (Klima and Bellugi 1979). English morphology involves affixes which are added to the stems (plural, past tense, progressive, comparative, superlative, possessive) and freestanding grammatical words (future, prepositions, infinitival "to", and determiners). Because ASL uses other grammatical methods (such as spatial arrangement in place of several types of prepositional phrases), signs for many function words and morphemes (e.g., *at, to, the, -ing*) that are not needed in ASL were invented for SE (Wilbur 1987). These are translated into SE as separate signs, each requiring independent articulation in sequence; the result is that SE sentences have substantially more signs per sentence than ASL. Therefore, SE takes at least 50 percent longer to produce the same set of propositions than either of the two natural languages, spoken English and ASL, which are roughly comparable (Bellugi and Fischer 1972).

The constraint that SE should follow English morphology encourages sequentiality and *prevents* layering mechanisms from arising. For example, Supalla (1991) reports that despite pure SE input containing no spatially modified verbs or pronouns (and no known contamination by ASL signers), ten-year-old deaf students produced signing in which 80 percent of the verbs and 86 percent of the pronouns were spatially modified. The total absence of these devices in the teacher's signing suggests that these innovative spatial modifications will be treated as unacceptable errors by the teacher until they are completely eliminated from the students' signing and are replaced by the proper SE forms. Under these circumstances, grammaticalization of nonmanuals or manual sign modifications for functions like verb agreement cannot evolve. Furthermore, when adults (usually hearing) learn to sign English, they are already fluent in English and find it convenient to follow English principles, making innovations by this older population less likely. In essence, then, the dominance of English sequentiality of words and morphemes in this communication situation suppresses layering adaptations of SE.

Wilbur and Petersen (1998) studied two groups of fluent SE users, one which also knows ASL (adult children of deaf parents) and one which does not (teachers, parents, audiologists, speech-language pathologists). In this study, the signers who knew ASL were relatively diligent in using ASL nonmanual markers to convey information while producing SE (with or without speech), that is, they extended layering from ASL to SE. The signers who did not know ASL used minimal and occasionally incorrect nonmanual marking while signing SE. For example, some of their SE productions of yes/no questions had correct ASL brow raise on them, whereas other productions were inappropriately marked with brow lowering. Fully 81 percent of the yes/no questions produced by these signers were not correctly marked by ASL standards. Other nonmanuals (blinks, negative headshakes) clearly differed between the two groups even though both groups were supposed to be producing the same SE content. The signers who knew ASL were able to transfer nonmanuals to SE because SE has no specified nonmanuals of its own. As a group, the signers who did not know ASL but who are nonetheless fluent users of SE were not homogeneous in their use of nonmanuals because no such system has been developed for SE. If this is true for the general population of SE signers who do not know ASL, then it is clear that children are not presented with a consistent adult model of SE in the settings in which it is used.

Finally, the observation that there are systematic cues for intonation in signed languages provides insight into the universal structure of natural languages (Wilbur 1991, 1997, 2000b). One may infer that intonational information is a necessary component of the human linguistic and cognitive systems, and that at the prosodic level, the central processing mechanisms of the brain are indifferent to the modality in which such information is received by the peripheral mechanisms (ear or eye), so long as the information is present and appropriate to the linguistic content and communicative situation. There are clear differences between naturally evolved languages prosodically suited to their modality by appropriate layering (ASL and English) and artificial systems like SE which take structure from one modality (spoken English) and attempt to convey it in another modality (SE) without regard to modifications that might be appropriate for the production modality.

The solution that I am arguing for here is one where ASL is used as the initial language of communication and instruction for deaf children and where English is treated as a second language. That second language has a signed form (SE), a spoken form, and a written form. I have identified problems with SE and indicated why I do not think it should be the first method of communication and language instruction. However, I want to make it clear that I think there is a role for SE, and that this role is separate from signing and speaking at the same time. SE can be used to assist deaf children as they struggle to understand the differences between ASL and English (Schick 2003). It can be used to concentrate on English syntax and morphology and on its written form (reading and writing; Paul 2003; Mayer and Akamatsu 2003).

Speaking and signing at the same time is another matter altogether. First, it should be clear from the above description of ASL that it is impossible to sign ASL and speak English at the same time. There are cognitive, linguistic, and motoric reasons for the presence of English-based signing and the absence of ASL-based signing when speaking English.

Second, questions have arisen about the quality of speech that serves as input to deaf children in simultaneous communication situations. The Wilbur and Petersen (1998) study reported that in the production of simultaneous communication, speech duration increased as compared to producing speech alone. Slower, elongated speech such as that produced in simultaneous communication sounds less natural than speech produced alone. The source of these speech production modifications was not signer fluency (see similar findings in Whitehead et al. 1995; Schiavetti et al. 1996). Rather, the observed modality interaction is likely the result of the prosodic structural mismatches between spoken and signed English. Theoretically, simultaneous speaking and signing contains the same number of words in each modality as they both code English. However, the number of *syllables* in the two modalities and the rhythmic pattern are extremely unlikely to match (Wilbur 1990, 1993; Wilbur and Petersen 1997). There are numerous mismatches in the number of forms produced because SE frequently requires a separate sign for spoken English suffixes (e.g., *-s*); hence a single-syllable word in spoken English (e.g., *cats*) may be two separate signs in SE (e.g., CAT + plural). Every sign is given full metrical timing (e.g., full sign duration) regardless of whether its corresponding English translation is a lexical item or suffixal morpheme (Wilbur and Nolen 1986). Hence, the single spoken syllable for *cats* is matched by two full sign productions. Furthermore, spoken English has many words that have two or more syllables, but SE, which gets its basic vocabulary from ASL, contains mostly monosyllabic signs (Coulter 1982; Wilbur 1990). For example, the English word *eliminate* has four spoken syllables but only one signed syllable. Thus, in simultaneous signing and speaking, the number of syllables being produced is usually different in the two modalities.

SUMMARY

The research that has been reviewed here provides strong support for the use of ASL as a means of communication before the deaf child enters school, to develop cognition, socialization, and an age-appropriate knowledge base, as well as to provide a basis for learning English and English literacy. Its use should continue into the classroom. Consider the ways in which knowledge of ASL can be helpful in improving the learning of English and literacy proficiency with deaf children.

Conversational use of ASL models important features of ASL discourse, and discourse in general (Wilbur and Petitto 1983). As we have seen, ASL requires more obvious attention to recognizing the focus of the sentence in order to construct sentences in accordance with the requirement that the focus should be at the end of the sentence. This structural requirement, in turn, requires the signer to separate old and new information, placing the discourse old information prior to the new. Because deaf children do not understand when and how to push old information to the background and bring new information to the foreground, they frequently have difficulty with English structures which are designed for that purpose, including determiner usage (a/the), pronoun usage, and the stiltedness of the information flow in their paragraphs. The mechanisms for accomplishing these tasks in ASL are clear and consistent, so that children who know ASL come to the task of learning the English counterpart constructions with a strong base of understanding of the range of differences in meaning that need to be encoded in English syntax. That is, they would already know how to separate old from new information and have a sense of how conversational flow affects individual sentence structure. The task then becomes one of presenting these children with a situation in the form of "if this is what you mean in ASL, here's how you express it in English." When phrased this way, the task is not confounded by the necessity to also teach the notions of old and new; in short, we now have a typical bilingual learning environment.

Prosodic structure (intonation, stress placement) provides cues to the listener as to where sentences end and new ones begin, as well as providing cues as to whether the speaker intends to continue, plans to yield the floor, expects a response from the addressee, and other conversational controlling functions. These functions are only partially represented in the written form of English, through the use of punctuation and novelty uses of capitals, italics, bold, and graphic symbols ("!@$%#"). In ASL, sentence boundaries, signer intentions, and conversational controllers are all provided by cues other than the signs themselves. Various nonmanual cues provide overt information about phrasing and syntactic constituency. The difference between a string of words and a real sentence is the "sentence glue" that binds the words into phrases and the phrases into sentences. In ASL, eye blinks, head nods, and brow raising or lowering all signal the ends of clauses and sentences. The height of the hands signals whether the signer intends to continue, yield, or interrupt someone else (Wilbur and Petitto 1983). Deaf children who learn ASL first are prepared with full conversational fluency before they begin the task of learning to use English fluently. Full conversational fluency includes the signer's responsibility to ensure that the addressee can follow the topic—who is doing what to whom—and how much certainty the signer places in the truth of the assertions. These are all things that are coded in normal English usage, but are not part of the standard English lessons that are provided for deaf students.

Along the same lines, ASL provides clear cues to which noun phrase is the subject/agent and which is the object/undergoer. For many verbs, formation is adjusted so that the verb production starts at a location indexed to the subject and moves to a location indexed to the object (see Meir 1998 for a complete linguistic discussion). Information about subject and object in English is carried by some morphological information, such as case marking on pronouns and subject-verb agreement on the verb, but primarily by word order, such as subject before the verb and object after. Students with knowledge of ASL will find the correlation between word order and grammatical function of English syntax fairly easy to acquire. The use of nonmanuals and spatial modifications of sign formations is one of the reasons why ASL does not need separate signs for many of the concepts that (spoken/signed) English has separate words for. In this respect, the fact that ASL is a naturally evolved language in the visual/manual modality can be fully appreciated—more information is conveyed simultaneously than in comparable English renditions.

As we have seen in the section on the development of speech skills in deaf learners, early acquisition of ASL does not affect the development of speech production or speechreading skills. Deaf children who have deaf parents who use ASL as the primary means of communication perform at a level comparable to orally trained deaf children from hearing households with respect to speech skills. In addition, deaf children who know ASL have the further advantages of superior performance on measures of cognitive, linguistic, and social skills.

Finally, there is the fact that sign languages have no written form. This is also not a major concern. Consider the functions that writing serves: long-distance (not face-to-face) communication and preservation of documents for future use. For signed languages, these functions are easily served by digital movies. The history, stories, biographies, theatrical performances, poetry, and other linguistic expressions of American Deaf culture in ASL are preserved in video recordings (and earlier, on film) dating back to the beginning of the twentieth century. Early knowledge of sign language allows deaf students access to their history and culture, which, in turn, engenders pride in who they are. Through a bilingual, bicultural approach, we should see the elimination of what Johnson et al. (1989) call "the cycle of low expectations"—which they suggest is the primary cause of the failure of deaf education.

If the adults in the deaf child's environment do not know the local natural sign language, how can the child develop full sign language fluency? Parents trigger the language acquisition process, but they do not control its ultimate outcome. Instead, children acquire the language of their peers. The earlier the child is placed in contact with the natural sign language, the better the child will learn it. Strategies for accomplishing this contact include opportunities for the child to play with other signing children (deaf or hearing), signing babysitters, regular visits to the local Deaf clubs or schools, and other interactions with members of the Deaf community. Johnson et al. (1989) provided a number of additional suggestions, many modeled after the successful programs for Deaf people in Sweden. The critical factor is that the child must be placed in an appropriate language-learning environment. If the parents never become fluent in the natural sign language and can only just manage in SE, so be it. The focus should not be on what the parents can or cannot do. Rather the focus should be on the child's education, which requires communication in a natural language, on which all advanced learning is built. Early knowledge of sign language is a critical part of the solution, not part of the problem.

REFERENCES

Ahlström, K. 1972. On evaluation of the effects of schooling. In *Proceedings of the International Congress on Education of the Deaf*. Stockholm: Sveriges Laraforbund.

Allen, George D., Ronnie B. Wilbur, and Brenda S. Schick. 1991. Aspects of rhythm in American Sign Language. *Sign Language Studies* 72:297–320.

Baker, Charlotte, and Carol Padden. 1978. Focusing on the nonmanual components of American Sign Language. In *Understanding language through sign language research*, ed. Patricia Siple, 27–57. New York: Academic Press.

Battison, Robbin. 1974. Phonological deletion in American Sign Language. *Sign Language Studies* 5:1–19.

Bellugi, Ursula, and Susan D. Fischer. 1972. A comparison of sign language and spoken language: Rate and grammatical mechanisms. *Cognition* 1(3):173–200.

Bonvillian, John D., Veda R. Charrow, and Keith E. Nelson. 1973. Psycholinguistic and educational implications of deafness. *Human Development* 16(5):321–45.

Charrow, Veda R., and J. D. Fletcher. 1974. English as the second language of deaf children. *Developmental Psychology* 10(4):463–70.

Charrow, Veda R., and Ronnie B. Wilbur. 1975. The deaf child as a linguistic minority. *Theory into Practice* 14(5):353–59.

Coulter, Geoffrey. 1982. On the nature of ASL as a monosyllabic language. Paper presented at the Linguistic Society of America, San Diego, December 27–30.

Frishberg, Nancy. 1978. The case of the missing length. *Communication and Cognition* 11:57–67.

Hakuta, Kenji. 1986. *Mirrors of language: The debate on bilingualism.* New York: Basic Books.

Hirsh-Pasek, Kathy, and Rebecca Treiman. 1982. Recoding in silent reading: Can the deaf child translate print into a more manageable form? *Volta Review* 84(5):71–82.

Hoffmeister, Robert. 2000. A piece of the puzzle: ASL and reading comprehension in deaf children. In *Language acquisition by eye,* ed. Charlene Chamberlain, Jill P. Morford, and Rachel I. Mayberry, 143–64. Mahwah, N.J.: Lawrence Erlbaum Associates.

Hoiting, Nini, and Dan I. Slobin. 2002. What a deaf child needs to see: Advantages of a natural sign language over a sign system. In *Progress in sign language research: In honor of Siegmund Prillwitz,* ed. Rolf Schulmeister and Heimo Reinitzer, 267–77. Hamburg: Signum.

James, Deborah, and Mairead MacSweeney. 2005. *Phonological awareness of sign and rhyme and the relationship with reading in Deaf children whose preferred language is British Sign Language.* Paper presented at the Tenth International Congress for the Study of Child Language. Freie Universität, Berlin, July 25–29.

Johnson, Robert E., Scott K. Liddell, and Carol J. Erting. 1989. Unlocking the curriculum: Principles for achieving access in Deaf education. WP89-3. Available from Gallaudet Research Institute, Gallaudet University, Washington, D.C.

Karchmer, Michael A., and Ross E. Mitchell. 2003. Demographic and achievement characteristics of the deaf and hard-of-hearing students. In *The Oxford handbook of deaf studies, language, and education,* ed. Marc Marschark and Patricia E. Spencer, 21–37. New York: Oxford University Press.

Klima, Edward, and Ursula Bellugi. 1979. *The signs of language.* Cambridge, Mass.: Harvard University Press.

Liddell, Scott K. 1978. Non-manual signals and relative clauses in American Sign Language. In *Understanding language through sign language research,* ed. Patricia Siple, 59–90. New York: Academic.

———. 1980. *American Sign Language syntax.* The Hague: Mouton.

Lillo-Martin, Diane. 1993. Deaf readers and universal grammar. In *Psychological perspectives on deafness,* ed. Marc Marschark and Diane Clark, 311–37. Edison, N.J.: Lawrence Erlbaum Associates.

———. 1994. Setting the null argument parameters: Evidence from American Sign Language and other languages. In *Binding, dependencies, and learnability,* ed. Barbara Lust, Gabriela Hermon, and Jaklin Kornfilt, 301–18. Hillsdale, N.J.: Lawrence Erlbaum Associates.

Mayer, Connie, and C. Tane Akamatsu. 2003. Bilingualism and literacy. In *The Oxford handbook of deaf studies, language, and education,* ed. Marc Marschark and Patricia E. Spencer, 136–50. New York: Oxford University Press.

McDonnell, Patrick, and Helena Saunders. 1993. Sit on your hands: Strategies to prevent signing. In *Looking back: A reader on the history of Deaf communities and their sign languages,* ed. Renate Fischer and Harlan Lane. Vol. 20 of *International studies on sign language and communication of the deaf.* Hamburg: Signum.

Meadow, Kathryn. 1966. *The effects of early manual communication and family climate on the deaf child's early development.* Ph.D. diss., University of California, Berkeley.

Meir, Irit. 1998. Syntactic-semantic interaction in Israeli Sign Language verbs. *Sign Language and Linguistics* 1(1):3–33.

Moores, Donald. 1971. *Recent research on manual communication.* Minneapolis: University of Minnesota, Research, Development, and Demonstration Center in Education of the Handicapped.

———. 1974. *Educating the deaf: Psychology, principles, and practices.* Boston: Houghton-Mifflin.

Newport, Elissa, and Richard Meier. 1985. The acquisition of American Sign Language. In *The crosslinguistic study of language acquisition.* Vol. 1 of *The data,* ed. Dan I. Slobin, 881–938. Hillsdale, N.J.: Lawrence Erlbaum Associates.

Padden, Carol, and Vicky Hanson. 2000. Search for the missing link: The development of skilled reading in Deaf children. In *The signs of language revisited: An anthology to honor Ursula Bellugi and Edward Klima,* ed. Harlan Lane and Karen Emmorey, 435–47. Hillsdale, N.J.: Lawrence Erlbaum Associates.

Padden, Carol, and Claire Ramsey. 2000. American Sign Language and reading ability in deaf children. In *Language acquisition by eye,* ed. Charlene Chamberlain, Jill P. Morford, and Rachel I. Mayberry, 165–89. Mahwah, N.J.: Lawrence Erlbaum Associates.

Paul, Peter V. 2003. Processes and components of reading. In *The Oxford handbook of deaf studies, language, and education,* ed. Marc Marschark and Patricia E. Spencer, 97–109. New York: Oxford University Press.

Petitto, Laura A. 1993. Modularity and constraints in early lexical acquisition: Evidence from children's early language and gesture. In *Language acquisition,* ed. Paul Bloom, 95–126. Cambridge, Mass.: MIT Press.

Pinker, Steven. 1993. Rules of language. In *Language acquisition,* ed. Paul Bloom, 472–84. Cambridge, Mass.: MIT Press.

Power, Desmond. 1974. Language development in deaf children: The use of manual supplement in oral education. *Australian Teacher of the Deaf* 15.

Prinz, Philip. 2002. Crosslinguistic perspectives on sign language and literacy development. In *Progress in sign language research: In honor of Siegmund Prillwitz,* ed. Rolf Schulmeister and Heimo Reinitzer, 221–33. Hamburg: Signum.

Quigley, Stephen P., and Robert Frisina. 1961. *Institutionalization and psychoeducational development in deaf children.* Washington, D.C.: Council on Exceptional Children.

Quigley, Stephen P., and Robert E. Kretschmer. 1982. *The education of deaf children.* Baltimore: University Park Press.

Quigley, Stephen P., and Peter Paul. 1984. *Language and deafness.* San Diego: College-Hill Press.

Rönnberg, Jerker. 2003. Working memory, neuroscience, and language: Evidence from deaf and hard-of-hearing individuals. In *The Oxford handbook of deaf studies, language, and education,* ed. Marc Marschark and Patricia E. Spencer, 478–90. New York: Oxford University Press.

Schick, Brenda. 2003. The development of American Sign Language and manually coded English systems. In *The Oxford handbook of deaf studies, language, and education,* ed. Marc Marschark and Patricia E. Spencer, 219–31. New York: Oxford University Press.

Singleton, Jenny L., Samuel Supalla, Sharon Litchfield, and Sara Schley. 1998. From sign to word: Considering modality constraints in ASL/English bilingual education. In *ASL proficiency and English literacy acquisition: New perspectives,* ed. Philip Prinz, *Topics in Language Disorders* (special issue) 18(4):16–29.

Siple, Patricia. 1978. Visual constraints for sign language communication. *Sign Language Studies* 19:95–110.

Stevenson, Elwood A. 1964. A study of the educational achievement of deaf children of deaf parents. *California News* 80:143.

Strong, Michael, and Philip Prinz. 1997. A study of the relationship between ASL and English literacy. *Journal of Deaf Studies and Deaf Education* 2(1):37–46.

Stuckless, Ross. 1981. Real-time graphic displays and language development for the hearing-impaired. *Volta Review* 83:291–300.

Stuckless, Ross, and Jack W. Birch. 1966. The influence of early manual communication on the linguistic development of deaf children. *American Annals of the Deaf.* Part 1, 111(2):452–60; Part 2: 111(3):499–504.

Supalla, Samuel J. 1991. Manually coded English: The modality question in signed language development. In *Theoretical Issues in Sign Language Research.* Vol. 2 of *Psychology,* ed. Patricia Siple and Susan D. Fischer, 85–109. Chicago: University of Chicago Press.

Vallduví, Enric. 1991. The role of plasticity in the association of focus and prominence. In *ESCOL '90: Proceedings of the Seventh Eastern States Conference on Linguistics,* ed. Yongkyoon No and Mark Libucha, 295–306. Columbus: Ohio State University Press.

Van Patten, Bill. 1995. Cognitive aspects of input processing in second language acquisition. In *Studies in language learning and Spanish linguistics: In honor of Tracy D. Terrell,* ed. Peggy Hashemipour, Ricardo Maldonado, and Margaret van Naerssen. New York: McGraw-Hill.

———. 1996. *Input processing and grammar instruction: Theory and research.* Norwood, N.J.: Ablex.

Veinberg, Silvana C., and Ronnie B. Wilbur. 1990. A linguistic analysis of the negative headshake in American Sign Language. *Sign Language Studies* 68:217–44.

Vernon, McCay, and Soon D. Koh. 1970. Early manual communication and Deaf children's achievement. *American Annals of the Deaf* 115(5):527–36.

Wilbur, Ronnie B. 1979. *American Sign Language and sign systems: Research and applications.* Baltimore: University Park Press.

———. 1987. *American Sign Language: Linguistic and applied dimensions.* San Diego: College-Hill Press.

———. 1990. Why syllables? What the notion means for ASL research. In *Theoretical issues in sign language research.* Vol. 1: *Linguistics,* ed. Susan D. Fischer and Patricia Siple, 81–108. Chicago: University of Chicago Press.

———. 1991. Intonation and focus in American Sign Language. In *ESCOL '90: Eastern States Conference on Linguistics,* ed. Yongkyoon No and Mark Libucha, 320–31. Columbus: Ohio State University Press.

———. 1993. Segments and syllables in ASL phonology. In *Current issues in ASL phonology.* Vol. 3: *Phonetics and phonology,* ed. Geoffrey R. Coulter, 135–68. New York: Academic Press.

———. 1994a. Eyeblinks and ASL phrase structure. *Sign Language Studies* 84:221–40.

———. 1994b. Foregrounding structures in ASL. *Journal of Pragmatics* 22(6):647–72.

———. 1995a. What the morphology of operators looks like: A formal analysis of ASL brow-raise. In *FLSM VI: Formal Linguistics Society of Mid-America.* Vol. 2 of *Syntax II and semantics/pragmatics,* ed. Leslie Gabriele, Debra Hardison, and Robert Westmoreland, 67–78. Bloomington: Indiana University Linguistics Club Publications.

———. 1995b. Why so-called rhetorical questions (RHQs) are neither rhetorical nor questions. In *Sign language research 1994: Fourth European congress on sign language research, Munich,* ed. Heleen Bos and Trude Schermer, 149–69. Vol. 29 of *International Studies on Sign Language and Communication of the Deaf.*Hamburg: Signum.

———. 1996. Evidence for function and structure of wh-clefts in ASL. In *International Review of Sign Linguistics,* ed. William H. Edmondson and Ronnie B. Wilbur, 209–56. Hillsdale, N.J.: Lawrence Erlbaum Associates.

————. 1997. A prosodic/pragmatic explanation for word order variation in ASL with typological implications. In *Lexical and syntactic constructions and the construction of meaning,* vol. 1, ed. Kee D. Lee, Eve Sweetser, and Marjolijn Verspoor, 89–104. Philadelphia: John Benjamins.

————. 1999a. Typological similarities between American Sign Language and Spanish. *Actas de VI simposio internacional de comunicacion social (Santiago de Cuba)* 1:438–43.

————. 1999b. A functional journey with a formal ending: What do brow raises do in American Sign Language? In *Functionalism and formalism.* Vol. 2 of *Case studies,* ed. Michael Darnell, Edith Moravscik, Michael Noonan, Frederick Newmeyer, and Kathleen Wheatly, 295–13. Amsterdam: John Benjamins.

————. 1999c. Stress in ASL: Empirical evidence and linguistic issues. *Language and Speech* 42(2–3):229–50.

————. 2000a. The use of ASL to support the development of English and literacy. *Journal of Deaf Studies and Deaf Education* 5(1):81–104.

————. 2000b. Phonological and prosodic layering of nonmanuals in American Sign Language. In *The signs of language revisited: Festschrift for Ursula Bellugi and Edward Klima,* ed. Harlan Lane and Karen Emmorey, 213–41. Hillsdale, N.J.: Lawrence Erlbaum Associates.

————. 2003. Modality and the structure of language: Sign languages versus signed systems. In *The Oxford handbook of deaf studies, language, and education,* ed. Marc Marschark and Patricia E. Spencer, 332–46. New York: Oxford University Press.

Wilbur, Ronnie B., and George D. Allen. 1991. Perceptual evidence against internal structure in ASL syllables. *Language and Speech* 34(1):27–46.

Wilbur, Ronnie B., and Susan B. Nolen. 1986. Duration of syllables in ASL. *Language and Speech* 29(3):263–80.

Wilbur, Ronnie B., and Cynthia Patschke. 1998. Body leans and marking contrast in ASL. *Journal of Pragmatics* 30(3):275–303.

————. 1999. Syntactic correlates of brow raise in ASL. *Sign Language and Linguistics* 2(1):3–40.

Wilbur, Ronnie B., and Lesa Petersen. 1997. Backwards signing and ASL syllable structure. *Language and Speech* 40(1):63–90.

————. 1998. Modality interactions of speech and signing in simultaneous communication. *Journal of Speech, Language and Hearing Research* 41:200–12.

Wilbur, Ronnie B., and Laura A. Petitto. 1983. Discourse structure of American Sign Language conversations; or, how to know a conversation when you see one. *Discourse Processes* 6(3):225–41.

Wood, Sandra K. 1996. *Nose wrinkles in ASL: A discourse particle for co-construction.* Paper presented to the American Association for Applied Linguistics, Chicago, March 23–26.

10 | ENGLISH AND ASL: CLASSROOM ACTIVITIES TO SHED SOME LIGHT ON THE USE OF TWO LANGUAGES

SHANNON ALLEN

I came to the field of Deaf education twelve years ago with a background in linguistics and a love for children. Although I immediately became aware of the controversy around language and communication choices for deaf children, it has always been evident to me that American Sign Language (ASL), as a natural visual language, is the ideal choice for a deaf child's daily communication and education. It is also evident that English, as the dominant language of commerce and power in the United States and around the world, is a necessary choice. Both languages are equally capable of expressing all that a person might think, imagine, feel, wonder, know, or dream. I am passionate in my search for ways to allow the deaf students I teach to express themselves in ASL and English and to understand other people who express themselves in either language. It is not my purpose in this chapter to convince anyone else that this is what they should do. Rather, I offer practical methods for how to go about doing it and explain the basis for my attention to language forms in these particular activities.

In this chapter I describe three activities that I have used in kindergarten and first-grade classrooms with children who are deaf. This is the kind of essay that I am always looking to read as a teacher eager for more ideas that (a) uphold what I believe to be important for learning and teaching and (b) are practical to implement in my own classroom. As you will see, the activities I present here originated in the work of others, and in the spirit of reciprocation, I hope that readers will learn from what I have added or changed and make their own adaptations as well. This is also, I hope, an essay that researchers will read to see practical applications of theories and directions for further research, that administrators will read to find out how they can help teachers enact lessons that support bilingual ASL and English language development, and that parents will read to see what's possible for their deaf child.

Language Use

Depending on the language models they have at home and at school, deaf students may see sign language varieties that range from constructed manual codes for English, to pidgin Signed English, to native or near native ASL (Gee and Goodhart 1988, 54). English is used in spoken forms either along with signing, or by itself. It is also the language of print. For example, during a classroom discussion about a science experiment, students and teachers are using ASL. The teacher records the students' predictions about the outcome of the experiment on chart paper—in English. The process of translating from the students' signs to the teacher's writing is usually invisible. Because of this distribution, where codeswitching between the languages happens simultaneously with a change in modality, students have little basis for recognizing that there are, in fact, two distinct languages. Furthermore, for the most part, English remains the only language that is taught in school and tested in school, and it is the language that is problematized when it comes to deaf students' academic achievement. (Lane, Hoffmeister, and Bahan 1996, 333). Even in schools where ASL is recognized as a language of instruction, it may not be formally taught. There is no published ASL curriculum for deaf children (although there are several for teaching it as a second language to hearing students). Students can learn the rules of English when explicitly taught, but what they have internalized (to varying degrees) are rules of ASL (Bochner and Albertini 1988). Without conscious attention paid to ASL in the classroom, interference from ASL influences how English is learned (and not learned). Given these conditions, one approach to teaching deaf children both languages more effectively is to teach the differences between the two languages explicitly, with the identification of each language and instruction in translating between them—a consciously bilingual approach—a part of everyday experience. Three activities that I use to accomplish these goals are Doing Words, Morning Meeting, and ASL/English class.

Rationale for Attention to Language Forms

All three activities start with my belief that deaf students need to understand the differences between the use of the two languages, in both form and function. There have been different perspectives on whether second language learners should be specifically taught to attend to and correct the form of their utterances, and if so, how. Long (1988) and Nassaji (1999) both address the issue of focus on form as a positive instructional practice that does not conflict with the favored communicative or natural approach to language teaching. In fact, Nassaji argues that "a totally message-based approach is inadequate for the development of an accurate knowledge of language" (Nassaji 1999, 386). In the case of Deaf children learning English, it seems very clear that focus on form is a necessity, since a "natural approach" mimicking first language acquisition is hardly plausible given that auditory input is inaccessible or, at best, fractured. To learn a language "conversationally" requires that a learner have access to and engage in conversations; part of the learning takes place through the negotiation and interaction, but part of it takes place because a learner develops an "ear" for what "sounds right." Deaf children will not be able to use that skill in learning English and must have concrete reasons for the language rules they learn. In her review of research on negotiation in second language learning, Pica (1994) describes three conditions for what learners need to do for the second language to be learned: 1. comprehend the message (comprehensible input); 2. produce comprehensible output (given opportunities to organize and restructure the syntax of their output); and finally, 3. attend to the form of the language being learned (Pica 1994, 500). I believe that skillful translation between ASL and English allows for comprehensible input for very young children and enables them to produce comprehensible output, and that attention to language form in both languages develops the children's recognition of each language and their own proficiency in translating independently between the two.

As for ASL acquisition, as described earlier, language models in the child's environment present forms of ASL on a continuum from English to ASL, and from ungrammatical to native. As Gee and Goodhart (1998, 69) note, "different children are exposed to different parts of this continuum and to different degrees. But surely a logician exposed to such data could never induce a consistent grammar any more than a child exposed to an early pidgin can." Given this constraint, focus on form teaching in *both* languages seems of great benefit for a deaf learner. Research has shown that although focus on form does not alter the stages of acquisition, it can speed up the process (Pienemann 1984, cited in Long 1988). Support for such conscious attention to language is useful as Schmidt (1990, 3) explains, "because it ties together such related concepts as attention, short-term memory, control vs. automatic processing and serial vs. parallel processing. Conscious processing is a necessary condition for one step in the language learning process." Deaf children need to be made more conscious of the varieties of ASL they see and the translation process that occurs between "through the air" sign language and print language. They also must be taught how to be consistent and conscious in their own use of the two languages. Teachers who teach this way must understand the differences between ASL and English and be consistent and conscious in their use of the two languages. The activities I use in my classroom require me to think about my own use of language and model that metalinguistic experience for my students.

A NOTE ON THE CLASSROOM SETTING

There are a number of ways that teaching both ASL and English can happen in a classroom. How a teacher does so will depend on the ages and abilities of her students, as well as her own beliefs about classroom management and pedagogy. The three activities that I will describe below reflect my own beliefs. My readers may make different decisions to suit their own teaching style and student population.

I will describe the three activities in the order in which they have tended to happen in my classroom during a typical school day in the middle of the year for a kindergarten or first-grade class. At the beginning of the year, students practice expectations and procedures for all of these different routines, so that they can predict what will happen when they are at school. By the middle of the year, students are able to participate in these routines successfully, and that time is what I will describe here. Although I describe scenes from different lessons, they are typically a composite of various classes from the past few years, and all the names of students are fictitious.

Students begin their school day with breakfast and conversation between themselves and the classroom staff (myself and an aide). As they finish eating, they choose from a variety of activities: block building, drawing and writing, playing board games, taking care of a classroom pet, making projects with construction paper and glue, and so on. While they do this, each student also takes a turn coming to me for their word for the day. When everyone has received their word, we clean up and sit in a circle on the rug for Morning Meeting. From there, we commence more academic work such as math, reading, writing, and ASL/English. Typically our afternoons are for lunch, art and gym, and social studies and science. I will not describe reading and writing lessons here, although many of the same principles that I use during Doing Words, Morning Meeting, and ASL/English necessarily apply to those subjects.

Doing Words

Doing Words is an activity that I began telling other teachers about as soon as I tried it out in my own classroom, because I think it is so effective in helping the youngest school-age children to learn several things: that everything that is signed can be written, that they have important thoughts to express, and that ASL and English are different. They also learn many mechanics and conventions of print, including how to form letters beautifully without ever using a worksheet or drill approach. Although this activity requires almost no preparation on the teacher's part, it does require a lot of on-the-spot thinking about language. This procedure is based on the book *Doing Words* by Katie Johnson (1987), who adapted it from Sylvia Ashton-Warner's (1963) work described in the book *Teacher*. As with Morning Meeting, my goal here is to describe how I use it specifically for ASL and English development. For more details on the basic procedures, I highly recommend Johnson's book.

Doing Words is a daily activity. It works wonderfully in a kindergarten classroom when students are learning primarily through play for part of the day and are self-directed. While they attend to that important business, I can see each child individually for their daily word. A classroom aide can guide, mediate, and supervise play while I do this.

The procedure is very simple, but it packs in a lot. I sit at a table with markers and a stack of manila paper sentence strips. I call a child over. I ask, "What word do you want today?" The first time I do the activity, I simply explain to the children that they can tell me anything they want, and I will write the word in English for them. If a child has a hard time at the beginning, I follow Johnson's advice and ask, "Who do you love?" (Johnson 1987, 18). For the first few weeks of this activity, almost all the children ask for names of loved ones even when I don't use this prompt. It is a clear indication of the importance of people in children's lives, both socially and academically. Be forewarned: It is a good idea to know the spelling of your students' brothers' and sisters' names before starting this activity, because it is quite disappointing to ask for a sibling's name (indicated by a name sign) and then have the teacher not know how to spell it!

⤗

Kyle sits beside me at the table where I am sitting with my scissors, tape, sentence strips, and markers.

"What's your word today?"

Kyle is past the one-word stage. He gets whole sentences now. In fact, his sentences are usually the longest ones in the class. (At some point, there may be competitions to make the longest sentence, but we are not at that point. When we get there, the students quickly discern that the more friends' names you include in your sentence, the longer it is.) Kyle's use of ASL, however, is usually one- or two-word sentences. His English sentences are long because I expand on his language use, first in ASL, in order to make a sentence that accurately reflects the thought in his head. I must make sure I understand what he means, and in so doing, model for him not only that what people say is supposed to make sense but also that I care about what he has to say—what he thinks about is important enough to record, to tell others, and to reflect upon and remember. In clarifying what he means, I am also able to model ASL that is more complex than what he uses independently and yet is still hopefully within his zone of proximal development.

Today Kyle has a story to tell. He signs:

BIRD CL:holding-cylindrical-object-in hand PECK-at object

The story behind this is not transparent. I want to be sure I understand the complete thought that he intends in such a way that I can express it in coherent English and also model for him ASL that includes referents and background information. By asking him simple questions (e.g., Did you see birds? Where? One or many? What was in your hand?), I can expand the information he carries in his utterance and model back for him both an ASL and an English sentence that will be understood by others. Sometimes, while the student watches, I confer with the aide in the classroom about how to translate the ASL into English. This is an additional way of making the translation process more transparent. Eventually I have learned enough about what he is thinking to model for him:

YOU GO Z-O-O CUP CL:hold-cup FOOD (point to cup) BIRD PECK-at-food-in-cup

Kyle nods, and I tell him it's his turn to sign that.

GO Z-O-O BIRD FOOD CL:hold-cup PECK

I am not looking for him to copy my utterance exactly but to add enough clarity to what he said so that I can write an English sentence. And so I write, "I went to the zoo and a bird ate food from my hand." If I had written "Bird pecks," the important event that Kyle was remembering and reporting would not have been conveyed. I have also seen teachers who write exactly what they see a child sign, without translating it to English; in this instance, they might write, "Go zoo bird food peck." This is not an English sentence, does not capture all that the ASL does, and would not distinguish the two languages for the student.

Kyle takes his sentence strip and sits down at the table with a notebook into which he copies the sentence. When he first started getting words of the day, he simply traced the word using his finger after I wrote it and then read it to a friend. After a couple of months or so, when he seemed dissatisfied with a mere word after telling me entire stories, I began writing down sentences for him and he traced them as well. Since all of the students choose to write on their own during other times of the day, asking them to trace one very personally meaningful word or sentence was a simple way for them to practice letter formation. When they began copying sentences into their notebooks, their letters were written with a precision that other teachers familiar with kindergarten handwriting were surprised to see.

༄

What's important for this activity (and the others as well) is not only the procedure we follow but also the kinds of things we talk about while in the process. When I wrote the sentence as well as when Kyle traced it, I talked about the capital letter at the beginning of the sentence, the spaces between the words, and the period at the end. I told him I was writing it in English. I said, "You saw many birds, so I will write an 's' at the end of this word." "You went to the zoo last April, so I spell *go* like this: w-e-n-t." "You didn't sign I, because you were using ASL, but when I write your sentence in English, I need to write *I*." We might compare the number of signs and the number of words. When students begin Doing Words, I name each letter as I write it. I may show them that the handshape they used in their ASL sign is not the same as the English letter their word starts with. The number of things we can talk about is practically limitless. The students are interested in what I tell them about their sentence because their sentence is important to them. It is theirs.

Students progress from receiving words to trace with a finger, to sentences to trace, to sentences to copy, to sentences written as a horizontal list of words where only the words they don't already have are written for them, to writing sentences and stories on their own. Again, more details are in Katie Johnson's (1987) book.

The final step in Doing Words is to share the words and sentences with the class. In my classroom, we did this as part of Morning Meeting once they had sentences, but when it was one word each, the children, after tracing the word, went immediately and read it to a friend.

MORNING MESSAGE

At the school where I work, each classroom begins the day with a Morning Meeting (in some schools this is referred to as Circle Time). It is a time for the teachers and students to come together and greet one another, share news and announcements, and perhaps complete a group game or activity. It is also a great opportunity for language development. More details about Morning Meeting can be found in Roxann Kriete's (1999) book, *Morning Meeting Book*. I will not repeat that information here but will instead explain how I use the morning message to meet some of my ASL and English goals.

The morning message is ready when the students arrive in the classroom in the morning. Sometimes I use chart paper to write a new morning message every morning, or I may use sentence strip pocket charts to create the message (main-taining the same sentence strips over time for the repetitive parts of the morning message). In a class where students have less experience with English print, the morning message will be short and predictable.

⚜

One morning, the message read:

Good Morning Spring Rabbits!
Today is Monday, April 25, 2005.
Lashawn is first in line.
Today we will go to the Book Fair.
What is your favorite book?

The first line is always the greeting, and throughout the year, the students are exposed to a variety of greetings, both in English print and in ASL: "Good morn-ing," "Hello," "Happy Monday," "Welcome to April," and so on. For the young-est students, I use the same greeting consistently for a while so that they become familiar enough with it to recognize it when they see it again. The second line is always the date. Different formats can be introduced here too, such as "The date is ___/___/___." In my classroom, the third line is always about a classroom job, and again, I tend to use each one for a while. The fourth sentence always begins "Today we will"; this is obviously a sentence with more variety and the least pre-dictability, but I use verbs that are most important for the work students do in school: *make, help, read, write, draw, work, finish, start, go, see, watch,* and so on. This vocabulary will expand as the students experience more, read more, write more, and use expanded ASL vocabulary to talk about their school day. The last sentence requires a response from the students. They draw, write their name, or write a sentence in response to the final sentence, depending on what it asks, and when everyone has had time to do so, we begin Morning Meeting.

The children and I sit on the floor in a semicircle so that we can all see each other. A large piece of paper with the morning message written on it is tacked to the bulletin board next to me. After we greet one another around the semicircle, we read the morning message. Lashawn raises her hand when I point to the third sentence. She visibly sweeps her eyes across the line of print. She signs, hesitantly at first, pausing between the first two words, then more sure as though she is con-fident about this final part: TODAY BOOK F-A-I-R GO WILL.

A second teacher, who is in the classroom with us, watches Lashawn read this sentence and becomes puzzled after Lashawn signs TODAY BOOK.

"She left out the verb," the teacher says.

"She hasn't gotten to it yet; she's doing it in ASL," I explain.

Lashawn reads this way because that's what I've modeled for her and expected her to do. I teach the children to look at the English words, think about what they mean, look away from the print to make eye contact with their audience, and sign the meaning of the English in ASL. I do this by modeling each step, describing what I'm doing, and thinking "out loud" while I try to translate the English into ASL. The morning message is always short and predictable and therefore makes this complex task much more manageable for early readers.

Lashawn successfully read the sentence because she saw the English print, understood the words, and translated the meaning into ASL, using correct syntax and appropriate sign choices. She engaged in a process of translation, making meaning from English print and deciding how to relay the information in ASL. Her knowledge of both ASL and English came into play in this activity. I have taught Lashawn to do this because I want her to be able to use and understand both languages, and I believe that the process of translation requires her to think about each language and create meaning in a way that is both artistic and intellectually rigorous.

⚜

For students who may have prior experience with reading as a recitation of English words, I initially allow them to sign the sentences word for word and then tell them approvingly, "You read all the English words." In this way I acknowledge the skill that they have in recognizing and translating English words to signs. However, I make clear my expectation that reading involves comprehension and translation rather than simply decoding, as well as my expectation that we all use language that others will understand (in this case the other children will understand ASL better than the English) by then asking, "Now can you sign what that sentence means in ASL?" Eventually, students who see and use this process consistently wait to begin signing until they read the entire sentence and understand it. They will also become aware that English and ASL are different and separate languages even though we codeswitch between them frequently.

ASL/English

My first year teaching kindergarten, a speech teacher approached me about team-teaching a weekly structured ASL and English comparison class. This was something she had seen at another school and heard was very beneficial for the students. I immediately agreed, since I believed that students needed to see the similarities and differences between the two languages and to understand that, in fact, they were codeswitching between them when they went from spoken or written English to signed ASL.

We began with one class, just me, my new speech teacher friend, and our eight seven-year-old students. Over several years, it has grown into a schoolwide practice, with either one speech and language teacher or one ASL teacher and the classroom teacher working with groups of students for at least thirty minutes, once or twice a week. Sometimes it serves as an ASL lesson, sometimes more as a reading lesson, sometimes a writing lesson, and occasionally it is more focused on spoken English. In any case, the goals are to use a "one person, one language" approach and to clearly mark ASL as a signed, visual, spatial language, and English as a language that is spoken, speechread, written, and read.

Each week the co-teachers decide on the focus for the week. Sometimes we choose it based on an English structure we want to emphasize; at other times, we are motivated by something we think the students need to work on in ASL. At the very beginning and with the youngest students, we focus primarily on labeling what language we are using based on some key differences. The students learn that the four "rules" of ASL are (a) it uses signs, (b) it uses facial expression, (c) it is "voice-off," and (d) you must make eye contact with the person with whom you are communicating. The English "rules" are that it can be spoken, written, or read. When we first started with the initial group of kindergartners, they mistook the sign ENGLISH for the sign NIGHT, telling me that ENGLISH meant that it was dark outside. (The signs ENGLISH and NIGHT rhyme in ASL; that is, they are signs that differ on only one phonological parameter. Their difference is in the phonological parameter of location; in particular, the point of contact on the dominant hand. In the sign for ENGLISH, the dominant hand clasps the back of the nondominant hand (like two hands resting on the top of a cane, one on top of the other). In the sign for NIGHT, the wrist of the dominant hand rests on the back of the nondominant hand, and the dominant hand is cupped downward.) Now those same students can describe many features of the languages, comparing and contrasting how you can sign or write the same concept in either ASL or English.

A lesson on pronouns for first graders began with all of us in two lines facing each other. We had a pile of photographs of each student and teacher that we began passing through the line. The first person took one picture and pointed to the person it showed. The picture was then passed to the person in the photo, and then that person did the same thing. We went through the entire stack of pictures, and each student pointed either at themselves, the person directly across from him or her, or a third person. The students laughed as we tried to pass the photos quickly and keep track of who we were supposed to be pointing at. When we finished the entire stack, we then discussed how in ASL we sometimes use similar pointing gestures to refer to people. Who would you be talking about if you pointed to yourself? To the person you are talking to? How would you refer to someone who wasn't with you while you were talking? We gave examples of how you would name a person who wasn't with you, and then how you could refer to them again with indexing, or pointing to a particular space, even though the person wasn't there. A student named Nelson decided to demonstrate this for us by "hiding" where we couldn't see him and telling us to tell a story about him.

For the English lesson, we began by playing the same pointing game using written names for all of the participants. When they saw their own name, they pointed to themselves; when they saw the name of the person directly across from them, they pointed to that person, and so on. Lashawn made the connection between pointing to herself and the word *I*, which she and most of the other students already knew. We used this comment to talk about other words we could use instead of names. We introduced cards for *I*, *you*, *he*, and *she*. We made sentences about ourselves and the students using pronouns, and they immediately recognized who the sentences were about: The sentence that said, "He loves trains," could only be about Kyle; one that read, "She has long black hair," was certainly about Maria. We pointed out that in English, there was a different pronoun for talking about a girl or boy. The students took turns making similar sentences using ASL, and we wrote the sentences in English. Finally, we played our game again, using cards with pronouns written on them. The students were able to point to a girl when they read the word *she*, to a boy when they saw *he*, and to their partner directly across from them when the word *you* was on their card. Follow-up lessons involved the children reading sentences in English, signing them in ASL, and replacing names with the correct English pronoun.

Throughout these lessons, the designated ASL person (in this case, myself) led the conversations about ASL, and the designated English person led the conversations about English. Any writing was done by the English person, and both of us modeled thinking about translating when we went back and forth between the languages. The English teacher also used her voice throughout the lesson, and the students were encouraged to either use their voices or make approximate mouth movements as well. When they signed in ASL, they were reminded to turn off their voices and use facial expression where appropriate.

In any team-teaching situation, preparation beforehand is important to make sure that the lesson goes smoothly, with both teachers having the same idea about the lesson and their role. For planning, we think about several questions to guide us:

(1) What is the language feature that we want to teach?
(2) How will we teach it in both languages in a structured way?
    (a) How is the feature used in ASL?
    (b) Do the students already know it and use it?
    (c) How is the feature used in English?
    (d) What do students already know about it?
    (e) Can they understand it if they read it?
    (f) Do they use it in their writing?
(3) How can we contrast the features of the two languages?
(4) How can this structure be highlighted within a meaningful curricular content area and in communicatively interactive ways?
(5) Finally, how will students demonstrate their learning and what will they be accountable for and when?

As the classroom teacher, I focus on whatever structure we have chosen during other times in the classroom. The Morning Meeting question the next morning read, "Who can write some English words we use for talking about people?" In a writing mini-lesson later in the week, I "thought aloud" as I crossed out *Dad* and wrote the word *he* in a sentence about my father. When we read a story after lunch, we talked about whether the author used *I* or *she* to talk about the main character and how, when I read it in ASL, I might switch perspectives. The ASL/English lesson takes place only once a week, but the concepts are reinforced every day.

CONCLUSION

Like all teachers, I often struggle with what to teach, how to teach it, whether what I'm doing is actually helpful, or if the kids are learning everything I want them to (and what else they're learning along the way that I might not intend!). However, these three activities are ones that I almost always feel good about. I love seeing Kyle, Maria, Lashawn, Nelson, and all of the other students I teach talking about language and naming the languages they use. Sometimes one of them will start to read a sentence in English word order and then correct him- or herself, stating, "Oh, I need to translate to ASL." At other times, I may ask the class,

"I'm going to write now. Will I write it the same way I sign it?" They always shake their heads and tell me, "No, you have to write it in English!"

I must admit that the balance in my own as well as most classrooms for deaf students is still weighted more heavily toward instruction in English, and I constantly search for ways to make time for ASL for its own sake. I feel confident, though, that the students I teach also recognize that ASL is an important part of their lives, and they no longer view English as something as mysterious and dark as night.

REFERENCES

Ashton-Warner, Sylvia. 1963. *Teacher.* New York: Simon and Schuster.

Bochner, Joseph H., and John Albertini. 1988. Language varieties in the deaf population. In *Language learning and deafness,* ed. Michael Strong, 3–48. New York: Cambridge University Press.

Gee, James Paul, and Wendy Goodhart. 1988. American Sign Language and the human biological capacity for language. In *Language learning and deafness,* ed. Michael Strong, 49–74. New York: Cambridge University Press.

Johnson, Katie. 1987. *Doing words.* Boston: Houghton Mifflin.

Kriete, Roxann. 1999. *The morning meeting book.* Greenfield, Mass.: Northeast Foundation for Children.

Lane, Harlan, Robert Hoffmeister, and Ben Bahan. 1999. *A journey into the DEAF-WORLD.* San Diego: DawnSign Press.

Long, Michael. 1988. Instructed interlanguage development. In *Issues in second language acquisition: Multiple perspectives,* ed. Leslie Beebe, 115–41. New York: Harper and Row.

Nassaji, Hossein. 1999. Towards integrating form-focused instruction and second language acquisition in the second language classroom: Some pedagogical possibilities. *Canadian Modern Language Review* 55 (3):385–402.

Pica, Teresa. 1994. Research on negotiation. What does it reveal about second language learning conditions, processing, outcomes? *Language Learning* 44 (3):493–527.

Pienemann, Manfred. 1984. Psychological constraints on the teachability of languages. *Studies in Second Language Acquisition* 6 (2):186–214.

Schmidt, Richard. 1990. The role of consciousness in second language learning. *Applied Linguistics* 11:2.

11 | A Bilingual Approach to Reading

Doreen DeLuca and Donna Jo Napoli

Learning to read your native language can range from being a simple task to being enormously difficult. A lot depends on the writing system employed by your country, language, or culture.

Alphabets, excluding manual alphabets, are systems built on a correspondence between single written symbols and single sound segments. The prototype of an alphabet is a system in which every written symbol corresponds to one and only one sound segment and every sound segment corresponds to one and only one symbol. Spanish comes quite close to having such an ideal system. So when a child learns the alphabet and learns what sound segment each symbol corresponds to, the child can then sound out words accurately. As soon as the concept of reading sinks in, the child can fly ahead quickly. The Spanish-speaking child who is reading Spanish does not often stare at a written word and wonder what on earth it sounds like. And spelling bees don't make sense after early elementary school—everyone would win. Of course, there are different varieties of Spanish, and this description, if it took that into account, would be somewhat more complex. But on the whole, this is a representative picture of the situation.

Not all alphabet systems are anywhere near as close to the ideal as that described for Spanish. English, for example, has symbols that are not pronounced (e.g., the letter "1" in *walk*) as well as sound segments that are not represented by any symbol in the word (e.g., the sound [p] that many people insert after the sound [m] in *something*). English allows single symbols to correspond to a range of different sounds (e.g., the letter "s" corresponds to a different sound segment in each of the words *soon, sugar, present*). English allows single sound segments to be represented by a range of different written letters, including, sometimes, a sequence of written letters (e.g., the initial sound segments of these words: *silent, celery, psychiatrist*). The English-speaking child who is reading English does, on occasion, stare at a new word and wonder what on earth its pronunciation might be (think of *cough*). English-speaking countries have spelling bees, and it's hard to be the winner.

Regardless of how close a language's alphabet system comes to a one-to-one correspondence between written symbol and sound segment, reading tends to be mastered in alphabet systems relatively quickly. By the time a child is in fourth grade, chances are reading is no longer a daunting task. Alphabets are amazingly efficient and accessible that way. With just the twenty-six symbols of the Roman alphabet, for example, we can write all the words of the English language—tens of thousands of words.

Another kind of writing system is the character system, such as that used in China. In the prototype of a character system, each written symbol corresponds to an entire word. The character is not analyzable with respect to sounds. So one character that has the [p] sound segment in it may have absolutely nothing in common with another character that has the [p] sound segment in it. The written character corresponds not to the sound of a word, but to its meaning. So when a child faces a new character, that child cannot figure out what it means (there is no chance of sounding out here). Instead, the child must be taught each character. To learn to read 4,000 words, the child must memorize 4,000 characters.

To be sure, character systems, like alphabet systems, differ to varying degrees from the prototype. For example, some have words that are made by superimposing one (part of a) character onto another, particularly when the sense of the result is related to the senses of the two component characters. So if a child knows both of the component characters, he or she might have a chance at guessing somewhat accurately the sense of the new, composite character. Still, learning to read in a character system is a much more difficult task than in an alphabet system. Children continue to learn new characters through high school, and if they go on to the university, that learning continues. It is difficult to give a general statement about when it is likely that a child will have mastered enough characters to read a novel, for example, since countries with character systems vary quite a lot in their educational systems and in their societal attitudes toward those systems—both of which affect the rate of student learning. But you can be sure that reaching this level of competence takes many years longer than in a country with an alphabet system.

There are other kinds of writing systems, such as those in which each symbol stands for an entire syllable—called syllabaries. But it isn't necessary for us to go into them here. Alphabets represent one end of the spectrum and character systems represent the other in terms of ease of learning to read. And our initial look at just these two kinds of systems is enough to help us in our discussion of reading skills with respect to the deaf or hard of hearing person.

If you cannot hear the language, you cannot use sounding out as a method for learning to read in the same way a hearing person can. Therefore, even if the language you are trying to read uses an alphabet, the task for you is largely the same as if that language were written in characters. That is, you are likely to learn each word in the list—*pat, mat, bat, cat,* and so on—separately, as an unanalyzable whole.

Of course there is a meaning breakdown available. For example, once you have learned the word *kind* and the negative prefix "un-" and the adverb ending "-ly," you can look at the new word *unkindly* and figure out its meaning. Roots like *kind*, prefixes like "un-," and suffixes like "-ly" are called morphemes. They are meaning-bearing units. So some figuring out of new words is possible for the child who does not have access to the sounds; in particular, the child can recognize morphemes, break the word down into its composite morphemes, and take a stab at the meaning of the whole word.

Still, the task of learning to read an alphabet system is vastly more difficult for the deaf child than for the hearing child (although there is evidence that some profoundly deaf children develop phonological awareness that helps them in reading, but exactly how they develop this awareness and how they use it is unknown; see Goldin-Meadow and Mayberry 2001). Add to this the fact that for many children who have hearing loss, their native language is not the language they are learning to read, but, instead a sign language. So the child who uses ASL, for example, has the extra burden when learning to read of facing an entirely new language—with an unfamiliar lexicon and an unfamiliar syntax. It would be as though we put a hearing child who spoke English into a Chinese classroom and plopped a book in Chinese, written in Chinese characters, on the desk and said, "Read." Let's make it even more uncomfortable by having this be the child's first experience with reading.

The job of learning to read English is a heavy one for the deaf or hard of hearing child. We have been working on trying to lighten that burden by writing a book of five stories that employs a new method of developing reading skills.

THE CONCEPT OF READING

While writing has served humans well through several millennia, the very concept of reading and writing is sophisticated. A set of written symbols stands for a language. When you think of all the things that language comprises, that idea seems impracticable. Spoken languages, for example, have intonation that can be miraculously nuanced. Sign languages have modulations of movement in signs that can, likewise, be subtle and delicate in their significance. Whoever would have guessed that writing could do such a good job?

Actually, writing doesn't do all that. The reader does. The reader interprets the writing. That's why we can admire one director's production of a drama and perhaps be less enthralled by another's of that same drama. Reading is an activity. It requires energy on the part of the participant. It is an interpretive art.

But that art cannot begin until the reader masters the initial (and surprising) idea that written symbols on a page can convey language. That is task number one.

DIFFERENCES IN THE LEXICON

Clearly, the lexicon of one language is different from the lexicon of another. Since the child whose native language is a sign language is learning to read in a foreign language, she or he must master a new lexicon.

We tend to think that learning a new lexicon is a relatively simple task of memorization. If you want to learn how to say "eat" in Japanese, for example, you look it up in a dictionary or ask a Japanese friend. In fact, however, languages break down information in different ways. While we say "garden" in English for both a flower garden and a vegetable garden, we say "giardino" for the first, but "orto" for the second, in Italian. On the other hand, Italian has the word *bibita*, which covers refreshing beverages, like soda or juices, but not hot drinks or *drink* as in "one needs food and drink to live." There is no single word of English that covers exactly what the word *bibita* covers in Italian.

These same mismatches of the lexicon occur between sign languages and spoken languages. However, they occur in much greater number. That's because of the graphic nature of sign languages. While individual lexical items are rarely truly iconic (witness the fact that people who don't know American Sign Language [ASL] are unlikely to catch even the gist of a conversation in ASL), in the contexts of sentences, predicates can take on a distinctly pictorial nature. That is because signs that connote actions often vary according to who is doing the action or what physical object is being acted upon and even how that actor is acting upon the object.

One such kind of variation is due to the use of classifiers. This is perhaps best understood through exemplification. If a man hurries down the street, the 1 handshape may move quickly along a certain path (where 1 is a classifier for human beings; its use shows that a human is doing the action). If a cat hurries down the street, we may have the same speed and path (i.e., the same movement), but the bent 2 handshape will be used (where bent 2 is the classifier used for animals). If a car hurries down the street, the movement might remain the same but the handshape will change to 3 (the classifier for wheeled vehicles).

Why should 1 indicate humans, bent 2 indicate animals, and 3 indicate vehicles? There seems to be nothing iconic about this at all. Only the speed and path in these predicates seems graphic.

But things can get more complicated. If a woman in high heels hurries down the street, we may well use two hands quickly moving along the path, with the I handshape pointing down and tapping their way along (like the pointed heels of her shoes). If a very fat person hurries down the street, we may well use the dominant hand in a Y shape pointing down and rocking from side to side with or without the upturned palm of the nondominant hand as base as both hands move quickly along the path (showing the waddling nature of the gait). If a clumsy person makes that same action, we could use both hands in the 3 handshape moving like footsteps, but the 3s would be horizontal, that is, in a plane parallel to the ground (whereas for vehicles, the 3 would be in a plane orthogonal to the ground, unless the vehicle falls on its side).

The examples above all involve alteration of the action sign (the predicate) in accordance with the identity or other characteristics of the one doing the action (the agent argument of the predicate). But predicates can vary depending on characteristics of the other participants in the action (i.e., the other logical arguments of the predicate), as well. If a person is carrying something, the predicate CARRY will have a handshape appropriate to the object carried and even to the part of the object that is being touched while it is carried. So the action of carrying a bowl will use a different handshape from that used in carrying a bucket by holding it on the sides, which will be different from that used in carrying a bucket by the handle, and so on.

While all the above are examples of uses of classifiers, there are other ways in which predicates adapt to their logical arguments. If you look up the English word *eat* in an English-ASL dictionary, chances are you will find the sign of a flat

O handshape moving toward the mouth. But, in fact, if the proposition you want to convey in ASL is that a chicken ate, you wouldn't use the sign EAT. Instead, you'd use flat baby O tapping on the upturned palm of the nondominant hand—that is, you'd use the sign PECK. And if you wanted to convey the proposition that a cow ate, you'd have both hands in the A shape, making circles against each other (knuckles to knuckles, base of the palm to base of the palm)—that is, you'd use the sign CHEW-CUD. Different animals eat differently—so a sentence about a snake eating would use a different sign from one about a lion eating, and so on. The eating predicate will be appropriate to the manner in which the particular animal eats. This is because the predicate to a certain extent tries to "draw" (if you will) the eating action in the air.

On the other hand, English has many separate words for semantically related lexical items, whereas often ASL will simply modulate some aspect of the movement of one lexical item in generating the other. For example, English has *chair* and *sit*, two morphologically unrelated words, while ASL has a pair that use the same location, handshape, and palm orientation, but differ only by movement (CHAIR involves two quick taps, while SIT involves one slow movement to a resting contact point).

Additionally, sign languages may exploit polysemy to a greater extent than spoken languages do. So, for example, the word *run* in English can be used in many types of situations that have only a vague semantic similarity (compare: "Her stocking ran" to "His nose ran" to "The child ran" to "He ran the business," and so on). Several relatively low-information verbs have this property. But many more lexical items in sign languages have this property. So the sign WOW, for example, can correspond to the English words *awesome, amazing, struck with something* and so on.

Learning the lexicon of a second language is not just a matter of memorization; it's a matter of understanding how the other language breaks up world information.

DIFFERENCES IN SYNTAX

As we stated above, the syntax of a country's or locale's sign language is independent of the syntax of the country's or locale's spoken language. That's because sign languages arise independently of spoken languages.

Comparing ASL and English syntax, for example, we can find many disparate points. For one, ASL tends to incorporate relative spatial notions into predicates; English tends to use prepositions. So in expressing the proposition that the boy put the cat in the box, ASL might use the sentence

PAST CAT$_i$ BOX$_j$ BOY CARRY$_{i\text{-to-}j}$

This is to be understood as making the sign PAST, then making the sign CAT and indicating a spatial location (which we have designated with the locational index i), then making the sign BOX and indicating a different spatial location (designated by j), then making the sign BOY, then doing the predicate CARRY by having the hands in an appropriate shape to indicate carrying a cat-size animal and moving them from spatial location i to spatial location j, clearly moving downward into the spot j. English might use the sentence

The boy put the cat in the box.

Likewise, ASL tends to incorporate modifiers of the action into predicates; English tends to use modifying phrases. So if we wanted to convey the information that the boy placed the cat carefully in the box, the predicate CARRY could be altered in several ways, including using the nonmanual parameter. One might move the whole torso with the hands/arms from point i to point j, while pursing the lips or forming a tight O with the lips. English would just add the word *carefully* at some appropriate niche in the sentence.

There are other differences between ASL and English syntax besides the lack or presence of prepositions and modifiers of the action, and some of them are made obvious by this same example. The ASL sentence places the predicate in final position; the English sentence places it between the subject and the object. The ASL puts the topic as the first noun phrase—the cat. The English sentence begins with the grammatical subject. While the ASL sentence employs spatial indices, the English sentence employs the definite article *the*. The ASL sentence indicates past by a sign at the start, whereas the English sentence indicates past by inflecting the verb.

Before we go any further, we should point out that these differences are not due to any strangeness of either language. Lots of languages of the world behave very much like English with respect to each one of these particular grammatical characteristics. And lots of languages of the world behave very much like ASL with respect to each one of these particular grammatical characteristics. For example, Japanese is similar to ASL in word order—placing the predicate in sentence-final position and the topic in sentence-initial position. Chinese is similar to ASL in indicating time frame via lexical items ("in the future," "recently," etc.) rather than changes in the verb string.

What do these differences mean to the deaf child learning to read English? Let's look at just one of these differences for a moment—perhaps the one that seems most trivial: the use of definite articles. If you are a native speaker of English, have you ever tried to describe to someone who speaks another language how to use *the*? Why is it inappropriate to walk into a room that has no apples in it and say, "What do you think of the apple?" but fine to say, "What do you think of apples?" Why do you say "I'm going to school" without an article, but "I'm going to the hospital" with an article (at least in American English)? Why can you say "He's the boss" as easily as "He's boss," meaning the same thing? Go ahead; try to account for these data. Simple it isn't.

Likewise, if you are a native speaker of English and you have ever tried to learn to speak Spanish or French or Italian, you have probably had to work hard to learn when it is appropriate to use articles or to leave them out in these languages. And the use of the partitive in French—wow, now that's a tough one to describe. French language teachers can talk themselves into knots trying to explain the differences to American students. Basically, the Americans get a vague idea, but really learn to use the partitive properly only if they wind up being lucky enough to live in a French-speaking area for many months.

In other words, the syntactic differences between languages, even those that seem relatively small, can present a serious puzzle to our incipient reader. And most English sentences are going to be packed with multiple syntactic differences from their ASL counterparts.

So many complex differences thrown at the child at once can be overwhelming. And it is not surprising to find the overwhelmed child defeated at the outset.

OUR APPROACH

We start with a story that is told almost entirely in one-word utterances of English. And we choose words that translate easily into ASL. In other words, we push aside syntax and complications of mismatched lexical items. Under each English word, we give the corresponding ASL sign. In this way, the child can focus on the concept of reading itself while starting to build a lexicon in written English.

Later stories bring in mismatches in the lexicons of the two languages, allowing the child to notice those differences and enjoy them. The child can face the fact that this is part of the job of learning English. And, since both languages are given on the page, speakers of English and signers of ASL alike can develop a sense of respect for the richness of the others' language.

Even later stories introduce sentences, gradually bringing in differences between English and ASL syntax, while remaining careful not to load too many differences into any one sentence or story. The idea is to allow the child to grapple with each difference separately, increasing the child's chance of mastering them.

We also have several positive hooks to help the child learn to read: repetition, rhythm, rhyme, and semantic cohesion.

Many children learn to read by having the same story read to them over and over, so that they memorize the words. They can then figure out the written words on their own, since they know what words have to be on each page. Stories that are easy to memorize, therefore, can be wonderful ignitions for the reading motor. Some of the most effective aids to memorization are repetition and rhyme.

In our first story, both repetition and rhyme are employed in the English words. But repetition and rhyme are also employed in the ASL signs. Here is our first story:

"School Signs"

Ride
bump bump bump

School
jump jump jump

Friends
1 2 3

Trains
A B C

Cookie
yum yum yum

Music
drum drum drum

Dance
feet hands head

Colors
blue green red

Time
jump jump jump

Ride
bump bump bump

The repetition is obvious in both English and ASL, occurring in the second line of the first two couplets, the middle two couplets, and the final two couplets.

We used rhyme consistently in the English to help any hearing child memorize the story, since we are hoping that our method will help not only the deaf and hard of hearing child but also any child whose native language is not English, as they are trying to learn to read English.

The English rhyme does nothing to help the deaf child learn to read, however. The oral rhyme is lost to the child who cannot hear it. And the written rhyme seems equally lost. Indeed, in studies involving reading rhymed and unrhymed words, orthographic rhyme did nothing to enhance the memory of Deaf people when they were asked to recall the words they'd read. Recall on written rhymed words was, in fact, worse than on unrhymed words (Padden and Hanson 2000). This finding should be no surprise, really; Jacoby and Dallas (1981) found that orthographic similarity is not an aid to memory recall among hearing people. In other words, oral rhyme helps the hearing child learn to read—not orthographic rhyme. That's one of the many reasons why reading aloud to hearing children is of vital importance to their developing literacy skills.

ASL rhyme, on the other hand, can help the deaf or hard of hearing child in the task of learning to read. That is, for hearing and deaf or hard of hearing children, it's the phonology pattern that counts.

In a strong rhyme in ASL, three out of the four phonological parameters of handshape—movement, location, and palm orientation—are the same. So our first story is rich in strong rhymes: SCHOOL-JUMP, JUMP-DANCE, FRIENDS-HANDS, 1-2-3 , BLUE-GREEN, as well as RIDE (the nondominant hand)-C.

In a weak rhyme in ASL, two out of the four parameters are the same. So our first story revels in weak rhymes, as well: SCHOOL-COOKIE, JUMP-COOKIE, TRAINS-MUSIC, TRAINS-DRUM, DRUM-A, COLORS-RED, BLUE-B.

Further, as Corina and Knapp (2006) have shown, lexical entries of a sign language are most likely organized and accessed by our memory according to both their semantic and phonological properties. However, the phonological parameters of movement and location exert a stronger influence on the retrieval of signs during language perception or production than do the phonological parameters of handshape or orientation (Corina and Hildebrandt 2002; Dye and Shih 2006). Accordingly, we have used several signs with the same movement, in terms of going in X direction, then in –X direction, then back in X direction. Up-and-down motion is found in SCHOOL, JUMP, DRUM (where each hand does this movement but inverted in time). Sideways back-and-forth motion is found in DANCE, MUSIC, TRAIN. Both up-and-down and back-and-forth movement are found in COOKIE. Likewise, several signs use the location of an upward facing nondominant B hand: SCHOOL, JUMP, COOKIE, DANCE. Several use the (ipsilateral) dominant side of neutral space: 1, 2, 3, A, B, C. Several start from the lower part of the face: COLORS, BLUE, GREEN, RED. Several use the center of neutral space: FRIENDS, TRAINS, DRUM, FEET, HANDS. Two use parts of the nondominant forearm as location: MUSIC, TIME.

Additionally, we have exploited another hook common in works aimed at helping children learn to read: rhythm. Each couplet here has identical rhythm: The first line (which is a single word) is worth one beat; the second line (which is three words) is a duple and a beat, where the duple is in double-time. In other words, this story has a one, one-two-three cadence. This particular rhythm is an old tradition in ASL performances and is used in the famous "Bison Song" (Bahan 2006). The semantics mimics the rhythm. The word of the first line of each couplet is general, introducing a topic. The three words of the second line are either specific, getting into the details of the topic (as in TRAINS, 1 2 3) or are a response to the whole topic (as in COOKIE, YUM YUM YUM). That the final word of the second line of each couplet gets a full beat helps signal to the child that that couplet is ending. The regularity of rhythm matched to the regularity of meaning will, we hope, trigger memory in the same way jump rope songs or marching songs do. ASL storytellers use rhythm as a recall tool; we're now applying it to reading.

The above point about the semantic structure of our story brings us to our final reading hook. As Jacoby and Dallas (1981) have shown, semantics is an even more salient factor in memory recall than phonology. Stories that not only rhyme, but also make sense, are easier to memorize. So, while stories about a cat in the hat who swings a bat may be fun to make up and to read aloud, they are less easily memorized than stories about a cat who found a rat under a mat and that was that. Our first story is built around a day at school. The events are familiar to the point of being almost predictable to the child. Strong semantic connections, as in COLORS-BLUE-GREEN-RED and in DANCE-FEET-HANDS-HEAD, for example, are potent aids to memorization.

CONCLUSION

Reading is a complex activity, and learning to read in a foreign language that you cannot hear is that much more complex. By analyzing the chore, we have been able to try to isolate each subtask and then present the child with reading material intended to help master each particular subtask. Our hope is that these materials will be useful to any child whose native language is not English as that child approaches reading in English.

Additionally, should these materials be used in a classroom in which children with hearing loss have been mainstreamed, the child who knows ASL might well have an opportunity to teach the rest of the class how to sign the ASL properly.

What a lovely position for that child to be in! What a wonderful exchange of culture might take place in those classrooms!

Our first reading book, *Handy Stories,* will be published by Gallaudet University Press in 2008 or 2009, but we hope that teachers and parents will experiment with our approach right away, making up stories for the children they love.

REFERENCES

Bahan, Ben. 2006. Face-to-face tradition in the American Deaf community: Dynamics of the teller, the tale, and the audience. In *Signing the body poetic: Essays on American Sign Language literature,* ed. H-Dirksen Bauman, Heidi Rose, and Jennifer Nelson, 21–50. Berkeley: University of California Press.

Corina, David P., and Ursula C. Hildebrandt. 2002. Psycholinguistic investigations of phonological structure in ASL. In *Modality and structure in signed and spoken languages,* ed. Richard P. Meier, Kearsy Cormier, and David Quinto-Pozos, 88–111. New York: Cambridge University Press.

Corina, David. P., and Heather P. Knapp. 2006. Lexical retrieval in American Sign Language production. In *Laboratory phonology 8: Varieties of phonological competence,* ed. Louis Goldstein, D. H. Whalen, and Catherine T. Best. Berlin: Mouton de Gruyter.

Dye, Matthew W. G., and Shui-I Shih. 2006. Phonological priming in British Sign Language. In *Laboratory phonology 8: Varieties of phonological competence,* ed. Louis Goldstein, D. H. Whalen, and Catherine T. Best. Berlin: Mouton de Gruyter.

Goldin-Meadow, Susan, and Rachel Mayberry. 2001. How do profoundly deaf children learn to read? *Learning Disabilities Research and Practice* 16(4):221–28.

Jacoby, Larry L., and Mark Dallas. 1981. On the relationship between autobiographical memory and perceptual learning. *Journal of Experimental Psychology: General* 110(3):306–40.

Padden, Carol, and Vicki Hanson. 2000. Search for the missing link: The development of skilled reading in Deaf children. In *The signs of language revisited,* ed. Karen Emmorey and Harlan Lane, 435–48. Mahwah, N.J.: Lawrence Erlbaum Associates.

Part Three

American Sign Language in the Arts

12 Body/Text: Sign Language Poetics and Spatial Form in Literature

H-Dirksen L. Bauman

In his *Essay on the Origin of Language,* Jean Jacques Rousseau (1966) speculates that a society might just as well have developed "by the language of gesture alone." If this had happened, Rousseau muses, "We would have been able to establish societies little different from those we have. . . . We would have been able to institute laws, to choose leaders, to invent arts, to establish commerce, and to do, in a word, almost as many things as we do with the help of speech" (9). Rousseau's ruminations lead us to wonder about this gestural society: Although its economic and legal systems may have been "little different from those we have," what about the arts and literature? It seems safe to assume that literature, at the very least, would be quite distinct from that produced by a society of speakers. For starters, there would be no *language* and hence, no *literature* per se, as the terms *language* and *literature* stem, respectively, from the Latin *lingua* (tongue) and *littere* (letter). Much like the term *oral literature, sign literature* is an oxymoron at best and an outcast at worst.[1]

As it turns out, Rousseau's speculations were to come partially true, as formal deaf education had begun to develop in France by the time he had published his essay, a phenomenon that ultimately led to the growth of a Deaf, signing community which produced literary-like performances without recourse to speech or writing. Despite the existence of these signing communities and their literatures, they have gone largely unnoticed in literary criticism. While literary theory has historically turned a deaf ear to sign language, it is now time to turn a Deaf eye toward literary theory and practice. Like adding dye to a specimen to reveal the traces of previously invisible substances, a Deaf lens brings to light the previously embedded traces of phonocentrism in the very designs and definitions of literature. Not

---

1. Despite the original meanings of these terms, however, the past forty years of sign language studies have widened the definitions to account for the validation of signed languages as human languages.

surprisingly, these traces appear everywhere, and are especially pronounced in fundamental aspects of literature such as genre, text, audience, and criticism. Consider, for example, how "voice" infuses the genre of poetry with its foregrounding of the relationship between sound and meaning, or how integral phonetic writing is to the literary "text," or how implicated auditory perception is in the very concept of *audience*. These are but a few phonocentric traces evident in the critical apparatus we have constructed around the phonocentric category of literature.

As it examines the very construction of literature, a Deaf critical lens is bifocal. One focus is the magnification of the phonocentric heritage embedded in literary practice and criticism; the other is more speculative as we look through this theoretical looking glass to imagine what a purely signed literary theory and practice would be. Such speculation is at the very root of theoretical practice. The Greek *theoria* originally meant *a mental viewing, speculation*. Deaf theory insists that it, like the literature it engages, is a visual practice; as such, it both critiques phonocentrism and speculates on the possibility of a literary world created outside its reach.

Clearly one enduring discussion throughout thousands of years of literary history would have been structured differently: This is the question of the relations of the visual, spatial, and literary arts in general and the notion of "spatial form in literature" in particular. Conventional wisdom has described painting as a "spatial art" and poetry as a "temporal art." This commonsense alignment has greatly influenced how we have defined the material and experiential aspects of art and literature. The notion of spatial form, then, is no small matter. As W. J. T. Mitchell (1974) writes, "The concept of spatial form has unquestionably been central to modern criticism not only of literature but of the fine arts and of language and culture in general. Indeed, the consistent goal of the natural and human sciences in the twentieth century has been the discovery and/or construction of synchronic structural modes to account for concrete phenomena" (271). Spatial form, then, may be seen as an explanatory device that allows us to perceive whole structures that elude our immediate and local sensory grasp. Yet spatial form can also be thought of as an experiential phenomenon, as we are bound within space as a fundamental aspect of our being-in-the-world. Thus, when the notion of spatial form arises in literary studies, there is a lot at stake—ranging from the structural whole of literary production, to particular literary texts, to the reader's embodied experience of spatial form within the texts.

This chapter explores the notion of "spatial form in literature" through a Deaf lens. A critique of the current notion of "spatial form" is instructive, for it questions the relations between the fundamental elements of experience—spatiality and temporality—and the literary text and experience. A Deaf perspective on spatial form recovers a poetics of manual-visual language that has long been forgotten, thereby adding new and literal depth and perspective to a discussion of spatial form. The overarching goal of this chapter, then, is to use a Deaf critique of "spatial form" to shed some preliminary light on the emerging practice of a *Deaf literary theory*.

Background: Spatial Form in Literature

Although literary critics have discussed issues relevant to space for centuries, the current notion was branded by Joseph Frank's 1945 essay, "Spatial Form in

Literature" (Mitchell 1974). In this essay, Joseph Frank modernized G. E. Lessing's discussion of the relation between the visual and the temporal arts. In the *Laocoön*, originally published in 1766, Lessing claimed that the arts should stick to what they do best: Painting should paint a picture in space, and literature should tell a story in time.

> If it be true that painting employs wholly different signs or means of imitation from poetry—the one using forms and colours in space, the other articulate sounds in time—and if signs must unquestionably stand in convenient relation with the thing signified, then signs arranged side by side can represent objects existing side by side . . . while consecutive signs can express only objects which succeed each other . . . in time. (Lessing 1962, 91)

The tone here can only be described as "disciplinary" in both senses of the word—painting and poetry should perform their respective tasks within the parameters of their respective disciplines, without getting out of line. Joseph Frank, however, noted that modernist poets and writers like Eliot, Pound, and Joyce were indeed getting way out of chronological line. By breaking away from traditional narrative structure juxtaposing images and fragments, they created texts and images that can better be appreciated in their simultaneity than their sequence. For Frank, *spatial form* means that the author has halted the linear flow of time in favor of juxtaposed, often disjunctive arrangements of events, ideas, words and images. In modernist spatial form, the text becomes a literary version of collage where the reader may focus on the particular arrangement of images or perceive the whole of a text. In short, spatial form becomes another way of saying "anti-temporal."

Frank's notion of spatial form has come under vigorous attack for not being "spatial" per se, but rather a simple metaphor based on parochial notions of time and space. The scale of this critical debate can be measured by the sizeable bibliography on spatial form compiled by Smitten and Daghistany (1981). Amid this critical debate, Mitchell elevated the discussion beyond an attack on Frank to reveal deeper observations concerning spatial form. In his *Spatial Form in Literature: Toward a General Theory*, Mitchell writes:

> Far from being a unique phenomenon of some modern literature, and far from being restricted to the features which Frank identifies in those works (simultaneity and discontinuity), spatial form is a crucial aspect of the experience and interpretation of literature in all ages and all cultures. The burden of proof, in other words, is not on Frank to show that some works have spatial form but on his critics to provide an example of any work that does not. (Mitchell 1974, 273)

In short, Mitchell (1974) continues, "Everything points to the conclusion that spatial form is no casual metaphor but an essential feature of the interpretation and experience of literature" (278).

To begin, Mitchell critiques Lessing's and Frank's assumption that spatial and temporal form are discrete and opposing notions. "The whole notion of 'spatial' versus 'temporal' arts is misconceived," Mitchell (1987) writes, "insofar as it is employed to sustain an essential differentiation within the arts" (98). Indeed, we cannot even conceive of time without reference to space: "The fact is that spatial form is the perceptual basis of our notion of time, that we literally cannot 'tell time' without the mediation of space. All our temporal language is contaminated with spatial imagery: we speak of 'long' and 'short' times, of 'intervals' (literally, 'spaces between'), of 'before' and 'after'—all implicit metaphors which depend on a mental picture of time as a linear continuum" (Mitchell 1974, 274). Thus, as Frank pits spatial form against temporal form, he has artificially separated ultimately inseparable categories.

Further, just as spatial and temporal form cannot be separated, neither can spatial form be separated from any aspect of the production and reception of literary texts. In order to reveal the omnipresence of spatial form, Mitchell identifies four levels in which we can locate it in the experience of literature.

The first level is the "physical existence of the text itself" which is "unquestionably a spatial form in the most nonmetaphoric sense" (Mitchell 1974, 282). Although the text is always spatial because of its ineluctable materiality, some texts foreground their spatiality while others do not. Consider the difference between reading Chinese characters, a concrete poem, and a theoretical essay such as the one you are reading now. Yet even within the standard bearer of written language—linear print within the book—the very materiality of the text has an impact on its reception. What's more, the book is only one conduit for written language; others include baked mud, carved stone, papyrus, flesh, walls, sand, billboards, computer screens, skywriting, and spray paint. Whether we are aware or not, we always read the physical text as a culturally significant artifact.

The second level is what Mitchell (1974) calls the "descriptive" level, where "we attend to the world which is represented, imitated or signified in a work" (283). Picturing the reality represented in the text, Mitchell notes, "is clearly a spatial realm that has to be constructed mentally during or after the temporal experience of reading the text, but it is none the less spatial for being a mental construct" (ibid.). Imagine the differences among the spaces described in William Blake's cosmology, Sherwood Anderson's *Winesburg, Ohio,* or Wallace Stevens's jar on a hill in Tennessee. Although the spaces described by these authors are vastly different, they are all conjured up in the imagination of the reader.

The third level is the structural whole of a text, its architecture from beginning to end. We learn of this spatial dimension of a text early in our literary education as we graph a plot's introduction, rising action, climax, and denouement. Beyond this basic structural skeleton of prose, there are many other ways to conceive of a work as a spatialized whole. Whether an episodic novel, a haiku, a Shakespearean tragedy, or an improvisational slam, a literary work invites its readers or listeners to reflect on the work in its entirety, to sit back as if to see the text's blueprint reveal the underlying pattern. "The search for and momentary imposition of spatial patterns on the temporal flow of literature," Mitchell (1974) writes, "is a central aspect of reading" (284–85).

The fourth level of spatiality is difficult to discuss, Mitchell (ibid.) claims, because it "approaches that point where the interpretation of literature . . . converges with the experience of it" (ibid., 285). When we attempt to articulate the overall significance or meaning of a text, we frequently employ spatiality as a means of organizing our perception. "The familiar pattern in literary criticism— the claim that we do, at least for a moment, 'see the meaning' of a work coupled with our inability to state it in a verbal paraphrase—seems to me a phenomenon that rises out of a spatial apprehension of the work as a system for generating meanings" (ibid.).

By dividing literary experience into these levels, Mitchell's theory stands in contrast to Frank's more limited and specific notion of spatial form, in its search for a "general theory" that seeks to demonstrate the underlying spatiality that allows literature to be able to (literally) take place in the first place. This perspective expands the relevance of spatial form in literature from an isolated feature of modernism to the notion that literature is a particularly rich manifestation of the ways we humans experience the world. Mitchell (1974), then, comes to the conclusion that "the great virtue of perceiving spatial form in literature is not that we can hold up a spiral and say, 'There it is, *The Iliad* in a nutshell!' . . . It is to see the fiction, like the life it criticizes and represents, as an ecosystem, an organism, a human form, or to glimpse what Gaston Bachelard describes as 'the trans-subjectivity of the image,' a language of vision which may tell us things about ourselves and our poems that words alone cannot touch" (ibid., 299).

SPATIAL FORM IN LITERATURE: TOWARD A DEAF THEORY

The following notes toward a Deaf theory of spatial form aim to do just that: to illuminate ways that sign language affords literature a means through which the transsubjectivity of the image comes alive. In such a sign-based world, literary criticism might have been much more in line with Mitchell's approach to spatial form than to Lessing's or Frank's. Mitchell, who has always been attuned to the visual dimensions of literary production, has also written eloquently on the importance of sign language literature, though nearly a decade after he published *Spatial Form in Literature: Toward a General Theory* (Mitchell 1989, 2006). This chapter, then, builds on Mitchell's insights, making his general theory even more general by including sign language literature within the discussion of spatial form. This is not only a matter of adding another language to the discussion but also of adding another modality that allows us to see the relationships between text and space on a (literally) deeper level. Labeling this notion a "Deaf theory of spatial form" does not narrow the focus exclusively to the specific instance of sign language literature, but instead expands it to the whole body of literature as it reconnects discussions of gesture, space, language, and the body to the general notion of all linguistic and literary production.

We may now see that the very shape of the discussion of spatial form brings to light the traces of our phonocentric orientation. Had Lessing been writing in a society that "developed by the language of gesture," he would never have argued for the strict separation of spatial and temporal form, of painting and poetry. Rather, he would have described poetry as using forms in both time and space, for once the hand moves across space, it stitches time into space and space into time. The hand—like anything else for that matter—cannot move except through spatial/temporal displacement. The ensuing debate generated by the *Laocoön* would thus, in all likelihood, never have occurred in a society that used a manual-visual language. We may also presume that centuries later, Joseph Frank would never have called the modernist preference for juxtaposition in lieu of linear narrative "spatial form" per se. Juxtaposition—or the "ideogrammic method," as Ezra

Pound called it—might be described as one variety of a larger body of spatial form, but it would never be construed to mean "anti-temporal."

We must ask, then: What would a theory of spatial form that emerged out of the body of sign language literature look like? And more importantly, would this theory have any bearing on the practice of literature and literary criticism as a whole? In short, could a so-called "Deaf theory" also be a "general theory"? This is no easy question, for the answers could multiply based simply on how one defines *spatial,* not to mention *form* or *sign language literature* or even *in* for that matter. Whose space are we talking about? Are we referring to Newtonian absolute space that is at all times constant, or to Einsteinian space that is at all times relative, or phenomenological space that arises out of the body's interaction with the natural world? Do these spaces have any influence on the literary space of a sign poem? What is literary space, after all?

The default construction of "space" in a traditional sign language poetics has been formalist space, that is, space as a neutral and static constant, a container in which the poem takes place. This container is called "sign space"—a roughly two-by-two-foot cube in front of the body where most signing takes place. Within this cube, signing makes use of space as a formal property of the signed poem (or any signed discourse, for that matter). In the tradition of Clayton Valli's (1990b, 1995, 1996) poetics, space is a central element in sign language "rhymes." Movement paths of signs are described in terms of their *directionality*; palm *orientation* depends on intentional placement of the hands, nonmanual signals are often described as *raised* or *lowered* facial features; and *location* is obviously spatial, but becomes aesthetically important in the overall spatial composition of a text. Space, it appears, is everywhere. It is inescapable.

But is it limited to formal properties of a linguistic text, or is there another level of spatiality operating? Formalist descriptions of space are useful in describing the nuts and bolts and even the mechanics of a poem, but they do not shed light on the sources that make these elements possible in the first place. This chapter extends the notion of spatial form toward a general theory that reveals the spatial and visual-manual components inherent in *poiesis*, which originally meant, simply and profoundly, *to make*. And what is made, if not with the hands? A Deaf critical lens, then, magnifies not only contemporary cultural particularities but also transports us to a poetics of space and motion relevant to literary, poetic, and cultural practices in general.

To begin, we shall follow Mitchell's lead by utilizing his four-level heuristic. However, given such little space to discuss a topic as large as space, this chapter devotes its attention to the first two levels—the "physical existence of the text itself" and the "descriptive space" created by the text. The third level—the structure of the text—may be unique in some ways for sign literature, but not in ways that reveal anything not already touched upon in the discussion of the first two levels. A Deaf lens turned on the fourth, or "hermeneutic," level magnifies the role of the body in the production of meaning and literary experience in general and in particular texts.

The Difference a Body Makes

In the case of a sign poem, the text, of course, is not print on paper but rather a body in motion, either on stage or screen. As a result, Heidi Rose (2006) recognizes, "Sign language literally provides a new *space* for literature to exist." She then asks, "What are the implications of this new space?" (ibid., 131).

The immediate and most striking implication is that the body is not like any other linguistic object in space. The body, unlike a piece of paper, plays a formative role in the understanding and construction of space in the first place.[2] As French philosopher Maurice Merleau-Ponty (1989) recognizes, "[F]or us to be able to conceive space, it is in the first place necessary that we *should have been thrust into it by our body*, and it should have provided us with the first model of those transpositions, equivalents and identifications which make space into an objective system" (142). Here, Merleau-Ponty helps us to see what we overlook in our daily lives: that objective space could only be made intelligible as such through the body's cohabitation with a world of things.[3] The body does not simply move through an objective, absolute space, but is engaged in a deeply collaborative relationship with space. "The space in which normal imitation operates is not, as opposed to concrete space with its absolute locations, an 'objective space' or a 'representative space' based on an act of thought. It is already built into my bodily structure and is its inseparable correlative" (1989, 142). Given this originary projection of spatiality, it seems necessary that a general theory of spatial form be situated at the very site that makes space possible in the first place—its embodied source. In short, "[B]eing is synonymous with being situated" (1989, 252).

This helps to explain Mitchell's contention that spatial form pervades every aspect of literary experience. Mitchell (1974) approaches this notion as he writes, "We must suspect that the most complex and vividly imagined spatial form in literature is finally the labyrinth of ourselves, what Cary Nelson calls the 'theater of flesh' in which 'the verbal space becomes an emblem for the physical structure we inevitably carry with us'. At this point, spatial form of literature becomes the Logos, or incarnate word" (294). While both Mitchell and Nelson allude to the body as the source of spatiality, they do not explicitly state that the physical structure we carry within us is the common element that links together all aspects of spatial form. It appears, then, that the embodiment of spatial form is the most general source of spatiality that Mitchell was looking for in his "general theory." While embodiment is certainly not an exclusively Deaf issue, it is brought into greater focus through a Deaf lens—for the sign language poem is ontologically rooted in the body.

---

2. Keep in mind here that we are focusing on the very physical aspect of the text itself. Clearly, writing on paper—such as a map, linear writing, or hieroglyphics—can have enormous influence over our construction of space. However, for a moment, the discussion centers on the material properties of the text, not on their reception, which will be dealt with below, in the "descriptive" level.

3. Francois Billeter (1990) describes this originally dynamic projection of spatiality: "It is we and we alone who had to find the means of combining our visual impressions devoid of depth with the sense of space we had within us, to synthesize the two and conceive, by an act of imagination, of the existence of a space external to ourselves. Next we had to discover that this imagined external space enabled us to explore the outside world, and that consequently there was a possible equivalence between the space we projected outside ourselves and real external space. The invention of space and the discovery of the world resulting from it are events the memory of which we forget once our 'normal' perception of external reality is ensured, but which for all that leave an indelible mark deep down in our own subjectivity" (140).

Yet, oral and performance poetry are also grounded in the body. Clearly, the body is hyperpresent as performance artist Carolee Schneeman unravels a scroll from her vagina on stage in "Interior Scroll," or as slam poets sweat out their poems in front of raucous audiences, or in the many other ways that oral and performance poets have sought to reconnect the body with the text in search of the kinetics and immediacy of the signifying body. Sign poetry falls directly in line with this oral impulse in contemporary poetry, which, as Jerome Rothenberg (1983) writes, "is deeply rooted in the powers of song and speech, breath and body, as brought forward across time by the living presence of poet-performers, with or without the existence of a visible/literal text" (xiii). Yet while the oral impulse in contemporary poetry seeks to recover the voice's original role in poetry, the sign poet may be seen as recovering an even deeper and originary aspect of human language: *gesture*.

If "being" is synonymous with being situated in space, then gesture becomes a primordial means of claiming and designating our place in the world. Merleau-Ponty (1989) refers to the "initiating gesture" as that "which endows the object for the first time with human significance" (194). He continues, "Moreover, significances now acquired must necessarily have been new once. We must therefore recognize as an ultimate fact this open and indefinite power of giving significance—that is, both of apprehending and conveying a meaning—by which man [sic] transcends himself towards a new form of behavior, or towards other people, or towards his own thought, through his body and his speech."[4] As it mediates between the world of nature and of human meaning, the gestural component of language, according to Merleau-Ponty (1989), "*is* the subject's taking up of a position in the world of his meanings. The term 'world' here is not a manner of speaking: it means that the 'mental' or cultural life borrows its structures from natural life and that the thinking subject must have its basis in the subject incarnate" (193). We humans claimed space as our own through gesture, opening up a hermeneutic space in which meaning could hang its shingle.

As recent research (Corballis 2002; Armstrong, Stokoe, and Wilcox 1995; Stokoe 2001; Armstrong 2002; Armstrong and Wilcox 2007) has shown, it is likely that it was the hand and gesture that, quite literally, pointed the way toward being human through the use of symbols. "An arbitrary social convention is necessary to link vocal sounds to meanings," writes William Stokoe (2001), "and unless it was supernaturally established, such a convention could only have arisen after gestures and their meanings provided a set of paired forms and meanings for vocalizations . . . to represent" (227). Stokoe notes that the primary spatial distinctions—"in front of/behind, near/far, over/under, in/out . . . enter/emerge, arrive/depart, stay/leave"—are "most clearly, directly, and efficiently expressed not by the words of any spoken language but by visible gestures. The conclusion is inescapable: not only language but thought as well is firmly based in movement and vision" (unpublished ms.). When rudimentary gesture—and its syntactic elaboration, sign language—is understood as our primordial means of coming to

---

4. While Merleau-Ponty refers specifically to speech here, it is clear within the wider context of his chapter "The Body as Expression, and Speech" in *The Phenomenology of Perception* that speech is endowed with a wider meaning referred to as the "gestural sense"— in which the whole body is constantly "speaking."

language, the notion of spatial form expands to encompass the spatial nature of Being itself. Gesture leads to sign language and, thus, to the mental grasping of space, of carving out a place in which being may actually take place.

From this perspective, sign poetry is not a newcomer to the field of literature, but rather a primordial means of enacting the body's existential relation to language and space. We are now in the neighborhood of a more original notion of *poiesis*. The visual-manual modality was lurking, hidden and banished outside the domain of poetics, philology, and linguistics through the epoch of the voice. But now that sign language poetry has barged in, we may find ourselves in a more primordial contact with our being-in-the-world.

Take, for example, the deceptively simple poem "Hands" by Clayton Valli (1990; **clip 12.1**). The poem opens with a simple but enormous question: HANDS: WHAT? Indeed—hands: what *are* they? As Frank Wilson (1999) has shown so well, the story of the hand is epic when placed in the context of our evolutionary history—its connection with the brain, our survival, and our day-to-day living. (Think quickly: What have your hands done that enabled you to read these words?)

After asking, HANDS: WHAT? Valli uses the same 5 handshape to create the images of snow falling, flowers blooming, grass waving, leaves falling. After the leaves fall, he gathers these images together through a circular gesture and then ends the poem by offering these gathered images to the viewer through the sign EXPRESSION, which extends the hands from the body, the heart out into space, opening like a delta into a vast ocean of space.

Clearly, this is a Deaf poem as it calls particular attention to manual-visual languages and to the dexterity of the hand that may conjure imagery of the four seasons. As Lon Kuntze, the narrator of Valli's *Selected Works* (1995), explains, these images of cyclical perfection are also images that do not rely on sound to be understood. Hence, deafness and sign languages are associated with natural rather than pathological imagery. There is little doubt about the intentional connection between images of natural perfection and deafness.

Yet a phenomenological reading of space encourages us to follow the implications of this interpretation a step further: If sign language and deafness are natural, then this calls for a fundamental rethinking of "natural." Common (i.e., phonocentric) wisdom cannot fathom deafness-as-natural. And yet, it is Deaf people who have revealed a deeper understanding of the very nature of language—that it relies on deep neuroanatomical patterning rather than on any particular material or modality—that is, speech. In this light, Valli's question, HANDS: WHAT? is indeed a Deaf question, but it is not exclusively a Deaf question; it is also a human question. Indeed, what are the hands, anyway, and what can we learn about them from those who use them as their primary means of expression? An answer to Valli's question can be found in Martin Heidegger's Parmenides: "Man [*sic*] himself acts [*handelt*] through the hand [*Hand*]; for the hand is, together with the word, the essential distinction of man. . . . The hand sprang forth only out of the word and together with the word. Man does not 'have' hands, but the hand holds the essence of man, because the word as the essential realm of the hand is the ground of the essence of man" (80). In this light, we may see Valli's short poem as a quick reverie on the poetic potential of the hands and the nature of human beings and their language.

A Deaf theory of spatial form, then, magnifies the role of the hand in making meaning and poetry, invoking an originary *poiesis*. While the Deaf bard has ironically been banished from the domain of poetry, it is the Deaf bard who uses the very medium that may have signaled our way toward being human as we know it.

Co-embodiment of the Poetic Image

Now that the notion of embodiment of space has been addressed, we are better able to discuss the second level, that of descriptive space within a three-dimensional language. When we see Ella Mae Lentz conjure up a dew-speckled spiderweb, or Debbie Rennie enact the gunning down of a mother and child, or Peter Cook paint a falcon, a sun, and leaves, we witness performers given over to a spatiality other than that of the stage or screen. This is due, in large part, to the poet's ability to project clear images; yet this is only the beginning, for the viewer must also engage the image, making spatial sense of it. This level of descriptive space, then, is only possible insofar as it is a collaborative event, resulting in what was mentioned earlier as Bachelard's "transsubjectivity of the image."[5]

As a sign language poet's ability to convey clear images is a key element to a rich poetic experience, the sign poet must be in command of space; she must, unlike the written poet, be an actor, able to create a clear presence of space on stage. In his instructions to actors, Hollis Huston (1992) writes:

> To create a space that isn't here, you must see it, playing your eyes over its contours, its attractive points and trade routes. . . . If you see it, so will the spectator; if you lose sight of it, so will he. There is no hiding your mind, they see what you see, as you see it. . . . [T]he space may be smaller than your body, as wide as the world—the choice is yours, but you must, you will choose. Anyone can be at the mercy of space. Only a performer can take responsibility for it (68).

Like the actor, the sign poet assumes responsibility for space largely by seeing it, by living inside her own projection of it. This is a skill inherent in everyday sign discourse, as eye gaze holds crucial grammatical function; but in sign poetry, eye gaze also serves a heightened, more dramatic function that reveals a particular being-in-the-world in a particular space and time.

Consider, for example, Ella Mae Lentz's performance of Clayton Valli's "Dew on Spiderweb" (Valli 1995; **clip 12.2**). Lentz effectively brings to life the image of a dew-speckled spiderweb whose droplets shimmer in the moonlight. The image gains such a palpable existence as Lentz's eyes see it, and through this seeing, she calls the image into being. What the audience actually sees, then, is not so much this or that particular handshape, movement path, or palm orientation, but rather another body in the presence of an image. We see Lentz

---

5. The term *transsubjectivity* may imply identical images on the part of the poet and viewer, which may be misleading—for clearly they could not be fully identical. Perhaps the term *heterosubjectivity* of the image may be more accurate, implying a heterogeneous set of perspectives on the same image. As a nod toward Gaston Bachelard, whose thoughts are informative throughout this chapter, I have opted to keep *transsubjectivity*.

seeing an image, and we come as close as possible, though in face-to-face reversal, to sharing this image.

If we avoid the tendency to quantify and classify and instead grant the constitutive role that the poetics of body-space plays in sign poetry, we find it necessary to redefine the cornerstone of poetic experience: the image. In the dramatic realm of sign space, we experience the image as an event occurring as the performer is in the thrall of an image, projecting a clear physical topography of the imagination that beckons the viewer inside. This drama of spatial projection is so clearly communicated because it awakens and overlaps with the viewers' own experiences of spatiality embedded in their particular bodies. Indeed, the performer cannot go it alone; the poem is not complete until it is received by the viewer, who lends it the depth of her own spatial being in the world. "The crucial thing is the viewer's action," observes Francois Billeter (1990), who applies Merleau-Ponty's phenomenology to a type of viewer-response criticism for Chinese calligraphy: "On the simplest level, it is the viewer who gives body to the calligraphic element, who makes of it an object standing in a space which has depth. It is he who gives body to the character, who perceives it as a whole organized according to the laws of gravity and balance, because he projects on to it the intuitive knowledge that his body proper has of these laws" (203).

The viewer's action in perceiving a sign poem is similar, but not identical, to this process. In sign poetry, the viewer does not give body to a written text, but to another body, which is a very different phenomenon. As Merleau-Ponty (1993) describes, bodies share a unique intersubjective understanding:

> It is precisely my body which perceives the body of another person and discovers in that other body a miraculous prolongation of my own intentions, a familiar way of dealing with the world. Henceforth as parts of my body together comprise a system, so my body and the other person's are one whole, two sides of one and the same phenomenon, and the anonymous existence of which my body is the ever-renewed trace henceforth inhabits both bodies simultaneously. (353–54)

While this is true of any two bodies and their mutual combination, it is especially true of spectators of the signifying body.

> The communication or comprehension of gestures comes about through the reciprocity of my intentions and the gestures of others, of my gestures and the intentions discernible in the conduct of other people. It is as if the other person's intention inhabited my body and mine his. The gesture which I witness outlines an intentional object. This object is genuinely present and fully comprehended when the powers of my body adjust themselves to it and overlap it. (Merleau-Ponty 1989, 185)

The two sides of sign poetry—the performing body and the viewing body—together create the textual event. When the image is originally projected from a visual, spatial, kinetic, and kinesthetic body/text, the viewer's body understands what it means to inhabit particular spatial images. The space of the text emerges through a dialectic exchange, projected initially from the body of the poet to the body of the viewer and then back onto the collaborative body/text. This trans-subjectivity may also be called the *cohabitation of sign space*.

Because viewers play such an integral role, sign theory should not focus exclusively on the poems themselves, but should also be mindful of viewing practices. Sign poems are not so much read or seen as they are lived in from the inside. Any theory of spatial form would therefore be incomplete if it did not address the viewers' projection of their own spatiality onto the text. The performer and the viewer, then, may be said to co-project sign space, a phenomenon similar to what Gaston Bachelard calls the "transsubjectivity of the image."

Conclusion: Turning a Deaf Lens on Literary Theory

We may now summarize a few points that begin to chart a phenomenological theory of spatial form in (sign) literature. First, we should enhance our conception of space beyond a constant area in which signs take place; we should recognize that space is a co-creation of the body and its flexible, perceptual field, projected by the performer and the viewer. Second, we should perceive that space, time, vision, and movement are inextricably bound, that they can only be revealed through the other, a synthesis foregrounded by the depth of sign space. Third, we should grasp space at its source, noting that the very nature of our Being is predicated on spatiality. Finally we must acknowledge that gesture and its linguistically elaborated form, sign, play a fundamental role in the designation of our being-in-the-world. We may therefore look toward sign poetry as a means of enacting our primordial contact with language, space, and the body. While Mitchell expands the parameters of spatial form into a wider condition that permeates literature, we may now extend these parameters even further to encompass what Mitchell was looking for all along: the common element of the varieties of spatial form.

Recognizing this more general nature of spatiality brought to the fore through widening literature to include sign languages should have us pay attention to a wider variety of poetic expression. Mitchell (1974) notes that literary studies has, for some time, not paid enough attention to the spatial dimensions of literature, a result of the misalignment of poetry as a temporal art and painting as a spatial art.

> Instead of Lessing's strict opposition between literature and the visual arts as pure expressions of temporality and spatiality, we should regard literature and language as the meeting ground of these two modalities, the arena in which rhythm, shape, and articulacy convert babbling into song and speech, doodling into writing and drawing. At the moment the arbitrary ludic, anti-iconic aspect of language would seem to have the upper hand in literary criticism, with vision and spatial form treated as "merely metaphoric" aspects of literature, the imbalance cannot persist indefinitely in the face of the mounting evidence that consciousness is not simply a stream of verbal language accompanied by inchoate, formless feeling. At least half our brain is occupied in systematic thinking based in spatial forms that organize consciousness at the level of basic perception (Gestalten), conceptual patterns (Ideas), and poetic structures (images). (297–98)

What Mitchell describes here is a clear consequence of our phonocentric heritage. Perhaps the growing recognition and interest in American Sign Language studies and sign poetry may help to tip the scales back toward a visual, spatial, kinesthetic modality. As sign language is as natural an output of the human language mechanism as oral language, it is only a matter of time before the dam will well up and overflow with the pent-up poetic energy of the signing body. We are now beginning to see the manual *poiesis* emerge from the Deaf community. We thus stand at a moment in literary history in which we may witness the desegregation of literary modalities and the reincorporation of sign and gesture into the body of language.

REFERENCES

Armstrong, David. 2002. *Original signs: Gesture, signs and the sources of language.* Washington, D.C.: Gallaudet University Press.

Armstrong, David, and Sherman Wilcox. 2007. *The gestural origin of language.* Oxford: Oxford University Press.

Armstrong, David, William Stokoe, and Sherman Wilcox. 1995. *Gesture and the nature of language.* New York: Cambridge University Press.

Bachelard, Gaston. 1964. *Poetics of space,* trans. Maria Jolas. Boston: Beacon.

Billeter, Jean Francois. 1990. *The Chinese art of writing.* New York: Rozzoli International.

Corballis, Michael. 2002. *From hand to mouth: The origins of language.* Princeton, N.J.: Princeton University Press.

Frank, Joseph. 1963. *The widening gyre: Crisis and mastery in modern literature.* New Brunswick, N.J.: Rutgers University Press.

Heidegger, Martin. 1982. *Parmenides,* trans. Andre Schuwer and Rochard Rojcewicz. Bloomington: Indiana University Press.

Huston, Hollis. 1992. *The actor's instrument: Body, theory, stage.* Ann Arbor: University of Michigan Press.

Lessing, Gotthold Ephraim. 1962. *Laocoön: An essay on the limits of painting and poetry,* trans. Edward Allen McCormick. Indianapolis: Bobbs-Merrill.

Merleau-Ponty, Maurice. 1993. *The Merleau-Ponty aesthetics reader: Philosophy and painting,* ed. Galen Johnson. Evanston, Ill.: Northwestern University Press.

———. 1989. *The phenomenology of perception,* trans. Colin Smith. London: Routledge.

Mitchell, W. J. T. 1974. Spatial form in literature: Toward a general theory. In *The language of images,* ed. W. J. T. Mitchell, 271–99. Chicago: University of Chicago Press.

———. 1987. *Iconology: Image, text, ideology.* Chicago: University of Chicago Press.

———. 1989. Gesture, sign, and play: ASL poetry and the Deaf community. *MLA Newsletter* 21(2) (Summer):13–14.

———. 2006. Preface: Utopian gestures: The poetics of sign language. In *Signing the body poetic: Essays in American Sign Language literature,* ed. H-Dirksen L. Bauman, Heidi Rose, and Jennifer Nelson, xv–xxiii. Berkeley: University of California Press.

Rose, Heidi. 2006. The poet in the poem in the performance: The relation of body, self, and text in ASL literature. In *Signing the body poetic: Essays in American Sign Language literature,* ed. H-Dirksen L. Bauman, Heidi Rose, and Jennifer Nelson, 130–96. Berkeley: University of California Press.

Rothenberg, Jerome. 1983. Pre-Face. In *Symposium of the whole: A range of discourse toward an ethnopoetics,* ed. Jerome Rothenberg and Diane Rothenberg, xi–xviii. Berkeley: University of California Press.

Rousseau, Jean Jacques. 1966. Essay on the origin of languages. In *On the origin of language: Two essays,* trans. John H. Moran and Alexander Gode, 1–74. Chicago: University of Chicago Press.

Smitten, Jeffrey R., and Ann Daghistany, eds. 1981. *Spatial form in narrative*. Ithaca, N.Y.: Cornell University Press.

Stokoe, William. 2001. *Language in hand: Why sign came before speech*. Washington, D.C.: Gallaudet University Press, 2001.

———. A long perspective. Unpublished manuscript.

Valli, Clayton. 1990a. The nature of a line in ASL poetry. In *SLR 1987: Papers from the Fourth International Symposium of Sign Language Research*, ed. W. H. Edmondson and F. Karlsson, 171–82. Hamburg: Signum.

———. 1990b. *Poetry in motion*. VHS. Burtonsville, Md.: Sign Media.

———. 1995. *ASL poetry: Selected works of Clayton Valli*. VHS. San Diego: Dawn Pictures.

———. 1996. Poetics of ASL poetry. In *Deaf studies IV: Visions of the past, visions of the future, conference proceedings, April 27–30, 1995*, 253–63. Washington, D.C.: Gallaudet University Press.

Wilson, Frank. 1999. *The hand: How its uses shape the brain, language, and culture*. New York: Vintage.

13 | Tree Tangled in Tree: Re-siting Poetry through ASL

Michael Davidson

At a conference on disability studies, Simi Linton spoke about Casey Martin, the golfer who was denied access to the PGA national golf tour because, as someone with a mobility impairment, he needed to ride in an electric cart. As Linton pointed out, Martin's disability is not located in the game of golf—which he plays spectacularly—but in the rules by which golf tournaments are conducted. This prompted Linton to meditate on the seemingly unproblematic meaning of institutions and activities when they are limited to an able-bodied individual. The big question, she mused, is: "What is the game of golf?"[1] This is a not insignificant issue because it forces us to reevaluate impairment not from the standpoint of a physical condition but from the environment in which that condition gains meaning. Is golf radically different when it is played by someone who rides rather than walks from tee to tee?

The same question could be asked of poetry when it is regarded from the perspective of poets who utilize American Sign Language (ASL)—for whom poetry is no longer governed by the voice, page, or writing. Although poets often describe their work as emanating from the body and voice, these tropes mean something quite different when literalized by poets who sign their poems by and on the body and whose voice is removed from some interior space of the body and represented on its surface. When Walt Whitman (2002) claims that "my voice goes after what my eyes cannot reach," he suggests a metaphoric expansion of poetry beyond its phenomenological origins and extended through the medium of print.[2] But when Peter Cook of the Flying Words Project sends language "around the world" by throwing the fingerspelled letter L into space, language ceases to be a metaphor for extension and becomes, visibly, a "flying word" in space (Flying Words Project n.d.). On the model of Linton's golf metaphor, we

---

1. Linton's talk, along with the entire conference proceedings, was published in *PMLA* as "What Is Disability Studies?"

2. Whitman's remark occurs in section 48 of "Song of Myself."

might ask the big question, "What is poetry?" When considered from the stand-point of sign language, and more particularly for our own era, what is modernist poetry when its ocularcentrism is re-sited through sign?[3]

This latter question requires some contextualization. At the level of cultural production, ocularcentrism is manifested in the retinal aesthetics of modernist art. Cubism, Futurism, Constructivism, and Fauvism all have, at their core, a critique of single-point perspective in place since the early modern period. Post-Impressionist work in its various modalities fractures the unity of the object as well as the (presumed) perspectival integrity of the viewing subject. Literary counterparts to the visual arts—Imagism, Vorticism, Objectivism—emphasize visual clarity and economy against the expressivism and rhetorical abstractions of late Romanticism. The various metaphors for modernist distanciation, whether via Ezra Pound's ideogram, T. S. Eliot's objective correlative, Louis Zukofsky's object "brought to a focus," or Gertrude Stein's filmic repetition—privilege the eye in poetry as a way of achieving, as Pound said, "an intellec-tual and emotional complex in an instant of time" (Pound n.d., 4).

Such emphasis on the visual is reinforced by what Joseph Frank has called "spatial form" in modern literature. According to Frank, modernist literature as-pires to the condition of the visual arts by creating the illusion of a simultaneous apprehension—as though the entire work could be read all at once. Whether in Joyce's or Eliot's use of myth, Proust's epiphanic moments, or Woolf's stream-of-consciousness narration, modernist formal innovation jettisons linear, develop-mental narrative in favor of a "space logic" of simultaneity (Frank 1963, 13). Frank's ahistorical reading of modernism is, of course, symptomatic of New Critical formal values which, in an attempt to repudiate more biographical or his-torical contexts of literature, place emphasis on the literary work as a "verbal icon" (William Wimsatt) or symbol (I. A. Richards) or "miraculist fusion" of disparate particulars (John Crowe Ransom).

The "space logic" of modernism is a local version of a much larger epistemo-logical break within social modernity in which knowledge, far from being a disin-terested arena, is aligned with forms of power based on sight. Michel Foucault notes that within modernity, from the seventeenth century on, the body becomes increas-ingly governed and scrutinized through forms of "bio-power," those technologies and institutions that taxonomize and discipline bodies. With bio-power, the optical is invested with an ability to govern and control quite apart from its relation to the senses. Late-nineteenth-century sciences of statistics or eugenics or comparative anatomy and institutions such as the modern penal system or the asylum partici-pate in making the body visible for purposes of measurement and control. While it is tempting to find alliances between the institutions of bio-power and the racial politics of Pound, Marinetti, or Eliot, it is equally possible to see their verbal experi-mentation as a repudiation of the panoptical qualities of modern urban life.

Disability scholars have understood how Foucault's critique of bio-power relates significantly to persons with physical or cognitive impairments.[4] Shelley

---

3. Surveys and analyses of modernist ocularcentrism can be found in Levin (1993) and Jay (1993).

4. For a thorough treatment of Foucault's relationship to disability studies, see Tremain 2005.

Tremain (2005) refers to the "asylums, income support programs, quality of life assessments, workers' compensation benefits, special education programs, regimes of rehabilitation, parallel transit systems, prostheses, home care services, telethons, sheltered workshops, poster child campaigns, and prenatal diagnosis" by which bio-politics makes people with disabilities visible (5–6).

Many Deaf poets and storytellers make the institutionalization of oralist education, the historical attacks on sign language, and the (presumed) linkage between deafness and mental illness a centerpiece of their work. In one of their works, "I Am Ordered Now to Talk," Peter Cook and Kenny Lerner of the Flying Words Project compare the repression of sign language by oralist educators to an act of lobotomy. Their performance elaborates on a popular conflation of *deaf* with *dumb,* in every sense of the term, for which the historical incarceration of poor and indigent deaf persons in asylums was often a social remedy. The disciplining of deafness has had national implications as well. As Douglas Baynton (1996) and Jane Berger (2005) have pointed out, post–Civil War oralist education in the United States was directly tied to projects of national consolidation and citizenship. Deaf individuals, who in the antebellum period had created communities around residential schools in which ASL was encouraged, were now subjected to disciplinary action for using sign language. Manual signing became the visible representation of a deaf citizen's linguistic—and presumably characterological—deviance that had to be coerced back into the national fabric. In this respect, deaf persons joined Native Americans, immigrants, and ex-slaves whose visibility as noncitizen subjects was monitored by epidemiological and medical discourses.

MAN SEES HORSE: THE FLYING WORDS PROJECT[5]

Having rehearsed two dimensions of modernist ocularcentrism, one aesthetic and the other sociohistorical, I want now to look at recent poets who utilize ASL's relationship to the visual to elaborate a politics of space and, in the process, critique hearing culture by representing—and satirizing—its presumptive claims on normalized identity. Among the foundational documents of modernism, Ezra Pound's rendering of the sinologist Ernest Fenollosa's essay on the Chinese written character occupies an especially privileged position. When Pound encountered Fenollosa's work in 1913, he used it to break with what he took to be a Western, rationalist epistemology. By adopting Fenollosa's (now discredited) theory of the Chinese character as a method for poetry, Pound was able to launch a number of poetic projects, including his theories of Imagism and Vorticism, and the historical methodology of *The Cantos.* What was particularly valuable for Pound in Fenollosa's essay was its emphasis on the visual character of the ideogram, its ability to fuse both temporality (the characters map a sequence of actions) and space (the character combines several discrete images) in a single sign. The Chinese character, according to Fenollosa, joins radicals into a compound or cluster that maintains connections to concrete objects yet permits a dynamic movement

---

5. After writing this chapter, I discovered Jim Cohn's excellent study of disability, *The Golden Body: Meditations on the Essence of Disability* (2003), which features a chapter titled "Sun Tangled in Sun: Disability Freedom in the ASL Poetry of Peter Cook and Kenny Lerner."

FIGURE 1. "Man Sees Horse."

among them. Verbal language is based on an arbitrary relationship of word and thing, whereas Chinese pictorial language retains the image of the thing in the character, much as, in acoustic terms, onomatopoeia imitates natural sounds. When several characters are placed side by side, the visual, spatial properties of the objects are retained while permitting each to resonate with the other. As Fenollosa says, "A true noun, an isolated thing, does not exist in nature. Things are only the terminal points, or rather the meeting points, of actions, cross-sections cut through actions, snapshots" (Fenollosa 1936, 10).

To show how the ideogram provides a "vivid shorthand picture of the operations of nature," Fenollosa (ibid., 8) uses two phrases to illustrate his point. In the first, "Man Sees Horse," each character emphasizes dynamic, forward movement (ibid.). The character for "man" shows two legs striding forward; the character for the verb "sees" features an eye walking on legs; "horse" depicts the animal with four legs. Unlike the written English sentence, the Chinese characters contain the idea of movement in each visual figure rather than distributing various functions among the alphabetic symbols. The man who observes the horse is linked to the animal not merely through grammatical relations (subject, verb, object) but also by shared placement and physical properties; the eye literally *walks* toward the horse. Fenollosa (1936) summarizes his second example, "Sun Rises [in the] East," as "The sun . . . on one side, on the other the sign of the east, which is the sun entangled in the branches of a tree" (ibid., 33). The middle sign, "rises," combines both: the sun rising above the horizon plus the trunk-line of the tree-sign. "East" ceases to be an abstract position on the compass but is concretized in an image of the sun seen through trees in the morning. Pound adapted this principle of layered images in the construction of much larger poetic units, juxtaposing one concrete image with another without transitions or connectives. It is ironic that the most characteristic feature of modernist poetry in English—an extended

FIGURE 2. "Sun Rises [in the] East."

montage of disconnected elements—was, in part, derived from a misreading of Chinese written language in order to suit a visualist imperative.

Dirksen Bauman (1997) notes that Pound's experiments with the Chinese character hint at a "phantom limb phenomenon where writers have sensed language's severed visual-spatial mode and went groping after it" (316). What would happen, he continues, if the "deaf poet had been mythologized as the blind poet has been; would literature have developed differently?" Perhaps with this question in mind, Bauman challenged Peter Cook and Kenny Lerner, the Flying Words Project, to translate some of Fenollosa's phrases into ASL, and the result is a sequence of transformations of the sinologist's core phrases (**clip 13.1**). Lerner and Cook's often droll response is perhaps not what Bauman had in mind when he suggested this translation project, but their performance highlights something important about the ways that signing poets re-site or resituate poetry in the act of reciting it. At one level, Cook, who is deaf, attempts to respond as accurately as possible to the phrases that his hearing partner gives him, an intention signaled by his adoption of a Zen-like pose of concentration before beginning each translation. At another level, however, he extends the logic of Fenollosa's project by generating new phrases out of minimal examples in an increasingly chaotic semiotic package, all the while using Lerner as the hearing straight man who assigns the translation tasks. From "Sun Tangled in Branches of Tree" or "Man Sees Horse" Cook signifies on the act of translating, taking on its darker associations with "traduce" and "violate" by following out the surreal logic of each sign and by performing his own variations on Lerner's words. If the point of Fenollosa's example is to unite subject and object through the visual image, then that unity is vividly realized in a poet who is himself both the producer and text of his poem.

Take, for instance, the first example: "Sun Tangled in Branches of Tree":

A tree in the early morning sun,
As the sun nears the branches
It burns down the whole tree,
And the sun moves across the sky.[6]

In English, we hear the subordinate phrase "as the sun nears the branches" as referring to the sun seen through leaves. Cook literalizes the phrase, collapsing observer and object in the signs for SUN and TREE, both of which feature the right arm raised vertically. Cook "hears" the verb *nears* as meaning that the tree literally approaches the sun, a proximity that Cook reinforces by allowing his right

---

6. This series can be seen on The Flying Words Project's collected videos, *The Can't Touch Tours: Current Works (1990–2003)*. Lacking a printed version of the poem and relying on Lerner's spoken version of it, I have created my own lineation based, admittedly, on English syntactic patterns. This raises the interesting question of what constitutes the "line" in ASL poetry and whether it can be mapped onto print. Clayton Valli (1990a) has attempted to relate ASL poetry to traditional English versification, finding in the repeated patterns of handshapes an equivalent to traditional English lines. However important Valli's thesis, it is based on a rather traditional, blank verse model (indebted, no doubt, to his own affection for Robert Frost) and does not deal with the manifold differences between patterns in manual signing and in English prosody.

hand to sign TREE while his left gradually brings the SUN sign closer and closer to the tree until the tree is figuratively "burned down." Cook transfers SUN to his right hand and moves it to his right while the flickering embers of the TREE continue to burn.

When the same phrase is rendered a second time, the absurd logic that links "tangled" with "burned down" goes through an even more extreme variation:

Sun in early morning sun.
As the sun approaches the sun
The sun burns down the sun
And the sun drifts across the sky.

Here the sign TREE has been replaced (burned down?) by the sign SUN, leading to the cosmic, comic collision of two suns. By mapping ASL signs onto Chinese ideograms, by combining handshapes for TREE and SUN, Cook is able to generate novel meanings while retaining the principle of homology and repetition that animates Fenollosa's essay.

In his second example, "Man Sees Horse," Cook builds on the supposed difference between subject and direct object in English. In variation number one, the poem is straightforward: "walking person sees horse through fence." In variation two, the seeing man becomes a "rubber necked man" whose head stretches through a fence to see the horse. In variation number four, a "rubber-eyed man" projects his eyes out of his head toward the horse, and his eyes then rebound back into the eye sockets. Picasso's disembodied figures in *Guernica* were never so physically rendered! Here, instead of the mimetic economy that Pound celebrates in the Chinese character, Cook creates scenarios that focus on the destruction of horses, trees, sun, and man when language is removed from its voice and allowed to move through its own spatial logic. Furthermore, Cook produces rather unfaithful translations of Lerner's phrases as well, playing havoc with Pound's ideal of translation based on fidelity to an original.

By speaking of signing poets *re-siting* poetry, I am relying on a pun that, like Derrida's neologism "différance," must be seen to be understood. In substituting an "a" for an "e" in the French word "différence," Derrida signals language's unspoken difference from itself, the spatial differing and temporal deferring that are the basis of meaning making (Derrida 1982). Similarly, in *Of Grammatology,* Derrida deconstructs Saussure's famous model of the sign (which, fortuitously for my purposes, utilizes both the image of a tree and a horse). In his schematic representation of the sign, Saussure shows how the relationship between the words *arbor* or *equos,* and the material tree or horse is based on an arbitrary association between sign and referent, as it is in all oral languages; there is no necessary relationship between the phonemes that make up the word and the concept invoked (Saussure 1966, 67). But as Derrida points out, Saussure assumes that the written sign is simply the outer representation of language's "internal" structure, a passive sign of a phonocentric intent. For Saussure, as with Plato, writing is secondary to its originary, oral form and as such is underwritten by a metaphysics of presence, a phonocentrism based on the Logos or Word of God (Derrida 1976, 27–73). Unlike spoken language, writing—*écriture*—represents in its material form the difference from presence that is the foundation of language. As Derrida concludes, "the play of difference, which, as Saussure reminded us, is the condition for the possibility and functioning of every sign, is in itself a silent play" (Derrida 1982, 5).

Despite the rich implications of this "silent play" for the semiotics of signing, Derrida does not take sign language into account and thus fails to consider work like that of Peter Cook that would seem to complicate a phonocentric metaphysics. After all, if writing is not the material representation of a prior phonetic sign but "the condition for the possibility and functioning of every sign" (ibid.), then presumably ASL signing would be a form of writing as well.[7] In ASL poetry, meaning is established through a body that is also a text; a tree can be literally tangled in a tree, thus challenging the interiority of the voice as something located within or prior to the body. By severing meaning from an ontologically grounded Logos and locating it on the expressive body, we may see "seeing" from an entirely different vantage.

In the Name of the Father: Clayton Valli

If ASL poetry asks us to reconsider the ocularcentric nature of modernist poetry, it also questions the "voice" upon which so much poetic theory is based. Does the use of ASL mean that Deaf poets have no purchase on the revived oral tradition that emerged during the 1960s and 1970s? Is there no reciting in ASL? Deaf scholars have pointed out the paradoxical fact that the closest analog to ASL storytelling is the ancient oral tradition, insofar as both stress face-to-face contact between poet and audience.[8] Both rely on audience participation in knitting community together, and both stress qualities of variation, facial expression, and face-to-face exposure. Although, as Christopher Krentz (2006) points out, this conflation risks aligning ASL poetry with the oralist education encouraged by Alexander Graham Bell, it does point to the fuzzy boundaries between signed, spoken, and written poetries (ibid., 52, 3). For some Deaf activists, however, any rapprochement with the spoken is anathema. I have discussed the scandal of speech in signed poetry elsewhere, but I want here to say something about the ability of ASL to represent the voice that has implications for a politics of Deaf community (Davidson 2002). In order to make this point, I want to look at Clayton Valli's "Snowflake" (1990b), a poem that may seem on the surface to have nothing to do with either the social or the spatial but which, in its manipulation of linguistic codes, ultimately speaks to the isolation of the deaf individual in audist culture[9] (**clip 13.2**).

"Snowflake" is a small allegory about a deaf child of hearing parents that parallels Valli's own upbringing in an oral household. "Snowflake" is divided into three segments. Part one describes a gray day when all of the leaves have fallen from the trees and where the landscape is barren and empty. The fall of a snowflake suddenly reminds the poet of a moment in the past, a memory of a small

---

7. Jennifer Nelson (2006) remarks that Derrida's theory of meaning as *différance* can be applied to social identities as well.

8. On the connection of orality and ASL poetry, see Krentz (2006).

9. "Snowflake" can be seen on the videotape *Poetry in Motion: Original works in ASL* as well as on the *Signs and Voices* DVD. I have been aided in my reading of this poem by David Perlmutter, to whom I extend my thanks.

boy's face. That moment is described in part two as an interchange between the
deaf boy and his hearing father. Part three returns to the present, the snow now
covering the ground. A falling snowflake once again distracts the poet, but now
it seems part of the white landscape rather than an isolated fleck. Parts one and
three are in the present, serving as temporal bookends for part two, the "social"
portion of the poem, in the past. Although the entire poem is signed, Valli makes
use of at least four modes of manual signing in order to display the various levels
on which signed communication occurs. In the first case, the father brags to his
friends in fluent English about his son's vocal skills. Valli signals the father's fluency in English by an expansive use of ASL that the child interprets as gibberish.
Here, the representation of English fluency, seen from the standpoint of a deaf
child, is a series of empty signs, the equivalent of "blah blah blah." Second, the
father then turns to the child, switching to a more careful intonation, signaled in
this case by a combination of signing, silent vocalization, and fingerspelling. The
father asks, in a slow, deliberate manner, "What is your name?" and "How old
are you?" The third mode is that of the child's attempts to respond orally to his
father—"My name is . . ." and "I am five . . ."—which are rendered in Signed Exact
English (SEE), a form of signing that uses ASL signs but follows English word
order and fingerspells English grammatical morphemes. The child never has a
chance to finish his phrases because the father interrupts him to celebrate the son's
success. As the father changes modes to relate to his friends and then to his child,
so Valli adjusts his representation of speech in each speech act situation. As the
child adjusts his signifying function to accommodate English expectations, so Valli
changes from ASL, to fingerspelling, to SEE.

The fourth mode, the "snowflake" frame, contains or brackets the "speech"
frame but also provides a poetic alternative to a discursive binary of speech/
silence. Here Valli exploits the richness of ASL, utilizing extensive variations on
handshapes, body position, facial expression, and visual puns to create a wintry
landscape as a metaphor for alienation. The use of repeated handshapes in various
positions assists in creating rhythm, much as rhyme or alliteration links elements
in traditional English verse. In describing the wintry landscape, for example, Valli
uses the number 5 handshape (all five fingers spread out) as it appears in the sign
TREE (the right hand and arm placed vertically on top of the left hand horizontally
extended in front of the chest, directed across the body). TREE morphs into a swirl-
ing motion in front of the face to suggest a tree full of leaves. This sign is followed
by a downward motion of the 5 handshape to signify leaves falling. From the erect
tree, to the tree full of leaves, to the tree bereft of leaves, a single handshape displays the transformation of a tree in winter.

In this section of the poem, Valli deploys a familiar trope of romantic dejection in which the poet is alienated from the social world, unable to translate the
natural landscape into his own condition. The world seems flat and gray; a cloud
covers the sun, blending foreground and background into a blank emptiness. Then
the poet observes a falling snowflake, a moment that begins a process of reflection upon a particular face and moment in the past that lifts the poet out of dejection and into time. This Coleridgian change from blank nature to memory,
present to past, coincides with the child's verbal alienation from his father. But
as in Coleridge or Wordsworth, the ability to remember and thus enter time permits a larger, more expansive view. The isolated snowflake and solitary deaf child

of part one merge into a common landscape in part three. The child *is* the father of the man, not by living beyond him (and the symbolic regime he represents) but by rearticulating childhood isolation in his own (signed) terms. Valli, the mature poet, depicts an earlier version of himself, marginalized in an oralist universe, who has now transcended childhood and audism by translating both into sign.

PARADOX: PATRICK GRAYBILL

The Oedipal trajectory of Valli's poem testifies to an important theme among deaf poets surrounding the issue of generation and language. Because most deaf persons live in families with members who are hearing, multiculturalism is a given and bilingualism a (hoped for) horizon. As the documentary *Sound and Fury* indicates, generational issues within Deaf culture are often linguistic: whether, in a household of hearing and deaf members, to raise a child in ASL or to reinforce oralism via cochlear implant or other medical intervention. Valli's poem quietly articulates tensions that exist between nonsigning, hearing parents and their deaf children. With the advent of new hearing technologies—cochlear implants, hearing aids—along with oral education and mainstreaming, the cultural heritage of the Deaf world seems in jeopardy. Many ASL poems deal with generational tensions around language use, and in the case of Patrick Graybill's (1990) "Paradox," those tensions are figured through race and gender (**clip 13.3**).

In "Paradox" Graybill describes a black woman singing a love song that, as in the Valli example, triggers a reflection on his own relationship to his hearing parents. A rough paraphrase of the poem looks like this:

> A woman, who is black, sings a song. As the pianist plays the piano, she sings a song whose title is "My man, where is the man I love?" White and black keys of the piano bounce up and down as her voice rises. There are women in the audience with men among them. All watch the singer as she cries out, "My man, where is the man I love?" The piano keys, black and white, come to a stop. In a white and black room, women rise and applaud the singer—men as well—applaud for a long time. The woman smiles, bows, walks over to someone seated. Her man! So that for her, the meaning of the song is just a song, nothing more.
>
> But for me, deep inside myself, I am haunted by those words: "My man, where is the man I love?" My mother can hear and can sign. My father can hear but cannot sign. For me the story rings true throughout my life; "My man, where is the man I love?"

This seemingly simple tale contains a more complex story about how cultural differences are articulated. Graybill's poem divides the world into racial and gendered categories. The woman is black; there are women *but also* men in the audience; the piano keys are black and white; the women applaud, *and so do the men*; the room is white and black. Such contrasts reinforce racial and gender difference at the same time that the repeated refrain reinforces a level of common ground. The black singer sings a love song for someone who is a projection of the song, not the man in the club where she sings. Graybill sings a song for his father who, like the addressee of the woman's song, is also not in the room. Despite differences of race, gender, and audiology, Graybill is able to empathize with a black hearing woman by re-siting her desire onto his.

"Paradox" exposes the degree to which signing itself is a "site" of affective relations. The refrain, "Where is the man I love?" is "heard" differently by Graybill, for whom the interrogative in the title refers less to a place than a potentiality in language: "Where in language does the father whom I love live?" The black and white room where the song is heard, the black and white keys of the accompanying piano, the black and white features of the two singers, hearing and deaf, become contrastive features that heighten the common affective core between the two artists.

RE-SITING POETRY

Where is the politics of Deaf community in these very different examples? Peter Cook's reconfiguration of Chinese phrases, far from providing a satisfactory aesthetic closure, opens up the images to collision, violence, and semantic indeterminacy. While Valli's lyric draws upon a romantic trope of dejection, it represents that mode through an indictment of paternalist oralism, one made all the more poignant by the poet's identification of himself as the subject of the father's vocalization. Graybill draws on a black blues song to express his distance from his hearing, non-signing father. These themes and strategies may not strike hearing persons as being particularly political, but for a bicultural d/Deaf audience, they embody a kind of double consciousness that interprets literary conventions through a deaf optic. Pound drew upon the Chinese ideogram to assert the primacy of visual images over the distancing effects of rhetoric. Peter Cook draws upon Pound's ocularcentric poetics to generate an imagism based on the signifying body and on the generative potential of handshapes to suggest new, unexpected meanings.

I might make one further observation about the term *siting* that goes beyond the spatial implications of sign language toward the social world in which ASL is used. I am referring here to the ways that d/Deaf poets are sited in social spaces of the Deaf world: residential schools, deaf clubs, special education classrooms, deaf rap and slam competitions, and, more recently, videotapes and DVDs. Certain cities—Rochester, Hartford, Philadelphia, Fremont, Baltimore, Washington, D.C.—have an almost mythic status within the Deaf world, equivalent to the great modernist metropoles of Paris, London, and Zurich. These places are identified not only with deaf schools but also with the communities that form around them, the institutions and businesses that support these communities, the families that raise children—hearing and deaf—within them. Peter Cook's oralist education at the Clarke School in Massachusetts, Clayton Valli's training at the Austine School for the Deaf, and Patrick Graybill's experiences at the Kansas School for the Deaf and Gallaudet University must be considered as foundational elements of their work, as significant to their creative life as Paris to the expatriate generation of writers. The history of modern poetry is a material history of publishers, magazines, journals, and essays on the Chinese written character. Coffeehouses, bars, and salons become important adjuncts of literary professionalism, to be sure, but the fact of the book and its reception makes literary community largely a matter of print. For the Deaf poet, shared cultural traditions are sited around specific performances, no one of which is ever quite the same. The proliferation of videos and DVDs notwithstanding, the fact of the signed poem and its reception makes literary community uniquely a matter of space. Presence may be represented by the metaphor of a snowflake, but it can never be dissevered from an audience before which the figure is enacted.

So what is golf? I return to Simi Linton's initial question to ask, again, what is the field on which the game is played and how does that field include and exclude certain players? In the case of poetry, the game concerns language, and, as Wittgenstein (1967) observes, "what belongs to a language game is a whole culture" (8). Wittgenstein is discussing the situated nature of cultural values—the fact that aesthetic ideals of beauty are products of specific class-based values. Translated into our terms with ASL poetry, we might say that what belongs to the language game called poetry, at least within hearing society, is a set of self-evident values concerning poetry's association with the voice and sound. But an equally potent principle of poetry is its ability to challenge linguistic norms. As a genre, poetry is enriched most when its rules are broken, when its formulae and rhetorics are challenged. Ezra Pound had just such a challenge in mind when he advocated the "direct presentation of the thing" against the inflated rhetoric of late Victorianism; the Chinese character became his alternative. Pound's and Williams's fetish of the visual image and objectivist thing-in-itself invented the subsequent language games of modernism by erasing the word in pursuit of the world. The "whole culture" interpellated within the language game of modernism knows the score and reads the page.

For Peter Cook, Clayton Valli, and Patrick Graybill, Wittgenstein's phrase means something else. What belongs to the language game of ASL is a "whole culture" that lives in a colonial relation to the spoken word. Deaf poets' transformations of handshape, body position, diction, and register continue a modernist effort to defamiliarize language, to see differently. But they signify on sight as well, bringing into vivid presence the body and expressiveness that have been the dream of poetry since the romantics. In an era in which poetry in the academy has fallen on hard times, ASL performance offers an opportunity to revivify the art, not by adding increments to an existing canon, but by rethinking the metaphors of vision and presence upon which poetry has been erected. When ASL poetry is brought into the poetry classroom—and into the ASL classroom as well—we may begin to understand rhyme anew when tree is tangled in tree.

REFERENCES

Bauman, H-Dirksen L. 1997. Toward a poetics of vision, space, and the body. In *The disability studies reader*, ed. Lennard J. Davis, 315–31. New York: Routledge.
Baynton, Douglas. 1996. *Forbidden signs: American culture and the campaign against sign language.* Chicago: University of Chicago Press.
Berger, Jane. 2005. Uncommon schools. In *Foucault and the government of disability*, ed. Shelley Tremain, 153–71. Ann Arbor: University of Michigan Press.
Cohn, Jim. 2003. *The golden body: Meditations on the essence of disability.* Boulder, Colo.: Museum of American Poetics.
Davidson, Michael. 2002. Hearing things: The scandal of speech in Deaf performance. In *Disability studies: Enabling the humanities*, ed. Sharon L. Snyder, Brenda Jo Brueggemann, and Rosemarie Garland-Thomson, 76–87. New York: Modern Language Association.

Derrida, Jacques. 1976. *Of grammatology,* trans. Gayatri Chakravorty Spivak. Baltimore: Johns Hopkins University Press.

———. 1982. Différance. In *Margins of philosophy,* trans. Alan Bass. Chicago: University of Chicago Press.

Fenollosa, Ernest. 1936. *The Chinese written character as a medium for poetry,* ed. Ezra Pound. San Francisco: City Lights Books.

Flying Words Project. n.d. Chinese translations. *The can't touch tours: Current works (1990–2003).*

Frank, Joseph. 1963. *The widening gyre: Crisis and mastery in modern literature.* Bloomington: Indiana University Press.

Graybill, Patrick. 1990. *Poetry in motion: Original works in ASL.* VHS. Burtonsville, Md.: Sign Media.

Jay, Martin. 1993. *Downcast eyes: The denigration of vision in twentieth-century French thought.* Berkeley: University of California Press.

Krentz, Christopher. 2006. The camera as printing press: How film has impacted ASL literature. In *Signing the body poetic: Essays on American Sign Language literature,* ed. H-Dirksen L. Bauman, Jennifer Nelson, and Heidi Rose, 51–70. Berkeley: University of California Press.

Levin, David Michael, ed. 1993. *Modernity and the hegemony of vision.* Berkeley: University of California Press.

Linton, Simi. 2005. What is disability studies? *PMLA* 120(2):518–22.

Nelson, Jennifer. 2006. Textual bodies, bodily texts. *Signing the body poetic: Essays on American Sign Language literature,* ed. H-Dirksen L. Bauman, Jennifer Nelson, and Heidi Rose, 118–29. Berkeley: University of California Press.

Pound, Ezra. n.d. A retrospect. In *Literary essays of Ezra Pound,* 3–14. New York: New Directions.

Saussure, Ferdinand de. 1966. *Course in general linguistics.* New York: McGraw-Hill.

Sound and Fury. 2000. Dir. Josh Aronson. New York: Aronson Film Associates and Public Policy Publications.

Tremain, Shelley, ed. 2005. *Foucault and the government of disability.* Ann Arbor: University of Michigan Press.

Valli, Clayton. 1990a. The nature of a line in ASL poetry. *SLR '87: Papers from the Fourth International Symposium on Sign Language Research,* ed. W. H. Edmondson and F. Karlsson, 171–81. Hamburg: Signum Press.

———. 1990b. Snowflake. *Poetry in motion: Original works in ASL.* VHS. Burtonsville, Md.: Sign Media.

Whitman, Walt. 2002. Song of myself. In *Leaves of grass and other writings,* ed. Michael Moon. New York: Norton.

Wittgenstein, Ludwig. 1967. *Lectures and conversations on aesthetics, psychology, and religious belief,* ed. Yorick Smythies, Rush Rhees, and James Taylor. Berkeley: University of California Press.

14 | *Nobilior est vulgaris:* Dante's Hypothesis and Sign Language Poetry

David M. Perlmutter

To the memory of Clayton Valli (1951–2003)

More than seven hundred years ago, Dante (1305)[1] articulated with amazing clarity the concept of "natural language" that many twenty-first-century people still fail to grasp:

> Vulgarem locutionem appellamus eam quam infantes assuefiunt ab assistentibus cum primitus distinguere voces incipiunt; vel, quod brevius dici potest, vulgarem locutionem asserimus *quam sine omni regula nutricem imitantes accipimus.*
>
> I call "vernacular language" that which infants acquire from those around them when they first begin to distinguish sounds; or, to put it more succinctly, I declare that vernacular language is *that which we learn without any formal instruction,* by imitating our nurses. (emphasis mine—DMP)

I am greatly indebted to Sharon Allen and Merrie Davidson for working with me on ASL poetry; to Sharon Allen, Peggy Swartzel Lott, Rachel Mayberry, and Carol Padden for help with the text; to Sharon Allen, Rain Bosworth, Page DuBois, Nigel Fabb, Michael Flynn, Pascal Gagneux, Sharon Kwan, Peggy Swartzel Lott, Ceil Lucas, Rachel Mayberry, Donna Jo Napoli, Irina Nikolaeva, Carol Padden, and Jonathan Saville for their comments on earlier versions of this chapter; to Françoise Santore for checking my French; and to Linda Murphy for bibliographical assistance. Responsibility for all errors and inadequacies is mine alone.

1. Botterill (1996, xiii–xiv) places Dante's writing of the manuscript in the period 1303–1305. The quotations from Dante and their English translations cited here are from Botterill (1996, 3).

In Dante's time, the spoken language or vernacular that children learned without instruction differed considerably from the written language. Today we think of them as different languages: Old Italian and Latin (the latter—no longer anyone's native language—was governed by consciously promulgated rules that had to be taught). Dante pointed out that not all peoples have this kind of language, which he called "secondary to us," noting that "few . . . achieve complete fluency in it, since knowledge of its rules and theory can only be developed through dedication to a lengthy course of study." He continues:

> Harum quoque duarum *nobilior est vulgaris:* tum quia prima fuit humano generi usitata; tum quia totus orbis ipsa perfruitur, licet in diversas prolationes et vocabula sit divisa; tum quia naturalis est nobis, cum illa potius artificialis existat.
>
> Of these two kinds of language, *the more noble is the vernacular:* first, because it was the language originally used by the human race; second, because the whole world employs it, though with different pronunciations and using different words; and third, because it is natural to us, while the other is, in contrast, artificial.

Dante is saying that natural language preceded the development of consciously promulgated rules of grammar, that it is universal, and that it is natural to us. His claim that it is the "more noble" was daring at a time when the vernacular was viewed as a degenerate form of the written language.

Dante aimed to show that the vernacular is "illustrious, cardinal, aulic, and curial" and "to teach a theory of [its] effective use" (Botterill 1996, 45), with recommendations about what would enable it to achieve the highest poetic expression.[2] By writing poetry in it himself, he was, in essence, testing a hypothesis:

Dante's Hypothesis:
Natural language has what it takes to serve as the vehicle of poetry.

The result was *La divina commedia,* which established a literary standard for Italian and is considered by many to be one of the finest works of poetry ever written.

Dante's definition of *vernacular language* as "that which we learn without any formal instruction" includes the sign languages of Deaf communities. Only recently, however, has it become possible to test his hypothesis against these languages in a serious way.

The Emergence of ASL Poetry

At the dawn of the twenty-first century, there are people known as American Sign Language (ASL) poets. Their work is published on videocassette or DVD. Conferences are held where ASL poetry and literature are discussed. All this is relatively new, having emerged only in the 1970s and 1980s.

---

2. After discussing the range of Italian vernaculars (in what may have been the world's first dialect survey), he opts for the one used by vernacular poets "which belongs to all Italy, is called the Italian vernacular" (Botterill 1996, 45).

Poetic expression in ASL certainly existed earlier. A rhythmical example of what could be called "folk verse" in ASL was recorded on film by Charles Krauel in the 1930s (Dannis 1994).[3] Schools for deaf people and Gallaudet College had rhythmic signed cheers to support their sports teams. To find further antecedents of poetry in ASL, one must ask what literary experiences Deaf people had in their own language. Deaf culture has always nourished a strong story-telling tradition that continues to the present day. Deaf clubs were a venue for storytelling and signed performances. Introducing films made by the National Association of the Deaf in 1913, Veditz (1913) laments that they had insufficient funds to film "performances in sign language." It is unclear to what extent, if any, such performances would have included what could be called poetry in sign language. In the nineteenth century, sermons were an important literary experience for both Deaf and hearing people. In a brief filmed memoir in ASL based on his experiences at the school for deaf children in Hartford, Connecticut in the nineteenth century, Hotchkiss (1913) says that two of the teachers were "like actors and provided great entertainment for the children, so much so that the children would rather miss dinner than miss their sermons on Sunday evenings."[4] He performs one of their homilies, which has elements of poetic form. This suggests that there may have been types of poetic expression in ASL early on which, in the absence of a written form of the language or other means of preserving them, have been lost.

An early discussion of poetic expression in ASL (Klima and Bellugi 1976, 1979) reports on "art sign": signed renditions of English-language poems and a haiku in both English and ASL. In these works, signs stood for English words and were signed in a graceful or artistic manner, but this was not yet original poetry in ASL.

For a long time, the development of a poetic tradition in ASL was hindered by Deaf people's lack of awareness that ASL was a full-fledged language distinct from English. Whatever differences were noticed between the way thoughts were expressed in sign and in English were interpreted as evidence that sign lacked grammar and was not real language. Lou Fant, a native signer and a founding member of the National Theater of the Deaf, expressed it clearly:

> Like most children of deaf parents, I grew up with no conscious awareness that ASL was a language. I thought of ASL as an ungrammatical parody of English. It was not until I reached my mid-thirties [in the late 1960s] that I was relieved of this conception. My enlightenment came from people who were not native users of ASL. They were people who had come into the field of deafness with no preconceived notions, and bound to no points of view regarding deaf people and their language. They looked at the signed language of deaf people with fresh eyes and described to people like me what the situation really was. (1980, 193)

Deaf people's belief that ASL was not a language had been nurtured by an educational system that granted it no legitimacy and viewed it only as an obstacle to their learning English. Linguists as well dismissed sign language as a manual

---

3. This is cited by Padden and Humphries (1988, 77–79), by Peters (2000, 66–67), and by Peters (2001, 138).

4. Translated from ASL by Merrie Davidson.

coding of speech and therefore unworthy of linguists' attention (Perlmutter 1987). Following Stokoe's (1960) pioneering research, the linguistic study of sign languages produced abundant evidence that they are full natural languages differing structurally from coterritorial spoken languages in significant ways.

These results facilitated a fundamental change in consciousness among Deaf people. The discovery that they had a full-fledged language of their own led many Deaf people to think of themselves in a new way: as a linguistic and cultural minority in the larger society.[5] This encouraged the development of a literary culture that included not only stories with roots in the culture's storytelling tradition but also theater and poetry in ASL. The founding of the National Theater of the Deaf in 1967 was an important milestone. The advent of the videocassette recorder in the 1970s made it possible to publish and disseminate literature in ASL on videotape, which, in turn, reinforced the idea that Deaf people have a culture of their own.

Linguistic research on ASL and changing attitudes toward linguistic and cultural minorities in American society had a profound and salutary effect on the American Deaf community. Stokoe's work at Gallaudet College ensured that successive generations of college-educated Deaf people would be exposed to the idea that ASL is a full-fledged language. ASL poet Ella Mae Lentz tells how this idea influenced her:

> When I entered Gallaudet College in 1971 I studied with Professor Eastman. The class was sign language translation for theater. During the course Professor Eastman said that American Sign Language and English were equally sophisticated. I argued, saying, "No, that can't be! English is a far more complex language. ASL is nothing more than broken English." We debated this issue throughout the semester: "Yes, it is!" "No, it isn't!" "Yes it is!" "No it isn't!" until finally I understood his points. . . . With this I was inspired to move on.
>
> Later I took a creative writing class because I like poetry. I had been writing poetry in English for a while. The professor, however, was very progressive and said, "Why don't you write your poetry in sign language?" I thought, "Well, why not?" So I did. I would begin signing my poem, then try recomposing it on paper. I had a hard time making the transition from motion to a static form. (Rutherford 1984)[6]

It is clear that linguistic research played a key role in bringing about the conditions that led Lentz to become an ASL poet. Before ASL was thought of as a language, there would have been no such course as Sign Language Translation for Theater, and no teacher would have suggested to a student like Lentz that she write poetry in sign.

---

5. This change in consciousness is described and analyzed by Padden and Humphries (1988), especially chapter 5. See also Parasnis (1996), Padden and Humphries (2005), and the chapters in this volume and the references they cite.

6. The English translations of both quotations from Lentz are taken from the voice-over on the published videotape.

The development of ASL poetry was also facilitated by linguistic discoveries that brought aspects of ASL structure to signers' conscious awareness. As Lentz notes:

In the past few years, people have become more aware of ASL's richness and scope. . . . Research continues to uncover linguistic principles which artists are now using as tools. By applying this knowledge, we expand the creativity of our language, and we no longer feel restricted by the written form of English. The poetry form began to change. (Rutherford 1984)

There are significant parallels between the conditions faced by ASL poets in the twentieth century and those faced by Dante in the thirteenth. Both had to break away from the literary preeminence of the written language (Latin for Dante and English for ASL poets). Bards and minstrels performed in the vernacular of Dante's day, just as there were performances in deaf clubs and folk verse in ASL. Like Dante's vernacular, ASL was not recognized as a language, much less as a literary language. It was viewed as a degenerate form of English, much as Dante's vernacular was viewed as a degenerate form of Latin. Neither language was thought to be an appropriate vehicle for poetry.

ASL poet Clayton Valli tells how he came to write poetry in ASL:

My family had a tradition of reunions at our old summer house. We had an old summer house and every year we gathered there. One summer our house burned down. We had planned for the gathering. We were shocked. We all felt funny at the thought of never meeting there again. The summer house was always on my mind. But I went ahead and started school at NTID [National Technical Institute for the Deaf]. But I couldn't let go of the summer house. I carried it with me everywhere. I got the idea of writing a poem about it. So I started writing something; it was difficult. But I wasn't happy with the little I wrote. I put it aside. Later I felt the urge to write again. I thought I had the idea. And I had the inspiration, but I couldn't get it down on paper. And then I thought—why not create the poem in sign language? So I did. I liked it! I liked playing with the signs and revising the poem.

My only problem was my memory. How could I remember the poem? I decided to code the signing with English glosses. I would compose the poem in ASL, and then use an English word to represent the ASL sign. So then I had a page of English glosses just to help me remember the poem.

I never mentioned this to friends or showed them my poetry. I don't know why not. I just never felt comfortable in sharing it. I kept it to myself.

Then in 1980 I attended a workshop in Tennessee, a summer workshop. We were studying how to teach ASL. It so happened that a woman named Ella Mae Lentz said, "I am an ASL poet." I thought, "She's an ASL poet!" I was thrilled! I thought I was the only one. But I'd found another person like me.

Later, I buttonholed her and asked if we could discuss poetry. We worked out a time to meet. I couldn't wait. When the time came, I was so excited. We sat and shared. It made me more inspired to continue with my poetry. (Valli 1990a)[7]

While Dante (1305) cites troubadours and poets who wrote in the vernacular before him, Valli began to write poetry in ASL in the absence of any model. Here we see how he overcame the lack of a written language, as well as his isolation as he began to create poetry alone, with no audience other than himself, in a language in which he had never seen a poem.

GOALS OF THIS CHAPTER

The discovery that sign languages are natural languages challenges Dante's Hypothesis in ways he could hardly have imagined. How are the physical resources of sign languages (the hands, face, and body) used to create poetry? To what extent are poetic forms in sign and the resources that sign languages offer the poet like those in spoken languages, and to what extent are they different? To what extent does sign poetry exploit the possibilities of the visual modality?

Like sign poetry itself, these questions are new. For sign poets, the challenge is to discover the poetic resources and possibilities of sign languages. Poetry in sign languages breaks new ground. There is no poetic tradition to guide sign poets, to provide poetic forms, or to rebel against. For analysts and theorists of poetry, the challenge is to discover the poetic forms sign poets use, the resources sign languages make available to poets and how poets use them to achieve poetic effects, as well as the extent to which sign poets exploit the possibilities of the visual modality. Sign poetry raises basic questions about what is intrinsic to poetry and what is due to the modality in which it is written. This chapter addresses some of these issues by examining one ASL poem: Clayton Valli's (1995) "Deaf World" (**clip 14**).

My first goal is to determine whether this poem exhibits evidence for the line.[8] Since sign poems are published as performances on videotape or DVD with no written text to indicate poetic form, the existence of the line is not obvious. Furthermore, what belongs to the poem as text must be separated from what belongs to a particular recorded performance. In metrical or rhymed poetry in spoken languages, meter and/or rhyme delineate the line. To whatever extent sign poetry is metrical, the nature of its meter remains to be discovered. There is no counterpart of rhyme that consistently marks the ends of lines.[9] Consequently, I appeal to structural properties of "Deaf World," which provide robust evidence for the line and the hemistich (half-line).

---

7. Translated from ASL by Merrie Davidson.

8. In this, I follow Valli's (1990c) pioneering study, in which he points out some ways that patterns of handshape, movement, and nonmanual signals delineate the line in his poem "Snowflake" and Ella Mae Lentz's poem "Circle of Life."

9. Valli (1990c) uses the term *rhyme* much more broadly to refer to many aspects of the linguistic signal that are repeated for poetic effect.

My second goal is to investigate how the poet uses the language for poetic effects. What in the structure of ASL enables him to delineate the poem's poetic structure and give "Deaf World" its emotional impact? My third goal is to make explicit some of the poetic resources of ASL, focusing especially on those with no direct counterparts in spoken languages.

I also argue that "Deaf World" does not exploit the full range of possibilities of the visual modality. The poet limits himself to the more restricted set of resources provided by ASL grammar, but tweaks the language's grammatical constraints in interesting ways. Finally, I reexamine Dante's Hypothesis, asking what makes natural languages suitable vehicles for poetry.

THE POEM

To give the reader an overview of the poem before analyzing it in detail, I provide a rough translation which lacks the economy, elegance, and visual force of the ASL original,[10] followed by a transcription of the ASL text.[11]

Deaf World
by Clayton Valli

I was born into a world thrust on me
Shackled with hearing aids—noises noises noises in my ears
Music—noises noises in my ears
Voices on the silver screen—little noises back and forth
Noises noises noises noises in my ears

But I see
I see the rocks strewn over the ground—Behold, they are deaf
I see the still waters of the lake—Behold, they are deaf
I see the trees that grace the land—Behold, they are deaf
I see the mountains against the sky—Behold, they are deaf
I see the clouds on high—Behold, they are deaf
This whole world is deaf! It's like me!

Not that—That world is not like me
Not that—This world is mine!

---

10. Translation of poetry is always difficult, if not impossible. The difficulties are compounded for translation from a non-Indo-European language such as ASL to English, and even more for translation from a signed to a spoken language. As in all poetic translation, the translator is often torn between the conflicting demands of fidelity to the words of the text and fidelity to its poetic feeling. Some discrepancies between this translation and the transcription of the ASL text below are due to the translation's incorporating elements of the ASL original that are expressed by facial expression or by face and body orientation (not reflected in the transcription), or to the attempt to give the translation some of the poetic feeling of the original. Discussion of the problems inherent in translation of a poem such as this is beyond the scope of this chapter.

11. I follow the standard convention of representing ASL signs by capitalizing their English glosses. Where more than one English word is needed to gloss an ASL sign, the words are connected by hyphens. "CL:" indicates a classifier sign.

I	BORN	CL:BIG-BALL	THRUST-ON-ME
HEARING-AIDS-PUT-ON-ME	EMIT-NOISES$_E$	EMIT-NOISES	EMIT-NOISES$_E$
MUSIC	EMIT-NOISES	EMIT-NOISES$_E$	
CL:SCREEN	MOVIE	EMIT-NOISES	EMIT-NOISES
EMIT-NOISES$_E$	EMIT-NOISES$_E$	EMIT-NOISES$_E$	EMIT-NOISES$_E$
SEE			
ROCK	Classifier-Predicate[12]	THEY[13]	DEAF
WATER	Classifier-Predicate	THEY	DEAF
TREE	Classifier-Predicate	THEY	DEAF
MOUNTAIN	Classifier-Predicate	THEY	DEAF
CLOUDS[14]	Classifier-Predicate	THEY	DEAF
CL:BIG-BALL	DEAF	IT-LIKE-ME	[NOT-]IT-LIKE-ME[15]
[NOT-]THAT	THIS	MINE	

The poet begins by describing the hearing world: It was thrust on him, hearing aids were put on him, and he was subjected to unintelligible noises (indicated by a sign glossed as EMIT-NOISES or EMIT-NOISES$_E$ when signed at the ears). The signer's facial expression shows his increasing irritation with these bursts of unintelligible noise. This world is symbolized by human contrivances (hearing aids, music, movies) that make irritating noises.

Turning his face and body to the right, he signs SEE and begins to describe a beautiful landscape, mentioning rocks on the ground, the waters of a lake, trees, mountains, and clouds, using classifier predicates to indicate the place of each in

12. Each line has a different classifier predicate that describes one element of the landscape. For example, the classifier predicate in the first line (bent-5 handshape) indicates objects of indeterminate roundish shape on the ground, while the one in the second line (B handshape) indicates a flat surface, for example, a lake or pond. For studies of classifiers in sign languages, see Emmorey (2002) and the references cited there.

13. This is a deictic sign in an elevated style that would be used in addressing an audience, as in a sermon, for example, rather than in an informal conversation. This sign is discussed further in the sections titled Tripartite Structure in the Last Line and in the Poem, The Role of the ASL Deictic and Reference System, and The Manual Aspect of the Modality: The Role of Dominance Shift.

14. The sign transcribed as CLOUDS and the following classifier predicate are the same sign, which has a double status: It can be used as a noun to mean "clouds" or as a classifier predicate meaning "clouds move."

15. The negation is enclosed in brackets in this sign and the next because it is expressed by a nonmanual signal.

the landscape. His face shows increasing elation as he discovers that each is deaf. In contrast to his irritation at the unintelligible noises of the hearing world, he is elated to discover the beauty and harmony of this world and the fact that it is deaf like him.

To contrast the two worlds, the poet uses a common grammatical device of ASL. Each world has a locus in the signing space. References to that world are made by reference to that locus. The orientation of the signer's face and body indicates which world is being described. Initially the signer's face and body are oriented toward the locus of the hearing world on his left. To describe the Deaf world, he shifts their orientation to its locus on his right.

The contrasting orientations of the signer's face and body in the two major parts of the poem are but one of many formal contrasts between them. Although they do not have the kind of parallel structure they would need to qualify as stanzas, for convenience I refer to the first and second parts of the poem as the first and second stanzas.

EVIDENCE FOR THE LINE AND THE HEMISTICH IN THE SECOND STANZA

Evidence for the Line

Line structure is particularly clear in a passage in the second stanza:

ROCK	Classifier-Predicate	THEY	DEAF
WATER	Classifier-Predicate	THEY	DEAF
TREE	Classifier-Predicate	THEY	DEAF
MOUNTAIN	Classifier-Predicate	THEY	DEAF
CLOUDS	Classifier-Predicate	THEY	DEAF

Each line consists of four signs and is about one element of the landscape (rocks, lake, trees, mountains, or clouds). Syntactically, each line consists of two sentences: a noun followed by a classifier predicate that reveals its shape and position in the landscape and THEY DEAF. The line is the unit of both semantic and syntactic parallelism.

Three devices make the description of the landscape vivid. First, the classifiers are signed at successively higher levels of the signing space, mirroring the position in the actual landscape of the objects described. Second, as each element of the landscape is described, the signer's gaze fixes at the appropriate level of the depicted landscape and moves upward, one step at a time, gazing in turn at the rocks, the lake, the trees, and the mountains until, when the clouds are described, his eyes gaze upward, as if watching the clouds. Eye gaze marks each line as different from the others. Third, in the deictic sign THEY, the hand points toward the location of the preceding classifier predicate, its angle matching that of the accompanying eye gaze. The position of the classifier predicate in the signing space and the angle of the eye gaze and of the hand in the deictic are different in each line, giving it unity and distinctness from the others.

These lines all display the same patterning. If they are lines of poetry, these parallels are explained as instances of the parallelism among lines that is common in poetry.

These structural parallels function together to produce much of the poem's emotional impact. We see the signer making a series of discoveries, each reinforcing the others. Each is a new discovery because it is about an additional element of the landscape, but each is also the same discovery: What is described is deaf. The structure of the line brings out both the newness and the sameness of each discovery. The signer looks at the harmony and beauty of the landscape to discover that each element, starting with the rocks on the ground and moving upward, step by step, to the clouds in the sky, is deaf, just like him. His face expresses his increasing elation as he discovers that each is deaf. His elation reaches a peak in the next line: "This whole world is deaf! It's like me!"

This is the emotional core of the poem. The poet's use of eye gaze makes viewers feel they are seeing the landscape through the signer's eyes. With him, they discover that the world of nature is a deaf world in two senses. It doesn't require hearing to be appreciated, and in this world, deafness abounds and human deafness is as natural as that of the rocks, the lake, the trees, the mountains, and the clouds.

These lines connect with Deaf viewers' life experiences. The commentary and video letter on the DVD version of Valli (1995) point out that the deictic sign signed at successively higher levels of the signing space is a near-pun on the ASL sign GROW-UP, which is like the deictic but signed with the palm down, while in the deictic, it faces up. This association with GROW-UP in the description of the Deaf world suggests growing up deaf in a world of nature that is also deaf—a strong and beautiful image.

These lines also recreate the experience of many Deaf people born to hearing parents, thanks to the pun in the poem's English title "Deaf World." Often used in English to refer to the Deaf community, here this phrase also refers to the world of nature, where each element of the landscape is deaf. Isolated in the hearing world by their deafness, many deaf children of hearing parents have to discover the Deaf community for themselves. These lines recreate their elation as they discover a new world in which there are others like themselves. The signer's face reflects his elation at his discovery of the deaf/Deaf world in both senses.

The beauty of this passage lies in the way it unfolds with a new discovery in each line. The structure of the line, with each vivid image and the realization that this, too, is deaf gives the poem much of its emotional impact.

Evidence for the Hemistich

Evidence for the hemistich (half line) in "Deaf World" comes from the pattern of repetition of THEY DEAF in these five lines, which is too strong to be ignored. If each line consists of two hemistichs (indicated by the brackets), the unit of repetition is the second hemistich.

[ROCK   Classifier-Predicate]_{Hemistich}   [THEY   DEAF]_{Hemistich}

[WATER   Classifier-Predicate]_{Hemistich}   [THEY   DEAF]_{Hemistich}

[TREE   Classifier-Predicate]_{Hemistich}   [THEY   DEAF]_{Hemistich}

[MOUNTAIN   Classifier-Predicate]_{Hemistich}   [THEY   DEAF]_{Hemistich}

[CLOUDS   Classifier-Predicate]_{Hemistich}   [THEY   DEAF]_{Hemistich}

Evidence that the first hemistich is a structural unit of the poem comes from the fact that the first hemistichs are parallel semantically, syntactically, and morphologically. Semantically, each is about one element of the landscape and sketches its appearance and position in the landscape. Syntactically, each is a sentence of the form [Noun Classifier-Predicate], each with a different subject and classifier predicate. The morphological parallelism of the classifier predicates is heightened phonologically: All use handshapes with all fingers extended (although in the first and last lines, where they describe objects of a roundish shape, the fingers are bent). Each hemistich consists of two signs. The first hemistichs are structurally parallel at multiple levels of linguistic structure.

The division of the line into hemistichs brings out the two sides of the signer's discovery in each line. The first hemistich announces and describes a new element of the landscape. The second confirms that it, too, is deaf.

Evidence for a Caesura

The claim that a line consists of two hemistichs entails the claim that the boundary between them (the caesura) is a major break because it separates the two major poetic constituents of the line. A way to test this claim is to see where it places the caesura and whether there is evidence for a major break at that point.

First, the caesura comes at the break between the line's major syntactic constituents; each is a complete sentence with a subject and a predicate.

A second piece of evidence for a caesura comes from a shift in hand dominance. One-handed signs are made with the "dominant" or "strong" hand: the right hand for right-handers, the left hand for left-handers. In the published performance of "Deaf World," the signer is right-handed, but the first sign of the second hemistich, the deictic sign THEY, is signed with the left hand in each line. This is a shift in hand dominance. One doesn't arbitrarily shift dominance; there has to be a reason for it. One function of this shift is to mark the caesura.[16]

This evidence for the caesura belongs to the poem as text. Additional evidence can come from the way it is performed. In Jed Gallimore's published performance, the face suggests a break where we have posited a caesura. His mouth breaks into a smile and his eyes squint slightly as he begins to sign THEY DEAF. The caesura is also where a signer might pause.

---

16. Its other functions are discussed in the sections titled Tripartite Structure in the Last Line and in the Poem, The Role of the ASL Deictic and Reference System, and The Manual Aspect of the Modality: The Role of Dominance Shift.

The fact that the caesura comes at a major break in syntactic and semantic structure is a phenomenon familiar from spoken languages, but the shift in hand dominance is unique to sign languages. Both types of evidence support the hemistich and the caesura as constructs common to spoken-language and sign-language poetic structure.

POETIC STRUCTURE IN THE FIRST STANZA

Setting aside the first four signs, most signs in the first stanza divide naturally into lines:

HEARING-AIDS-PUT-ON-ME	EMIT-NOISES$_E$	EMIT-NOISES	EMIT-NOISES$_E$
MUSIC		EMIT-NOISES	EMIT-NOISES$_E$
CL:SCREEN	MOVIE	EMIT-NOISES	EMIT-NOISES
EMIT-NOISES$_E$	EMIT-NOISES$_E$	EMIT-NOISES$_E$	EMIT-NOISES$_E$

Each line consists of four signs. The second line has only three, but the persistent pattern of four signs per line is clear evidence for the line as a structural unit in the first stanza. Each is about a source of sound (hearing aids, music, movies) and how the poet perceives it.

The fourth line, with four repetitions of EMIT-NOISES$_E$, is the transition to the second stanza as the signer's face and body begin to turn toward the locus of the Deaf world. The poet could have chosen any number of repetitions of EMIT-NOISES$_E$. Four is the right number because in this poem a line consists of four signs.

Even the contrasts between the two stanzas bring out the parallels between them. The objects of perception in the first stanza are human contrivances (hearing aids, music, movies), while those in the second stanza are elements of the natural world (rocks, water, trees, mountains, clouds). In the first stanza, the signer's face shows his irritation with the discordant and unintelligible noises he hears, while in the second stanza, it shows his delight with what he sees in the natural world and his realization that all those things are deaf. Both stanzas focus on objects in the external world, how the poet perceives them, and his emotional reaction to them.

While the first stanza consists of four-sign lines, the evidence for hemistichs is scant. One could view the second hemistich as the unit of repetition of EMIT-NOISES, but repetition of this sign is not confined to the second hemistich. Nor are the first hemistichs structurally parallel. This lack of evidence for the hemistich in the first stanza is not accidental, but plays a role in the poem's overall structure (cf. the section The Role of Syntactic Structure).

ADDITIONAL LINES

The first line tells how the poet was born into a world he did not choose: I BORN CL:BIG-BALL THRUST-ON-ME. It adheres to the pattern of four signs per line.

The second stanza begins with the sign SEE signed quickly. With the shift in orientation of the face and body, it marks the transition to a visual world. The stanza's last line differs from the preceding five: CL:BIG-BALL$_j$ DEAF IT$_j$-LIKE-ME [NOT-]IT$_k$-LIKE-ME.[17] Yet it consists of four signs divided into two hemistichs. The first hemistich shares a formal element with the other hemistichs in the second stanza: It is a sentence. It has the same predicate DEAF as the second hemistich in the preceding five lines and means "[This] whole world is deaf."

The second hemistich of the last line consists of two sentences each consisting of the same sign, but they contrast in meaning. The first means "It's like me" and refers to the world of nature that has just been described and discovered to be deaf. The second means "It's not like me" and refers to the hearing world of contrivances that produce unintelligible noises.

This sign is a predicate that has two arguments whose reference is indicated in three ways. First, the hand in the Y handshape moves back and forth along the line determined by the loci of the signer and the world with which he is comparing himself. The reference of the second argument is also expressed through eye gaze and the orientation of the signer's face and body. In the first occurrence of "it's like me," the signer looks at and faces the locus of the Deaf world; in the second, he looks at and faces the locus of the hearing world. The line along which the hand moves, eye gaze, and the orientation of the signer's face and body all express the contrasting reference of "it" in IT-LIKE-ME.

The negation of the second occurrence of IT-LIKE-ME is expressed nonmanually. The sign is immediately preceded by a head shake with a squinting facial expression that continues while IT-LIKE-ME is signed. These nonmanual signals express negation, so the second instance of IT-LIKE-ME means "it's not like me," where "it" refers to the hearing world.[18]

Tripartite Structure in the Last Line and in the Poem

The last line of the poem consists of only three signs: [NOT-]THAT—THIS—MINE. NOT- is enclosed in brackets because it is expressed by a nonmanual signal. The first two signs, glossed here as THAT and THIS, are instances of the same sign: the deictic THEY that appears in THEY DEAF in the second stanza. Here the deictic is signed by the left and then the right hand, pointing toward the loci of the hearing and Deaf worlds in turn. Each time the signer faces the locus in question, fixing his eyes on it. The different reference of the two instances of the deictic is indicated by the orientation of the face, by eye gaze, and by the angle of the hand.

The deictic is negated the first time it is signed: It means "*not* that [the hearing world]." Its negation is expressed in two ways in Jed Gallimore's performance. The first is facial expression. The squinting negative facial expression that accompanies the head shake, associated with the second instance of IT-LIKE-ME in the previous line, continues the first time the deictic is signed, expressing negation. This negative facial expression is gone the second time the deictic is signed; the signer

---

17. NOT is enclosed in brackets because it is expressed not by a sign but by a nonmanual signal. The contrasting reference of IT is glossed with contrasting subscripts: The first IT has the subscript j to indicate reference to the Deaf world, while the second has the subscript k to indicate contrasting reference.

18. To express this sign and its reference and negation, the English translation adds a line not present in ASL.

opens his eyes and faces the locus of the Deaf world to which the deictic refers as he signs THIS MINE ("This [world] is mine"). Second, the first time the deictic is signed with a dismissive flick of the wrist, signaling his rejection of the hearing world. The second time the hand not only points to the locus of the Deaf world, but remains in position while the final sign MINE is signed. The poem ends with the two signs THIS MINE simultaneously displayed.

The last line makes two strong assertions that express the poem's message. The poet affirms both his rejection of the hearing world and his identification with the Deaf world. The formal devices he uses set it off from the rest of the poem and make it the strongest line in the poem. It stands in stark contrast to the rest of the poem in four ways.

First, the last line breaks the pattern of four signs per line; it has only three.

Second, the three signs have a uniformity of form that the signs in no other line exhibit.[19] This is the only line in the poem built on only one handshape.[20] All three signs are articulated at chest level and have similar movements. The uniformity of the three signs in the last line gives it a visual strength and unity that no other line has.

Third, the last line is symmetrical. The first sign is articulated to the left, the second to the right, the third in the center. No other line in the poem exhibits such symmetry.

Fourth, and strikingly, the last line displays *three* shifts in hand dominance. In ordinary signing, all three signs would be signed by the strong hand, but in the poem, they are signed in turn by the weak hand, the strong hand, and the weak hand. Dominance shifts with each sign in this line. The first shift marks the break between the second stanza and the last line. The other two formally divide the line into three parts, marking its tripartite structure.

Why does the last line contrast so strongly with the other lines? Why does it have a tripartite structure instead of their four-signs-per-line, two-signs-per-hemistich structure?

The last line's contrasts with the other lines set it apart from the first two parts of the poem; it constitutes the third major structural unit by itself. For a single line to function in this way, it must be strong enough to stand on a par with the first two stanzas. This is one reason it contrasts so strongly with the other lines. Since the poem is published not as a written text but as a filmed performance, the last line must be different enough not to be interpreted as part of the second stanza. The fact that it begins with a shift in dominance reinforces its separation.

Recognizing the last line as the third major structural unit of the poem means that the poem itself has a tripartite structure. The last line has a tripartite structure because it encapsulates the tripartite structure of the entire poem. The first two signs of the last line indicate the two worlds, just as the first two parts of the poem describe them. The third sign is the climax of the last line, just as the last

---

19. The sole exception is the last line of the first stanza, in which the same sign occurs four times.

20. Even the last line of the first stanza, which has four repetitions of the same sign, uses more than one handshape, since handshape changes from O to 5 twice in each repetition of the sign.

line is the climax of the poem. Each sign in the last line stands for one of the three major parts of the poem.

The first deictic sign, which refers to the hearing world, is negated. ASL has a sign NOT that expresses negation, but the poet does not use it. If he did, the last line would conform to the pattern of four signs per line: NOT THAT THIS MINE. This, however, would completely destroy the last line's effectiveness. Gone would be its unity, based on its three signs' uniformity in handshape, type of movement, and chest-level articulation.[21] Gone would be the line's left-right-center symmetry. Gone would be the tripartite structure through which the last line recapitulates the structure of the poem itself. The last line can express negation while maintaining its uniformity, its symmetry, and its tripartite structure because ASL grammar allows negation to be expressed by the face and head (reinforced in performance by a wrist flick) while the hand signs the first deictic sign, preserving the last line's uniformity, symmetry, and tripartite structure.

The last line's power is due, in part, to its economy of means. Its three signs are alike in handshape, in being articulated at chest level, and in type of movement. The first two signs' deixis is reinforced by the signer's eye gaze and by the orientation of his face and body. Eye, face, hand, and body go first toward the locus of one world, then toward the locus of the other, uniting to emphasize the contrast between the two worlds.

The last line's staying power comes from the fact that the deictic, signed by the strong hand, remains in place while the weak hand signs MINE. Held in place at the end, the signs THIS MINE remain in viewers' memory. Strikingly, as the last sign MINE is signed, for the first time in the entire poem, the signer looks directly at his audience. By making eye contact, he signals that he is no longer in the role of someone describing his experiences in the two worlds but is communicating with his audience directly as he affirms his identification with the Deaf world.

Some Ways Linguistic Structure Contributes to the Poem's Impact

The Role of the ASL Deictic and Reference System

The ways ASL expresses deixis and reference play such an important role in this poem that it is hard to imagine how it could succeed without them.

First, the role of loci in ASL grammar is essential to the poem's economy of means. The poet never has to say which world he is talking about; the orientation of the signer's face and body and the direction of his eye gaze tell us.[22] Loci are exploited again in the last two lines, supplemented by the orientation of the

---

21. Unlike the open B handshape of the signs in the last line, NOT has the closed A handshape, and unlike their place of articulation at chest level, NOT is articulated on the chin.

22. The shift to a visual world at the beginning of the second stanza (expressed by the sign SEE and the shift in the orientation of the signer's face and body and in the direction of his eye gaze) is what motivates "But I see" at the beginning of the second stanza in the English translation. "But" announces a shift, and "I see" puts us into a visual world. Repetition of "I see" through most of the second stanza corresponds to the orientation of the signer's face and body toward the locus of the Deaf world.

hand in IT-LIKE-ME and the deictic sign, so that eye, face, and hand unite to express contrasting reference to the two worlds.

Second, in the second stanza, the way eye gaze combines with the classifier predicates and the angle of the deictic sign enables us to see the landscape through the signer's eyes and share his discoveries and elation.

Third, the ASL deictic system can express more contrasts than English demonstratives, which provide only a two-way contrast between *this* and *that*. A five-way contrast among positions in the signing space (maintained by the classifier predicates, the deictic sign, and eye gaze) indicates the relative positions of the elements of the landscape.

The deictic sign (glossed as THEY in the second stanza, but as THIS and THAT in the last line) has multiple functions. As a deictic, it points to the locus of each element in the landscape and those of the two worlds. As a pronominal, it serves as the subject of DEAF. It marks an elevated style such as would be used in a sermon.[23] Like an honorific, it honors each element of the landscape and gives the description of the Deaf world a special aura. These effects come from a sign whose prominence is enhanced because each occurrence involves a shift in hand dominance, which marks the caesura in the second stanza and the tripartite structure of the last line. The deictic gives the poem's last line its symmetry and its uniformity in handshape, movement, and chest-level articulation. The near-pun between the deictic and the ASL sign GROW-UP suggests the powerful image of growing up deaf in a world of nature that is also deaf. Finally, in the last line, the deictic is used to reinforce the poem's central theme in a subtle way. Earlier it occurred five times in "deictic DEAF." In the last line, it reappears in "deictic MINE." The unstated equation makes itself felt: DEAF [is] MINE.

For readers who do not know ASL, French can provide another perspective on the ASL original. In my translation below, the deictic *voilà* lets us visualize the signer pointing to each element of the landscape as he discovers it is deaf. Suffixing *–ci* and *–là* to the French demonstrative *celui* mimics the ASL deictic's ability to refer to the hearing and Deaf worlds in turn.

> Mais je vois
> Je vois les roches éparpillées sur la terre—les voilà qui sont sourdes
> Je vois les eaux des lacs et des mares—les voilà qui sont sourdes
> Je vois les arbres qui embellissent le paysage—les voilà qui sont sourds
> Je vois les montagnes dressées contre le ciel—les voilà qui sont sourdes
> Je vois les nuages qui circulent là en haut—les voilà qui sont sourds
> Ce monde-ci tout entier est sourd—sourd comme moi!
>
> Pas celui-là, celui-là ne l'est pas
> Pas celui-là, celui-ci est à moi![24]

---

23. In the English translation, *they* performs the deictic's pronominal function as subject of *deaf*. Like the ASL deictic, *behold* directs the hearer to look at each element of the landscape and belongs to an elevated register not used in conversation but which could be used in a sermon.

24. The next-to-last line of this French translation corresponds to the last part of the previous line in the ASL original. It most naturally forms a couplet with the last line, both set off from what precedes.

The Role of Syntactic Structure

We have seen evidence that "Deaf World" consists of two major parts: (a) Each describes a different world; (b) each is performed with the face and body oriented toward a different locus in the signing space; (c) they display different repeated elements and patterns of repetition; and (d) they incorporate symbols drawn from different sets: human contrivances and the world of nature. Differences in syntactic structure also reinforce the contrast between the two worlds.

The key to understanding syntactic structure in the first stanza is the verb glossed loosely as EMIT-NOISES or EMIT-NOISES$_E$. In terms of Padden's (1988) typology of plain, inflecting ("agreement"), and spatial verbs, this is a spatial verb.[25] Hence it can indicate both the source of the noises and where they are directed. For example, when the sources are music and movies, EMIT-NOISES is signed first in neutral space where MUSIC and CL:SCREEN MOVIE were signed, then EMIT-NOISES$_E$ is signed at the ears to indicate that they make noises in his ears.

As a verb, this sign is the predicate of a sentence each time it occurs. Consequently, the line HEARING-AIDS-PUT-ON-ME EMIT-NOISES$_E$ EMIT-NOISES EMIT-NOISES$_E$ consists of four sentences. The same holds of the last line in the first stanza: EMIT-NOISES$_E$ EMIT-NOISES$_E$ EMIT-NOISES$_E$ EMIT-NOISES$_E$. These two lines thus consist of eight sentences. In the line: [CL:SCREEN MOVIE EMIT-NOISES]$_{SENT}$ [EMIT-NOISES]$_{SENT}$, the hands' placement in the part of the signing space where CL:SCREEN MOVIE was signed shows that the movie on the screen is the source of the noises. The same holds for the line: [MUSIC EMIT-NOISES]$_{SENT}$ [EMIT-NOISES$_E$]$_{SENT}$. The essential point is that each occurrence of EMIT-NOISES is the predicate of a separate sentence. Consequently, there are four sentences each in the first and last lines and two each in the other two. This contrasts with syntactic structure in the second stanza.

[HEARING-AIDS-PUT-ON-ME]$_{SENT}$ [EMIT-NOISES$_E$]$_{SENT}$ [EMIT-NOISES]$_{SENT}$ [EMIT-NOISES$_E$]$_{SENT}$

[MUSIC EMIT-NOISES]$_{SENT}$ [EMIT-NOISES$_E$]$_{SENT}$

[CL:SCREEN MOVIE EMIT-NOISES]$_{SENT}$ [EMIT-NOISES]$_{SENT}$

[EMIT-NOISES$_E$]$_{SENT}$ [EMIT-NOISES$_E$]$_{SENT}$ [EMIT-NOISES$_E$]$_{SENT}$ [EMIT-NOISES$_E$]$_{SENT}$

[Noun Classifier-Pred]$_{SENT}$ [THEY DEAF]$_{SENT}$

[Noun Classifier-Pred]$_{SENT}$ [THEY DEAF]$_{SENT}$

[Noun Classifier-Pred]$_{SENT}$ [THEY DEAF]$_{SENT}$

[Noun Classifier-Pred]$_{SENT}$ [THEY DEAF]$_{SENT}$

[Noun Classifier-Pred]$_{SENT}$ [THEY DEAF]$_{SENT}$

In the second stanza, syntactic structure is uniform: Five successive lines have the same structure. Each sentence has an overt subject and predicate. Syntactic structure and poetic structure are fully congruent: Each sentence in syntactic structure corresponds to a hemistich in poetic structure and vice versa. The absence of such congruence is a key reason why there is scant evidence for the hemistich in the first stanza. The first stanza consists mostly of one-sign sentences, while these five lines don't have even one one-sign sentence.

---

25. Key evidence for this comes from the contrast between EMIT-NOISES-AT-EACH-OTHER and EMIT-NOISES-PAST-EACH-OTHER (cf. Padden 1988).

These syntactic differences between the two stanzas contribute significantly to the poem's emotional impact. In the first stanza, the lack of syntactic regularity, of balanced subject-predicate sentences, and of congruence with the poetic structure, as well as the predominance of staccato-like one-sign sentences, has a disordered, fragmented effect that accentuates the discordant picture the first stanza paints of the hearing world. After this relatively chaotic syntactic structure, as the signer shifts his body and eye gaze, we are suddenly in the ordered Deaf world with uniform syntactic structure, balanced subject-predicate sentences, and congruence between syntactic and poetic structure. All this reinforces the second stanza's picture of an orderly, harmonious Deaf world. The poet uses syntactic structure to accentuate the contrast between the hearing and Deaf worlds—the major theme of the poem.

The Role of Handshape

This contrast is further accentuated by the poet's use of handshape. In ordinary signing, signs with a change from one handshape to another are extremely common. Yet in the second stanza, all the signs use the same handshape throughout. That this is not accidental can be seen in the sign MOUNTAIN, which has two variants. The common variant has the closed A handshape followed by the open 5 handshape, but here the poet uses an alternative with only the closed A handshape. The other variant of MOUNTAIN would break the pattern in the second stanza, which consists entirely of signs with only one handshape. The second stanza's complete avoidance of signs with more than one handshape reinforces the feeling of stability and harmony in the landscape of the Deaf world.

In the first stanza, however, in the sign that indicates emission of irritating noises, the handshape changes abruptly from the closed O handshape to the open 5 handshape. This sign accounts for eleven of the nineteen sign tokens in the first stanza, and in each the handshape changes twice. These twenty-two brusque handshape changes have a jarring and discordant effect in a poem where all the other signs use only one handshape. These handshape changes occur in one-sign sentences, giving them prominence and heightening their fractured effect. The frequent repetition of this jarring handshape change accentuates the first stanza's discordant picture of the hearing world, while the stability of handshapes in the second stanza reinforces its ordered syntactic structure and the harmonious picture it paints of the Deaf world.

WHAT DOES "DEAF WORLD" REVEAL ABOUT THE POETIC RESOURCES OF SIGN LANGUAGES?

The Issues

The poetic devices in "Deaf World" raise questions about the poetic resources of sign languages in general. To what extent are they shared with spoken languages? Does the visual-manual modality give sign languages poetic resources unlike anything in spoken languages? Do they take advantage of the full range of possibilities this modality offers?

Mentioning sign poetry to nonsigners often elicits the response that it must be like dance, with graceful, rhythmic movements of the hands, arms, and body.

This suggests that sign poetry embraces the full range of possibilities the visual modality offers, with poetic resources unlike anything in spoken languages. However, this is not the case in "Deaf World," which exploits only aspects of the modality mediated by ASL grammar.

Poetic Resources Shared with Spoken Languages

Syntactic and semantic structure, structural parallelism, the degree of congruence between syntactic and poetic structure, and patterns of repetition all contribute to delineating lines and hemistichs in "Deaf World" and to the contrasting pictures of the hearing and Deaf worlds. These devices bring out commonalities between poetry in signed and spoken languages. Poets in both modalities exploit words' phonological properties, as Valli exploits handshape in ASL, to achieve poetic effects. To discover what is distinctive in sign poetry, we now turn to the poetic devices in "Deaf World" that are particular to sign languages.

The Visual Aspect of the Modality: Valli's Description of the Landscape

When describing the landscape in the second stanza, the poet seems to be painting a picture in the air, using classifier predicates and the visual modality to place each aspect of nature in its place in a beautiful landscape. What makes classifier predicates different from other signs in this respect lies in ASL grammar: Their relative position is used to indicate that of the objects described. The fact that the placement of the classifier predicates in "Deaf World" is meaningful, while that of most other signs is not, follows from ASL grammar.[26] Similarly, the deictic functions of eye gaze, of the deictic sign, and of the orientation of the signer's face and body are all mediated by the notion of locus in ASL grammar. What initially appears to be the use of the visual modality to paint a picture in the air is really the use of two fundamental elements of ASL grammar: classifier predicates and loci. Poetic devices that may appear to be due to the visual modality are actually due to ASL grammar. Of the many ways the visual modality could be exploited, in "Deaf World" it is exploited only in ways mediated by ASL grammar.[27]

The Manual Aspect of the Modality: The Role of Dominance Shift

Perhaps the clearest example in "Deaf World" of a poetic resource unique to sign languages are the shifts in hand dominance that the poet exploits for three kinds of effects. First, dominance shift has an aesthetic effect. Having THEY and DEAF

---

26. In the first stanza, Valli exploits the position of EMIT-NOISES to indicate the noises' source. EMIT-NOISES is a "spatial verb"—another class of signs whose position is meaningful (cf. footnote 25). A poet can exploit the position of signs whose position is *not* meaningful for aesthetic or poetic effects, as Valli does in his poem "Hands" (Valli 1990b, 1995), where the poem's four central lines are articulated in a circle in the signing space. This use of the signing space is reminiscent of concrete poetry in spoken languages, where aesthetic or poetic considerations govern the arrangement of words on the page.

27. The extent to which ASL grammar itself exploits the possibilities of the visual modality is an interesting question that is beyond the scope of this chapter.

signed by different hands in the second stanza yields a visual balance that would not be possible if both were signed by the strong hand. In the last line, the contrasting reference to the two worlds presents a symmetrical picture with the deictic signed on opposite sides of the signing space. Second, with the deictic THEY signed by the weak hand in the second stanza, it remains in place while the strong hand signs DEAF, enabling us to see THEY DEAF displayed on the two hands simultaneously. In the last line, the deictic THIS is held in place after MINE is signed, heightening the prominence and visibility of the last sentence: THIS [is] MINE. Third, dominance shift delineates poetic structure, marking the caesura that divides the line into hemistichs in the second stanza and dividing the poem's last line into three parts.

While dominance shift has no counterpart in spoken languages, it is not just a poetic response to the aesthetic possibilities of the visual-manual modality. There is evidence that hand dominance is mediated by a constraint of ASL grammar:

> STRONG-ACTIVE: The strong hand (the right hand for right-handers, the left hand for left-handers) is used as active articulator.

The evidence comes from its interaction with a phonetic constraint proposed by Mathur and Rathmann (2006) to account for the ill-formedness of inflected verb forms that would require radioulnar pronation of the strong hand. Perlmutter (2006) proposes that STRONG-ACTIVE is a phonetic implementation constraint in ASL grammar and is outranked by Mathur's and Rathmann's phonetic constraint. This correctly predicts that the inflected forms in question can be articulated by the weak hand in those cases where their articulation by the strong hand would violate Mathur's and Rathmann's phonetic constraint. This is an argument that STRONG-ACTIVE is a constraint of ASL grammar. Violations of STRONG-ACTIVE are independently attested and are mediated by ASL grammar. In violating STRONG-ACTIVE for poetic purposes, Valli is violating a grammatical constraint that signers sometimes violate for other reasons.

Segmental vs. Nonsegmental Expression of Information

Lines of verse are built on countable elements. In "Deaf World," the line consists of four signs. In other types of verse, the countable elements may be syllables or morae. Because ASL can express negation with the face and head, it can be expressed without disrupting the tripartite structure of the last line of "Deaf World" or the pattern of four signs per line in the preceding one. This is a poetic resource of ASL. Is it unique to sign languages?

What is essential is not that negation is expressed with the face and head, but that it is expressed nonsegmentally. This is possible in certain spoken languages as well, as in the Aboh dialect of Igbo, a Benue-Congo language spoken in southeastern Nigeria, where tone can express negation. For example, to say "he is going" in Aboh Igbo, one would say ọ je kọ, with low tone on all three syllables, while to say "he is not going," one could say ọ je kọ, with high tone on the first two syllables and low tone on the third.[28] This would enable a poet to express negation

---

28. I am indebted to Larry Hyman for calling my attention to Aboh Igbo and providing these examples.

without affecting the number of countable elements in the line. Spoken languages also have affixes that express negation or other semantic content without increasing the number of countable elements.

Nonetheless, ASL grammar provides more channels to express information than spoken languages do. Nonmanual channels include eye gaze, head shakes, facial expression, and the orientation of the face and body. The mouth can express manner adverbials such as "carelessly" (tongue slightly protruding) or "attentively" (lips pursed). The mouth's shape can express small size or thinness. Puffed cheeks can express large size or fatness.[29] The number of distinct channels that can express semantic content in ASL is potentially a poetic resource.

ASL's distinct channels are a poetic resource in another respect as well: Their combined effect can be greater than any of them would have alone. In "Deaf World," the placement of the classifiers in the signing space, the signer's eye gaze, and the angle of the hand in the deictic sign are coordinated in the description of the landscape. In the poem's last line, eye, face, hand, and body together go first toward one locus, then the other. The poet exploits the coordination of these channels for poetic effect. With fewer channels and less semantic content expressed nonsegmentally, such poetic effects in spoken languages may be more limited.

Does "Deaf World" Take Full Advantage of the Visual Modality?

The distribution of articulation between the two hands offers a good illustration of the relation between "Deaf World" and ASL grammar. As shown by Battison (1978), in ASL signs where both hands move, they both have the same handshape and their movements are either the same or mirror images. This holds throughout "Deaf World." If the poem took full advantage of the possibilities of the visual modality, there would be no reason for it to obey these grammatical constraints. In "Tears of Life" (Valli 1995), however, the weak hand in the G handshape expresses the shedding of a tear as the signer reflects on the stages of life, while the strong hand signs the rest of the poem. This violates Battison's constraints on signs in which both hands move, but in a limited way: The weak hand articulates the same sign again and again. This is not full-fledged signing by the weak hand.

This example illustrates the two ways ASL poetry relates to ASL grammar. In the general case, it obeys ASL grammatical constraints. By relaxing them, one at a time and in limited ways, a poet can achieve specific poetic effects. Only rarely, and to achieve such effects, does Valli depart from ASL grammar.

Similarly, STRONG-ACTIVE, which makes the strong hand the active articulator in signs in which both hands do not move, is obeyed throughout "Deaf World," except where Valli shifts hand dominance at the caesura in the second stanza and in the poem's last line. These violations would not have the same effect if this constraint were violated throughout the poem. Adherence to it elsewhere makes the violations stand out and gives them their poetic effect.

---

29. Intonational functions (e.g., the marking of yes/no questions, wh-questions, and topics, which in ASL are marked in the zone of the face above eye level) are not considered here because they are nonsegmental in both modalities and therefore irrelevant to the comparison. Wilbur (2000) discusses a wide range of phenomena expressed through nonmanual channels in ASL.

If "Deaf World" took full advantage of the possibilities of the visual modality, it could include movements of the hands, arms, and body unlike anything in signing. It could be like dance, as some nonsigners imagine sign poetry to be. None of this is found in "Deaf World," which does not use movements or parts of the body not sanctioned by ASL grammar. The medium of "Deaf World" is not the visual modality, but ASL. The poet has revealed some of ASL's poetic resources by responding to the challenge of using only what ASL grammar makes available to produce a work of verbal art. Valli's work shows that by itself, ASL is all a poet needs to create poetry. This suggests a way to refocus Dante's Hypothesis:

> Dante's Hypothesis:
> Natural language has all it takes to serve as the vehicle of poetry.

In What Sense Are Natural Languages "More Noble?"

Dante claimed that natural languages are "more noble," that is, more suited to poetry than language based on consciously promulgated rules. The evidence for poetic structure in "Deaf World" strongly supports Dante's Hypothesis, which raises a question: Why? What guarantees that a natural language can serve as the vehicle of poetry? What makes it "more noble?"

Natural languages are part of nature. They are what results when children learn a language without explicit instruction. This gives them a richness of structure for poetry to exploit. In just five lines in the second stanza, "Deaf World" exploits patterns at all these levels:

Discourse level:

Face and torso are oriented toward the locus of the Deaf world as the Deaf world is described.

Semantic level:

a. Each line describes one aspect of the landscape and says it is deaf.
b. Each hemistich has one noun phrase of which one thing is predicated.

Syntactic level:

a. Each of the two hemistichs in a line is a sentence.
b. Each sentence has an overt subject and predicate.
c. Syntactic parallelism in first hemistichs: noun + classifier predicate
d. Unit of repetition in second hemistichs is a sentence: THEY DEAF.

Grammar of classifier predicates:

Placement of classifiers in the signing space reflects the relative position of the objects described.

Deictic and referential level:

a. Angle of the hand in the deictic sign reflects locus of referent.
b. Eye gaze reflects locus of referent.

Word level:

Four words per line, two per hemistich

Phonological level:

a. Only one handshape per sign
b. All classifier predicates use handshapes with all fingers extended or bent.

Phonetic level:

Caesura marked by shift in hand dominance.

The contrasting pictures of the Deaf and hearing worlds conveyed by the meaning of the signs (the semantic level) are reinforced by the poet's use of contrasting devices at other levels of linguistic and poetic structure. The beautiful and ordered Deaf world is described with an ordered poetic structure in which each line and hemistich and the caesura are all clearly demarcated, the latter exploiting dominance shift at the phonetic level. This contrasts with the first stanza describing the hearing world, where the lines are not divided into evenly balanced hemistichs. At the syntactic level, the lines describing the ordered Deaf world consist of two sentences, each with a balanced internal structure with an overt subject and predicate. This picture of stability is reinforced at the phonological level by the use of signs with only one handshape. The syntactic structure in the first stanza, by contrast, is not uniform from line to line and consists mostly of staccato-like one-sign sentences with two abrupt handshape changes that have a disordered and fragmented effect. The syntactic differences result in total congruence between syntactic and poetic structure in the second stanza and a dissociation between syntactic and poetic structure in the first. The second stanza uses parallel classifier constructions to make the description of the landscape vivid. At the deictic and referential level, the angle of the deictic sign and the eye gaze enable us to see the landscape through the signer's eyes. All this occurs in just five lines.

The simultaneous exploitation of linguistic patterns at multiple levels of structure plays a major role in making "Deaf World" poetry rather than prose. The fact that all natural languages have structure at multiple levels for poetry to exploit is what makes them suitable vehicles for poetry. This is the linguistic reality behind the insight Dante articulated more than seven hundred years ago.

REFERENCES

Battison, Robbin. 1978. *Lexical borrowing in American Sign Language.* Silver Spring, Md.: Linstok Press.

Botterill, Steven. 1996. *Dante, De vulgari eloquentia* [On the eloquence of the vernacular]. Cambridge Medieval Classics 5. New York: Cambridge University Press.

Bragg, Lois, ed. 2001. *Deaf world: A historical reader and primary sourcebook.* New York: New York University Press.

Dannis, Joe, producer. 1994. *Charles Krauel: A profile of a Deaf filmmaker.* VHS. San Diego: Dawn Pictures.

Dante Alighieri. 1305. *De vulgari eloquentia* [On the eloquence of the vernacular]. Unfinished manuscript. First published Paris, 1577. Prepared for publication by Jacopo Corbinelli. Page references are to Botterill 1996.

Emmorey, Karen, ed. 2002. *Perspectives on classifier constructions in sign languages.* Mahwah, N.J.: Lawrence Erlbaum Associates.

Fant, Louie. 1980. Drama and poetry in sign language: A personal reminiscence. In *Sign language and the Deaf community: Essays in honor of William C. Stokoe,* ed. Charlotte Baker and Robbin Battison, 193–200. Silver Spring, Md.: National Association of the Deaf.

Hotchkiss, John. 1913. *Memories of old Hartford.* Motion picture film. National Association of the Deaf. Reissued on VHS in *The preservation of American Sign Language: The complete historical collection.* 1997. Burtonsville, Md.: SMI/Sign Media.

Klima, Edward S., and Ursula Bellugi. 1976. Poetry and song in a language without sound. *Cognition* 4:45–97.

———. 1979. *The signs of language.* Cambridge, Mass.: Harvard University Press.

Lentz, Ella Mae. 1995. *The treasure: Poems by Ella Mae Lentz.* VHS. Berkeley: In Motion Press.

Mathur, Gaurav, and Christian Rathmann. 2006. Variability in verbal agreement forms across four signed languages. In *Laboratory phonology 8: Varieties of phonological competence,* ed. Louis Goldstein, Douglas H. Whalen, and Catherine T. Best, 287–314. Berlin: Mouton de Gruyter.

Padden, Carol A. 1988. *Interaction of morphology and syntax in American Sign Language.* New York: Garland.

Padden, Carol, and Tom Humphries. 1988. *Deaf in America: Voices from a culture.* Cambridge, Mass.: Harvard University Press.

———. 2005. *Inside Deaf culture.* Cambridge, Mass.: Harvard University Press.

Parasnis, Ila, ed. 1996. *Cultural and language diversity and the Deaf experience.* New York: Cambridge University Press.

Perlmutter, David M. 1987. No nearer to the soul. *Natural Language and Linguistic Theory* 4:515–23.

———. 2006. Some current claims about sign language phonetics, phonology, and experimental results. In *Laboratory phonology 8: Varieties of phonological competence,* ed. Louis Goldstein, Douglas H. Whalen, and Catherine T. Best, 315–38. Berlin: Mouton de Gruyter.

Peters, Cynthia. 2000. *Deaf American literature: From carnival to the canon.* Washington, D.C.: Gallaudet University Press.

———. 2001. Rathskeller: Some oral-traditional and not-so-traditional aspects of ASL literature. In *Deaf world: A historical reader and primary sourcebook,* ed. Lois Bragg. New York: New York University Press.

Rutherford, Susan D., producer. 1984. *American culture: The Deaf perspective.* Part 3 [of 4]: *Deaf literature.* VHS. San Francisco: San Francisco Public Library, with the assistance of Deaf Media.

Stokoe, William C. 1960. Sign language structure: An outline of the visual communication systems of the American Deaf. Studies in Linguistics 8. Buffalo, N.Y.: University of Buffalo.

Valli, Clayton. 1990a. How I came to write poetry. In *Poetry in motion: Original works in ASL: Clayton Valli.* VHS. Burtonsville, Md.: SMI/Sign Media.

———. 1990b. *Poetry in motion: Original works in ASL: Clayton Valli.* VHS. Burtonsville, Md.: SMI/Sign Media, Inc.

———. 1990c. The nature of a line in ASL poetry. In *SLR '87: Papers from the Fourth International Symposium on Sign Language Research,* ed. William Edmondson and Fred Karlsson, 171–81. Hamburg: Signum Press.

———. 1995. *ASL poetry: Selected work of Clayton Valli.* VHS, reissued as DVD. San Diego: Dawn Pictures.

Veditz, George W. 1913. *The preservation of the sign language.* Motion picture film. National Association of the Deaf. Reissued on VHS in *The preservation of American Sign Language: The complete historical collection.* 1997. Burtonsville, Md.: SMI/Sign Media. English translation in Bragg (2001, 83–85).

Wilbur, Ronnie. 2000. Phonological and prosodic layering of nonmanuals in American Sign Language. In *The signs of language revisited,* ed. Karen Emmorey and Harlan Lane, 215–44. Mahwah, N.J.: Lawrence Erlbaum Associates.

15 | Flying Words:
A Conversation between
Peter Cook and Kenny Lerner

The Flying Words Project is a two-person act featuring Peter Cook and Kenny Lerner, who collaboratively compose and perform American Sign Language (ASL) poetry. While ASL is their primary medium, Flying Words' performances also incorporate elements of spoken word, mime, and dance. This interview began with a question from the editors, and the artists simply ran with it in an e-mail exchange between the two of them.

Their poem "Need" can be seen on the accompanying *Signs and Voices* DVD (**clip 15**). It is performed in a hotel room; as Peter and Kenny explain in their conversation, they often create and rehearse poems in hotel rooms while on the road performing. Peter and Kenny can be contacted at flyingwordsproject@yahoo.com.

EDITORS: Can you tell us a little about the way you two work?

KENNY: You want to start, Peter?

PETER: First of all, time is a luxury for us nowadays. We don't have much time to get together because we simply live too far apart. In the old days, we lived in the same house and were able to create poems on the spot daily. Kenny would be able to wake me up at 2 A.M. to work on new ideas! That's why I live five hundred miles away from him—so I can sleep!!! But when we do get together in person to create new work, we can talk about an idea and see it from different perspectives. For example, when working on a poem called "Psych Hospital: White Padded House," Kenny had this idea about characters in a psych ward who have different kinds of addictive personalities. This was from an old poem we created during our college years and later stopped using. I can't remember why we stopped using it. Perhaps we lost interest in it or it didn't fit into our show. Perhaps the momentum in the poem wasn't right.

KENNY: We actually have many bits and pieces of ideas and images floating around. Some of them will never get into any of our poems. But every so often, we'll have a new idea and it is missing something. We'll suddenly realize that an old idea fits it perfectly. . . . Maybe it's just one old image that needs to be re-worked and something will just fall into place.

PETER: That's true. At the same time, we have had great ideas that we simply didn't have the techniques to express properly. Sometimes we have an old poem that contains an image that we love to use, and then we create a new poem and find that the image from the old poem fits into the new poem and becomes stronger. We simply clip it out of the old poem and put it in new poems. It works great! Sometimes our fans will come to us and say, "Hey! I have seen that image before in another poem!" I think that's cool because we are giving our fans a déjà vu experience! Anyway, I remember I had a discussion with Clayton Valli about his poetry. We were playing with some of the images in his poem and creating new ones. He said to me, "Gee, I wish I could change my poem." I said to him, "Why not? You can do that. You own that work!" He shook his head, saying, "Once it's on videotape, it cannot be changed." I never see the works that Kenny and I create as finished products.

KENNY: Our work is constantly changing. Once we develop a poem, we need to perform it. . . . Something happens in performance that makes problems clear. . . . We'll realize that a particular image isn't clear enough or we're not happy with the feel of a piece. I recently suggested a small change in "Wise Old Corn #1," which is a poem we wrote almost ten years ago!

Getting back to the psych hospital poem—it has gone through many changes. We had an idea that didn't work. Both Peter and I had worked in psych ward settings, so we had a number of relatively true characters and situations. We began thinking about how individuals who are addicts are forced to do horrible things. . . . People get involved in crime. . . . People kill other people . . . and their addictive behaviors are bad for their own lives and those around them.

PETER: Yes, about these characters. They were interesting. I think we had at least four different characters but we ended up with only two. Why? Simply because the momentum wasn't right. The poem has its own momentum. No matter how important the images are or how powerful they are, if the momentum isn't strong, we simply throw them out!

KENNY: So as a result, we had to throw out the greatest character of all. It was a lady who would literally forget what had happened only moments before. . . . She was so perfect for this poem because it is about how nations can be addicted and how nations behave like individuals. If they are addicted to something like oil, they can start wars . . .

PETER: But we don't want to preach to our audience about the moral issues in our country. So we use the characters as metaphors for what has happened in our country. On the human level, I think people are lured into these things. Why? We all do experience these kinds of addictions.

Kenny, allow me to go off the point. . . . A good poem is like a good movie. There are some movies that will last forever because they have universal messages to which everyone can relate. A movie like *Citizen Kane* will last forever for a number of reasons. It is easy to follow yet powerful enough to hold our attention to the end of the movie. It also uses amazing cinematic techniques that changed the way films are made. Some of our poems will last a long time too, and others won't. The poem "Charlie" will last forever because it is about a dog who goes through combat training. Kenny and I love dogs. Everybody loves dogs. We know the impact of a war on people's lives. People also are addicted to stories about things that they never experience. We haven't changed this poem much since we first created it. It had a strong foundation: strong techniques such as handshape rhymes and repetition of images. People still want to see it performed. On the other hand, we sometimes create poems that last for just a few years because they may be too trendy to keep performing over many years.

KENNY: But we write them anyway. I always want to create the greatest poem ever written, but of course, I'll never succeed. You always want your work to last, but you need to express yourself whether it will last or not!

"Charlie" is a good example of how we work. Peter was reading a book on training dogs for war, and I was reading one on the Ho Chi Minh Trail, a system of trails and tunnels that helped the Vietnamese to defeat us. The poem had good ideas but it just wasn't working. Peter gave up for the evening and foolishly went to bed within five hundred miles of me.

PETER: It was a very short sleep . . .

KENNY: I sat there agonizing over this poem and then I was struck by the idea of this one image we could replay throughout the poem. . . . It became a kind of string that connects the entire work. It is of the dog running in slow motion and jumping up to bite the padded arm of his master. This image made the whole poem work. So I went in and woke up Peter . . .

PETER: Did I mention that it was 2 A.M.? Kenny was excited and showed me the idea while I was in bed. I thought it was a great idea! I loved the image of the running dog. It set up the mood for the poem. It held the poem together.

KENNY: If it was such a good idea, why weren't you willing to get up and try it?

PETER: Hello??? Did I mention it was 2 A.M.?

KENNY: You have to understand that back then, we had no video. So we had already lost many great ideas. We'd get the idea at night, go to bed, and by the morning, we'd forgotten an image or forgotten the rhythm. . . . Some of our best ideas were gone forever. I was determined not to forget this one.

PETER: Yes, I was simply too young to understand what it meant to lose an image or idea. You need to age to be a poet. So I said good night to Kenny.

KENNY: You were also too stupid to realize I would never give up. . . . There was no way Peter was going to sleep until we had tried my idea. . . . I knew if we tried it, we wouldn't forget it, but Peter refused to get out of bed.

PETER: For God's sake!!!! How many times have I said it?? It was 2 A.M.! But Kenny was right about that. . . . He was so determined. I couldn't get rid of him, so I said, "OK, I'll do it, but I stay in my bed!"

KENNY: He performed it lying there on his back in bed! But it was obvious that the idea worked and the poem has changed very little since that night. In fact, it is our most requested poem!

PETER: So, what I learn from this experience . . . what I learn from this wisdom . . . the witness protection program looks very appealing to me . . .

Kenny, you mentioned some things about how we work. Have we actually worked? I mean, we're always coming up with ideas. I think it's good that we always tell each other how we feel about our ideas. We never feel insulted if we tell each other an idea is bad because it is often bad. (And I might add, we have had several great ideas simply because we misunderstood each other.)

KENNY: Yes, it's easy for us to work together. Sometimes we struggle over the work itself, but not with each other. If something isn't good enough for one of us, we don't do it. Peter is a fountain of creativity. Sometimes we'll have an idea and I'll say, "try it again" . . . and he'll come up with the same image, but a little bit better. And I'll say, "do it again." And he'll come up with something a little different. It's amazing how many times we find the right image by simply prodding one another.

I tend to have many little ideas . . . like the Charlie idea we were talking about. I'll get a million of them. That's why I'm angry about the witness protection program. It's harder to get my many thoughts to Peter when I don't know where he is! Once I can find him, Peter will brood on an idea and then suddenly suggest a huge change. I remember one time he came back to Rochester from a trip with an idea about a poem we had called "Romero." The new idea completely changed the poem. Then I started hammering away at it again with my little changes and ideas.

PETER: We have so many poems that are completed because we took out the original ideas. We learned to let the original idea go so the poem would become stronger. We had one original idea that we were holding for three years. We kept working and working on the poem ("Wise Old Corn"). It wasn't working until one day, we took out the original idea. BAM! It worked!!!

KENNY: "Wise Old Corn" started off as one big poem and then broke itself down into three different poems that all go together. We perform them separately quite often. It's interesting. Sometimes an idea will develop in a couple of days. Last summer we were at the 36th Annual Poetry Festival in Rotterdam. We met this amazing poet from Romania named Constantin Abolut. He is a very simple old man with a simple style that elicits simple but powerful poetry.

Peter and I joined a workshop with poets from all over the world translating Constantin's various works. I'd like to add that we've been working on one series of poems called "Screen Door" for several years now. As we tried to translate Constantin's poem "Intruder" into ASL, we saw ourselves slowly but steadily moving farther and farther from actually translating the poem. Instead we were creating our own work loosely borrowing from Constantin's style. We literally showed him what we were doing and asked if it was okay. I was a little worried because he was strict about some of the other poets' translations, but he gave us nothing but encouragement. In a matter of a few days, we had created a short poem that we both love. Meanwhile, we are still stuck on "Screen Door"!

PETER: I'd like to go back to where Kenny was fuming about my relocation. Honestly, it does have a price. We don't have the opportunity to get together as often as we'd like to. For a few years, we were not able to create new ideas. Some of our poems became stale. . .

KENNY: Yeah, you can be working on something really good, but if there is too much time between work periods, you lose the motivation and the poem dies.

PETER: It was our dark ages. Truly dark. It's very difficult to hold onto ideas or create new ones without each other's feedback. I need to be simulated . . .

KENNY: You also need spelling lessons. . . . It's "stimulated" . . .

PETER: I can spell "relocation"!
    Anyway, I was invited to teach at the New York School for the Deaf in the nineties. I met a teacher who was very much into video technology. She came to me with exciting news. She told me it was possible to talk with someone through video online. I realized that this technology would solve our problem, making my escape impossible. Oh well . . .

KENNY: Actually, even with the witness protection program, after the dark ages, we were able to work together and come up with new ideas. We would fly to a city for a show, practice all day, and then work on new ideas all night. We'd do the show and fly home the next morning. Often we went back to our hotel in the evening after the show so we could work more on the new ideas and then videotape them so we wouldn't forget.

PETER: That's why we called one of our videotapes *The Can't Touch Tours.* No time to see wonderful things in other cities. Too busy . . . Then the video technology came. Bless them and, of course, curse them!
    We can have a rehearsal online. Kenny, at his Rochester office, can watch me and practice his voicing while I move around at my loft in Chicago five hundred miles away . . .
    Because of this technology, we were able to get rid of the stress of last-minute rehearsals in person. It is a wonderful break for us!

KENNY: It also allows us to work on new ideas. It can still be frustrating, especially because the technology has not developed enough to allow me to wake up Peter when I get a really good idea!

[Kenny and Peter are interrupted by themselves. When they return, they take up another topic.]

KENNY: I remember when we first started working together, we had several problems. For one thing, the Deaf President Now protests at Gallaudet were just beginning. We caught quite a bit of flack from people who didn't like the idea of a hearing person and a deaf person working together. It was frustrating for us because we were simply good friends with a great working relationship. We never thought about deafness or hearingness. But we were told that I was controlling Peter because he is deaf.

PETER: For the record, Kenny never control me in any way. Did I do this right, Kenny?

KENNY: It should be "controlled," not "control."

PETER: Really?

KENNY: Yes, change it. . . . NOW!

PETER: OK. For the record, Kenny never controlled me in any way.

At that time, I was labeled as not a Deaf poet because my works didn't have themes related to Deaf culture.

KENNY: Of course, this is absurd. One doesn't have to focus on a particular theme to be presenting a culture. In our work, we are always trying to show our ideas, not say them. Peter's skillful use of ASL everywhere he performs is showing the power of his language and his culture. People, deaf and hearing, are amazed wherever we go. So we don't need to say in a poem, "ASL is a language!" or "There is a powerful Deaf culture!" That is clear no matter what theme we choose to focus on. And we write what we write. We have found that when we try to force a particular theme, you can be sure it will be an unsuccessful poem.

I also have to add that we do create some poems with deafness as a theme. It's not like we're against these ideas! "Lost Culture," " I Am Ordered Now to Talk," and the recent poem that we ripped off from Neruda called "Ode to Words" are all examples of deaf themes in our poetry.

PETER: I think it is important for poets to express their feelings regardless of who they are. I do not believe in using deafness as a theme to define who is a Deaf poet. I believe that people who are masterful in manipulating their language are true poets, deaf or not. Don't get me wrong. I am stubborn and proud of my culture. I am damn proud of being Deaf. I will wear a T-shirt with a big "D" on it. It is simply not necessary to focus on deafness as a central theme in order to be a poet. "I Am Ordered Now to Talk" is my strongest anti-oral poem. Instead of signing, I use my voice and read aloud. The poem is about being forced to talk. I love the irony that I have to read it aloud. Yes, deaf people can't hear me speaking it aloud. I am aware that it is aimed at hearing audiences and that it affects them powerfully. The deaf audiences only get the real impact of the work by seeing the look of anguish on hearing peoples' faces. Lately, I have been experimenting with video and visual media so that Deaf audiences will have access to the poem. Also, it amazes me that after all these years, and all the poems that we've created in ASL, a lot of people, especially scholars, always use "I Am Ordered Now to Talk" in their presentations. I often wonder about their reasons for picking this poem over other sign poems. I find it simply ironic.

KENNY: We're running out of time, so maybe we can try to sum this all up. Our goal is to have fun and to play with language and ideas. In this conversation, we didn't really focus on the spoken words in our poems, but we work together on the spoken words just as we work on the sign language. We are a team and yet we are also individually able to express ourselves freely. I feel like we are extremely lucky. I like what we create, I enjoy performing the work, and I get to see a great friend regularly—a friend who, I might add, lives five hundred miles from me. How many friends do you see because you have to get together regularly with them for an upcoming job? The funny thing is that our relationship has almost entirely consisted of work. We met for the first time to work and we have worked ever since. But for us, work is play! Who could ask for anything more?

16 | Visual Shakespeare: *Twelfth Night* and the Value of ASL Translation

Peter Novak

The translation of Shakespeare's *Twelfth Night* into American Sign Language (ASL) reflects a confluence of cultures, where the nature and process of theatrical translation has been revisited and, to some extent, re-envisioned. This chapter describes and annotates the process of transmuting an oral/aural text into a visual/manual one—of transmuting Shakespeare's verbal wordplay into a poetry of sight. The translation stands at the center of two distinctly different cultures: the hearing world with Shakespeare as one of its greatest poets, and the American Deaf community with its visual/manual language and literature. The product of these two languages and literatures creates a new "text"—a literature of the body—a corporeal artifact that will expand conventional notions of language, text, and performance. There are two ideal outcomes from the continuation of translation projects like this one. First, perhaps this cultural fusion will help ASL translation and performance become more widely recognized both within the canon of scholarly study and as a source of rich and creative performance techniques in theater, film, and other forms of visual representation. Second, Shakespeare's work will emerge reconsidered in purely kinetic terms as a newly constructed cultural artifact along a vast history of interpretations and performances.

The translation began with funding from the Digital Media Center for the Arts (DMCA) at Yale University. The core translation team was comprised of four translators—two deaf and two hearing: Adrian Blue, Robert De Mayo, Catherine Rush, and Peter Novak. Beginning at Yale in the library of Trumbull College and continuing for sixteen months at various locations and houses, this team of four was joined by other artists along the way: Peter Cook, Jackie Roth, Frank Dattolo, Troy

This chapter is part of a larger project of translating some of Shakespeare's works into American Sign Language. An ASL/English website that features video clips from the translation and professional production, essays, and information about Shakespeare's life, career, and theater, along with lesson plans for teachers, can be found at www.aslshakespeare.com.

Kotsur, Sabrina Dennison, and Dennis Webster. The digital recording of the translation was done in part at the DMCA and also wherever we could set up a black background and video camera.

The ASL version of *Twelfth Night* raises questions about the nature of theatrical translation. It forces the translator to construct a new approach to performance and to other historical, theatrical, cultural, and critical features of translation. Each of these aspects of translation is affected by the visual and manual modality of ASL. The syntax of this language cannot be conveyed in the two dimensions of written text. As a result, videotape recording is fast becoming the textual choice for ASL literature and is the archival medium for translating *Twelfth Night* into ASL. This chapter includes several clips that illustrate the complexity of the translation and the significance of ASL as a performed language. Some clips were filmed in a television studio with a black background. Others are from the theatrical production of the translation that occurred in Philadelphia, produced by the Amaryllis Theater and performed at the Prince Music Theater. Though they are similar, the material differences between the studio translation and the theatrical performance could and should be analyzed for stylistic, literary, and cultural significance in the same way that Shakespeare's original is examined through both textual and performance criticism.

Robert Wechsler, writing about the devaluation of literary translation in America, contends that without translation, there would be little poetry in our own language. "Ah, but we have the original Shakespeare," he writes, "we're very lucky. However, the rest of the world is even luckier because it has new translations of Shakespeare every year, full of different sorts of beauty and power. We can see Shakespeare interpreted on stage by actors and directors, but not in language by translators" (Wechsler 1998, 28). As Americans, we have the unique opportunity to have Shakespeare translated on the stage through a language and culture that allows us to really *see* Shakespeare's words for the first time. This chapter is an introduction to the translation and to some issues and questions that such a visual text elicits.

BODY LANGUAGE

Twelfth Night is Shakespeare's only play that both opens and closes with music. With Orsino's initial command, "If music be the food of love, play on," an ASL translator of Shakespeare's most character-driven comedy is immediately thrust into interpretive and performance-related dilemmas. Roger Warren and Stanley Wells, co-editors of the Oxford edition of the play, write: "It is almost as if the printed text is a blueprint for the total experience of words and music together—which of course is how Shakespeare has conceived it, 'hearing' the musical phrases, played and repeated, blending with the spoken text" (Warren and Wells 1994, 28). It's a daunting process to think about translating a play so reliant on music and the spoken text into a nonspoken, nonmusical language. But the distance between Shakespeare and sign language is not so great as one might expect.

Speaking Shakespeare's language on the stage requires physical dexterity and articulation of thought through movement and gesture. Shakespeare's language was visceral, intended for the playhouse, where words were conveyed to thousands of theatergoers each day in London's teeming theatrical venues. Words and

movement combined in the visual presence of an actor, where visual and auditory cues were inextricably linked. J. L. Styan (1967) writes, "Shakespeare's identification with his character worked so strongly within him that physical gesture
forced itself upon the lines, moving the actor to reproduce its muscular activity.
Shakespeare wrote a gestic poetry" (56). An ASL translation enhances this gestic
element in Shakespeare's language without removing the "tone." Neither does it
eliminate the intricate rhymes and puns based on homonyms, or the articulations
of speech that help the listener move through a dependent clause to the end of a
thought. Rather, an ASL translation searches for a new paradigm of communication that reimagines Shakespeare's spoken text through visual reproduction. All
previous conceptions of language, rhyme, rhythm, pun, and voice itself must now
begin with the body, with that "gestic poetry" of an Elizabethan dramatist.

But how to "write" a language of the body? Numerous methods of notating
three-dimensional movement have been attempted throughout the centuries, with
varying degrees of success. In 1928 the most extensive form of notation for dance
was developed by Rudolf von Laban (1879–1958). His system, which attempts to
record a wide range of human motion, is a complex system of signs and symbols.
Sophisticated though it is, "Labanotation" lacks a method to transcribe the complicated linguistic structure and grammar of ASL. It was created to document
large body movements, not the intricate patterns and movements of the face and
hands together that ASL demands. It wasn't until the 1970s that linguist William
Stokoe began his method of transcribing sign language on paper in an attempt to
record the complexities of the language and to offer a method of reading ASL.
Other systems such as Signwriting and Hamburg Notation System (HamNoSys)
have become popular among linguists who have attempted to study signed languages around the globe.

All ASL translators face the daunting and frustrating task of trying to find an
appropriate way to notate their translations. Every individual, unless trained in
the complicated systems named above, has a different way of glossing an English
word, idea, or sentence in ASL. Usually, the words that serve as glosses of ASL
are written in English, which is why many people wrongly consider ASL a reduced version of English. For example, below are Malvolio's lines on the left,
glossed by two different members of the translation team on the right:

Shakespeare

"There is example for't: the Lady
of the Strachey married the yeoman
of the wardrobe." (II, v, 39–40)

Translation Member 1

STORY HAPPENED BEFORE, HONOR,
WOMAN=RIGHT FELL IN LOVE SEWER
PERSON, WOMAN LEVEL HIGH, MAN LEVEL
LOW, MEET IN MIDDLE MARRY

Translation Member 2

2H-STORY 2H-HAPPEN RT-BEFORE / RT-
HONOR, RT-WOMAN / LF-MAN, LOW-LEVEL /
RT-FALL-IN-LOVE-LF (MEET IN THE MIDDLE) /
MARRY

Perusing the written transcriptions of this relatively simple sentence from the
play, it becomes almost impossible to gain the full meaning of the glosses. One

person glosses "sewer person" while another glosses the same signs as "low-level." The second team member uses "2H" to indicate two-handed signs, and either "LF" or "RT" to indicate directionality or hand dominance. Even with individual glossing styles, translation team members may not remember what exactly they meant by "sewer person" or "low-level" only a few days after a translation session. In fact, when reading the glossed script again, the translation team mistook the gloss "SEWER" to mean something akin to the gutter, when in reality it was a "sew-er" or a person who sews. It is an important sign that the second translator failed to include, because it referred to the "yeoman of the wardrobe" in Shakespeare's original.

The confusion that results from various and individual methods of glossing is the primary reason for immediately rehearsing and videotaping the translation a few pages at a time. The digitized translation became an important tool both for continuous work and for later analysis of it. The ability to "reread" the translation allowed the translation team to review earlier moments in the process and to make changes accordingly, often clarifying earlier translations or making visual parallels with later moments. "Movement," as Keir Elam (1980) notes, "is continuous, and is open to analysis only through the overall syntactic patterns of a (preferably filmed) stretch of kinesic behavior" (71). Videotape or film allows us to identify and understand those language movements in ASL within the full range of their expression alongside the facial expressions that ASL requires in order to convey meaning.

While Malvolio's lines above are relatively simple to follow, others grew so complicated that the written translation merely says "see videotape" when glosses were ultimately too time-consuming and difficult to produce. There were brief moments when the text existed only in the physical memory of the translation team until it could be refigured on our bodies in front of the video camera—a process not unlike anonymous scribes remembering their lines for a scribe who later recreated the written text for printing. This process also highlights a philosophical component of the task of English-to-ASL translation: This is neither a literary translation nor a "creative art" but rather, in the words of Robert Wechsler (1998), a "performing art." But the intrinsically performative and visual nature of ASL requires a new analysis of performance texts, one based on the understanding of the ASL translation *as* literature and performance simultaneously. A better "performance" of the translation on videotape actually makes a better translation. See for example this short moment when Sir Toby Belch tries to convince the disguised Viola that Sir Andrew Aguecheek, a coward by nature, is a virile knight looking for a fight (**clip 16.1**). Dennis Webster's performance of Sir Toby Belch in the Amaryllis Theater production in Philadelphia invests the translation with a performance that cannot be separated from the textual elements of the signs alone. His bearded, slovenly physicality is matched by an over-the-top presentation of bravery, swordplay, and grandeur. For the line "Souls from bodies hath he divorced three," Webster presents an image from classic films and cartoons. Using a 1-classifier on one hand to act as a sword, he swipes across the 3-classifier of his other hand to signify three people who immediately drop dead. He uses another 3-classifier that rises up from the three dead bodies to show their souls ascending toward heaven. He ends it by adding the sign of the cross, which was not included in the translation CDs, but now becomes a fixed element of the

translation for future study. Performance imbues the translation with the physicality and style of the individual signers.

Class and Gender

American Sign Language can render historical and social notions of gender and
power onto the body in ways that English cannot. In ASL, status, class, or power
is visually relational; those with greater status are located in space over and above
those with lesser status. With the ability to render these relationships on the body,
ASL transforms hidden or historical assumptions and meanings in English into
visual constructs and images. Consider the simplicity of the words *thee, thou,* and
you. While contemporary audiences might think words like *thee* and *thou* are more
formal, they were actually more familiar in Shakespeare's day. ASL has an
honorific form of *you* that illustrates status and class more clearly. We used these
distinctions throughout the translation to indicate levels of relationships or shifts
in power.

In another example, Malvolio's line "The Lady of the Strachey married the
yeoman of the wardrobe" manifests a clear separation of classes (II, v, 39–40).
Christina Malcolmson (1991) argues that gender operates only through its relationship to class structures in *Twelfth Night* and that ontologically, women always
occupied a lower position of status. The play, she writes, "was written during a
period before a woman's place was imagined as a separate sphere, since, for the
Renaissance, a woman was considered to be analogous to other social inferiors
in a hierarchical society" (30). The translation renders this status visually. For
Malvolio, if a woman of higher status (the Lady of the Strachey) marries a man
of lower status (the yeoman of the wardrobe), then the woman's status decreases
while the man's increases. Notice how this is foregrounded spatially through the
levels at which Malvolio places these two individuals and the locations where they
meet in space around his body (**clip 16.2**). This example illustrates one of many
ways in which aspects of materialist feminist or new historical readings of the play
can be literally "incorporated" into the ASL text.

The performative nature of ASL in translation also allows for visual augmentation of simple narrative structure. Take for example Malvolio's lines below
in which he fantasizes about being married to his mistress Olivia. Christina
Malcolmson argues that

> Malvolio's crime is not that he, as a gentleman, wants to marry a count-
> ess, or even that a steward wants to marry his mistress; it is that he will
> use his new position to disrupt traditional customs and rituals, and that
> such use of his "prerogative" will be motivated by an ambition to estab-
> lish his superiority and to impose his will on others. (1991, 32)

The prim and proper steward, inflamed by the power gained by marrying up,
sends for his new wife's cousin, Sir Toby Belch, whom he plainly despises:

> Seven of my people with an obedient start make out for him. I frown the
> while, and perchance wind up my watch, or play with my—some rich
> jewel. Toby approaches; curtsies there to me. (2.5, 55–58; **clip 16.3**)

The translation allows for visual augmentation of the text, providing nuance and explication of character in ways that the original cannot. In ASL, the imposition of Malvolio's will assumes abusive undertones. When "Toby" (not "Sir Toby") finally arrives before Malvolio, rather than simply "approaching," Toby is heaved into the room, skids across the floor, and leaps up to face the steward. Malvolio then provides a disapproving look until Toby finally "bows" to him in humiliation. It's not just that Malvolio will impose his will on others, as Malcolmson argues, it's that he is so decidedly tyrannical and overreaching with his newfound authority. ASL allows Malvolio's imagined fantasy to be played out visually. Malvolio can physically objectify and control the images in his fantasy by performing them on his own hands. It's as though he is the director of his own play and can control the objects of both his desire and derision.

The ASL translation of *Twelfth Night* also elicits different features of character. Throughout the translation, Malvolio's inner concupiscence threatens to burst through his prudish pretense in ways more visually evocative than the English original. Adrian Blue addresses this moment in chapter 17 of this volume. Take, for example, Malvolio's description of the young girl disguised as the boy Cesario who waits at the gate outside Olivia's house:

Olivia
    Of what personage and years is he?

Malvolio
    Not yet old enough for a man, nor young enough for a boy: as a squash is before 'tis a peascod, or a codling when 'tis almost an apple. 'Tis with him in standing water between boy and man. He is very well-favoured, and he speaks very shrewishly. One would think his mother's milk were scarce out of him. (1.5, 149–55; **clip 16.4**)

In English, there is nothing overtly sexual to a modern audience about these lines; however, the bawdiness of Malvolio's lines is blatantly obvious in ASL. Malvolio chooses vividly phallic imagery to describe Cesario, a strategy that functions both as a comic visual joke—since Cesario is really female—and as a reminder that the part was originally played by a young boy who hadn't yet reached maturity. While describing the young boy, Malvolio uses signs designating vegetables and fruit. But the signs have a double meaning and the images are of a boy whose penis (squash) has not yet matured and whose testicles (apples) have not yet dropped (grown heavy). As he shows the difference "between boy and man," he locates Cesario somewhere in the middle, using a 1-classifier to resemble a semi-erect penis. But Malvolio seems oblivious to the sexual nature of the signs he uses, contributing to the disruption of social norms and rituals in a comic display of ASL double entendre.

VERSE, RHYME, RHYTHM, AND PUNS

The persistent problem for any translator of Shakespeare's plays is the issue of verse structure. Shakespeare varies his use of language from the rhythms of blank verse and rhymed tetrameter to simple narrative or elaborate description in naturalistic prose, providing actors and audiences written and aural clues to comic or dramatic structures. J. L. Styan (1967) writes about *Twelfth Night* particularly, arguing that most of the scenes without Sir Toby flow in an "aura of poetry" but that Act III, Scene iv questions that flow because of Shakespeare's amalgamation of forms.

> Here the Malvolio and Viola plots are pursued together, and the mood passes successively from Olivia's "mad" poetic anguish to the witty taunting of the "mad" Malvolio in prose; then it passes to Olivia's verse and again back to prose for the farce of the duel, finally rising to verse for the resurgence of the romantic plotting as Antonio the sea-captain re-enters to save "Sebastian." (161)

In addition to these sudden changes in verse and prose, Shakespeare includes rhymed lyrics in songs and extensive puns or plays on words. Each of these modes of language presents different challenges to a visual translation of the play and is translated using a variety of linguistic strategies.

French translators of Shakespeare, for example, have to grapple with the differences in "classical" verse structure. In French, that metric structure is the alexandrine line consisting of twelve syllables with major stresses on both the sixth syllable and the last syllable. The closest foot-based verse would be iambic hexameter. In English, verse meter is essentially a convention of patterned stresses. Stress is a natural aspect of the sound of individual words. Meter, however, is an artificial construct imposed upon language. While sound is what establishes the natural stress of a word in English and some other spoken languages, sound cannot be the basis for word stress and therefore metrical structure in ASL. Similarly, the hearing concept of rhyme, which is based upon a "musicality" of identical sounds made from the primary stress to the end of a word, is equally foreign in ASL. But ASL does have a powerful visual rhyming structure that challenges the standard definition of rhyme as an aural experience. Every sign can be broken down into four basic components: hand configuration, location, movement, and palm orientation. If two signs have identical hand configurations, movements, and locations, then they have a strong visual rhyme. If they have a similar hand configuration only, it is a weak rhyme. However, if an entire story is told in the same handshape, it has a strong rhyme. Because of its visual/manual modality and lexical and semantic use of space, the translation of Shakespeare into ASL took advantage of movement, location, and handshape in order to establish patterns of rhyme throughout *Twelfth Night* (Valli 1996, 253).[1]

The most easily identifiable of these three elements is handshape, and ASL has a category of signs known as "classifiers" that are commonly defined as a set

---

1. See poet Clayton Valli's definitions of ASL rhyming structures according to a visual and kinetic model rather than an auditory and written one in his article, "Poetics of ASL poetry" in *Deaf Studies IV* (Washington, D.C.: Gallaudet University Press), 253. Valli differentiates among six separate manifestations of ASL rhyme based on visual perception, defining rhyme as a repetition of "handshapes, movements, nonmanual signals, locations, palm orientation, handedness, or a combination of these."

of signs that are made with a specific handshape and represent a noun's shape, size, and location as well as other defining physical characteristics. Classifiers do not have precise counterparts in English, and transcribing them is often difficult because of their specific movements. They can represent individuals, vehicles or animals, and inanimate objects; they "represent some mimetic elaboration to convey, for instance, a more precise description of an event or of a quality" (Klima and Bellugi 1979, 13). Classifiers can be used in an infinite number of ways (within circumscribed boundaries, of course), providing ASL users with enormous creative flexibility.

While it is possible to tell a story based on the use of one classifier handshape or on the creative interplay of two or more classifier shapes, stories and narrative structure usually involve several classifiers. In the following eight lines from *Twelfth Night*, Maria continues to warn Feste of the dangers of alienating Olivia's affections:

Maria
>   Yet you will be hanged for being so long absent, or to be turned away—
is not that as good as a hanging to you?

Clown
>   Many a good hanging prevents a bad marriage; and for turning away, let summer bear it out.

Maria
>   You are resolute, then?

Clown
>   Not so, neither; but I am resolved on two points.

Maria
>   That if one break, the other will hold; or, if both break, your gaskins fall.

Clown
>   Apt, in good faith, very apt. (1.5, 20–24)

Leaving the bawdiness of the lines aside, Maria's main argument to Feste is that his economic base will be eliminated, that without Olivia's money, he is as good as dead. The pun here is on three words, *resolute, resolved,* and *points.* Neither the Arden nor the Oxford edition of the play distinguishes between the words *resolute* and *resolved.* The difference may be in Feste's performance of the word *resolved.* Rather than meaning "decided," perhaps the word could be "re-solved," as in paid. The *Oxford English Dictionary*'s fourth definition of the word *solve* is "to clear off; to pay or discharge," so that Feste's line means, in essence, I am paid, or "solvent" from two points, or houses—both Olivia's and Orsino's.[2] "Points" according to Warren and Wells, are "matters. He [Feste] does not have the chance to say what these are, since Maria intervenes with her pun upon

---

2. "Solve, v." *Oxford English Dictionary*, 3d ed., ed. John Simpson. OED Online. Draft March 2000. Oxford University Press. Apr. 16, 2000.

'points' meaning laces holding up breeches" (Warren and Wells 1994, 103). The translation, however, provides a clearer meaning to the entirety of their dialogue, giving Feste a response central to Maria's economic argument. The translation links all three words (*resolved, resolute,* and *points*) into a visual pun using three different classifier shapes: the 2-classifier, 5-classifier, and F-classifier. It can be described as something like this:

Maria
    You are "decided?" (2-handed F-classifiers)

Clown
    Definitely. Well, not really, but I "profit" (2-handed F-classifiers) from both houses. [The sign for PROFIT moves down the front of the body from chest level and into Feste's pockets, drawing the path of suspenders.]

Maria
    [repeats his image of money in pockets] If one side is cut off (2-Classifiers "scissors"), you still have the other, but if both sides are cut off, your pants will fall.

The last image is of Feste's bare legs, dangling in the air, penniless and without clothing: It is indeed an "apt" metaphor, as Feste says, resulting from his long absence from Olivia's house (**clip 16.5**).

ASL has the advantage of allowing one performer to use another's body to create an interplay of meaning with specific signs. One person may make a specific sign, and another then adds to it or changes it with his own hands. Sign-play often involves more than two hands to create complex images and relationships among characters, objects, or events. An example of this sign-play comes from one of the most challenging aspects of the translation: Shakespeare's manipulation of the lyrics to the popular ballad from Robert Jones's *First Book of Songs or Airs,* which was printed in 1600. Shakespeare includes the lyrics, performed by Feste and Sir Toby during the "kitchen scene," when Malvolio chastises the revelers for their merrymaking. The performance of this scene is a delight to watch as Sir Toby plays on Malvolio's signs for dance and rhythm, using the same 2-classifier handshape to tell Malvolio to go hang himself. Later, as a further rebuff to Malvolio, and prompted by Malvolio's word *farewell,* Sir Toby begins to sing Jones's popular ballad. Feste joins him in the song:

Malvolio
    My masters, are you mad? Or what are you? Have ye no wit, manners, nor honesty, but to gabble like tinkers at this time of night? Do ye make an alehouse of my lady's house, that ye squeak out your coziers' catches without any mitigation or remorse of voice? Is there no respect of place, persons, nor time in you?

Sir Toby Belch
    We did keep time, sir, in our catches. Sneck up!

Malvolio
    Sir Toby, I must be round with you. My lady bade me tell you, that, though she harbours you as her kinsman, she's nothing allied to your disorders. If you can separate yourself and your misdemeanors, you are welcome to the house; if not, an[d] it would please you to take leave of her, she is very willing to bid you farewell.

Sir Toby Belch
    'Farewell, dear heart, since I must needs be gone.'

Clown
    'His eyes do show his days are almost done.'

Malvolio
    Is't even so?

Sir Toby Belch
    'But I will never die.'

Clown
    'Sir Toby, there you lie.'

Malvolio
    This is much credit to you.

Sir Toby Belch
    'Shall I bid him go?'

Clown
    'What an if you do?'

Sir Toby Belch
    'Shall I bid him go, and spare not?'

Clown
    'O no, no, no, no, you dare not.' (2.3, 95–105)

Both the Deaf audience and the hearing audience here share a common issue—no one in the audience is certain to know the lyrics of this late sixteenth-century song. The double meaning in Feste's line, "Sir Toby, there you lie," was an especially difficult one to translate, compounded by the rhyming of the lines. In instances throughout the translation where Shakespeare plays with the double meaning of words, often both meanings are included in the gestures and signs of the translation. In this case, *lie* means both a mistruth and death. In this clip, notice that Feste forces Toby's hand to make the sign for LIE by moving the 5-classifier across Toby's chin. The same handshape then becomes the earth that covers Toby's dead body, and Feste closes the image with a cross on top of the grave (**clip 16.6**). Classifiers presented us with the clearest way to manipulate Shakespeare's words and to make corresponding images articulated in space through the physicality of the performer.

CONCLUSION

In *An Apology for Poetry*, Sir Philip Sidney (1970) defines *poetry* as "an act of imitation: for so Aristotle termeth it in the word mimesis, that is to say, a representing, counterfeiting, or figuring forth—to speak metaphorically, a speaking picture" (18). The image of a "speaking picture" represents perhaps half of the equation in the ASL translation of *Twelfth Night*. That an image "speaks" to us at all is an audist metaphor for knowledge and discovery, of giving voice to something which has no voice as a means of authentication. A picture, like a metaphor, "represents" the real or actual, but fails—as all signs do (whether oral signs, in the shape of spoken language words, or visual signs, in the shape of sign language signs) to capture the essence of the thing itself. But when Sidney describes poetry as a "figuring forth," he nicely reveals the requirement of a morphology—a figure or shape or bodily manifestation—in poetry. More important, the phrase connotes a progressive movement or process, as in forward momentum or kinetic evolution. To redraw Sidney's definition, the ASL translation process is a "picture figuring forth"—in constant motion, mimetically and physically "representing" as it flows through both space and time.

The importance of Sidney's definition lies in its assignment of an epistemological value to spatial representation. Oftentimes the reliance on Shakespeare's written texts overshadows the fact that the plays are written to be performed in the three dimensions of theatrical space. Our understanding of language, literature, and poetry is bound by spatial metaphors, just as space is integral to any definition of art, sculpture, dance, and theater. The more original work in ASL poetry and the more translations we have, the more opportunity exists for an intertextuality of spatial form and visual images. The metaphors in our language influence the creation of our art and, as W. J. T. Mitchell (1974) writes, "Spatial form is no casual metaphor but an essential feature of the interpretation and experience of literature" in all ages and cultures (278). ASL poetry then paints for us a spatial dynamic, a rendering of text as the body moves through space. By combining the performance and dramatic texts, the ASL translation reveals a new definition of the textualized body and creates an important artifact for further critical study.

REFERENCES

Elam, Keir. 1980. *The semiotics of theatre and drama*. New York: Methuen.
Klima, Edward, and Ursula Bellugi. 1979. *The signs of language*. Cambridge, Mass.: Harvard University Press.
Malcolmson, Cristina. 1991. "What you will": Social mobility and gender in *Twelfth Night*. In *The matter of difference: Materialist feminist criticism of Shakespeare*, ed. Valerie Wayne, 29–57. New York: Harvester Wheatsheaf.
Mitchell, W. J. T. 1974. Spatial form in literature: Toward a general theory. In *The language of images*, ed. W. J. T. Mitchell, 271–99. Chicago: University of Chicago Press.
Shakespeare, William. 1994. *Twelfth night, or what you will*. Oxford edition. Edited by Roger Warren and Stanley Wells. Oxford, UK: Clarendon.
Sidney, Sir Philip. 1970. *An apology for poetry*, ed. F. Robinson. Indianapolis: Bobbs-Merrill.
Styan, John L. 1967. *Shakespeare's stagecraft*. New York: Cambridge University Press.

Valli, Clayton. 1996. Poetics of ASL poetry. In *Deaf studies IV: Visions of the past, visions of the future conference proceedings, April 27–30, 1995,* 253–63. Washington, D.C.: Gallaudet University Press.

Wechsler, Robert. 1998. America's woeful devaluation of literary translation. *Chronicle of Higher Education,* Opinion and Arts (October 2), B4.

17 | ASL in Performance: A Conversation with Adrian Blue

Adrian Blue is a director, translator, storyteller, playwright, and actor. His plays include *Deaf Heroes; A Nice Place to Live*, written with Catherine Rush; and *Circus of Signs*, which won the Cleveland Critic's Circle Award. He has directed and acted in numerous plays produced by the National Theatre of the Deaf, the Wheelock Family Theater in Boston, the Cleveland Sign Stage, and other venues. In addition, Adrian has translated more than thirty plays and novels, including children's books and several Shakespearean plays. He served as master translator for the ASL Shakespeare Project's production of *Twelfth Night*, in which he also played Malvolio. Currently he is filming an ASL production of *Much Ado about Nothing*, which he translated with Catherine Rush and in which he plays all the characters.

EDITORS: Did you grow up in a Deaf family?

ADRIAN: Yes, my father is Deaf. My mother was hearing, but she had Deaf influence in her family. Her grandparents were deaf. They used home signs. My mother's mother was the first interpreter in Boston in the 1930s and 1940s. There was no code of ethics then. The attitude was: "I'm here to save the deaf." That sort of thing.

EDITORS: How did you get started working in theater?

ADRIAN: In Rochester and in Boston, when I was about sixteen, I'd go out to the street and be a mime and collect money that way. I'd go to where the people were good hearted and they gave money.

EDITORS: Had you seen other mimes performing?

ADRIAN: Yeah, on TV. Noncaptioned days. Mostly clowns. I loved to watch them. But I didn't have any kind of formal training, I used gesturing. I knew sign, because my father is Deaf, though he grew up oral. I went to a school for the deaf very young, and my mother communicated with a mixture of home sign and talking. But when I did mime, I used gestures.

EDITORS: Where did you go to school?

ADRIAN: I went to the Horace Mann School for the Deaf in Roxbury, Massachusetts, near Boston. It was considered an oral school, but at the time I was enrolled, the students signed a lot with each other. It was impossible for the school to keep the students from signing, even though the classroom instruction was oral.

EDITORS: How did you move from performing mime to directing?

ADRIAN: During my younger days I struggled to communicate with the hearing world. I'd ask myself, "How can I get my thoughts across?" I would mime and gesture. I started that way. That enabled me to achieve some sort of communication with hearing people. One thing led to another and then I discovered scripts for plays and screenplays.

With miming and clowning, there's no written literature, so focusing on the written script was new to me. I enjoyed the challenge of moving from a basic, gestural communication to working with written English and ASL.

This change pleased me for another reason, too. Miming and clowning were fine for a while. But the white makeup and all that . . . I moved away from it. Still, I had an abiding interest in the performing arts, so I moved into directing. Then I discovered I didn't want to act, I wanted to direct.

EDITORS: What was the first thing you directed?

ADRIAN: My mime shows. The germ of directing was: "Oh, I have an idea . . ." and I'd get others to act it out so I could stay off the stage and direct.

My first mimed stage performance grew out of this scenario: There's a fly in an elevator with three people. One says, "No, no, you shouldn't kill the fly." Another says, "Kill it. It's bothering me." The third person becomes the negotiator. That was my first experience directing. If I were to direct it today, it would probably become an hour-long play.

A lot of things about acting don't suit me. When I was an actor, after the performance, they'd call me to the stage to take a bow. I had a hard time with that because in my view, my job was finished. I had changed my clothes. I wanted to get out. If acting never required me to bow, maybe I would have continued.

EDITORS: Did you see the work of other Deaf actors and directors in those days?

ADRIAN: Yes. It was seeing the National Theater of the Deaf that changed me. They had professional actors on a full stage with a thousand people in the house. And everyone paid to see them perform! It was professional: The sets moved, there was good lighting and an intermission. That level of professionalism was a goal for me to achieve, a position to aspire to as an artist. I looked at that and said, "Wow!" The audience gave them respect. That's what I wanted—to work where my art would be respected.

EDITORS: When did you start working with the National Theater of the Deaf?

ADRIAN: In the 1980s. In 1976 I attended a summer program with the National Theater of the Deaf, but I was too young to hire—about seventeen. Four years later they were looking for an actor; I went for an audition, and this time I got in. I worked with them on and off for the next ten years. One year I left for another opportunity, and then they called me back and I worked for two years on tour. Then I left again, and again they called me back for one year on tour. You know, living out of a suitcase, I could do it for three weeks—but not for a year.

But directing a Little Theater of the Deaf production with children, that was wonderful. I directed for the National Theater of the Deaf many many times, probably more than I acted for them. That was a big step, a big opportunity. It fueled my passion for directing.

Among the pieces I directed were "The Light Princess," "A Child's Christmas in Wales," "Wonderful 'O'," and a lot of other James Thurber stories. When I directed, the first thing in my mind was that each movement should tell a story in itself. Not just, "Move over there." Each frame has a story in it; the next frame continues that story. Whether working on film or stage, a director has to keep in mind that each movement is alive and telling a story as well. It's the same when you paint a picture.

EDITORS: The National Theater of the Deaf employs both Deaf and hearing actors. Was it hard to direct both at the same time?

ADRIAN: Not really. When I direct, I direct the Deaf actors. There's a voice artist who voices what's being signed, not the other way around. When someone's voicing, I always have an interpreter beside me letting me know if it sounds right or not. The older I became, though, the more uncomfortable I felt having hearing actors on stage. I asked myself, "Why are you there? Why are you on stage? What's the reason for speaking?"

So I became more sensitive; when I chose plays, I was careful to find a reason to use voice on stage other than accessibility for hearing audience members. For example, in the play *Much Ado about Nothing,* I was careful to find a reason for voicing that would enhance the overall play. I turned it into a spy story set in the 1940s. Don Pedro is a hearing character who can sign. His friend is also hearing, but doesn't sign. Don Pedro would look over to see what the Deaf actors were doing, and then he'd tell the other actor what the Deaf actors were saying. So that validated the use of voice.

So just to say that we need to have voice in order to make it accessible is not enough for me. I need a dramatic reason. It's easy to make sign understandable for a hearing audience. But that's not my interest.

EDITORS: Can you tell us about your play *A Nice Place to Live,* co-written with Catherine Rush, which focuses on the Deaf community on Martha's Vineyard in the 1800s? At that time, when there were many deaf people living on the island, both deaf and hearing islanders used sign. Did you produce the play solely in ASL, or did you use both sign and voicing?

ADRIAN: Both. We wanted the play to be signed and spoken. After Catherine and I finished writing the play, we went back to square one and asked why we wanted voicing. The whole story takes place on an island where everyone has to interact with everyone else. There are seven deaf characters and five hearing characters. We decided to create the character of an older doctor who knew everyone in the town. In fact, he had delivered almost everyone in the town, so he knew them well. He was hearing.

In one scene, the doctor was in a store and as he left, he said to the clerk, "I'll see you tomorrow." The clerk was hearing, but he signed, "Thanks for coming. I'll see you tomorrow." After the doctor walked out, he wondered, did the clerk sign or did he speak? Is he hearing or deaf? He couldn't remember.

The bottom line is that the islanders are so integrated that they don't know which people are deaf and which are hearing. Everyone signs. The only way you would know if someone was deaf is if you yelled and they didn't turn around. This was the actual situation on Martha's Vineyard at that time. In her book about this island community, *Everyone Here Spoke Sign Language,* Nora Groce quotes a woman as saying: "I never knew who the deaf and hearing people were. There was no difference. We all signed." We wanted to capture that in our play.

Let me describe how we used voicing to dramatic effect. We had two hearing women having tea on one side of the stage. They gossiped about what the other people onstage were doing. In this way, everything got explained.

EDITORS: So did the audience not know who was hearing and who was deaf?

ADRIAN: The audience saw and knew. Everyone signed, except two people who had just moved to the island. One boy was hearing and he fell in love with a deaf girl, and, as you might imagine, he learned sign so fast. He didn't want to leave the island because he was in love with that girl. We added this love story to spice it up. In the true history, a hearing boy from outside the island came to a town meeting, which was being run by deaf people. The hearing boy asked a hearing islander, "Are deaf people allowed to vote?"—a question that had never occurred to the hearing man. Every adult on Martha's Vineyard voted. But the question had a ripple effect among the townspeople. It had never been an issue until the boy brought it up. In its wake, members of the community asked themselves, "Who am I? Am I deaf or hearing?" Before that, there was no difference. They identified themselves as fishermen or farmers or shopkeepers or whatever. Then the boy asked that question, and the deaf people realized that it was insulting. Of course deaf people should have the right to vote.

In the last part of the play, the townspeople asked the statehouse in Boston whether deaf people could vote. They received a letter saying it was up to them. So the people of the town were happy again. But the very asking of the question left a scar that was there for decades.

EDITORS: Let's talk about your work as a translator. Can you tell us about the process of translating *Twelfth Night*?

ADRIAN: We were a group of four: Catherine Rush, who is hearing; Peter Novak, who is hearing and was then a Ph.D. student at Yale; Robert De Mayo, who is Deaf; and me. The four of us started and finished the project together. But in the middle, we brought in a few different actors to join us in translating for two weeks. After that, we decided to keep working with our original group of four. It took eighteen months to translate the play, line by line, half an hour to three hours on one page. Arguing and disagreeing. We each brought our own expertise and skill to the tasks. Peter is a Shakespearean scholar, Catherine is a dramaturge, Robert is a translator. All four of us worked together to figure out the what, why, and how. One thing I learned is that Shakespeare is a bawdy guy.

EDITORS: Was it difficult to translate the bawdy parts?

ADRIAN: Yes. The sexuality wasn't obvious. It was implied and often ambiguous. Shakespeare played with the language. He never used directly sexual language. The first responsibility of a translator is to be faithful to the text—the words that Shakespeare used. We had to deliver the same level of ambiguity. But we couldn't be too obscure; we had to make sure that, by the end, the audience understood. It was a balance between trying not to be too obvious and making sure the meaning was captured.

EDITORS: Can you give us an example?

ADRIAN: Let's look at the speech about young innocent fruit, in Act I, Scene v of *Twelfth Night*. Someone comes to the door and Olivia asks Malvolio about the visitor.

> Olivia
>   Of what personage and years is he?

> Malvolio
>   Not yet old enough for a man nor young enough for a boy;
>   as a squash is before 'tis a peascod, or a codling when 'tis almost an
>   apple. (I.v.149–52, **clip 16.4**)

I described the vegetable, the squash, which isn't yet ripe, and the apples, which aren't yet ripe. I never signed PENIS or TESTICLES, but the way the signs are made clarify the intention. It was important that the actor who played Olivia not react in an obvious way (for example, by gasping) to the double meaning. She had to just say, "Let him in." But she couldn't react as though something bawdy had been said.

EDITORS: Do you think that rendering Shakespeare in a visual language like ASL highlights particular aspects of the text?

ADRIAN: There's so much imagery in the words Shakespeare chose. When a hearing audience goes to a performance of Shakespeare, they might not be sure of the meaning of a certain word. That can be a problem, but it shouldn't be. You need to relax and let it come in. You need to back off—not try to follow it word for word—and let it come to you. It's the same way with sign. You see the images.

  For example, consider this exchange in the beginning of *Twelfth Night* about hunting a deer (a hart):

> Curio
>   Will you go hunt, my lord?

> Duke
>   What, Curio?

> Curio
>   The hart.

Duke
    Why, so I do, the noblest that I have. (I.i.16–19)

The homophony of HART and HEART brings up a double meaning that doesn't exist for these two signs in ASL. So I conveyed the double meaning through the verb. I used a cross on my fingers to represent the cross hairs in taking aim—the verb AIM—and then I moved my fingers to my heart to suggest it's like taking aim at the heart.

Often in translating poetry, I look for similar handshapes or similar movements. Many translators do that. Rhyme can be heard or seen. Handshapes and movements allow visual rhyme. But I add a third poetic device that works in a way that is similar to but distinct from rhyme: I look at the nouns and verbs and I try to find a connection. Classifiers allow us to create the images that make these grammatical connections. The ambiguity I described (using the verb AIM pointed at the deer and then moved to the heart) is conveyed through the verb's location rather than through nouns.

EDITORS: In translating *Twelfth Night,* how did you distinguish between a speech and a song?

ADRIAN: Peter Novak, the director, decided that the songs would use only classifiers, no real lexical items. Just the image, instead of the voice. But we added captions. We projected the words, huge, across the stage, so you could see them out of the corner of your eye while you watched the actors sign with classifiers. The ASL poet Peter Cook performed the songs. He played the clown.

EDITORS: How do you show a distinction between poetry and prose?

ADRIAN: The prose is just ordinary signing. The poetry is more stylized. Not overly so, but there's repetition of handshape and of movement of the hands. We didn't really follow the Shakespearean metrics. The ASL would have suffered if we did. It was word choice, where we placed the word, things like that that made it poetry.

Translation has its limitations. Not every line can be rendered in an artful way. It took us eighteen months to finish this play, and we paced and debated. There were a few points we still weren't satisfied with, but we had to let it go.

EDITORS: Tell us about *Much Ado about Nothing.* You're working on this project now, right?

ADRIAN: Hopefully we'll start filming soon. We showed clips from the film at the annual meeting of the Modern Language Association in December 2005. Catherine and I were commissioned by a theater company to translate it. The deal fell through after we had spent six months on it and were three-quarters of the way through. So we decided to go ahead and finish. And then we had to figure out what to do with it.

I do all the acting; I perform all the characters. I've had this obsession for maybe thirty years about playing all the characters in a play. This was my chance. I found a wonderful cameraman, a friend of ours. We'll film for three weeks in my basement this summer. We just need four black walls, a black ceiling, and a black floor. Later, we'll add voicing by one actor for all twenty-one characters.

EDITORS: When you play a female role in *Much Ado,* do you feminize your signs?

ADRIAN: Not really. I'm careful about the sign choice. I choose signs a female would use. Sometimes if there's a way that a woman signs something, I might do it the female way—for example, with a sign such as WORK.[1] But I wouldn't do anything stereotypical. I follow Shakespeare. The costumes are more than enough to show the character is a woman. I don't want to go overboard. I want to focus on the translation.

EDITORS: Can you tell us about a particular line or speech in *Much Ado* that was difficult to translate?

ADRIAN: In the script there was something about "black and white" that was mispronounced by the character Dogberry. So I signed BLACK on the chest, where WHITE is normally signed, and WHITE on the forehead, where BLACK is normally signed. We used the wrong location for the signs to show that they were mispronounced, so to speak.

At another point Dogberry says, "Nice to meet you," but says it with poor pronunciation. So we signed it normally, except instead of bringing the fingers of the two hands together for MEET, we moved them apart from each other. We changed the direction of the movement to show the mispronunciation.

EDITORS: What's your next project?

ADRIAN: For a long time I've considered doing C. S. Lewis's *Chronicles of Narnia.* I would love to translate that for film. I enjoy the beautiful imagery, the landscape, the magic. I can see those images coming alive in ASL. And I'd love to translate and produce Georges Feydeau's work.

REFERENCES

Groce, Nora Ellen. 1985. *Everyone here spoke sign language: Hereditary deafness on Martha's Vineyard.* Cambridge, Mass.: Harvard University Press.
Shakespeare, William. 1623/1972. *Twelfth Night,* ed. Charles T. Prouty. New York: Penguin.

---

1. Typically when a woman signs WORK, the S hand of the dominant hand has the palm oriented down. At times, when a man signs WORK, both S hands are vertical.

Contributors

Shannon Allen has worked as a teacher with deaf children for ten years. She holds a BA in Linguistics and an M.Ed in Deaf education. She is currently Lead Teacher for ASL and English Bilingual Education at the Pennsylvania School for the Deaf. She is also a doctoral student at the University of Pennsylvania in the Reading/Writing/Literacy program. Her research focuses on bilingual language and literacy planning for Deaf education.

H-Dirksen L. Bauman is a Professor of Deaf Studies at Gallaudet University where he directs the graduate program in Deaf studies. He is the co-editor of the book/DVD project, *Signing the Body Poetic: Essays in American Sign Language Literature* (University of California Press, 2006). He has published articles on sign language poetics, audism, and bioethical issues in Deaf studies and is the executive producer of the documentary film, *Audism Unveiled*.

Adrian Blue is a director, translator, storyteller, playwright, and actor who has been in theatre professionally for the last thirty-six years. He has directed more than sixty productions and translated more than thirty plays and novels, including children's books and several Shakespeare plays.

Brenda Jo Brueggemann is an Associate Professor of English, Women's Studies, and Comparative Studies at Ohio State University where she also serves as co-coordinator for both the ASL program and the Disability Studies undergraduate minor and graduate specialization. She is the author, co-author, editor, and co-editor of several books in disability studies and Deaf studies.

Teresa Blankmeyer Burke is a bioethicist and philosopher at Gallaudet University. She has worked in bioethics since 1986, starting her career by writing position papers for California Health Decisions, a grassroots advocacy organization. In addition to teaching at Gallaudet University, she currently serves as a consultant and instructor to the Ethics Institute at the University of New Mexico.

Peter S. Cook is an internationally reputed Deaf storyteller/poet. He has traveled extensively around the country and abroad with the Flying Words Project to promote ASL Literature with Kenny Lerner since 1986. Peter has appeared in "United States of Poetry" (PBS) produced by Emmy winner Bob Holman and was featured at the National Storytelling Festival, Illinois Storytelling Festival, Hoosier

239

Storytelling Festival, Tales of Graz in Austria, Deaf Way II, and the Millennium Stage at the Kennedy Center. Peter has worked with Deaf students in Sweden, Norway, Denmark and Japan. He was invited to the White House to join the National Book Festival in 2003. Peter lives in Chicago and teaches in the ASL-English Interpretation Department at Columbia College. He loves to tell stories to his son.

David Corina is currently a faculty member at the Center for Mind and Brain at the University of California, Davis and holds appointments in the departments of Linguistics and Psychology. He received his Ph.D. in Cognitive Science from the University of California, San Diego, and an MA in Linguistics from Gallaudet University. He researches the neural organization of language and cognition in deaf and hearing individuals. He receives support from NIH-NIDCD, NIH-NIMH, and NIH-NIBIB.

Michael Davidson is Professor of Literature at the University of California, San Diego. His books include *The San Francisco Renaissance: Poetics and Community at Mid-Century* (Cambridge UP, 1989), *Ghostlier Demarcations: Modern Poetry and the Material Word* (U of California, 1997) and *Guys Like Us: Citing Masculinity in Cold War Poetics* (U of Chicago, 2003). He has also published eight books of poetry, most recently *The Arcades* (O Books, 1998). Davidson has written extensively on disability issues and is completing a book on disability and cultural forms entitled *Concerto for the Left Hand: Disability and Cultural Studies.*

Doreen M. DeLuca has a BS Degree in Elementary Education and is certified in Deaf Education. Her Interpreter training work was completed in New Jersey and she is RID certified. Doreen has been working as a freelance Sign Language Interpreter in the Washington, D.C., and Philadelphia areas since 1990. She has taught ASL at Swarthmore College since 1999. She is co-author of a children's story book with a bilingual approach to reading for deaf children and their hearing peers, forthcoming from Gallaudet University Press. She is married and the mother of three.

Kristen Harmon is Associate Professor of English at Gallaudet University, Washington, D.C. In addition to her work in Deaf studies, Kristen has published academic articles in Disability Studies, ethnographic studies, feminist theory, and literary theory. She is also a creative writer with published short stories and creative non-fiction.

Tom Humphries is Associate Professor and Associate Director of Education Studies and Associate Professor in the Department of Communication at the University of California, San Diego. He is author and co-author of several books and papers including *A Basic Course in American Sign Language* (TJ Publishers, Inc., 1980), *Learning American Sign Language* (Allyn & Bacon, 2004), *Deaf in America: Voices from a Culture* (Harvard University Press, 1988), and *Inside Deaf Culture*, (Harvard University Press, 2005).

Sotaro Kita is a Reader in the School of Psychology at the University of Birmingham in the U.K. His main research area is psychology of language and communication. His research foci include gestures that spontaneously accompany speech and language development in children.

Heather Knapp is a doctoral candidate in Cognitive and Perceptual Psychology at the University of Washington. She investigates the neuropsychological representation of sign language phonology, specializing in visual and attentional aspects of sign perception. She received her M.A. in Linguistics from the University of Texas at Austin, and her B.S. in Neurobiology and Physiology from Purdue University. Her research is supported by pre-doctoral Ruth L. Kirschstein National Research Service Award (NRSA) F31 DC006796-01 through NIH-NIDCD.

Robert G. Lee is a Research Assistant in the American Sign Language Linguistic Research project as well as a doctoral student in linguistics at Boston University. He is also a Certified ASL-English interpreter. Robert is author or co-author of a number of chapters and articles about interpreting as well as the syntax of ASL.

Irene W. Leigh, a bicultural deaf psychologist, is Professor in the Clinical Psychology doctoral program at Gallaudet University in Washington, D.C. Her presentations, research, and approximately fifty publications, including three books, have focused on deaf people and issues related to identity, multiculturalism, parenting, attachment, depression, and cochlear implants. Her service includes various voluntary positions within the American Psychological Association as well as a National Research Council panel. She is a member of various Deaf/deaf organizations.

Kenny Lerner is the voice of the Flying Words Project and has been writing with Deaf poet Peter Cook since 1986. Flying Words was featured at the Peoples Poetry Gathering in New York City and at the thirty-sixth Poetry International Festival in Rotterdam, the Netherlands. Peter and Kenny have also done a ten-week run at the Theatre de Lucernaire in Paris, France. In addition, Kenny was the principal organizer of the First National ASL Literature Conference held in Rochester, N.Y., in 1992. Kenny works at the National Technical Institute for the Deaf tutoring the history courses and teaching modern American history. He lives in the country with his wife, his sons, and two dumb dogs.

Kristin A. Lindgren teaches courses in literature, writing, Deaf studies, and disability studies at Haverford College in Haverford, Pennsylvania. Her recent work appears in *Gendering Disability* (Rutgers University Press, 2004), *Disability/Teaching/Writing: A Critical Sourcebook* (Bedford/St. Martin's Press, 2007), and *Illness in the Academy* (Purdue University Press, 2007). She is currently completing a study of feminism, narrative, and disability.

Donna Jo Napoli is Professor of Linguistics at Swarthmore College. She completed undergraduate and doctoral degrees at Harvard University and then taught at several universities before settling at Swarthmore. She has published extensively in theoretical linguistics and in the past decade has worked on reading materials to enhance literacy skills, including materials designed specifically for deaf and hard of hearing children. She is the mother of five and also publishes fiction for children. http://www.donnajonapoli.com

Carol Neidle is Professor of Linguistics and Director of the American Sign Language Linguistic Research Project (ASLLRP) at Boston University (http://www.bu.edu/asllrp/). ASLLRP researchers have been engaged in syntactic research (cf. Neidle et al., *The Syntax of American Sign Language: Functional Categories and Hierarchical Structure*, 2000), development of SignStream (software to facilitate linguistic annotation and analysis of visual language data), collaboration with computer scientists on sign language recognition from video, and dissemination of a growing corpus of annotated video data.

Peter Novak is an Associate Professor at the University of San Francisco (USF) where he also serves as chair of the Performing Arts Department. He received his doctorate in Dramaturgy and Dramatic Criticism from the Yale School of Drama and is the former Dean of Trumbull College at Yale University. He co-directs the Performing Arts and Social Justice major at USF, training young artists to engage the world through performance.

Aslı Özyürek is a research scientist at the FC Donders Center for Cognitive Neuroimaging and Max Planck Institute for Psycholinguistics in Nijmegen, the Netherlands. Her main research concerns the relations between spontaneous gestures and speaking process in adults and children as well as crosslinguistic studies of sign languages, including Turkish and German sign languages and homesign systems.

David M. Perlmutter is Professor Emeritus of Linguistics at the University of California, San Diego. He has also taught at Brandeis University, M.I.T., and three Summer Linguistic Institutes. The central thrust of his research has been to confront linguistic theory with data from the widest possible range of languages, which led to discoveries about the role of grammatical relations in clause structure and to evidence for syllable structure in ASL. He pioneered the teaching of linguistics by actively involving students in grammar construction and has served as president of the Linguistic Society of America.

Ann Senghas is an Assistant Professor of Psychology at Barnard College, where she conducts research on language development. She completed her doctoral studies at the Massachusetts Institute of Technology in 1995, followed by postdoctoral work at the Sign Language Research Center at the University of Rochester, and at the Max Planck Institute for Psycholinguistics in the Netherlands. She began studying Nicaraguan Sign Language in 1989, and has traveled to Nicaragua nearly every summer since then.

Ronnie B. Wilbur conducts research on the structure of natural signed languages. Her current projects include: (a) using robot-vision techniques to perform automatic sign recognition (with Avinash Kak, Purdue); (b) automatic recognition of ASL facial expressions (Aleix Martinez, Ohio State); (c) a basic grammar of Croatian Sign Language (with Ljubica Pribani, University of Zagreb); and (d) the role of event structure and nonmanuals in sign language syntax and semantics.

Index

Page numbers in italics denote figures.